Engaged Anthropology

Engaged Anthropology

POLITICS BEYOND THE TEXT

Stuart Kirsch

UNIVERSITY OF CALIFORNIA PRESS

University of California Press, one of the most distinguished university presses in the United States, enriches lives around the world by advancing scholarship in the humanities, social sciences, and natural sciences. Its activities are supported by the UC Press Foundation and by philanthropic contributions from individuals and institutions. For more information, visit www.ucpress.edu.

University of California Press
Oakland, California

Library of Congress Cataloging-in-Publication Data

Names: Kirsch, Stuart, author.
Title: Engaged anthropology : politics beyond the text / Stuart Kirsch.
Description: Oakland, California : University of California Press, [2018] | Includes bibliographical references and index.
Identifiers: LCCN 2017044672 (print) | LCCN 2017048855 (ebook) | ISBN 9780520970090 (e-edition) | ISBN 9780520297944 (cloth) | ISBN 9780520297951 (pbk.)
Subjects: LCSH: Public anthropology—Papua New Guinea. | Indigenous peoples—Land tenure—Papua New Guinea. | Indigenous peoples—Legal status, laws, etc.—Papua New Guinea. | Mineral industries—Environmental aspects—Papua New Guinea.
Classification: LCC GN671.N5 (ebook) | LCC GN671.N5 K58 2018 (print) | DDC 323.11—dc23
LC record available at https://lccn.loc.gov/2017044672

27 26 25 24 23 22 21 20 19 18
10 9 8 7 6 5 4 3 2 1

To Janet

CONTENTS

ILLUSTRATIONS

MAPS

FIGURES

ACKNOWLEDGMENTS

A project like this—spanning decades, continents, islands, and oceans—would not have been possible without the support of many individuals and organizations. I reiterate my appreciation to all the people with whom I collaborated on the Ok Tedi case (see Kirsch 2006, 2014). I am grateful for the insight and assistance of the West Papuan political leaders John Rumbiak and Octovianus Mote, as well as the trust of the refugees living in Papua New Guinea. Rosa Moiwend made my visit to Jayapura and Biak in 2014 possible with her guidance, introductions, and translations. My research on the integrated conservation and development project in the Lakekamu River basin in 1994 was facilitated by Bruce Beehler and Cosmas Makamet. I am grateful to the late chief John Salea for his help during my research in Solomon Islands in 1998–99, to Marita Foley and Nick-Styant Browne of Slater and Gordon, and to Dorothy Wickham for sharing her knowledge of the area. I am indebted to Peter Iroga of the *Solomon Star* for facilitating my archival research in Honiara in 2014, and the former Anglican Bishop of Malaita, Terry Brown, for introducing me to Peter. Bill Graham, the public advocate for the Marshall Islands Nuclear Claims Tribunal, was responsible for my involvement, along with Holly Barker and Barbara Rose Johnston, in the initial phase of the Rongelap case in 1999. Fergus Mackay of the Forest Peoples Programme invited me to contribute affidavits to the Inter-American Commission on and Court of Human Rights, for which I relied on the guidance of Carla Madsian in Suriname in 2009 and Laura George and David James in Guyana in 2014. I also thank the captains and *toshaos* of the communities I visited.

The manuscript for this book was drafted while I was a visiting fellow at the Kellogg Institute for International Studies at the University of Notre

Dame in fall 2016. I am grateful for this opportunity and convey my appreciation to the director, Paolo Carozza, as well as Denise Wright, the Kellogg staff, and the other postdoctoral fellows. The Center for Southeast Asian Studies at the University of Michigan supported my attendance at meetings on West Papua in New York City and Washington, DC, in 2011, and my visit to West Papua, Indonesia, in 2014. The Office of the Vice President for Research, the College of Literature, Science, and the Arts, and the Department of Anthropology at the University of Michigan funded archival research in Solomon Islands in 2014 and my attendance at hearings of the Inter-American Court of Human Rights in San José, Costa Rica, in 2015. My work in Guyana and Suriname was supported by the Forest Peoples Programme, the Association of Indigenous Village Leaders in Suriname, and the Amerindian Peoples' Association of Guyana. The Dean's Office at Mount Holyoke College and Conservation International funded my research in the Lakekamu River basin in Papua New Guinea. The project in the Marshall Islands was commissioned by the Public Advocate's Office of the Nuclear Claims Tribunal. Work on the Ok Tedi case and the Gold Ridge lawsuit was supported by Slater and Gordon in Melbourne, Australia. Additional funding for research in Papua New Guinea was previously acknowledged in *Reverse Anthropology* (Kirsch 2006, xi–xii) and *Mining Capitalism* (Kirsch 2014, xi).

Chapter 1 includes passages from "Is Ok Tedi a Precedent? Implications of the Settlement," in *The Ok Tedi Settlement,* edited by Glenn Banks and Chris Ballard (ANU Press, 1997); "Anthropology and Advocacy," which appeared in *Critique of Anthropology* in 2002; and "Indigenous Movements and the Risks of Counterglobalization," published in *American Ethnologist* in 2007. Chapter 3 incorporates material from "Regional Dynamics and Conservation in Papua New Guinea," published in *The Contemporary Pacific* in 1997; and "Social History of the Lakekamu River Basin," in *A Biological Assessment of the Lakekamu Basin, Papua New Guinea,* edited by Andrew L. Mack (Conservation International, 1998). Chapter 5 draws extensively from "Lost Worlds: Environmental Disaster, 'Culture Loss,' and the Law," published in *Current Anthropology* in 2001. Chapter 6 includes a commentary on "Science, Property, and Kinship in Repatriation Debates," which first appeared in *Museum Anthropology* in 2011.

This project has benefited from questions and feedback received when I presented portions of the text at Bennington College, Bowdoin College, the British Museum, Central European University in Budapest, el Centro de

Investigaciones y Estudios Superiores en Antropología Social in Mexico City, Emory University, the Hans Arnold Center in Berlin, the University of Heidelberg, Ostello di Indemini in Switzerland, the University of Kent at Canterbury, the University of Manchester, McGill University, Memorial University of Newfoundland in St. Johns, the University of Michigan, Michigan State University, the University of Notre Dame, the University of Oslo, Princeton University, Universidad del Rosario in Bogotá, Rutgers University, the University of Sussex, the University of Toronto, Trinity College in Connecticut, the University of Tromsø in Norway, Schloss Überstorf in Switzerland, and Yale University.

I am also grateful to the following individuals for their comments on various chapters: David Akin, Doc Billingsley, Cat Bolten, Ramstad Jorun Bræk, Paolo Carozza, Rosalva Aída Hernández Castillo, Chip Colwell, Courtney Cottrell, Bill Donner, Julia Eckert, Kelly Fayard, Gillian Feeley-Harnik, Dario Gaggio, Ilana Gershon, Diana Glazebrook, Budi Hernawan, Eleanor King, Tina Lee, Chris Loperena, Debra MacDougall, Fergus MacKay, Keir Martin, Mike McGovern, Mariana Mora, Regev Nathansohn, Danilyn Rutherford, Warner Schiffauer, Sarah Swanz, Margaret Triyana, Holly Wardlow, and Jessica Worl. Mike Wood generously commented on the manuscript, although, like the other individuals and organizations mentioned here, he cannot be held accountable for its shortcomings. The project also benefited from conversations with and suggestions from Chris Ball, David Bond, Ben Burt, Beth Conklin, Catherine Coumans, Jatin Dua, Steve Feld, Daniel Goldstein, Dorothy Hodgson, Huatse Huazejia, Bruce Knauft, Andrew Lattas, Clive Moore, Lynn Morgan, Ron Niezen, Steve Nugent, Tony Oliver-Smith, Davide Orsini, Alcida Ramos, Elisha Renne, Olivia Serdeczny, Andrew Shryock, Karen Sykes, Jim Trostle, and Ximena Warnaars. Discussions with members of the interdisciplinary workshop "Ethnography-as-Activism," funded by the Rackham School of Graduate Studies at the University of Michigan, and with the students in my seminars on engaged anthropology and the anthropology of property at the University of Michigan and the University of Tromsø influenced the final argument.

I also thank the Southeast Asian bibliographer at the University of Michigan, Fe Susan T. Go, for her resourcefulness in tracking down hard-to-find materials; Jeri Sawall for copyediting the first draft; Randal Stegmeyer for preparing the images; and Bill Nelson for the elegant maps. Comments from the reviewers, including Ron Niezen, helped bring several key themes into sharper focus. I am grateful to my editor, Reed Malcolm, for his support and vision for the project; Victoria Baker for the index; Bonita Hurd for her astute editing; and Geraldine Gudiño García, Zuha Khan, Tom Sullivan, and the managing editor, Kate Warne, at the University of California Press for their help in bringing this book to fruition.

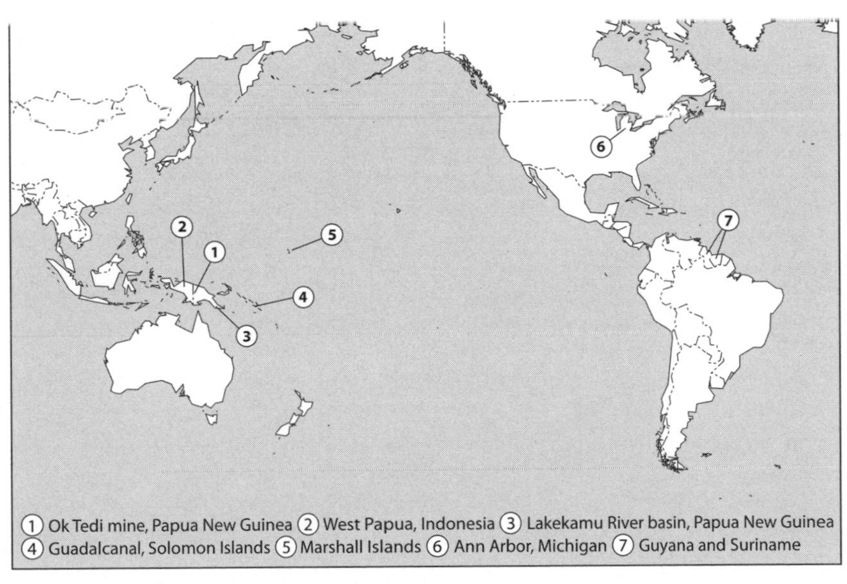

MAP 1. Case studies discussed in this book. Labels correspond to chapter numbers.

Introduction

ENGAGED ANTHROPOLOGY. ANTHROPOLOGY as advocacy. Activist anthropology. Collaborative anthropology. Militant anthropology. Public anthropology. Despite their differences, all of these projects share a commitment to mobilizing anthropology for constructive interventions into politics. They can be understood as a series of experiments in making anthropology relevant and useful. Examples include participation in social movements, collaborating with activists and nongovernmental organizations, advising lawyers, writing affidavits, and producing expert reports. These are the primary modes of engagement discussed in this book, which draws on my personal experiences, although they do not exhaust the contributions anthropologists can make to politics (see Low and Merry 2010). These practices offer a valuable supplement to more conventional forms of ethnographic research, as they introduce anthropologists to unfamiliar research sites and interlocutors, suggest alternative topics for inquiry, and yield novel insights. Engagement opens up new avenues for pursuing anthropological research.

These experiments in engaged anthropology can be seen to pick up where the influential literature on writing culture and cultural critique of the 1980s left off (Clifford and Marcus 1986; Marcus and Fischer 1986; see also Hale 2006; Ortner 2016; Starn 2015). The writing culture movement responded to the "crisis in representation" provoked by Edward Said's (1978) *Orientalism* and related developments in literary and postcolonial theory, especially the need to pay greater attention to power and history. Anthropologists in North America came to question the processes through which ethnographic knowledge is produced (Rabinow 1977), including the construction of ethnographic authority (Clifford 1988). On the other side of the Atlantic, Marilyn Strathern's (1988) pathbreaking *Gender of the Gift* similarly treated ethnographic narratives as "fictions" in the sense of being deliberately conceived for particular analytic purposes, emphasizing the constructed nature of representation rather than its opposition to truth or facts. Articulated at a historical moment dominated by the intersection of decolonization and globalization (Clifford 2015), and motivated by "challenges from feminists, political activists, native anthropologists, and others" (Besteman and Haugerud 2013, 2; see Said 1989, 210), these discussions encouraged anthropologists to "develop a critique of Western imperialism as well as anthropology's complicity with colonialism and other forms of domination" (Besteman and Haugerud 2013, 2).

While engaged anthropology follows the general trajectory established by the writing culture movement in addressing questions about political accountability and responsibility, there are a number of significant differences. Whereas the debates on writing culture focused on the *politics of representation,* engaged anthropology is primarily concerned with the *politics of participation,* addressing the roles anthropologists are increasingly called to play as expert witnesses, authors of social impact studies, contributors to social movements, and so forth.

The writing culture debates addressed the question of reflexivity *within the text,* including the influence of the author's political commitments and positionality on ethnography. In contrast, engaged anthropology is concerned with reflexivity *beyond the text,* examining how ethnographic knowledge and anthropological ideas like the culture concept are increasingly deployed by a range of actors, including activists, lawyers and judges, social movements, states, and diverse publics. Such practices encourage anthropologists to ask "how we understand our work, strategically, as a mode of social action and intervention in relation to and collaboration with the projects of those we study," as Faye Ginsburg (1997, 14) points out. Writing about her work with cultural activists, Ginsburg (1997) argues that "reflexivity [should] be more than textual, and that it [should] begin by considering how our research is part of a social world shared with our subjects."[1]

The critique of ethnographic representation by the contributors to the writing culture debates gave rise to a generation of experimental ethnographies that transformed the genre (Marcus and Fischer 1986). In contrast, the practice of engaged anthropology involves taking risks in how we conduct research and make use of ethnographic knowledge. Moving beyond conventional relationships with our informants and their political projects also means that the success of these interventions is far from guaranteed.

The writing culture movement also contributed to a major schism in the discipline, anthropology's version of the "science wars." While the resulting disputes over empiricism and interpretation have largely been resolved, or at least pushed to the back burner, they occasionally boil over.[2] Debates about engaged anthropology are equally contentious. Critics of engaged anthropology object to the politicization of research. They complain that engaged anthropologists chase ambulances rather than pursue intellectual questions. Some even argue that short-term engaged-research projects are a poor substitute for good ethnography, rejecting their value as a complementary practice. This is similar to the way critics of the writing culture movement objected to reflexivity, arguing that it was antithetical to empiricism rather than recognizing it as a serious effort to rethink ethnography's assumptions and reveal its blind spots.

The writing culture movement was deeply influenced by postcolonial politics and poststructuralist critique of the relationship between power and knowledge. Engaged anthropology takes the responsibilities associated with these concerns seriously (Low and Merry 2010, 203). These projects respond in part to the relationships that emerge in the process of conducting ethnographic research, especially the obligations of reciprocity that are central to these interactions (Kirsch 2002a). But engaged anthropology also seeks to address larger concerns about social justice, structural violence, and environmental degradation that are often rooted in colonial history and exacerbated by globalization and contemporary forms of capitalism. Most importantly, the participants in these projects recognize that anthropologists have more to contribute to the solution of these problems than their texts.

Given the centrality of reflexivity to the debates about writing culture, it is surprising that relatively little attention has been paid to the challenges, complications, and contradictions of engaged research. This omission is closely related to the way that most of the existing literature on engaged anthropology falls into two categories. On the one hand are problem-centered ethnographic accounts organized by concerns about social justice (e.g., Checker 2005; Johnston and Barker 2008). On the other are programmatic statements that call for rethinking the discipline's relationship to politics through activism (e.g., Hale 2006, 2007; Scheper-Hughes 1995). But given their pragmatic focus, case studies addressing social problems tend to be less reflexive than other anthropological writing, perhaps out of concern that acknowledging the author's political commitments might undermine the authority of the text. The more didactic literature on engaged anthropology exhibits similar omissions, given its emphasis on promoting engagement at the expense of revealing its vulnerabilities and shortcomings. Neither genre pays sufficient attention to the actual practices of engaged research and their implications for both scholarship and politics.

Consequently, I ask not only whether engaged anthropology produces "good enough" ethnography (Scheper-Hughes 1989, 28) but also whether engagement is good for anthropology and contributes to desirable political outcomes. In her analysis of liberal projects of reform, Elizabeth Povinelli (2002) questions whether progress is possible without critically examining the underlying institutions and practices. Anthropology's response to the "crisis in representation" and the need to address questions about power and history can be seen as the internal critique of the discipline that helped make contemporary experiments in engaged anthropology possible. In writing this book, my goal is to bring attention to the practices of engaged anthropology parallel to the examination of fieldwork and ethnography by the contributors to the writing culture movement. My purpose is not to critique engagement, however, but to better understand its contribution to anthropology, ethnography, and politics. I do so by examining my experiences as an engaged anthropologist.

MOTIVATION

This book is intended to enhance recognition and understanding of engaged research in anthropology and related social sciences. Despite the attention garnered by such arguments, I do not subscribe to the point of view that all ethnographic research should be activist or engaged. Political engagement is not always appropriate or welcome, and many anthropologists would be reluctant participants. More importantly, the diversity of approaches in anthropology is one of its greatest assets (Strathern 2006). Attempts to impose narrow agendas on the discipline ignore this fundamental insight. In contrast, acknowledging the value of engaged research has the salutary effect of expanding the possibilities and potential contributions of anthropology.

There are several reasons why engaged research has become so prevalent in recent years. The nearly universal recognition that culture is a valuable resource (Comaroff and Comaroff 2009; Strathern 1995; Turner 1991), and potentially a form of property (Brown 2003; Hirsch and Strathern 2004), increases the demand for anthropological skills and ethnographic knowledge. Given the face-to-face relationships that develop over the course of ethnographic research, the people who provide access to the intimate details of their lives feel entitled to make reciprocal demands on anthropologists (Kirsch 2002a), and in many contexts such requests take the form of preconditions for gaining access to research sites.

Anthropologists are also aware of the critical response of previous generations of informants to ethnographic representation of their practices (e.g., Scheper-Hughes 2000). This includes our penchant for publically sharing information ordinarily regarded as private (Herzfeld 1997; Shryock 2004). In contrast, engaged anthropologists seek to cultivate alternative relationships through collaboration on shared political projects. The rise of nongovernmental organizations since the 1980s has also multiplied the possibilities for engagement.[3] This includes participation in social movements that extend across international borders, incorporating differently positioned actors who deploy complementary modes of access to power, discourses of persuasion, and political leverage (Escobar 2008; Juris 2008; Keck and Sikkink 1998; Kirsch 2014).

It has also been suggested that greater academic precarity leads scholars to search for new ways to market their skills (Goldman and Baum 2000, 2). But it is more than economic opportunity that motivates these undertakings. In an era of diminished expectations for academic careers, many anthropologists seek alternative sources of fulfillment or rationales for conducting research, including the desire to contribute to positive social change. Such ambitions coincide with the revised expectations of funding agencies and society at large regarding the responsibilities of scientists and scholars (Nowotny, Scott, and Gibbons 2001), including the obligation to specify how their work will benefit the subjects of their research and have a positive impact on society (Page and Strathern 2016).

Scholars also come to identify with the subjects of their research and consequently seek to protect their interests. This occurs across the disciplines. For example, many of the biologists with whom I have worked became conservationists when the species they spent decades observing became endangered.[4] Other scholars, including scientists studying global climate change, are driven by their research findings to intervene in public policy. Anthropologists concerned about the welfare of their informants regularly invoke their political obligations in their writing, emphasizing their responsibility to bear witness to both physical and structural violence. If the discipline took a "dark turn" (Ortner 2016) in its focus on the "suffering subject" (Robbins 2013) during the decades that followed the writing culture movement, it was because anthropologists no longer assumed that the problems of the world were someone else's concern. It is the desire to both understand and actively respond to these issues that motivates anthropologists who pursue contemporary forms of engaged anthropology, giving rise to the need to examine how these experiments are changing the field.

STATUS

Anthropologists have a long tradition of addressing political concerns in their work, from the pioneering contributions of Franz Boas on racism and immigration quotas (Pierpont 2004), to Sol Tax's (1975) "Action Anthropology" founded in the 1950s, Kathleen Gough's (1968) critique of anthropology and imperialism in the 1960s, and teach-ins against the Vietnam War organized by Marshall Sahlins and Eric Wolf at the University of Michigan during the 1970s (Sahlins 2000, 205–70; Heyman 2010), to name but a few exemplars from the past. Nonetheless, it is important to recognize that engaged anthropology has never been the most prominent or prestigious trend within the discipline, despite efforts to identify and promote alternative genealogies for these practices (Lassiter 2005; Cook 2015).[5]

The primary reason for the second-class status of engaged research is its reputation for applying existing ideas rather than contributing to knowledge production and the development of social theory. The former is regarded as conventional or conservative, while the latter is associated with creativity and innovation and, thus, is more highly valued. The preference for pure or basic science over applied or engaged research continues to dominate many, if not most, academic fields, even though comparable distinctions have been discredited in other domains, resulting in more pluralist views of knowledge. However, the split between knowledge and practice is more pronounced in academic settings in the global north than in the global south, where establishing relationships between the two is often seen as more urgent.[6]

There are two common flaws in the persistence of this division. First is the assumption that the results from engaged research projects apply only to the problem at hand and, consequently, fail to yield generalizable findings or insights. In contrast, the examples presented in this book show how engaged anthropology results in ideas whose value transcends the initial research agenda. Second is the failure to acknowledge that most scientific research proceeds inductively from in-depth study of specific phenomena and concerns. Engaged anthropology is no exception. It can also be seen as where the rubber meets the road, providing opportunities to develop, test, and refine anthropological understandings in the real world, which is difficult, if not impossible for other forms of ethnographic research. Consequently, one of my goals in writing this book is to destabilize the prevailing dichotomy between purely academic and engaged forms of research in anthropology.

The historical status of engaged anthropology has affected its position in the disciplinary division of labor. Until recently, the dominant pattern has been for anthropologists to become involved in engaged research projects only after establishing their academic careers. Before Nancy Scheper-Hughes (1995) wrote her manifesto on the "primacy of the ethical" in response to violence in post-Apartheid South Africa, or reported on the inequities of the global organ trade (Scheper-Hughes 2005), she used the language of medical pathology to describe kinship, rural sociality, and schizophrenia (Scheper-Hughes 1979), provoking the "ire" of her informants in Ireland (Scheper-Hughes 2000). Similarly, in his classic essay on long-term fieldwork among the Kayapo in Brazil, Terence Turner (1991) divided their history into two distinct epochs, before and after political self-recognition, which turned on their appreciation of the value of culture. The change also demarcated a shift in his ethnographic praxis: only after becoming an established professor at the University of Chicago did Turner help set up the Kayapo Video Project and become involved in their struggle against the Altamira Dam on the Xingu River. These are not criticisms but prominent examples of how the status of engaged anthropology has shaped ethnographic research practices.

Only in the post-writing-culture era have anthropologists begun to frame their initial research projects in response to their political commitments. In *A Finger in the Wound,* Diane Nelson (1999, 46) describes her earlier work as a "solidarity activist" with people from Guatemala, although in hindsight she questions some of her original assumptions: "I have found 'the people' to be rather more heterogeneous, 'the state' less clearly bounded, *gringas* less magically welcome, and my accounts to be far more 'partial'—in the sense of incomplete—than I had acknowledged." Kim Fortun's (2001) *Advocacy after Bhopal* was one of the first ethnographic monographs in this period to be explicitly framed as a work of political engagement; she not only collaborated with local activists pursuing compensation for the chemical disaster in India but also "studied up" at home to examine whether similar disasters were possible in the United States.

In *Crude Chronicles,* Suzana Sawyer (2004, 22) describes how she worked with the leaders of an indigenous organization in Ecuador who challenged the expansion of petroleum extraction in their territories: "As such, my research dispensed with any pretentions of 'objectivity'; it was unabashedly invested and engaged. Yet such highly enmeshed research afforded a methodological richness that could not be gotten any other way. Establishing where my political allegiances lay was critical to my being able to collaborate with [the organization, which] would never have had me otherwise. . . . Thus," she concludes, "I consciously chose to build a research project based on political engagement rather than sociological detachment" (Sawyer 2004, 22). Shannon Speed (2007, 2) notes that she "came to the discipline as an activist" and describes how her political commitments shaped her research on human rights in Chiapas, Mexico. In most of the engaged ethnographies from this period, including my own (Kirsch 2014), relatively circumscribed discussions of engagement are used to position these projects politically and methodologically rather than being the primary focus of the work. Even in more recent ethnographies by Daniel Goldstein (2012) on violence and insecurity in urban Bolivia, and by Angela Stuesse (2016) on race and labor rights in the American South, questions about engaged or activist research methods are addressed in separate chapters rather than integrated into the text, perpetuating the division between ethnographic knowledge and political engagement.

The historically low status of engaged research within anthropology is also evident in the lack of institutional recognition and rewards. Nancy Scheper-Hughes (2009, 4) refers to the work of engaged scholars as "double time," or moonlighting, labor undertaken in addition to their day jobs. This was literally true for my participation in Australian legal proceedings against the owners of the Ok Tedi mine, given the time difference between Melbourne and Ann Arbor, which meant that conference calls with lawyers took place in the middle of the night for me. Another aspect of working a second shift is that engaged anthropology is undervalued labor, counted as either community service (Scheper-Hughes 2009, 3) or, in my case, service to the field. Thus composing an affidavit for a court case was implicitly compared to the duties of a committee member for the American Anthropological Association rather than recognized as an extension of my research.

The widespread failure to acknowledge the value of these kinds of activities has led some scholars to argue that engaged or activist research practices should be formally recognized by the academy (Hale 2007). However, inviting administrative oversight runs the risk of standardizing, homogenizing, and potentially compromising these projects, much as the institutionalization of social movements diminishes their capacity for contributing to radical change (Piven and Cloward 1978). To some extent, this has already started to occur as universities promote engagement in the form of local outreach, attracting corporate sponsorship of research, being quoted by traditional media or actively participating in social media, or providing service learning opportunities for students, activities that are potentially valuable and interesting but which differ substantially from the political projects discussed in this book.

Despite my concerns about bureaucratization, there is a need for greater appreciation of the alternative temporalities of engaged research projects in relation to fixed tenure clocks and research assessments. Similarly, it is important to recognize that engaged research lacks the certainty of more conventional forms of research in terms of guaranteeing academic outputs, as the status of the project may remain unresolved, publication may compromise the interests of one's informants, or the project may fail for reasons beyond the investigator's control. Greater institutional flexibility may be required to accommodate the elements of risk-taking in these projects, which contribute to the dynamic and innovative potential of engaged research.

CRITICISM

Being reflexive about engaged research requires acknowledging the concerns raised by its critics. As Charles Hale (2006, 101) notes, complaints that engaged anthropology "lacks objectivity or has become politicized" have been tempered by insights from feminist theory (Haraway 1988), which suggest that anthropologists are always already politically positioned as a result of power relations between researchers and subjects, the questions that orient their studies, and interpersonal relationships between anthropologists and their interlocutors (Behar 1993; Macdonald 2002). For example, James Ferguson (1999, 24–37) describes how the liberal politics of social anthropologists at the Rhodes-Livingstone Institute led them to assume that Euro-American narratives about modernity and progress were applicable to Africa. The primary response to these revelations about the nature of scholarly inquiry has not been futile efforts to purify anthropology from politics by retreating to prior understandings of objectivity in the social sciences (Latour 1993), which is no longer seen as possible or even desirable. Instead, these discussions have underscored the need to make explicit how politics and positionality influence scholarly research.

Critics of engaged anthropology also object to the heroic representation of its practitioners. The expression "anthropologist as hero" is usually attributed to the literary critic Susan Sontag (1966), although she was writing about the identification of the French structuralist Claude Lévi-Strauss with the indigenous peoples of the Amazon and his estrangement from the modern world, not engaged anthropology. "A Hero of Our Time" was the original title of Sontag's (1963) review, which was subsequently reprinted as "Anthropologist as Hero" in her collection *Against Interpretation* (Sontag 1966). The latter phrase invokes romantic accounts of anthropologists who intervene in distant conflicts, saving their informants from harm. But such clichés and declensionist narratives are more prominent in fiction and popular film than in scholarly publications, in which anthropologists are more likely to be depicted as bureaucrats of adventure rather than as heroic figures (Peacock 2002, 68).

Michael Brown (2014, 273) takes these objections one step further, arguing that the rhetoric of engaged research "needs victims and heroes, or better yet, heroic victims[,] . . . leading to frustratingly thin accounts . . . [that] oversimplify morally complex situations." In part, he is referring to the phenomenon of "ethnographic refusal," in which anthropologists withhold evidence that might complicate representations of their research subjects or jeopardize their political projects (Ortner 1995). For example, engaged anthropologists may fail to describe dissenting points of view or the opinions of those who decline to participate in social movements. Avoiding discussion of internal conflict results in a romanticized view of resistance (Ortner 1995, 177; see also Abu-Lughod 1990) and homogenized representations of communities (Agrawal and Gibson 1999; Creed 2006). This tendency may be exacerbated in the case of the short-term research projects that are incapable of producing the nuanced "thick description" associated with long-term ethnographic research (Geertz 1973), as I discuss in several of the chapters.

Taking sides in political conflicts also poses the risk that engaged anthropologists will lose access to informants who possess alternative perspectives or political views. Conversely, my experience suggests that advocacy can actually provide access to a wider range of interlocutors and facilitate participation in events from which anthropologists who remain neutral may be excluded (Kirsch 2002a). Taking a stance on controversial topics can also create opportunities to discuss these issues with participants on both sides of the debate (Loperena 2016). However, access to confidential information obtained through participation in political struggles can increase demands on engaged anthropologists to protect the interests of their informants, especially when "writing in the eye of a storm," as Diane Bell (2002) argues. Nonetheless, engaged anthropologists can revisit their work and offer more detailed accounts once the political stakes have changed. I discuss questions about ethnographic refusal and the political commitments of engaged anthropologists more thoroughly in the ensuing chapters.

Other critics express concern that political advocacy will compromise the ability of anthropologists to present evidence or provide expert testimony in court (see Cove 1996; Paine 1996). Although this is an important issue, lawyers and legal systems do recognize the professional "duty of care" anthropologists have to their informants (Edmond 2004). Consequently, the two models of the anthropological expert, as either a "reasonable and objective professional" or an "advocate" (Edmond 2004, 210), should not necessarily be treated as binary opposites (Fergie 2004, 50). There are also distinctive national traditions with respect to the treatment of anthropological testimony, variations across judicial forums, differences among judges, and contrasting views among opposing lawyers with respect to anthropological contributions to legal proceedings. In addition, it is important to recognize that such testimony is usually presented within an adversarial contest of competing experts. When I have asked lawyers whether my track record of supporting indigenous land rights and criticizing the mining industry disqualifies me from contributing to legal proceedings on these subjects, the response has always been that my testimony is more valuable as a result of my experience and commitments.

A final question is whether anthropologists who consult for corporations or are embedded in the military should also be seen as doing engaged anthropology. It is inappropriate to use political agreement or disagreement with these activities as the criterion for defining engagement. Rather, the critical issue is accountability (Goldstein 2012, 40), whether the information gained through ethnographic research is used to benefit the subjects of anthropological research or applied in ways that might increase their exposure to harm.

Marilyn Strathern (1987) describes the awkward relationship between feminism and anthropology, although elsewhere she demonstrates the value of putting the two in conversation with each other (Strathern 1988). Similarly,

I think it is important to acknowledge the potential awkwardness between academic research and political engagement without forgoing the benefits from their interaction.

ANTHROPOLOGY BEYOND THE TEXT

I became an engaged anthropologist by accident rather than design, as my initial steps along this path were unplanned. I was conducting ethnographic research on ritual, magic, and sorcery in a Yonggom village on the Ok Tedi River in Papua New Guinea in the late 1980s when I became concerned about pollution from a large copper and gold mine in the mountains to the north. In the ensuing years, I became involved in the struggle by the affected communities to protect their environment and livelihoods, although I did not anticipate that these interactions would eventually become the focus of my research.

In chapter 1, which describes my participation in the lawsuit against the Australian owners of the Ok Tedi mine, I discuss several issues that engaged anthropologists rarely address in their published work. I begin with the influence of politics on how social scientists frame their analyses. Next, I describe two interactions I was previously reluctant to write about, both examples of ethnographic refusal; it is only with the passage of time that I am able to write about these events without jeopardizing my informants or compromising their political objectives. In the second half of the chapter, I consider how participation in engaged research projects results in relationships that influence our work in unexpected ways. In particular I examine debates with colleagues, corporate efforts to discipline expertise, the legal colonization of anthropological knowledge, negotiating difference with nongovernmental organizations, and collaboration with communities. Although I have previously examined the Ok Tedi case in considerable detail (Kirsch 2006, 2014), many of these "backstage" encounters are presented here for the first time. This discussion also establishes the terms of reference for analyzing the other projects presented in the book.

The second chapter is based on long-term research and collaboration with West Papuan refugees and political exiles. Not far from the village on the Ok Tedi River where I conducted my original research was a refugee camp inhabited by several hundred people from the Indonesian side of the international border with Papua New Guinea. They were part of the 1984 exodus of more than ten thousand people in protest against Indonesia's military occupation of West Papua. Although I initially kept my distance from the refugees because of their suspicion of outsiders, they eventually invited me to work with them as well. Many of the refugees speak the same language as the Yonggom, although they refer to themselves as Muyu. Several of my early publications addressed the situation along the border, although later I began writing about the politics of representation in West Papua and its consequences. This work was constrained by government restrictions that prevented me from conducting research on the Indonesian side of the border. When I finally had an opportunity to visit West Papua in 2014, I learned about the different strategies of mobilization pursued by political actors living in Indonesia and by refugees and political exiles residing in other countries. My contribution to the West Papuan independence movement has thus far been limited to academic writing and participation in various forms of "solidarity politics" (see Nelson 1999). These experiences show that effective political engagement with the objectives of our interlocutors may prove to be elusive.

The other case studies in the book are the result of short-term interventions. In chapter 3, I ask whether conservation and development projects introduced in Papua New Guinea during the 1990s offer a viable alternative to destructive forms of resource extraction like the Ok Tedi mine. Ethnographic research in the Lakekamu River basin showed that competing land claims and alternative visions of development posed significant obstacles to the implementation of the project. But the desire to reduce future environmental threats led me to overstate its potential in my previous work. This suggests the need to consider how aspirations for better outcomes can influence the work of engaged anthropologists.

My participation in the lawsuit against the Ok Tedi mine provided me with the skills, experience, and opportunity to work on related projects. Chapter 4 addresses my contribution to a lawsuit against the Gold Ridge mine near Honiara, the capital of Solomon Islands. One of my responsibilities as a consultant in that case was to examine local property rights. When the litigation failed and Guadalcanal was engulfed by civil conflict, I was unable to return. Drawing on archival research conducted in the Solomons in 2014, I describe how my earlier work on land rights helps explain the subsequent outbreak of violence. In contrast to the assumption that the findings of engaged research are of little value beyond the initial context, I show how ethnographic data from these projects may be put to new uses in changed circumstances.

I discuss my work as a consultant for the Nuclear Claims Tribunal in the Marshall Islands in chapter 5. The focus of the project was the experience of people relocated from Rongelap Atoll after their exposure to radiation from nuclear weapons testing by the American military in 1954. My contribution to this project focused on their discourse about culture loss, especially how the concept of cultural property rights helped make their losses visible. These findings were subsequently incorporated into international discussion about noneconomic loss and damage associated with climate change, which considers those aspects of environmental impacts that cannot be reduced to purely financial terms, including attachments to place, the value of preexisting livelihoods, and various forms of local knowledge. This shows how the analysis of local contexts can have global significance. These discussions are of considerable importance to the people living in the low-lying atolls of the Marshall Islands, which are vulnerable to rising sea levels.

In chapter 6, I describe how research on controversial topics may have negative political repercussions even when the researcher is trying to identify common ground among the protagonists. The subject is recent debates about the repatriation of Native American human remains at the university where I teach. In a talk presented at a roundtable discussion of these issues, I explained how the participants in these debates draw on different domains in staking out their respective positions: archaeologists make reference to science, university administrators emphasize property law, and Native Americans invoke kinship when referring to the human remains in the collections of the archaeology museum. Yet all three groups recognize the value of these domains in other contexts. The response to my participation in these events suggests that when debates are polarized, attempts to show how different points of view are constructed may result in political backlash. The chapter illustrates some of the risks entailed in writing about contested issues.

In the final chapter, I examine the anthropologist's role as expert witness. Chapter 7 presents two affidavits on indigenous land rights I submitted to the Inter-American Commission on and Court of Human Rights. The first affidavit addresses the detrimental consequences of Suriname's refusal to recognize the land rights of the Kaliña and Lokono indigenous peoples, including the destructive impacts of bauxite mining on land taken from them for a nature reserve. The second case is concerned with the title to indigenous land granted by Guyana to the Akawaio people of Isseneru, which excludes land subject to mining permits previously issued to outsiders.

The chapter considers how these affidavits have to be simultaneously legible to audiences with overlapping but sometimes incommensurable frames of reference, including lawyers and the legal system, the communities participating in these proceedings, and the discipline of anthropology. I also needed to reconcile my support for the Akawaio land claim with concerns about their use of mercury in artisanal gold mining, which can have significant environmental and health impacts, ensuring that my affidavit did not exacerbate the problem.

I take up the larger questions raised by these examples in the conclusion, including the problematic dichotomy between purely academic and engaged forms of research, by showing how the findings of these projects are of value beyond their initial objectives and context. Engaged anthropology also offers new sites for research, such as the adjudication of culture in legal proceedings. It identifies novel topics for research, such as culture loss. It also suggests the need for caution when writing from a distance, when seeking solutions to problems, and when debates are polarized. It can generate valuable suggestions for future research, such as hypotheses concerning the role of contested land rights in civil conflict and how competing political claims may be fashioned from shared domains. Thus a key dimension of engaged research is its capacity to contribute to larger debates rather than being purely instrumental in scope. Finally, I consider whether engaged anthropology produces "good enough" ethnography, as well as whether it is good for the discipline and helps to achieve positive political outcomes.

PROPERTY DISPUTES AND LEGAL CLAIMS

All of the cases discussed in this book address questions about property, a topic with a long and distinguished history in anthropology, as well as recent developments that make it a "dangerously interesting term to use" (Strathern and Hirsch 2004, 7).[7] Although engaged anthropology takes many forms and addresses multiple questions, it is not unusual for anthropologists to become involved in conflicts relating to property, whether land rights, compensation claims, or cultural property rights. This is especially the case when working with indigenous peoples, given their long histories of dispossession and contemporary struggles for recognition.

The legal proceedings discussed in chapter 1, for example, include efforts by the mining company to preempt the rights of local landowners as well as their access to subsistence resources. The independence movement described in chapter 2 seeks sovereignty over the Indonesian territory of West Papua. Chapter 3 describes how overlapping and contested land claims among the four sociolinguistic groups living in the Lakekamu River basin in southeastern Papua New Guinea have delayed the establishment of a conservation and development project. The extension of secondary land rights to plantation workers in Solomon Islands, described in chapter 4, exacerbated anxieties about indigenous control over land that date back to the colonial period, and were the flash point for civil conflict. In chapter 5, I describe how forced relocation owing to exposure to radiation in the Marshall Islands resulted in the loss of specialized forms of knowledge dependent on access to specific resources. My university's treatment of human remains as property was vigorously contested by Native Americans in the Midwest, who view them through the lens of kinship rather than ownership, as discussed in chapter 6. In both of the cases from the Amazon discussed in chapter 7, indigenous peoples seek to compel the state to recognize their land rights. In Suriname, this was seen as essential to preserving their freedom. In Guyana, collective land rights are central to Akawaio identity, in contrast to the importance of private property elsewhere in the country. Consequently, this book can also be read as a discussion of indigenous property disputes and the contributions anthropologists might make to their resolution.

Many of the contests over land, territory, and cultural property discussed in this book ended up in court: the Ok Tedi case in the Supreme Court of Victoria in Australia, the dispute over the Gold Ridge mine in the High Court of Solomon Islands, claims for damage to property and persons as a result of U.S. nuclear weapons testing in the Nuclear Claims Tribunal in the Marshall Islands, and the disputes with Guyana and Suriname in the Inter-American Commission on and Court of Human Rights in Costa Rica and Washington, DC. Comparison of these cases provides insight into how different legal institutions influence the form and content of the claims being advanced.

Although indigenous rights are increasingly recognized and protected by the law (Anaya 2004; Gilbert 2016), indigenous peoples must present their claims in legal systems historically used to facilitate their dispossession. Such proceedings might be seen to further colonial hegemony by compelling indigenous peoples to express themselves in alien language (Das 1989, 316; Dirlik 2001). Given that the law generally favors the interests of elites (Comaroff and Comaroff 2006), the juridification of these conflicts might be seen to domesticate indigenous politics (see Eckert et al. 2012a, 4).

Countering the arguments of "hegemony theorists" are scholars who view the mobilization of the law from below as a means to democratize power (Santos and Rodríguez-Garavito 2005; Eckert et al. 2012b) and a valuable "weapon of the weak" (see Scott 1987). Access to international courts and tribunals may also permit indigenous peoples to transcend political conflicts that have stalemated at the level of the state (Kirsch 2007). This is an important debate, and the examples presented in this book contribute to our understanding of the risks and benefits of legal activism. Rather than limit myself to considering these questions in the abstract, I have long since thrown in my lot with the indigenous peoples described here—from the Yonggom in Papua New Guinea to the Akawaio in Guyana—who brought their claims to international courts in response to their frustration with local politics, in the hope of gaining support for their cause, and to further their pursuit of justice. In other words, I am trying to influence the debate between hegemony and counterhegemony theorists through my participation in these legal proceedings.

Consequently, in the chapters that follow, I describe both how I became involved in these projects, and their outcomes. In all of the legal cases described here, I was invited to participate by community members, the nongovernmental organizations with which they collaborate, or their lawyers, and sometimes all of them at once. At times, people were frustrated that they needed to enlist an outsider to help make their claims legible in court. But they also recognized the value of anthropological expertise in these legal proceedings and in relation to their political struggles more broadly.

CATEGORIES OF PRACTICE

New scholarly projects are often accompanied by the proliferation of specialized terminology, and recent attention to engaged anthropology is no exception. Although there is an understandable desire for precise delineation of these terms, there is considerable overlap in practice (Low and Merry 2010, S207; Goldstein 2012, 39). In my early work on the Ok Tedi case, I stressed the role of advocacy, comparing anthropologists to lawyers who act on behalf of their clients, and underscored my willingness to take sides because remaining neutral—given the unbalanced power relations—was equivalent to endorsing the status quo (Kirsch 2002a). Although I sometimes use *activism* as a synonym for *engagement* when explaining my work to others, I generally avoid using the term when writing about my own experiences. My primary reservation about the category of "activist anthropology" (Hale 2006) is that it can shift attention away from the people or community seeking to bring about change.[8] This may be why Charles Hale (2007, 105) defines *activist research* as the practice of "align[ing] oneself with an organized group in a struggle for rights," although his definition is unnecessarily restrictive (Goldstein 2012, 41). Of these terms, *engagement* is defined the most broadly (Low and Merry 2010), although in this book I am explicitly concerned with *political* engagement.[9]

Applied anthropology refers to the long-standing practice of using anthropological perspectives to design and sometimes implement solutions to specific problems. As Roy A. Rappaport (1993, 296) notes, applied anthropologists typically work for institutional clients rather than the people directly affected by the problem. Consequently, "whatever values motivate or guide the study are not necessarily the anthropologist's, usually remain inexplicit, and are sometimes even covert" (Rappaport 1993, 296–97). Even so, I would not want to exaggerate the differences between applied and engaged anthropology, as many of these projects could be defined either way. For example, both of the social scientists I collaborated with on the Rongelap case refer to their work as applied anthropology (Barker 2004; Johnston and Barker 2008).

A related category is public anthropology. This refers to writing for new audiences and the possibility of contributing "to a transformation of the way the world is represented and experienced" (Fassin 2013, 628). It also includes contributions to both traditional and new social media, from newspaper editorials to blogs. Although some scholars use the categories of "public" and "engaged" anthropology interchangeably (see Eriksen 2006), *public anthropology* almost always refers to writing texts rather than to other forms of participation. It also tends to refer to documents produced for consumption by educated readers in the anthropologist's country of residence, in contrast to sharing information with the participants in our research projects and the communities in which they live, although in some cases the two may overlap.

The final category of practice is collaborative anthropology. In one sense, anthropology is always collaborative given its reliance on interlocutors for information. When anthropologists mobilize their research to help their informants achieve their goals, both parties may benefit (Hale 2006; see Oldfield 2015). Other collaborative projects involve training community members to conduct research on their own behalf, without necessarily contributing to discussions within the discipline (see Lassiter 2005). Similar reservations apply to forms of applied anthropology that emphasize the production of "deliverables" to clients at the expense of participating in debates in the field (Mosse 2013). Although these initiatives have their own value and goals, they differ from the projects discussed in this book, which are explicitly intended to contribute to debates in anthropology and social theory.

As I have suggested, there has been a discernable shift in attitudes toward engaged anthropology in recent years, moving from entrenched skepticism toward popular acceptance. Thus, defining these categories of practice too narrowly may exclude some scholars who identify as engaged or activist anthropologists. This includes the primary distinction I make between the production of texts for academic or public consumption and other activities that constitute engaged research as a category of practice. Even though I fully acknowledge the power of the written word to change the world, and recognize the complementarity of political engagement and ethnographic writing, for the purposes of this project I focus on the contributions of anthropology beyond the text.

ONE

How Political Commitments Influence Research

BACKSTAGE IN THE OK TEDI CASE, PAPUA NEW GUINEA

A CONVERSATION ABOUT RESORTING to violence in the dispute over the Ok Tedi mine still wakes me up at night. It was 1995, and the legal proceedings were moving very slowly. I was in the town of Kiunga, meeting with the leaders of the campaign against the mine, most of whom I had known for several years. Out of frustration, one of the men suggested that they blockade the Fly River, stopping the ships that supply the mine and deliver its ore to international markets. Others expressed support for the idea. However, I reminded them of their decision to take the mining company to court rather than trying to achieve their goals by force. We also discussed the human toll of the civil war in Bougainville, which was precipitated by conflict over the Panguna copper mine, and the likelihood of comparable violence and loss of life if they blockaded the river. Support for taking matters into their own hands gradually dissipated.

Since the late 1980s, I have participated in the political campaign and legal proceedings that sought to limit the destructive environmental impact of the Ok Tedi copper and gold mine in Papua New Guinea.[1] This work followed two years of ethnographic research with the Yonggom people living downstream from the mine. In local media and scholarly publications, I sought to call attention to the environmental problems caused by pollution from the mine. I contributed to a social and environmental impact study of the communities along the Ok Tedi and Fly Rivers that was sponsored by the mining company. I subsequently advised the lawyers representing the affected communities in legal proceedings against Broken Hill Proprietary (BHP), the majority shareholder and managing partner of the mine. I also collaborated with nongovernmental organizations critical of the mining industry in Australia, Europe, and the United States and wrote regular updates on the situation for NGO publications, including *Cultural Survival Quarterly* (Kirsch 1993, 2002b, 2004a). I prepared expert reports on the Ok Tedi case and participated in forums on the extractive industries and indigenous peoples sponsored by the United Nations (Kirsch 2003) and the World Bank (see Kirsch 2014, 202–4).

My work as an engaged anthropologist also provided both the data and the motivation for scholarly publications in journals and books. My participation in these events shaped my arguments and conclusions. Rather than claim to be neutral and objective about the Ok Tedi conflict, I acknowledged my political commitments. I was sympathetic to the concerns of the people whose lives and livelihoods were being affected by pollution. I was openly critical of the mining company for its reckless disregard of its environmental impacts and, to a lesser extent, the state for its failure to regulate the mining industry. I occasionally clashed with colleagues whose opinions on these issues differed from my own. Although I did my best to account for the complexity of the events I was writing about, inevitably there were gaps and blind spots in my analyses.

To illustrate these dynamics, I consider how my involvement in the campaign against the Ok Tedi mine has influenced my research and writing. In addressing these issues, I hope to demonstrate the value of paying closer attention to what happens "backstage" in engaged research projects. I begin by considering how politics affects the way anthropologists frame their arguments. I do so by examining debates with other scholars about whether the conflict over the Ok Tedi mine is better understood in economic or environmental terms. I then turn to the question of ethnographic refusal (Ortner 1995), in which anthropologists produce romanticized accounts of political resistance by withholding evidence of internal conflict. Here I explain why I previously refrained from writing about several conversations that occurred at pivotal moments of the campaign against the Ok Tedi mine, including the discussion about blockading the Fly River in 1995, and why I am comfortable doing so now.

I also describe my interactions with the primary actors in the Ok Tedi case, including the mining company, lawyers, NGOs, and the people living downstream from the mine. These relationships have influenced my research and writing in a variety of ways. When other social scientists offered competing interpretations of the conflict, I felt compelled to respond. The mining company tried to control all of the available expertise about the region and silence its critics, including me. My participation in the legal proceedings made demands on my work that might be considered incompatible with contemporary recognition of ethnographic knowledge as partial and situated. Despite our overlapping political commitments, collaboration with NGOs was contingent on negotiating the differences in our perspectives and priorities. Similarly, my participation in the campaign and lawsuit against the mining company affected my relationships with people who were also potential informants—for example, by limiting my ability to accurately convey the opinions of people who opted out of the legal proceedings. My goal is to encourage engaged anthropologists to be more forthcoming in how they address comparable dilemmas and navigate similar challenges in their own work. This discussion also introduces key ideas used in analyzing the other examples of engaged anthropology described in this book.

FRAMING DEBATES

Anthropologists are often affected by and contribute to the framing of political debates (see Bateson 1972; Goffman 1974). After completing my dissertation research with the Yonggom in 1989, I gave a presentation at the University of Papua New Guinea on the impact of pollution on the people living beside the Ok Tedi River, published an op-ed on the subject in the *Times of Papua New Guinea* (Kirsch 1989a), and addressed these issues on a national radio show in Port Moresby. The prevailing view in the capital at the time was that excessive demands for compensation were impeding economic progress in Papua New Guinea (see Toft 1997). Complaints about the environmental impact of the Ok Tedi mine were readily subsumed into this larger national narrative. The failure to distinguish between the legitimate grievances of the people living along the Ok Tedi and Fly Rivers and other demands for resource rents delegitimized protests against the environmental impact of the mine.

Whereas my work framed the conflict downstream from the Ok Tedi mine in environmental terms, other social scientists writing about these issues emphasized conflicts associated with the distribution of economic benefits. In his influential "social time bomb" explanation of the uprising against the Panguna copper mine in Bougainville, Colin Filer (1990) argues that mining projects initiate a downward spiral of social disintegration. Compensation payments to communities living in the vicinity of mining projects fail to meet expectations as people move from local resource produc-

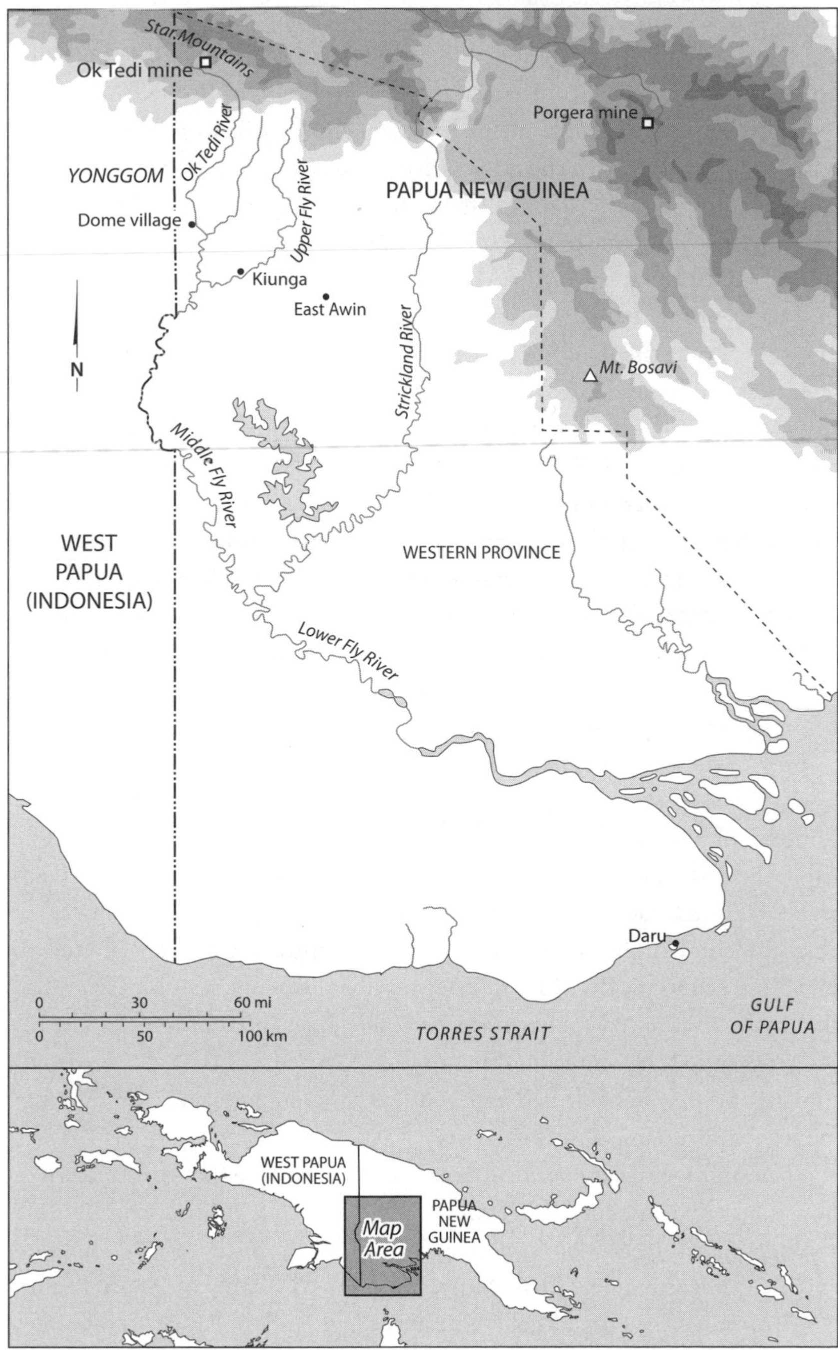

MAP 2. The Ok Tedi mine and the Fly River, from the Star Mountains to the Gulf of Papua, Papua New Guinea.

tion and traditional modes of exchange to participation in the capitalist economy of accumulation. Sons inherit deals their fathers made with the mining company and find them wanting. The cycle of dissatisfaction and renegotiation repeats with increasing frequency until no credible leaders remain and no deal with the mine will do. At that point, approximately fifteen years into the life span of the average mining project in Papua New Guinea, the social time bomb explodes.

Rolf Gerritsen and Martha Macintyre (1991) also focus on the distribution of economic benefits from mining companies to local communities. They argue that the dynamics of investment and development, which they refer to as the "capital logic of mining," dictate a pattern of expenditure that frustrates and ultimately infuriates local communities. Like Melanesian big men managing their lesser allies, mining companies hold their constituents at arm's length, spending to solve problems as they arise. The process generates an asymptotic curve of dissatisfaction that peaks just below the line separating conflict from calm. Yet maintaining this delicate balance is inherently risky, for events need only nudge the curve slightly to provoke a crisis. In addition, Gerritsen and Macintyre (1991) observe that Papua New Guinea's economic dependence on the mining industry leads the state to view rural communities as rivals for their share of mining revenues.

Both of these arguments frame mining conflicts in economic terms. Filer (1990, 70) notes that the key factor uniting the people living on the island of Bougainville was "nothing less than the hole in the middle of it," and that the rift in the body politic paralleled the underlying transformation of the landscape. He subsequently observed that the uneven "spatial distribution" of environmental impacts and benefits from compensation contributed to social and economic divisions in Bougainville (Filer 1997a, 104). He argued that compensation payments exacerbate fault lines in communities already predisposed to fragmentation (Filer 1997a).[2] Gerritsen and Macintyre (1991) similarly point to unfulfilled expectations for compensation and development as the primary sources of strife.

These arguments had political consequences, because they diverted attention from environmental impacts by suggesting that mining conflicts are driven primarily by economic motives. The mining industry readily embraced this view. For example, Gavin Murray and Ian Williams of Placer Pacific, which operated the Porgera gold mine in the highlands of Papua New Guinea during the late 1980s, claimed that the central issue in the Ok Tedi case was "stakeholder identification and consultation," referring to the economic interests of the people living downstream, rather than environmental degradation (Murray and Williams 1997, 200). Similarly, Ok Tedi Mining criticized conservation organizations for focusing on the mine's environmental record while ignoring the economic benefits provided by the project, including jobs, taxes, and foreign exchange earnings (Kirsch 2014, 77). As Roy A. Rappaport (1993, 299) warns, however, monetization operates according to "a logic that reduces all qualitative distinctions to mere quantitative differences, a logic that, as it were, attempts to 'bottom line' the world." While there may well be people in Papua New Guinea willing to trade a few feet of mud in their gardens and a few acres of dead trees for a winning lottery ticket, it hardly relieves mining companies of their responsibility to limit their environmental impacts, nor can the most toxic effects of mining on the environment and human health ever be made good with monetary compensation.

In contrast, ethnographic research with the communities downstream from the Ok Tedi mine led me to emphasize the consequences of environmental degradation for people whose lives and livelihoods depend on subsistence production. Pollution from the mine has affected the gardens where they grow bananas and other crops, sago stands that produce the starch that is the mainstay of their diets, and the fish, crayfish, turtles, and other riverine animals that were previously an important source of protein in their diets. The operation of the mine has also resulted in widespread deforestation along the Ok Tedi and Fly Rivers, affecting more than two thousand square kilometers of rain forest. Many of the birds and other animals that once lived along these rivers have migrated elsewhere. This led me to describe how the impact of pollution from the Ok Tedi mine has been so catastrophic for the Yonggom and their neighbors that "much of what they once took for granted about their natural environment no longer holds true" (Kirsch 1997b, 153).

My attention to environmental degradation and its consequences provided an important corrective to the prevailing focus on economic issues. I felt a responsibility to challenge the emphasis on monetary compensation in national debates that allowed the mining company to continue discharging millions of tons of finely ground tailings and waste rock into local rivers every year as long as they increased compensation payments to the people affected by the project. I also sought to help raise international awareness of the environmental problems downstream from the mine. Yet framing the conflict in environmental terms led me to downplay its economic dimensions rather than recognize the value of both perspectives and examine how they are interrelated.

It was only in 1999, when the mining company belatedly admitted that the environmental impacts of the project were far greater than previously acknowledged, concluding that the operation of the mine was "incompatible with its environmental values" (Barker and Oldfield 1999, 1), that I no longer felt compelled to persuade readers that the Ok Tedi mine was an environmental disaster. Public recognition of the severity of the problem provided me with an opportunity to reassess my earlier work rather than continue to defend claims made while "writing in the eye of a storm" (Bell 2002). Consequently, I acknowledged the ways that indigenous views on mining and the environment are shaped by "the complex longings, dreams and . . . choices" of people living on the margins of the global economy (Coumans 2004, 90). I also discussed local desires for economic benefits, as poignantly expressed by an elderly woman who told me she hoped that a successful resolution to the lawsuit would allow her to "taste some sugar before I die" (Kirsch 2006, 26). I explained how damage to the resources on which they depend forced them to purchase alternatives, resulting in their impoverishment. And I described how the Yonggom and their neighbors, like other people living in rural Papua New Guinea, generally aspire to greater participation in the national and global economies (see Gewertz and Errington 1991; Smith 1994).

In contrast to my willingness to revisit my earlier arguments, many of my colleagues writing about these issues elected to double down on their original positions, asserting that reports about the environmental impacts of the Ok Tedi mine were exaggerated. After the initial lawsuit was settled out of court in 1996, the anthropologist Colin Filer (1997c, 90) argued that while logging was more damaging to the environment in Western Province than mining, it received less attention because impacts from the mine were more photogenic. Similarly, the geographer Richard Jackson (1998, 207), a long-term consultant for Ok Tedi Mining, argued that "the destruction of a few square kilometres of swamp forest was a small price . . . to pay" for the economic benefits provided by the mining company, even though his estimate of the damage ended up being wrong by a magnitude of a thousand. Filer (1997c, 87) also wrote disparagingly about what he described as an "envelope of environmental paranoia which conflated local perceptions of physical and social change, making it difficult for other stakeholders to distinguish real grievances from imaginary fears," while failing to take into consideration the complexities of risk assessment for the people living downstream from the mine, who lacked access to independent scientific information or prior exposure to industrialized forms of development. Yet pollution from the Ok Tedi mine is expected to last for hundreds of years along parts of the river, and large portions of the landscape will never return to pre-mine conditions (Tingay 2007).

Years later, Filer continued to attribute the conflict over the Ok Tedi mine to the mishandling of public relations rather than the severity of its environmental impacts: "The big mistake was to discount the interests and opinions of foreign journalists, lawyers, academics and scientists who did not count as 'stakeholders' in PNG's national policy framework" (Filer, Banks, and Burton 2008, 185).[3] Anthropologist Martha Macintyre similarly denied that pollution was a contributing factor to mining conflicts in Papua New Guinea, arguing that people living near the Lihir gold mine "embrace the discourses of environmentalism and impending ecological catastrophe primarily to use them as leverage in negotiations with the mining company" (Macintyre and Foale 2004, 249), suggesting that local expressions of concern about the environment are largely strategic.

Although it may seem churlish to criticize colleagues for expressing views they might wish to recant, these were not offhand or idle remarks; they were assertions committed to print without regard to their political consequences or, in hindsight, their accuracy. I have two reasons for including their comments here. First, they illustrate how I had to fight uphill against more senior colleagues who consistently ignored or downplayed the gravity of the environmental problems on the Ok Tedi and Fly Rivers, undermining the legitimacy of concerns expressed by people affected by the Ok Tedi mine. And second, these examples are meant to challenge the view that my work is compromised because I acknowledge my political commitments, in contrast to scholars who claim their research is neutral or apolitical. All of us have been affected by the politically charged circumstances in which these debates took place. Filer's (1999) primary concern has been to contribute to the rationalization of the state's economic policies in contrast to its ad hoc responses to landowner demands. Jackson's (1998) objection was that the mining industry was being unfairly blamed for the failures of the state. Macintyre and Foale (2004) sought to discredit the claims of NGOs writing about mining in Melanesia. Yet these scholars have been reluctant to examine how their own political projects influence their views on the relationship between mines and communities in Papua New Guinea.

Only recently has the long struggle to elicit recognition of the negative impacts of the mining industry in Papua New Guinea finally persuaded some of the industry's staunchest supporters. After spending years defending the mining industry from its NGO critics, Martha Macintyre (2015, 144) finally acknowledged, "Environmental destruction, social discord, widespread corruption, and new inequalities have been the legacies of every mining project in Papua New Guinea to date." However, her belated recognition of these negative impacts has not been accompanied by reconsideration of her earlier scholarship on the subject.[4] This suggests the need for greater attention to the way scholars frame their work, how such frames are influenced by politics, and how they influence our findings.

ETHNOGRAPHIC REFUSAL

In the midst of a heated political struggle, it may be difficult to practice full disclosure. Only with the passage of time am I able to write more explicitly about certain events, including the discussion about blockading the Fly River in 1995. Another pivotal conversation I avoided writing about took place the following year. The lawsuit against BHP and Ok Tedi Mining had just been settled out of court for an estimated $500 million in compensation and commitments to tailings containment (Tait 1996, 19). Yet the agreement was nearly canceled before it could be ratified by the plaintiffs. One of the leaders of the campaign against the mining company was having second thoughts after initially approving the deal. He pointed out that the impacted communities would not have sufficient control over the compensation funds. He was also concerned that the only way to enforce the implementation of the settlement was to return to court in Australia, a high bar that would require support from their Australian lawyers, attract fierce opposition from the mining company, and take years to produce results.

We were meeting in the capital, Port Moresby, and planned to fly to the town of Kiunga the next day to begin collecting the signatures needed to finalize the settlement. Suddenly the disaffected plaintiff announced that he no longer supported the agreement. The lawyers were unable to dissuade him and reluctantly concluded that they would have to abandon the settlement and return their A$7 million fee. However, I persuaded the lawyers that we should travel to Kiunga as planned to discuss the issue with the other plaintiffs before making any irrevocable decisions. The dissenting leader and I stayed up late into the night discussing what would happen if the settlement failed, given that the law firm lacked the resources to continue litigating their case in court. But when the lawyers and I arrived at the airport very early the next morning, still unsure what would happen, we were surprised to see him waiting for us. He did not board our flight but promised to join us in Kiunga the following day to present the agreement to the other plaintiffs for their approval. Although I subsequently wrote about the strengths and weaknesses of the settlement agreement (Kirsch 1997c), I never revealed how close the case was to utter failure.

My reluctance to write about either of these incidents is an example of ethnographic refusal. Sherry Ortner (1995, 179) argues that anthropologists may "sanitize the internal politics of the dominated" in order to avoid subjecting their informants to external criticism or delegitimization. She also describes two other forms of ethnographic refusal. She is critical of anthropologists who focus exclusively on the material dimensions of protest movements, ignoring their cultural, religious, and ideological foundations. She also suggests that anthropologists writing about political resistance may fail to adequately represent the complex subjectivities of their informants. The refusal to address these issues results in accounts of political resistance that are ethnographically thin.

Why did I avoid writing about these interactions? Sharing these stories might have compromised the goals of my informants and put them at risk. Revealing their deliberations about violence could have exposed them to retribution by the state. Publicizing their discontent with the out-of-court settlement might have jeopardized its implementation. Consequently, writing about these interactions would have violated my ethical responsibility to protect my informants. I also wanted to avoid the appearance of taking credit for these decisions, as it is impossible to know what might have occurred in my absence. The revelation of my participation in these conversations could also have been exploited by parties seeking to discredit the campaign against the mining company by attributing its direction and leadership to outsiders. To the extent that engaged research provides access to confidential information, anthropologists may have to choose between protecting the interests of their informants and revealing internal political dynamics. Although withholding information may result in partially sanitized accounts of resistance, as Ortner (1995) argues, the pressure to do so may dissipate over time, allowing anthropologists to revisit their earlier work without compromising their responsibilities to their informants.

CORPORATE DISCIPLINE

My participation in a social and environmental impact study sponsored by Ok Tedi Mining offers insight into how corporations seek to discipline expertise. In 1991, the mining company hired a consulting company based at the University of Papua New Guinea to conduct research on the communities downstream from the Ok Tedi mine (Filer 1999). The project was initiated by a faction of the mining company that—with an eye to the causes of the 1989 civil war in Bougainville—was concerned that opposition to the Ok Tedi mine might also become a runaway train.[5] The research was intended to get a handle on local discontent before it became too great to manage. In the second year of the project, I was invited to conduct an assessment of the Yonggom and Awin villages where I had previously conducted ethnographic research.

As might be expected, working on a project sponsored by the mining company resulted in some awkward interactions. When I returned to the village where I lived during my dissertation research, I was both excited to see my old friends and anxious about their response to my participation in the social impact study. Several people expressed concern that the mining company might have co-opted my loyalties. I was also criticized by someone I had not previously met, as he had recently returned to the village after living elsewhere for a number of years. However, most of the people in the village expressed confidence that I would adequately convey their concerns to the mining company, although their comments were also intended to remind me of our long-standing relationships and my ongoing responsibilities to them.

When visiting another Yonggom village to the north, where I had previously attended a pig feast, the criticism was even stronger. One of the other members of the research team was traveling with me at the time, so everyone spoke in English and Melanesian Tok Pisin. Toward the end of the meeting, one of the men interrupted the conversation by handing me a letter addressed to the mining company. Then, abruptly switching to Yonggom, he warned me that if he did not receive a positive response to his message within two weeks, he would come after me with an ax. His comments were unexpected and jarring, especially since the Yonggom rarely make violent threats, which are considered dangerous to both parties. I realized, however, that he was not just speaking to me in his native tongue but deliberately addressing me in a common language, excluding my expatriate colleague from the conversation. By speaking to me in Yonggom, he invoked the solidarity of belonging to the same linguistic community, which neutralized the threat while still conveying a sense of urgency and importance in his demand.

My final report for the project described many of the problems that subsequently became the basis of the lawsuit against the mine, including the consequences of environmental degradation for the people living downstream and the failure of the mining company to adequately compensate them for their losses. Although the mining company never challenged the validity of my social impact study, efforts were made to limit its circulation, with the executive who commissioned the study reportedly telling another member of the research team that he intended to "bury Kirsch's report so deep that it will never see the light of day." However, in the introduction to my social impact study I cited the American Anthropological Association (1971, 19) code of ethics, which stipulates that "no reports should be provided to sponsors that are not also available to the general public and, where practicable, to the population studied," signaling my intention to publish my findings (Kirsch 1995, 26).[6]

While completing the study, I was asked to contribute a short account of the social and environmental impacts of the Ok Tedi mine to a special issue of *Cultural Survival Quarterly* on "societies in danger" (Kirsch 1993). I chose my words carefully to convey the magnitude of the problems without alienating the management of the mine, which was funding the social impact study. However, I encouraged American readers to write to the CEO of Amoco, which was one of the shareholders in the project at the time. Despite my effort to present a balanced assessment, the manager of the consulting company chastised me for "trying to play both sides against the middle" and informed me that the mining company instructed him not to renew my contract.

Several weeks after the original lawsuit against the mining company was filed in 1994, I was contacted by the mining executive responsible for having me fired. He was seeking my services as an adviser. He argued that the mining company would do a better job protecting the interests of the downstream landowners than a profit-seeking Australian law firm. Shortly after declining their generous offer, I received a letter from the lawyers representing the mining company, who threatened me with a lawsuit—given my participation in the social impact study—if I continued to assist the plaintiffs and their solicitors in the case. On the advice of the lawyers representing the plaintiffs in the case, I ignored their letter. But the implications of their actions were chilling: the mining company sought to either co-opt or silence all of the available expertise on its social and environmental impacts.

Despite their lucrative offer and subsequent legal harassment, I was occasionally asked to assume a back-channel role as a liaison between the mining company and the lawyers representing the plaintiffs. One of the senior executives at the mining company periodically called me to share information and solicit feedback about corporate proposals to settle the conflict. For example, he described a plan to construct a tailings dam in the lowlands along the Ok Tedi River, which would have destroyed what was left of that watershed while protecting the Fly River. The proposal never advanced further for reasons not shared with me and, presumably, took into account my warning about the likelihood of a violent response from several thousand Yonggom people who would have been displaced by the dam. Another proposal was to transfer BHP's shares in the mining project to a trust fund and continue operating the mine as before, which was subsequently implemented when the company negotiated its exit from the country. After the company shared this information with me, I was encouraged to speak with the lawyers from Slater and Gordon, who represented the Yonggom and their neighbors. Only after the case was settled did I learn that these conversations had been approved by the mining company over the objections of their legal representatives, as well as vetted by the senior partners of the law firm representing the plaintiffs in the case. In a spy novel, having frank conversations with parties on both sides of a dispute might foster suspicions that someone is a double agent; but in this case there was no duplicity, as everyone understood that I was politically aligned with the people living downstream from the mine. This relationship was the reason why the mining company continued to keep me in the loop and sought my assistance in vetting proposals.

After the case was settled out of court in 1996, mining company executives tried to persuade me they had learned from their mistakes, conveying the message that even though they may have been wrong in the past, they were now doing everything in their power to rectify the situation. This is an example of how liberal subjects optimistically claim to have overcome previous failures without critically examining the underlying institutions or practices responsible for the problem (Povinelli 2002). They wanted me to convey their message to the communities downstream and sought my advice on how to improve their relationships with them. But I remained skeptical of the mining company's commitment to fundamentally alter its decision making and, consequently, declined to endorse its plans for the future.

After the case was settled, I was invited to submit an editorial to *Anthropology Today* describing how international networks of "landowners, ecological activists, anthropologists and lawyers" are able to exert pressure on transnational corporations (Kirsch 1996a, 14). When the article appeared in print, I was surprised to learn that the editor of the journal had contacted the mining company to ascertain whether it objected to its publication and allowed lawyers for the company to contribute several footnotes.[7] This shows how corporations can wield influence over anthropology and anthropologists in a manner not ordinarily matched by our informants, as no one at the Royal Anthropological Institute, which publishes the journal, thought to contact the people living downstream from the mine to ensure that their views were properly represented. The same was true when the editors of *Third World Quarterly* invited Royal Dutch Shell to respond to an article on the relationship between political instability and economic opportunity, which raised questions about the company's practices in Nigeria (Frynas 1998, 2000; Detheridge and Pepple 1998).

It is also worthwhile comparing my response to the litigation against the mining company as an engaged anthropologist and the neutral stance adopted by other social scientists working in the region. None of the other contributors to the social impact studies published the results of their research or otherwise made them available to the public, nor did they provide assistance or advice to the plaintiffs in the case. Consistent with their claim to neutrality, they rejected overtures to assist the lawyers representing the mining company, although the project sponsor at the company remained in contact with several of us during the lawsuit. Information generated through research with members of the communities affected by the mine was made available to the company but not to the participants in the study. Thus scholars who asserted their neutrality during the lawsuit against the Ok Tedi mine provided information to the protagonists on one side of the dispute while depriving the communities on the opposite side of potential benefits from their research.

Whereas a common criticism of engaged anthropologists is that their political commitments prevent them from interacting with people who possess alternative points of view, my participation in the Ok Tedi case facilitated my interaction with the key players in the conflict. This included most of the people living along the river system, local activists, international NGOs, managers at the mine site and executives at corporate headquarters in Melbourne, politicians, and lawyers on both sides of the case. Advocacy rather than neutrality allowed me to participate in, and contribute to, the struggle against the environmental problems caused by the mining project.

Other anthropologists have explained their decision to work for the mining industry in a variety of ways: by their desire to improve relations between mining companies and communities, their recognition that downsizing the academy requires anthropologists to find new markets for their skills (see Goldman and Baum 2000, 2), or their understanding that corporations are more willing than indigenous groups to pay for anthropological advice (Filer 1996, 26). They also argue that they are more likely to effect positive change by working within the corporation than by critically addressing these issues from the outside, even though their ability "to publicize those insights may be restricted, and their reporting may be biased by their operating environment" (Coumans 2011, S33).[8] Mining companies tend to treat the findings of ethnographic consultants as proprietary business information and impose restrictions on what anthropologists publish. These controls may be enforced by the threat of legal action or the termination of their contracts. As the managing director of another mining company in Papua New Guinea once told me in frustration while objecting to the draft of an article I showed him before its publication, "I never had any trouble from the anthropologists who work for me!" Because anthropologists have been reluctant to address corporate restrictions on their research, these interactions are more widespread than has been recognized.

LEGAL COLONIZATION OF ANTHROPOLOGY

Anthropologists are increasingly called upon to provide information to lawyers and legal proceedings. I contributed several affidavits to the second phase of the Ok Tedi litigation, which ran from 2000 to 2004, after the plaintiffs returned to court because the mining company refused to stop discharging tailings into the river system as stipulated by the original settlement agreement. In one affidavit, I was asked to address the legitimacy of the process through which the mining company encouraged plaintiffs to opt out of the renewed legal proceedings in return for increased monetary compensation. The mining company collected signatures from a small number of people claiming to represent the villages affected by the mine on agreements that promised additional compensation in return for allowing the mine to continue operating as before. Once signed, the Community Mine Continuation Agreements became legally binding on everyone living in the village as well as members of future generations.

The lawyers representing the indigenous plaintiffs asked me to evaluate these agreements. I spoke to them in the middle of the night from a pay phone in the hallway of a college residence at the University of Cambridge, where I was attending a workshop. Normally I would have deferred expressing my opinion until I discussed the issues with people from the affected communities. However, the lawyers needed to file an injunction immediately. My response was that allowing one or two people to sign the agreements on behalf of an entire village—and future generations—violated local property rights. This is especially important in Papua New Guinea, where the constitution and the legal system recognize and protect customary land rights. I made reference to a map illustrating how land ownership is often independent of village residence, which I had previously produced for the social impact study sponsored by the mining company. I described how the people in this area historically resided in isolated homesteads or small hamlets, whereas nucleated villages are a relatively recent artifact of colonialism (Welsch 1994, 88).[9] Land rights are held by individual members of a lineage, and no one has the authority to make decisions about another person's land. Given that the mine continuation agreements were fundamentally concerned with the environmental impact of the mine on their land, I argued in my affidavit to the court that they were invalid.[10]

It is reasonable to ask whether anthropological arguments produced in support of legal claims can be considered "good enough" ethnography (Scheper-Hughes 1989, 28; see Macdonald 2002). I subsequently had an opportunity to view film footage shot in the town of Kiunga and in several of the Fly River villages about the same time I was composing my affidavit (Cavadini and King 2010). The legal tactics of the mining company initially confused people. Very few of them realized that signing the compensation agreement prevented the other members of the village from participating in the lawsuit against the mining company (Kalinoe 2003). Their confusion gradually turned into anger against the individuals who signed the agreements without obtaining their permission. One man's house was attacked and his family was forced to flee. The people depicted in the film challenged the authority of the signatories to determine what happens to their land, much as I had argued in my affidavit.

The gap between my legal work and ethnographic writing on the Ok Tedi case has never been substantial, as I frequently included materials produced for legal claims as examples in articles published in mainstream anthropology journals. This was possible because of my long-standing research in the area, which began years before the legal proceedings, in contrast to the short-term and problem-focused research I have conducted for the other court cases to which I have contributed, as I discuss in subsequent chapters. The continuity between the claims I make in legal venues and the arguments I present in academic publications might be viewed in a positive light, as consistency is generally considered a hallmark of reliable ethnography. But it can also be argued that legal claims made on behalf of clients belong to a genre of writing that is very different from ethnography (Foster and Grove 1993; Macdonald 2002), even though I treat them as commensurate. My stake in the truth value of these claims—given that submitting an affidavit requires an oath that the information presented is accurate to the best of one's knowledge—might also appear to contradict the postmodern recognition that all knowledge claims are partial and situated (Haraway 1988; Strathern 2004; Macdonald 2002).[11] But anthropologists have gradually backed away from the strongest versions of this argument, acknowledging that calling attention to how categories are socially constructed does not preclude their continued use. That we can deconstruct how we come to know the world does not mean that the associated facts no longer matter (see Latour 2004).

The increasing interpenetration of anthropological and legal knowledge, which Gary Edmond (2004, 220) refers to as the "legal colonization" of anthropology, means that when anthropologists become involved in litigation, all of one's publications, not only affidavits, may eventually have to be vetted by lawyers. This was true for me during the Ok Tedi case, although I recall only one occasion when I was asked to modify something I had written. I sent the draft of an article to a lawyer with whom I had worked for several years. He objected to a quote attributed to one of the key plaintiffs in the case, who had told me it was "too late to save the river." The lawyer knew the speaker in question well and suggested that, while the statement may have reflected his frustration at the time of our conversation, his views on the subject had changed over time. The lawyer also expressed concern that attributing the quote to the plaintiff might prejudice their case, given that one of the proposed solutions was environmental remediation. He encouraged me to use a more generic description of the speech act, such as "one landowner said." The lawyer did not press me to alter or delete the quote, only to avoid identifying the plaintiff by name. Our exchange raised important questions about how to treat the speech of informants who become public figures. In this case, my informant's standing in the legal proceedings made him vulnerable to public scrutiny. Although I frequently refer to the same speaker by name in other contexts and quote from his public speeches, he made these remarks to me during a private conversation. Keeping the source of the quote anonymous was an appropriate way to resolve the lawyer's concerns. Even though this decision might also be seen as another example of ethnographic refusal, anthropologists have historically recognized the importance of providing our informants with anonymity to protect them from harm.

Despite working closely with the lawyers in the Ok Tedi case for many years, including multiple occasions during which we were in each other's company for one or two weeks at a time, there were a number of critical junctures at which anthropological input was considered irrelevant or unwanted. For example, the original causes of action in the case were composed without anthropological feedback and included assertions that were not supported by ethnographic evidence, such as the claim that the Yonggom have chiefs who can speak on behalf of others, in contrast to the absence of formal political leadership, and that they are hunter-gatherers, despite their reliance on horticulture. In legal proceedings, strong statements of claim may be presented with the recognition that not all of them will stand up in court, and that claims that do go forward can be amended as needed. My close working relationship with the lawyers also failed to translate into participation or consultation on either settlement agreement. On a practical level, the lawyers negotiating these agreements were unaccustomed to consulting with anyone other than their clients in similar proceedings. Moreover, the negotiations moved rapidly and there was limited opportunity to solicit my opinion, especially given the time difference between Melbourne and Ann Arbor. However, I suspect that the lawyers were also content not to receive input or feedback that might have made reaching a settlement more difficult.

Anthropologists who produce evidence for legal claims also face other risks. A number of anthropologists and other social scientists have had their field notes subpoenaed (Watts 2010, 283–84; see Weiner 1999), even though they are ordinarily considered confidential documents. Participation in legal proceedings can also affect anthropologists' relationships with their informants. During the litigation, I was not able to conduct research on other topics, as the court case was all people wanted to talk to me about. When the second case was abruptly settled out of court without achieving its primary goal of stopping the mine from discharging tailings into the Ok Tedi River, people were disappointed and angry with their lawyers.[12] Had the circumstances been slightly different, they could easily have blamed me for the outcome, jeopardizing my ability to continue doing research in the area. Another risk for scholars who contribute to legal proceedings is that the resulting commitments might lead them to continue defending their positions over time, rather than remaining open to new evidence, ideas, and interpretations, which is a fundamental requirement of scholarship.

The juridification of political claims (Eckert et al. 2012b) also creates risks for the plaintiffs involved. It can have a funneling effect in which the number of active participants is restricted. The plaintiffs may become dependent on technical evaluations—including both scientific evidence and legal interpretations—that may be at odds with their own perceptions or understandings of what is right or just. There are also opportunity costs associated with legal claims, which may discourage activists from pursuing complementary political strategies or forging alliances with other parties, such as the trade union representing the mineworkers or communities facing comparable threats. Corporate defendants, moreover, are able to outspend plaintiffs and their lawyers, which means that finances can dictate when and how a case is settled, as occurred with both lawsuits against the mining company.

Nonetheless, these legal proceedings may have beneficial "unlocking effects" that help overcome political stalemates in domestic arenas, "reframing effects" that identify new political strategies and activate novel coalitions, "participation effects" that enhance political agency, and positive "socioeconomic effects" through political recognition and redistribution (Rodríguez-Garavito and Rodríguez-Franco 2015; see Gilbert 2017, 73). In the second case against the Ok Tedi mine, public pressure forced the mining company to transfer its shares in the project to a development trust established in Singapore, a decision that ultimately cost BHP Billiton several billion dollars in lost revenue (Kirsch 2014), although the distribution of these funds continues to be contested, as I describe below.

NEGOTIATING DIFFERENCE WITH NGOS

What are the similarities and differences between the articles and reports produced by anthropologists and nongovernmental organizations? What are their respective methods, standards for evidence, and priorities? Although it is important not to overgeneralize, NGOs tend to conduct research that documents existing policy positions, in contrast to ethnographic research, which is usually driven by open-ended questions. NGO personnel may have limited background knowledge, fail to acknowledge the influence of their political positions on their results, take shortcuts because they operate under strict time constraints, or be overly influenced by their funders (Cooley and Ron 2002). One example of the way NGOs routinely cut corners is their use of press releases in which quotations are ghostwritten by the organization and attributed to speakers after the fact, although the news media, when reporting these statements, rarely acknowledges this practice. NGOs also draw on their own cultural categories rather than those of the people with whom they work (Rabinow 2002, 14; Kirsch 2007). Their reports are rarely subject to independent review. On a more positive note, NGO staff members are able work on several related projects at a time, affording them a broader perspective, whereas anthropologists in the academy have responsibilities that limit their engagements beyond the university.

When engaged anthropologists collaborate with NGOs, they exchange information with each other. Scholars generally lack experience negotiating these relationships, which can lead to tensions or conflict, as the following example suggests. On one occasion, I learned that an NGO planned to distribute documents that exaggerated the public health impacts of pollution in the river system downstream from the Ok Tedi mine, incorrectly suggesting that it was the cause of birth defects. As written, the report would have falsely alarmed the people living along the river, so I asked a contact at the mining company to help me obtain more accurate medical information to share with the NGO. When I subsequently explained how I acquired these documents, my NGO contact felt that I had violated their confidence by discussing their plans with my contact at the mining company. Similar conflicts occur among NGOs as well. For example, when a prominent NGO in Australia scheduled a series of roundtable discussions between environmental groups and mining company representatives, other NGOs broke off their relationships with the participants in these meetings, fearing they had been co-opted by the process. Anthropologists who work closely with mining company personnel may face similar suspicions from members of the NGO community, compromising their relationships.

The differences between academic research and NGO reports are gradually decreasing as the studies produced by NGOs become more reliable. People increasingly move between academic institutions and NGOs during the course of their careers, transferring research questions and standards with them. In general, NGOs have been more willing to take advantage of new sources of information available through the Internet and social media than their academic counterparts. This allows them to provide valuable perspectives and critical analysis that may not exist anywhere else. However, there are questions about the reliability of these accounts, given that much of the information available on the Internet has not been checked for factual errors or bias. The reliance of NGOs on information that circulates freely on the

Internet is exacerbated by the restriction of academic works behind expensive paywalls established by publishers, impeding the flow of information and ideas between scholars and NGOs.

Academics and NGOs also operate according to alternative temporalities, with civil society being obliged to respond to urgent problems, and scholars having the luxury to write about them after they have become historical events. Given the journalistic sensibility of NGOs, their reports may become outdated in relatively short order, whereas academic writing, which is intended to produce analyses that transcend the moment of publication, is usually out of date by the time it is published. The difference might be described in terms of timeliness versus timelessness, both of which have their merits, although the lag time in the publication of academic work tends to decrease its value to people working for NGOs. Even though the work of NGOs and the work of academics are converging in many ways, their reliance on different sources of information and the alternative temporalities in which they operate suggest that they will probably continue to operate in separate silos.

The contributions made by NGOs to the documentation and analysis of social problems indicate the value of continued interaction between the academy and nongovernmental organizations. However, there is skepticism on both sides of this relationship. Active members of civil society may be disdainful of academic research and the lack of commitment to causes and communities on the part of scholars, whereas prior valorization of NGOs in the academy has given way to dour criticism of the simplifications promoted by civil society in its campaigns. But the claim that the academy is directed solely toward knowledge production, whereas civil society is focused on action, is outdated if it was ever true (see Osterweil 2013). NGOs are also knowledge producers, and engaged scholarship in the academy is on the rise. Claims to the contrary are based more on the desire to purify the academy of politics than an accurate assessment of the relationship between the two.

Other factors also contribute to the tension between civil society and the academy, including the sense of political resignation that constrains our ability to envisage changes to the status quo. For example, as Frederic Jameson (1994, xii) notes, it seems easier to imagine the destruction of the earth than an alternative to capitalism. Such radical pessimism is more common in academic writing than in work produced by nongovernmental organizations, which are often criticized for being overly optimistic. At the same time, scholars who are critical of corporate claims about social responsibility or sustainability risk being scolded for their "low-minded sentimentality" for believing the worst about corporations and their motives (Sen 1999, 280, cited in Walker-Said 2015, 19). But scholarship and NGO-work need not be exclusive; indeed, they should inform one another. Academics need to interact with the world to test their ideas and formulate original hypotheses, and civil society can benefit from the perspectives scholars have to offer.

It might seem that my reluctance to criticize NGOs is another example of ethnographic refusal, especially since attending to the shortcomings of these organizations remains fashionable among anthropologists and other social scientists. But the NGO community was far more accurate than my peers in the academy in its diagnosis of corporate responsibility for the slow-motion environmental catastrophe downstream from the Ok Tedi mine. NGOs also played a pivotal role in the campaign against the mining company, in contrast to the belated recognition of the legitimacy of NGO criticism by social scientists studying the mining industry.

COLLABORATING WITH COMMUNITIES

In November 2005, the year after the second lawsuit against the Ok Tedi mine was settled out of court, there was a meeting of representatives from the communities affected by pollution in the town of Kiunga. The goal of the participants was to map out a new political strategy for their campaign after the precipitous end to the legal proceedings. Although the court case provided important resources for political mobilization, it also limited leadership roles and restricted their political options. The settlement left the campaign against the mine in disarray. Relationships between the supporters and critics of the Community Mine Continuation Agreements, which significantly weakened the lawsuit, were tense. The communities also faced a new environmental threat from acid mine drainage, caused by the exposure of sulfur-bearing rock to oxygen, which can render large areas inhospitable to organic life for centuries.

These issues led me to propose a regional summit meeting in Kiunga. The plan was supported by Eneco, a local NGO that coordinated political activities during the two lawsuits. A colleague working at the Mineral Policy Institute in Sydney raised funding for the meeting from two NGOs in Europe. I arrived in the town of Kiunga on the Fly River a week before the meeting and worked with Eneco to finalize the arrangements and set the agenda. I also traveled to the mining township of Tabubil to interview several executives from the company, including the manager for the environment, who briefed me on recent developments.

The meeting began with an impassioned plea by the organizers for the three hundred participants to set aside past disagreements and forge a shared political agenda. Representatives from each of the downstream groups were then asked to report on the situation where they lived. They described the hardships caused by pollution in their gardens, sago stands, forests, rivers, creeks, and lagoons. They described their difficulty in accessing clean drinking water, especially during the dry season. They expressed concern about acid mine drainage and frustration about the lack of independent information about the environmental impacts of the mine. They demanded that the mining company restore the river to the way it was before mining commenced. They complained about the value of the compensation payments they received, which they described as incommensurate with the damage to the environment and its impact on their subsistence practices. They also sought control over the trust fund established when BHP abandoned its shares in the project during the lawsuit. By charter, two-thirds of the dividends paid to the trust are set aside for use after mine closure. Only one-third of the remaining funds, or one-ninth of the total, is invested in the province where the mine is located; the rest is spent elsewhere in the country. The participants at the meeting argued that these proportions should be reversed. They also discussed various options for achieving their goals, from closing down the mine until their demands were met to challenging the legislation that permitted the mining company to leave the country without cleaning up the river in exchange for transferring its shares in the mine to the trust fund.

The members of Eneco had asked me to make two presentations at the meeting. The first covered the history of the two lawsuits against the mining company, including the final settlement agreement. In that talk, I acknowledged that the legal proceedings brought about significant changes, but I pointed out that recent parliamentary decisions precluded further legal action against the mining company, which was the favored course of action for most of the participants at the meeting.[13] My second presentation reviewed the environmental impacts of the mine and included updated information from my recent discussions with corporate executives. I also emphasized the gravity of the threat posed by acid mine drainage and encouraged them to consider whether the continued operation of the mine remained in their best interest.

FIGURE 1. Suki participant at the summit meeting about the Ok Tedi mine held in 2005, with handout on acid mine drainage. Kiunga, Papua New Guinea. Photo: Stuart Kirsch.

There were several dramatic moments during the three days in Kiunga. When the organizing committee met at the end of the first day, we stayed up late into the night discussing how to address the problems caused by the mine. For years, the people living along the river system consistently supported the continued operation of the mine provided that proper environmental controls were implemented and the communities affected by the project received a greater share of its economic benefits. I always respected their right to make this decision, even when the international NGO community was calling for mine closure. But given the impending threat from acid mine drainage, I strongly encouraged them to consider calling for the mine to close. The room fell silent for a moment or two until someone responded, "For how long?" Given the cumulative environmental impact from the mine, they could no longer support themselves and their families without the financial benefits provided by the mining company, so the thought of calling for early mine closure was almost inconceivable to them.

Discussion of this question continued during the following day at the public meeting. A member of the organizing committee addressed the participants using the call-and-response style of public speaking that has become popular, asking them: "Do you want the environment or money?" Only a few people responded by saying "environment." There was a loud murmuring as the participants discussed the question among themselves. Finally, someone called out in Melanesian Tok Pisin: *Tupela wantaim!,* or "Both of them at once," and the crowd loudly indicated its approval. In other words, they wanted more robust protection of the environment as well as compensation and economic opportunities.

During a break in the discussion on the second day, I was accosted by a group of men from several of the Yonggom villages on the lower Ok Tedi River. Speaking to me in Yonggom, they instructed me "not to change canoes in the middle of the river," as their Australian lawyers had done when they settled the second case, but to continue collaborating with them. Their insistence contradicted an objection previously raised by a law professor at the University of Papua New Guinea, who thanked me for contributing to the Ok Tedi case but suggested it was time for Papua New Guineans to assume responsibility for their political work. Alcida Ramos (2008), a Brazilian anthropologist working in Venezuela, reports similar comments from her Yanomami informants, who felt that anthropologists interfered with their ability to be political actors on their own behalf. This led Ramos to encourage anthropologists to "disengage" from political conflicts. Audra Simpson (2014) refers to this perspective as another form of ethnographic refusal, the rejection of being turned into the subjects of anthropological research.

But it is unclear whether people living in rural Papua New Guinea are able to turn to their own elites for assistance. The same law professor who encouraged me to "disengage" from the Ok Tedi conflict later helped pass a controversial amendment to the Environment Act of Papua New Guinea while serving as acting secretary for justice and attorney general. The amendment blocked all legal challenges to development projects after they have been approved by the government. It was rushed to a vote to stop a lawsuit seeking to prevent the Ramu nickel mine from implementing submarine disposal of tailings, in which mine wastes are discharged directly into the ocean. The amendment violated the constitutional right of Papua New Guinea citizens to review government decisions. It was one of the first acts of parliament to be overturned after a subsequent change of government; but it nonetheless achieved the desired result, as the lawsuit against the nickel mining company had already been dismissed.

On the last day of the meeting, the participants finalized a set of resolutions drafted by the organizing committee the previous evening. The plan was for the participants at the meeting to discuss the resolutions in their communities and return to Kiunga for a follow-up meeting several months later, which the governor of Western Province agreed to support. After the summit meeting, the members of Eneco collected several hundred signatures supporting the resolutions. They decided that the signatories should march through the mining township of Tabubil and formally present their demands to the managing director of the Ok Tedi mine. Although the managing director agreed to meet with the delegation, he simultaneously asked the national government to send a mobile police squad to protect the mine. Worried that a confrontation with the police force, which has a history of using excessive force, might turn violent, the organizers from Eneco canceled the protest.

These events, from the summit meeting to the hastily canceled protest march in Tabubil, convinced the governor of Western Province to fund a legal challenge to the acts of parliament that accompanied the settlement of the second lawsuit against the owners of the Ok Tedi mine. A finding by the Papua New Guinea Supreme Court that these acts were unconstitutional would have forced the mining company to negotiate a new series of agreements with the people living downstream from the Ok Tedi mine. Invalidating the previous agreements might also have provided an opportunity to reassess the Australian mining company's liability for the environmental impact of the Ok Tedi mine. As the provincial governor explained to me during a meeting the following year, one of the priorities for his second term in office was to find a way to clean up the river. However, I was dismayed to learn that his commitment to the lawsuit came at the expense of providing support for the follow-up summit meeting, which never took place.[14] When I sat down with the leaders of Eneco the year after the summit, it was their first meeting in several months. The political process I had hoped to help kick-start with the summit meeting was sidelined by the new litigation, which ultimately failed to make headway in court. In the meantime, the mining company hired a team of external mediators to renegotiate the compensation agreements with the communities downstream, furthering its control over the people affected by the mine.

My participation in the Kiunga summit meeting exceeded the bounds of conventional research practices in several ways, illustrating some of the complexities of doing engaged anthropology. First, I helped convene the meeting that I ended up studying. The original proposal for the summit was my initiative rather than theirs, although the leaders of Eneco immediately embraced the idea. I helped secure funding and set the date. I actively participated in the planning meetings, expressing my personal views. I was asked to make presentations on the mine's environmental impacts and the history of their legal struggle that combined information with strategic recommendations. Yet throughout the entire process, I took field notes like an ethnographer and subsequently included my observations of these events in several publications. These activities, like much of my involvement in the campaign against the Ok Tedi mine, are examples of how engaged anthropology is concerned with politics beyond the text. They also illustrate the kind of reciprocal relationships engaged anthropologists may have with community members, especially in the context of long-term research, and how these endeavors may include interactions in which the participants work collaboratively even when they do not always agree on the best course of action.

CONCLUSION

Engaged anthropology has the capacity to expand the possibilities of the discipline within and beyond the academy. My involvement in the Ok Tedi case led me to consider new research questions about indigenous movements and counterglobalization (Kirsch 2002a, 2007), environmental politics (Kirsch 2008), and corporate strategy (Benson and Kirsch 2010). In my first book, *Reverse Anthropology,* I analyzed Yonggom responses to the mine, including their view that pollution was the result of a failed social relationship with the mining company rather than a technical problem (Kirsch 2006). In *Mining Capitalism,* I expanded my analysis of the conflict by considering how corporations respond to criticism from indigenous political movements and their NGO allies (Kirsch 2014). While the first book was written from the heart in an effort to describe their experiences of loss, the second was written in anger at how corporations evade responsibility for the harm they cause. My experience working on the Ok Tedi case also led to new opportunities to learn about indigenous rights, property disputes, and environmental conflicts in other regions of the world.

In contrast to the concern that engaged anthropology may be fatally compromised by political commitments, such research is often subject to greater scrutiny than work written primarily for academic audiences. My publications on the Ok Tedi case have been closely examined by lawyers on both sides, government officials, local activists, and mining company executives. In some cases, readers were looking for flaws, mistakes, or contradictions that could be used to discredit my work. Despite having produced extensive rebuttals of other reports that were critical of the Ok Tedi mine (see Kirsch 2014, 69, 77), the mining company has never contested my findings apart from minor objections focused on competing interpretations of legal language. I suggest that, rather than signaling a weakness of engaged research, the challenges posed by interacting with colleagues, corporations, legal systems, NGOs, and communities strengthen the resulting accounts by holding anthropologists accountable.

This does not mean that engaged anthropologists fail to make mistakes. Indeed, the challenges posed by engaged anthropology suggest that this may be inevitable. Engaged anthropologists will occasionally practice ethnographic refusal to protect their informants or frame their work in ways that obscure other perspectives. But given the passage of time, it is possible to revisit and redress strategic omissions. Framing errors are hardly unique to engaged anthropology, as Orin Starn's (1991) famous essay on how symbolic anthropologists missed the revolution in Peru indicates. But the same standards for the validity and value of more conventional forms of ethnographic research—including internal consistency of ethnographic representations, the production of novel findings, and the willingness to reinterpret earlier results—are also incumbent upon engaged anthropologists.

In the introduction to this book, I defined engaged anthropology in terms of its contribution to politics. As the examples presented here suggest, another element of engaged anthropology is risk taking. The pressure to respond to a midnight phone call from Australia, the challenge of countering claims made by the mining company and its lawyers, and the willingness to conduct research in novel contexts and interact with unfamiliar interlocutors are among the things that provide engaged anthropology with its dynamic character. The opportunity to test anthropological knowledge against real-time events not only forces us to rethink our assumptions and expands what we are able to learn as anthropologists but also enhances our ability to use anthropology to help make a difference in the world.

It is important not to exaggerate the gap between engaged anthropology and other forms of ethnographic knowledge production. As this discussion about backstage interactions in the Ok Tedi case suggests, the work that I carried out on behalf of communities and in collaboration with lawyers and NGOs contains much of the same information as my academic publications. The changes I was asked to make strengthened my arguments rather than compromised their integrity. Doing engaged research also provided me with frequent opportunities to collect data in "natural settings" in which the participants debated important issues among themselves, in contrast to relying on "artificial data" produced through interviews and other research instruments (see Kirsch 2008, 54). At times my political commitments and positionality constrained my ability to investigate certain topics. But these compromises were offset by increased access to parties who might have been reluctant to share information with a neutral observer. Nonetheless, engaged anthropologists need to be willing to reevaluate and potentially revise their work rather than continue to defend their initial interpretations.

The possibility of remaining a neutral or passive observer may also be diminishing. Demands for collaboration come from below as the communities with which we work increasingly expect to benefit in some way from our research, as befits the reciprocal relationships established through ethnographic research, in which they share information with anthropologists (Kirsch 2002a). Related demands also come from above, as funding organizations and codes of ethics regarding the conduct of research increasingly require scholars to ensure that their work has tangible benefits for their subjects, especially individuals and communities chosen for particular characteristics, such as minority groups and other vulnerable populations, including indigenous peoples. At the same time, it would be wise to examine claims about neutrality made by anthropologists whose work is influenced by multiple obligations, including the requirement to serve the interests and agendas of funding agencies, meet the expectations of universities and departments to publish one's findings in specific formats and forums, and respond to corporate funding that imposes constraints on research projects as well as how the results can be used. For scholars working in contentious situations, the defensive impulse to deny that these interactions affect our findings runs the risk of turning anthropology into an antipolitics machine (Ferguson 1990). Rather than ignore these influences on our work, I encourage anthropologists to pay greater attention to how politics influences the ways in which they frame their research—a lesson from the 1980s writing-culture era that applies doubly to engaged research.

Ultimately, if their political commitments prevent engaged anthropologists from getting things right, their work will be of little or no value to their allies. The demand for accuracy, and sometimes the willingness to swear to its veracity, may be even greater for engaged anthropologists than for others in the discipline, both because the stakes are so much higher and because the results are subject to more careful scrutiny. Engaged anthropologists not only have to gain recognition from their peers, but they also have to meet the expectations of other actors in order to maintain their access to information and events, as well as for their work to have an impact.[15]

Consequently, I call for greater reflexivity in the practice of engaged anthropology by attending to conversations and interactions that are usually left unexamined in our accounts. Examining the "backstage" of engaged anthropology is also a general theme or metaphor for my discussion of the other projects described in this book. So, too, are the questions raised about ethnographic refusal and how politics influences the way anthropologists frame their research. My experience working on the Ok Tedi case, and in particular the kinds of relationships engaged anthropologists have with their interlocutors—including colleagues, communities, lawyers, and NGOs—have helped me navigate the challenges of the other projects discussed in this book. Attention to the issues raised here also helps me assess the aftermath of these engagements, including whether they produce "good enough" ethnography and whether they are good for anthropology and politics.

This chapter and the next, about political refugees and the independence movement in West Papua, Indonesia, address these questions in the context of long-term research, while the other examples in the book consider these issues in relation to short-term, problem-focused research projects, which possess their own challenges and opportunities.

TWO

When Contributions Are Elusive

WRITING ACROSS THE BORDER IN WEST PAPUA, INDONESIA

A DEFINING MOMENT IN MY RELATIONSHIP to the refugee community from West Papua—and my experiences as an engaged anthropologist—occurred during a male initiation ceremony in the rain forest near the Ok Tedi River in 1989 (see Kirsch 2006, 132–40).[1] A ritual expert named Kobarara, who was originally from Ninati village in West Papua, Indonesia, but who had been living in a refugee camp in Papua New Guinea since 1984, presided over the event. Most of the initiates were refugees from West Papua, although the other participants in the ritual were from the village where I had been conducting ethnographic research during the previous eighteen months. Late that night, there was a heavy thunderstorm, and everyone sought cover beneath a temporary shelter. With the rain drumming on the palm frond roof, two of the refugees confronted me about my participation in the initiation ceremony, asking me what I intended to do with the knowledge I had gained: Would I use it to help the refugees or assist their enemies? Their unexpected challenge encouraged me to reflect on the responsibilities of anthropologists to the people with whom they work, and on how I might help the refugees. These concerns have remained central to my work even though opportunities to contribute to their pursuit of independence in West Papua have remained elusive.

Since 1986, I have worked with people divided by the border between West Papua, Indonesia, where they are known as Muyu, and Papua New Guinea, where they refer to themselves as Yonggom. From 1984 to 1986, nearly twelve thousand West Papuans crossed the international border by foot to protest the Indonesian occupation of their territory (International Commission of Jurists 1985; see also May 1986; Wolfers 1988). The majority of the refugees came from the Muyu area close to the international border

(Kirsch 2006; Glazebrook 2008; Zocca 2008). Their departure was coordinated by the Organisasi Papua Merdeka (OPM), or Free Papua Movement, which has fought for political independence from Indonesia since 1965.[2] The first and largest group of refugees arrived in early 1984, several months after the violent reprisal by the Indonesian military against a peaceful protest and flag-raising in the capital city, Jayapura (Bell et al. 1986, 540–41). The refugees hoped their exodus would attract international attention, sympathy, and support for West Papuan independence (Kirsch 1989b, 2006; see also MacLeod et al. 2016, 172).

Since Indonesia gained control over the former Dutch colony of Netherlands New Guinea from the United Nations in 1962, its military has regularly committed human rights violations, including physical assault and torture, sexual violence, and extrajudicial killings (Anti-Slavery Society 1990; Budiardjo and Liong 1988; Hernawan 2013; MacLeod et al. 2016; Ondawame 2000, 2010). During a visit to Australia in January 2006, Juan Mendez, the special adviser to the UN secretary-general on the prevention of genocide, expressed grave concern about the fate of the indigenous peoples of West Papua, whom he described as being "at risk of extinction" (Voice of America 2009; see also Brundige et al. 2004, 2).

Control over the western half of the island of New Guinea provides the Indonesian state with access to valuable natural resources, including copper, gold, and nickel deposits; natural gas and petroleum; and timber and other forest products. This includes Freeport-McMoRan's Grasburg copper and gold mine, Indonesia's second-largest taxpayer and the world's largest polluter by volume (Leith 2003), and British Petroleum's Tangguh hydrocarbon project in Bintuni Bay, with more than 500 billion cubic meters of proven natural gas reserves. The operators of other resource extraction projects in the province, including timber concessions and oil palm plantations, pay little or no attention to their environmental impacts or infringement on traditional land rights (Lucas and Warren 2003, 75; Franky and Morgan 2015). Reforms promoting regional autonomy approved by the post-Suharto national government in 2001 have failed to deliver meaningful benefits or political control to the people of West Papua (Bertrand 2004; J. Septer Manufandu, pers. comm., 2010).

West Papua also offers access to arable land that is otherwise in short supply and consequently in great demand by the people of the densely populated island nation of Indonesia. Transmigration programs during the 1980s relocated between 85,000 and 145,000 peasant farmers and their families from

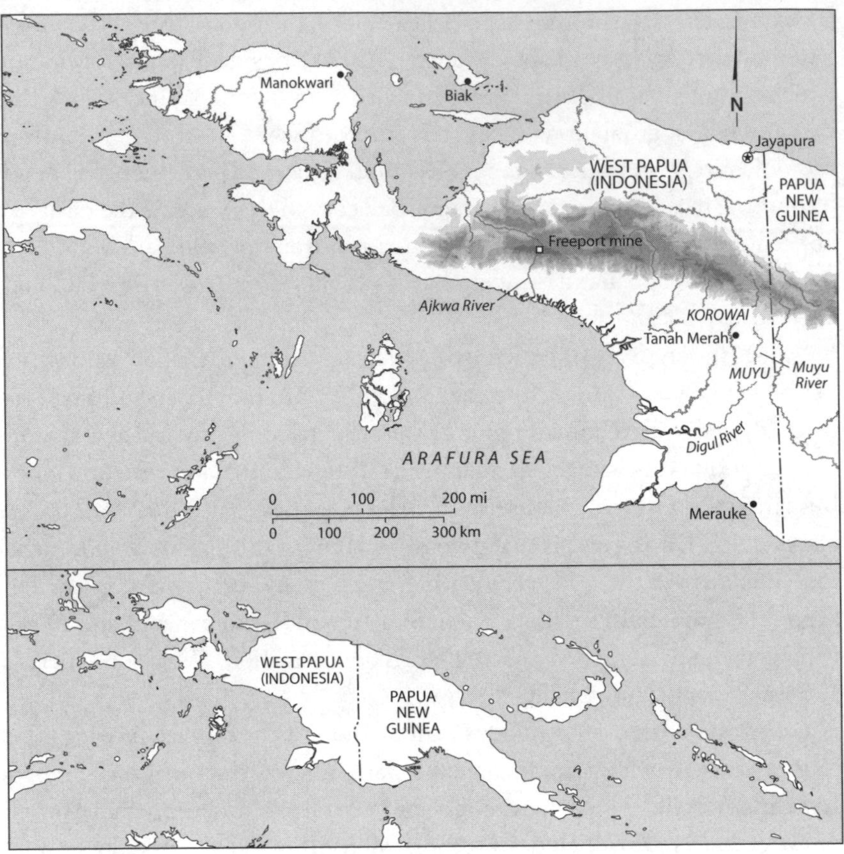

MAP 3. West Papua, Indonesia.

Indonesia's inner islands to West Papua (Elmslie 2002, 75). Another 216,000 migrants followed of their own accord during the same time period (Elmslie 2002, 75–76). According to some estimates, Indonesian migrants may already outnumber indigenous West Papuans (Elmslie 2010), although Papuans remain in the majority in the interior. Vast areas of land have been alienated from indigenous ownership and converted to smallholder agriculture and commercial plantations. Indonesian settlers dominate urban spaces and monopolize commerce, while Papuans are subject to pervasive racism, discrimination, and surveillance, resulting in substantial political and economic inequality. The Indonesian government continues to promote mega-development projects in West Papua, including the Merauke Integrated Food and Energy Estate, which plans to convert several million hectares of lowland rain forest into rice paddies, oil palm plantations, and sugarcane fields (Franky and Morgan 2015; Moiwend and Barber 2011).

My initial response to the challenge posed by the two refugees at the initiation ceremony was to write about the history of the border region and life in the refugee camps, adding an ethnographic perspective to existing accounts by political scientists and journalists and correcting a number of popular misconceptions about the refugees (Kirsch 1996b). Although my research with the refugees left me wanting to know more about conditions on the Indonesian side of the border, restrictions on travel and research in West Papua kept me from pursuing these interests (Kirsch 2002c, 54; see also Matbob and Papoutsaki 2006; McWilliams 2007, 15). Consequently, I began to examine how the Indonesian occupation of West Papua has been justified through the use of racist and primitivist stereotypes. This led me to write about the politics of representation in West Papua, including the way rumor mediates the experience of political violence along the border (Kirsch 2002c), and how reports about apocryphal lost tribes compromise support for the political aspirations of West Papuans (Kirsch 1997a, 2002c, 2010a).

At the time of my initial fieldwork on the Ok Tedi River in the late 1980s, West Papuan political resistance was organized almost exclusively by the paramilitary wing of the OPM, which waged low-level guerilla warfare against the Indonesian military. When I had the opportunity to interview the OPM general responsible for the southern region of West Papua in the village where I was conducting research, I was careful to limit my questions to his motives for joining the OPM and his aspirations for West Papua, and refrained from asking about their military activities. On the occasion when an armed OPM battalion marched through the village where I was living, I stayed inside my house, watching them pass by my window. My caution was a response to both their concerns about outsiders being spies and my personal reservations about their use of violence. The OPM's reliance on guerilla tactics reinforced negative stereotypes about the violent nature of West Papuans and benefited the Indonesian military by making the independence movement an easy target for condemnation and repression. Their paramilitary activities also made me reluctant to align myself politically with the independence movement despite my sympathy for their cause.

In contrast to my involvement in the Ok Tedi case, in which I played an active role in the struggle against the mining company, I have not been very successful in finding ways to assist the West Papuan refugees and their political leaders. It was only after the resistance movement shifted its focus to human rights activism and called for the demilitarization of West Papua in the mid-1990s that I felt comfortable seeking out opportunities to collaborate with political activists from West Papua at various workshops and NGO meetings in the United States and Europe. However, the fact that I have not conducted research in West Papua has affected my ability to contribute to their efforts. When I finally visited Jayapura and Biak in January 2014, the trip provided me with new perspectives on the differences between political activists living and working in West Papua and their counterparts in exile. Although I have collaborated with West Papuan refugees and activists for several decades, my participation in their activities has remained intermittent and limited. Nonetheless, these interactions have proven to be a valuable source of ethnographic material and ideas for scholarly research and writing.

These experiences suggest that the difficulty identifying constructive modes of political participation is greater than currently acknowledged in the literature on engaged anthropology. Indeed, it may be the primary constraint on anthropologists who wish to conduct engaged research. But even when the options for political engagement are limited, anthropologists are still able to contribute by writing about the situation. Describing my experiences working with West Papuan refugees and political leaders, including the transformations I have identified here, allows me to discuss the challenge of carrying out engaged research when the opportunities for making useful contributions are elusive.

WRITING LOCAL HISTORY

I began by writing about history along the border, starting with a coauthored op-ed commemorating the fifth anniversary of the refugees' exile for a newspaper in Papua New Guinea. In "Blood Brothers Separated by the Border," I sought to cultivate sympathy among the people living in the capital of Port Moresby for the West Papuan refugees by emphasizing the arbitrary imposition of the border, which divided families such that "one brother is a Papua New Guinean and the other a refugee" (Ketan 1989).[3] I subsequently published an article in a local journal that sought to rebut the claim that people living in the camps along the border were "traditional border crossers" rather than political refugees (Kirsch 1989b). The stakes in the designation were considerable: Denying their status as refugees would permit the state to ignore its international responsibilities, including protection against involuntary repatriation. It would also neglect their sacrifices and obscure their political motivation and objectives.

The international border between Papua New Guinea and Indonesia follows the 141st parallel without regard to the traditional territories of the people living in the area (Veur 1966).[4] Historically, marriage and long-distance trade partnerships connected people throughout the region (Schoorl [1957] 1993, 95). Large-scale pig feasts served as important nodes of exchange networks that established relationships between distant parties, including the members of several different sociolinguistic groups (Haan 1955; Kirsch 2006, 84–89; Schoorl [1957] 1993, 99–103; Welsch 1994). Some of the men attending these feasts also participated in male cult activities, like the initiation ceremony in which I took part, that were held in conjunction with these regional gatherings.

Before the colonial era, the Muyu and Yonggom lived in scattered homesteads and small hamlets that were vulnerable to attack, and consequently one of the few viable responses to the threat of violence or sorcery was to relocate. In some cases the entire settlement shifted location, while in other instances only those individuals who felt threatened left the area (Kirsch 2009c). Even though these population movements were usually temporary, in some cases they became permanent when the children of migrants acquired land rights after being adopted into local lineages. The broad dispersal of the Yonggom between the Digul and Ok Tedi Rivers, and the low population density in the area, facilitated conflict resolution through the separation of potential adversaries. In other cases, Yonggom or Muyu settlers forcibly displaced the Awin people living to the east, gaining control over their land.

Even before the border was finally surveyed in 1962, the division of their territory between colonial powers had significant consequences for the Yonggom. During the first two decades of the twentieth century, the Dutch permitted Chinese, Malay, and Australian bird-of-paradise hunters to enter Netherlands New Guinea, whereas they were banned by the Australian colonial administration. The foreign hunters traded steel tools and glass beads in return for help locating the display trees where the male birds-of-paradise could be found during mating season (Kirsch 2006, 33–35). Pacification also ended the head-hunting raids of the Marind-Anim and Boazi people along the Middle Fly to the south, opening up the former no-man's-land between these groups to settlement, including two Yonggom villages established on the north shore of Lake Murray. The Yonggom also moved to take advantage of new economic opportunities. Close proximity to the towns of Mindiptanah and Tanah Merah on the Dutch side of the border, as well as access to the more distant cities of Merauke, Hollandia (now Jayapura), and Sorong, attracted aspiring laborers from both sides of the border (Schoorl 1988; Kaipman 1974). The two colonial administrations, however, sought to discourage movement across the international border. They marked the trails between the two territories and regularly sent back border crossers they encountered on their patrols (Veur 1966).

The Dutch began to resettle local populations into nucleated villages during the 1950s (Schoorl [1957] 1993, 181–96) and the Australians followed suit in the 1960s and 1970s. People living close to the border were required to choose between what would turn out to be radically different futures. Lineages, families, and siblings were divided by these decisions. The people from Yat village, for example, which was literally split in half by the border, resettled in several villages in Dutch New Guinea, the town of Mindiptanah, and Dome village on the Ok Tedi River, where I was based during my initial field research.

In the late 1950s, the Dutch came under pressure to withdraw from New Guinea and relinquish control over the territory to the Republic of Indonesia, which had gained its independence in 1945. The Dutch responded in part by fostering an elite group of Papuan civil servants and encouraging expectations for independence (Webster 2001–2, 513). Similar aspirations spread to communities living in rural areas. Under the provisions of the New York Agreement, which the United States hoped would check Indonesia's turn toward communism, the Netherlands ceded its territory in New Guinea to Indonesia on August 15, 1962. The UN Transitional Authority played an official role in the transfer until May 1, 1963. In 1969, Indonesia selected 1,022 West Papuan representatives, who voted unanimously in favor of joining the Republic of Indonesia in what was officially called the Act of Free Choice, but which subsequently became known as the "Act of No Choice." The New York Agreement and the Act of Free Choice continue to figure prominently in West Papuan political narratives, as well as in reviews by the United Nations, the United States, and other parties addressing the legitimacy of Indonesia's territorial claim over West Papua.[5]

Even before the vote, however, there was resistance to the Indonesian presence in West New Guinea (Ondawame 2010, 63). The Organisasi Papua Merdeka was founded in Manokwari in 1965 as a paramilitary organization that used bows and arrows and vintage weapons to fight against the Indonesian occupation. Despite its lack of military success, the OPM gained broad support among both rural and urban populations. In April 1984, the

OPM coordinated the movement of six thousand Muyu across the border to Papua New Guinea (Glazebrook 2008, 6). The refugees abandoned some of their villages entirely, and the districts closest to the border were largely deserted. They were told by the OPM that they would be able to return home to claim their independence from Indonesia in the near future.

The Muyu established a series of refugee camps in Papua New Guinea, most of which were located adjacent to existing Yonggom villages, where they have close relatives and speak dialects of the same language. The villagers on the Papua New Guinean side of the border were outnumbered by their guests by as many as five to one. The resulting food shortages failed to attract national or international attention until a visiting pastor stumbled across a number of malnourished children and a series of recent graves at the Komokpin refugee camp in August 1984 (Smith and Hewison 1986, 213). Save the Children and the United Nations High Commissioner for Refugees were subsequently invited by the government of Papua New Guinea to provide food and medical care to the refugees living in the border camps.

When it became clear that the refugees were determined to stay in Papua New Guinea, the government formulated plans to relocate them away from the border. They established a resettlement center in East Awin, 120 kilometers to the east. The primary advantage of the site was its low population density. Its disadvantages, however, included relative isolation and inaccessibility; a swampy, malarial terrain; the lack of potable water; and the absence of sago palms, the staple food of the Muyu (Glazebrook 2008). Despite these problems, the government proceeded with its plan to resettle the refugees in East Awin, where they were also envisioned by some as a contract labor force for the local rubber industry. However, the majority of the Muyu refugees rejected the move to the relocation center in 1988 because it would have taken them farther away from their land and from their relatives who remained behind or who belonged to the OPM unit based near the border. They also rejected the move because it would have increased their dependence on the United Nations, which they criticized for abandoning them to the Indonesians in 1963 and 1969.

Despite their failure to bring about political change or even to provoke substantive reforms in West Papua, more than seventy-five hundred refugees continue to live in the border camps and the resettlement site (Glazebrook 2008).[6] Even though they have had to endure considerable hardship while in exile, the majority of the refugees remain committed to their original political objectives.[7] My rationale for writing about the history of the border region was to provide the context necessary for understanding the refugee movement. I also wanted to rebut the claim that they were traditional border crossers exercising their legal right to mobility, or economic refugees moving to seek employment in Papua New Guinea, and thus not subject to international protection. In contrast, the refugees unanimously identified with the OPM and explained that their goal was the independence of West Papua from Indonesia.

BEARING WITNESS

I was also concerned by the failure of external observers to take refugee perspectives and goals into account when reporting on the situation or making decisions about their future (Kirsch 1996b). This led me to write about the experiences of the West Papuan refugees in Papua New Guinea. In contrast to Nancy Scheper-Hughes (1995), who rejects the value of cultural relativism in arguing for the "primacy of the ethical," and Paul Farmer (2004), who emphasizes the need to focus on poverty rather than culture, I found that an ethnographic perspective was essential for an adequate understanding of life in the border camps. However, I agreed with Scheper-Hughes (1995) that anthropologists have a responsibility to "bear witness" to violence, both the physical acts themselves and their potential to reverberate as terror. By describing violence and its consequences, anthropologists can provide support for local political aspirations, bringing the resources of the discipline and the moral weight of the academy to bear on these problems (Kirsch 2006, 187). This was also my first attempt to address questions about the politics of representation.

I observed that discourse about refugees could be divided into three general categories: political, critical, and humanitarian. In political discourse, refugees attract attention and generate concern when they put diplomatic relations between states at risk. The ability of refugees to cross international borders raises questions about territorial integrity. The resulting discourse seeks to minimize complications arising from such population movements, including perceived threats to national security. The motivations of the refugees as political actors are largely ignored. Politicians, political scientists, and some journalists are the primary contributors to this discourse. Despite their deep historical and cultural ties to the people of West Papua, politicians in Papua New Guinea have generally been more interested in protecting their country's political and economic ties to Indonesia than addressing the concerns of the refugees (Maclellan 2015, 273). Papua New Guinea has never challenged the legitimacy of Indonesia's neocolonial occupation of West Papua (see Somare 2015, 294). It has also been reluctant to criticize Indonesia or its military for their treatment of West Papuans, and has made little effort to promote reform or to object to human rights violations in West Papua. Fighting its own war against the separatist movement in Bougainville also made it difficult for Papua New Guinea to support independence in West Papua (Kirsch 1996b, 233–34; Maclellan 2015, 273). In political discourse about refugees, national and economic interests take precedence over human rights violations and humanitarian concerns, and the political ambitions and experiences of the refugees are largely ignored.

Refugees become the subject of critical discourse when their predicament is invoked to promote particular theoretical agendas or political causes. Refugee voices are generally ignored in the resulting texts. The practical consequences of these arguments for the refugees are also overlooked. An example of the problems caused by critical discourse emerged in response to an article serialized in the *Times of Papua New Guinea*. The author asserted that the Indonesian military deliberately exposed West Papuans to cysticercosis, which can be lethal, through pigs infested with parasitic tapeworms that were introduced into West Papua as a form of biological warfare (Hyndman 1987; see Desowitz 1981). The author also incorrectly claimed that West Papuan refugees living in Papua New Guinea were carriers of the parasite (see Fritzsche 1988). Shortly after the article was published, an influenza epidemic resulted in several deaths in one of the refugee camps. During a postmortem sorcery divination, one potential cause of these deaths was described this way: "The Indonesians poisoned a pig the man had eaten, causing him to die." Unsupported assertions about biological warfare resulted in refugee fears of being poisoned by the Indonesian military, exacerbating their feelings of insecurity.

Another problem associated with critical discourse results from false or exaggerated claims. For example, sensationalist reports about helicopter gunships and armed river trucks patrolling the Fly River (Nietschmann and Eley 1987) and phantom OPM operations blockading the shipment of copper and gold from the Ok Tedi mine along the Fly River (Matthews 1992) were misleading, yet they had the potential to intensify refugee concerns. Such claims also encouraged West Papuans to pursue a military solution to their predicament, a strategy that not only had little chance of success but discouraged them from considering alternatives. Proponents of critical discourse neglect refugee interpretations of events and ignore the effect of their claims on the refugees themselves.

The third discourse about refugees is humanitarian. Its concerns are often pragmatic, ranging from the provision of food and medical care to integration of the refugees into the host society. A central feature of such discourse is its urgency, which may preclude effective consultation, even though participation is generally regarded as essential to the success of development interventions (Cernea 1985). A variety of external constraints, including funding, media attention, and regional political interests affect the delivery of aid to refugees in ways that may clash with their needs and interests. For example, the state's decision to close the border camps and withdraw humanitarian aid in 1988 backfired when the refugees refused to move to the resettlement center, temporarily leaving them without access to medical care.

Interested in producing an alternative to accounts that ignore the refugee point of view, I drew on Clifford Geertz's (1984, 124) invocation of the difference between experience-near constructs that consider how someone "might himself naturally and effortlessly . . . define what he or his fellows see, think, imagine, or so on, and which he would readily understand when similarly applied by others" (Geertz 1984, 12) in contrast to more analytic or experience-distant language employed by social scientists. I pointed to the Yonggom sentiment *iwari,* or "loneliness," as an example of an experience-near construct. Given the importance of social relations, being alone or lonely is a highly undesirable condition that evokes feelings of sorrow and shame. To quell a dispute between people from the village and the refugees living nearby concerning competition for scarce resources, an elderly refugee named Uran invoked his own predicament as a childless widower:

> We didn't come here to hunt on your land, but to gain independence for ourselves.
> The OPM told us to leave our homes, but to stay close to the border.
> We chose this village because our kin are here.
> We are one people.
>
> But I have no family of my own and live by myself.
> Look at me: I am not strong.
> I spend all of my time inside my house.
> No one comes to bring me meat.
> I have no wife, no brothers or sisters, and no sons or daughters to look after me.

> Every morning I wake up, make a fire, and see that there is nothing to cook.
> I just make a fire and wait to see whether anyone will bring me food.
> No one from my lineage lives here.
>
> I will stay in my house and die; they will bury me here.

When Uran described his isolation and feelings of loneliness (*iwari*) and abandonment, he shamed the villagers into feeling sorry for the refugees by reminding them of the hardships they have faced since moving to Papua New Guinea. This language can be contrasted with the more analytic and experience-distant language of national security or economic interests employed by outsiders when writing about the refugees.[8]

I also addressed the challenges faced by the West Papuan refugees living in the border camps. Instead of political solidarity, an emotional atmosphere of fear and mistrust dominates Yonggom social relations owing to concerns about sorcery (Schoorl [1957] 1993), and it is exacerbated by conditions in the refugee camps. The Yonggom ordinarily attribute responsibility for serious illness and death to sorcerers who intentionally harm other members of their society. In the border camps, sorcery accusations aggravate existing tensions among the refugees. For example, an individual's decision to move to the relocation center or back to West Papua may be interpreted as an admission that he was involved in acts of sorcery. There are also conflicts with people living in the neighboring villages over the use of scarce resources, which the refugees fear will result in retribution via sorcery.

These examples illustrate some of the common problems affecting West Papuan refugees living in the border camps in Papua New Guinea, experiences missing from other accounts of the situation. I recognized that writing about my ethnographic research with the refugees provided a perspective to which not many outsiders had access. But I also realized that I could not fully explain the reasons why the refugees moved to Papua New Guinea without addressing the situation in West Papua, which led me to shift my attention to questions about political violence.

RUMOR AND POLITICAL VIOLENCE

Writing about West Papua posed a challenge. Given that ethnographic authority is conventionally premised on "being there" (Clifford 1988; Geertz

1988), how could I write about a place where I have never been? Only a handful of anthropologists have been granted permission to conduct ethnographic research in West Papua since the 1960s, making it unlikely I would ever work there.[9] West Papua has also been an ethnographic "no-man's-land" between two very different traditions of scholarship that converge on the divide between Southeast Asia and the Pacific (see Rutherford 1996, 603; 1999). But given the paucity of attention to political violence in West Papua, and its importance for understanding the independence movement, I felt compelled to write about these issues anyway.[10] My work with the Muyu refugees provided a novel vantage point from which to address these issues, leading me to consider how rumors about political violence affect people living on both sides of the border.

Many of the rumors circulating along the border addressed questions about state-sponsored violence. But they also increased the impact of political violence by reinforcing and reproducing perceptions of terror. As Ann Stoler (1992, 182) notes, "Rumor can be damning and enabling." Through rumor, West Papuans simultaneously *experience* the threat of political violence and *express* their concerns about it. Such rumors are not simply a response to state-sponsored violence; they also generate terror in their wake.

While living near the border, I was witness to a variety of rumors circulating among the refugees. I later tracked the movement of related rumors across larger networks, including exchanges mediated through the Internet. Some of the rumors were concerned with the actions of the Indonesian military. Others addressed state-sponsored violence through the introduction of epidemic disease into West Papua. Some of these rumors were even more complex, including the transformation of local myths about cannibal women into media accounts of lost tribes that are seen to impede state plans for development. They also reveal the gendered nature of political violence in West Papua.

One rumor addressed the encroachment of Indonesian soldiers on the refugee camps, provoking panic and attempts to flee. At the time, cross-border incursions of Indonesian troops occurred periodically and occasionally resulted in refugee casualties. In one story that was told repeatedly, a woman from the refugee camps carried a large metal basin down a steep hill to collect water for her family. Barely able to balance the heavy container of water on her head, she struggled to make her way back up the hill. Approaching her house on the ridge, she saw a group of people milling agitatedly about. Indonesian soldiers had been seen on patrol, someone said, and were heading in their direction. In response, she overturned the pot, spilling out the water it contained, and frantically packed her belongings inside, preparing to flee along with the other refugees. Shortly afterward, however, the rumor was dispelled and the poor woman had to trudge back down the hill for water. The story always provoked considerable mirth despite its depiction of a moment of terror.[11]

Another rumor that spread through the refugee camps was the claim that their pigs were infected with the tapeworm that causes cysticercosis, which I previously described as an example of the detrimental effects of critical discourse. The issue arose in relation to a postmortem divination about the cause of a man's death, in which the participants asked whether it was the result of the Indonesian military intentionally infecting their pigs. Other questions raised during the divination also addressed state-sponsored violence or the threat of sorcery from neighboring villagers who objected to refugee use of local resources. The divination ceremony served as a forum in which the refugees could express concerns about their insecurity, but it also intensified their feelings of vulnerability.

Parallel rumors about West Papuans exposed to HIV/AIDS began to circulate in West Papua during the late 1990s. I learned about these rumors through the online newsgroup *Kabar-Irian* (1997a, 1997b, 1997c), which quoted an anonymous source claiming that Jakarta sent "prostitutes infected with [the] AIDS virus to purposely infect the local people [of West Papua]." At the time, West Papua had the largest number of HIV/AIDS cases per capita of any province in Indonesia (Butt, Numbery, and Morin 2002, 283). Sexually transmitted disease in New Guinea is often associated with anxiety about "modern" forms of sexuality, including prostitution (Clark 1997; see also Hammar 2010; Wardlow 2006). The rumor about prostitutes in West Papua infected with HIV/AIDS was therefore doubly threatening, for not only did it prey on local insecurities about these new forms of sexuality, but it also signaled the intrusion of political violence into one of the most private and intimate areas of life. Although this particular rumor singles out men as targets for exposure to disease, it also reveals a relationship between the violence of development and its consequences for women and their sexuality, to which I return below.

The relationship between political violence and terror is also at stake in recent debates about the role of public torture in West Papua. Despite major transformations in the governance of Indonesia since the fall of Suharto in 1998, these reforms have not been fully realized in West Papua, where the military continues to demonstrate repressive intolerance of political speech. In one instance of this, raising the flag of the "morning star," a key symbol of the West Papuan sovereignty movement, resulted in a fifteen-year prison sentence for the activist Filep Karma in 2004.[12]

A 2014 study of military violence in West Papua provides evidence that the incidence of torture has paradoxically increased since the fall of Suharto's repressive regime in 1998 (Hernawan 2014, 197). In contrast to covert use of torture intended to avoid public scrutiny and evade legal consequences, torture in West Papua frequently takes place in "front of a public audience, so anyone, including women and children, can witness" it (Hernawan 2014, 197). Budi Hernawan, a political anthropologist and human rights activist who has studied these violent interactions for many years, argues that they are intended to create a public spectacle. Torture, he asserts, is not just a state-sponsored crime but a mode of governance "employed by the Indonesian security services to intimidate civilians" (Hernawan 2014, 8). It is used to dehumanize West Papuans and legitimate military control over the contested province (Hernawan 2014). These acts of torture display the callous disregard for West Papuan lives expressed in the earlier rumors about the spread of fatal parasites and sexually transmitted disease. Even when the perpetrators of these acts are held accountable, they are tried not for torture or even assault but rather for disobedience by ignoring orders that prohibit violence against West Papuans (Hernawan, pers. comm., 2010).

These actions become even more powerful through their ability to terrorize people who do not observe the violence firsthand. Much like the Internet rumors about sexually transmitted disease, images of torture now circulate online. These videos are viewed by new audiences, drawing attention to the problems in West Papua, and have even been repurposed in political messages that promote independence (Rutherford 2012), reproducing the original acts of violence in new forms. In the process, the viewers of these images not only become witnesses to violence but also come to experience it themselves, thereby expanding the symbolic power of political violence and the role of terror in West Papua. The accessibility of these images on the web has also led to new conversations about political violence in Indonesia at the United Nations and in the U.S. government, as I discuss below.

LOST TRIBES

Other rumors are closely associated with the persistent denial that West Papuans are coeval with the modern world. A common example is the claim that they continue to live in the "Stone Age" (Rutherford 2014). Similar assumptions are involved in the trope of the lost tribe, which refers to the gradual integration of remote and marginal populations into larger political systems (Kirsch 1997d). As supposedly pristine versions of the indigenous, lost tribes are imagined to be the polar opposite of modernity. As such, they are sometimes thought to offer a potential antidote to its discontents. In this guise, stories about lost tribes may evoke nostalgia for a simpler past or suggest the possibility of relearning forgotten but fundamental truths. They also allow people to imagine places where modernity has yet to have a negative impact, absolving us of responsibility for colonizing the entire planet. Claims about lost tribes, however, can also be used to stigmatize the communities to which they refer.

In West Papua, claims about lost tribes refer to these groups not only as the antithesis of progress but also as an impediment to its achievement. In one story reported by Antara, a state-run news outlet, the local government planned to send a team to investigate rumors about a tribe of cannibal women who roam naked through the rain forest, armed with bows and arrows, and accompanied by a pack of dogs (Agence France-Presse 1999). The women are said to capture men from the surrounding communities, with whom they mate and conceive offspring, killing the men afterward. A similar report was circulated anonymously by the email newsgroup *Kabar-Irian* in 1999, which made reference to a "wild village of savage women who attack men and have sex with them all night long" (*Kabar-Irian* 1999d). Like the rumors about prostitutes with HIV/AIDS, these stories invoke the risks posed by the unrestrained sexuality of women. The threat is taken seriously by the state, as government and/or military expeditions prompted these accounts.

The claims about the women are apparently based on local myths that have been separated from their original source. In the Star Mountains of Papua New Guinea, the people of Telefolmin tell stories about a group of women known as Kundunang, fierce cannibals who, like the Amazons of Greek legend, are adept with bow and arrows and have only one breast. They are said to mate with wild dogs and give birth to offspring that fall into one of four categories: sons, daughters, male dogs, or bitches. To reproduce their original relationships, they consume the male children and female dogs (Jorgensen 1981, 83–84).

Significantly, reports of lost tribes in West Papua are linked to places that, before the Southeast Asian economic collapse in the mid-1990s and the subsequent demise of Suharto's New Order Indonesia, were the targets of major

FIGURE 2. *Lost in Papua* movie poster, depicting the reunion of the female protagonist with her ex-fiancé, who had been held captive by the members of an all-female village in West Papua. 2011.

development projects. Both of the groups described in these news accounts were said to live near Mamberamo, the site chosen by B. J. Habibie while he was Suharto's minister of research and technology, for one of the most ambitious and potentially disastrous development projects of the new century. The proposed agro-industrial complex would have cleared several million hectares of rain forest for steel mills, copper smelters, dams and hydroelectric power plants, pulp mills, paper factories, and one million hectares of rice (Carr 1998). Standing squarely in the path to modernity, which was to be introduced in the form of rapacious development projects, was a lost tribe of cannibal women who would have to be brought under state control. Like the rumors about HIV/AIDS, these accounts present uncontrolled female sexuality as a threat to both production and orderly reproduction. The same tropes were recently reproduced in the fictional Indonesian film *Lost in Papua,* in which the male protagonist from Java is held captive and raped by the residents of an all-female village in West Papua (Bahtiar 2011).

Rumors about lost tribes of cannibal women also provide a rationale for the taking of local land, even though the state already claims ownership of all arable land that is not under cultivation. Yet by consuming West Papuan resources without redistributing the benefits that result from production, the Indonesian state can be seen as the structural counterpart to mythical cannibal women who reproduce themselves at the expense of their male consorts and offspring. While sexuality is not the only idiom through which the contrast between "primitive" and "civilized" can be framed, it is a common medium for the expression of state power (Jolly and Manderson 1997). By representing women from West Papua as cannibals whose unrestrained sexuality—like that of the prostitutes with HIV/AIDS—poses a threat to men and modernity, the state claims legitimacy for the violent displacement of West Papuans from their lands in the name of development.

VIOLENCE AND THE SAVAGE SLOT

Claims about lost tribes are also central to contemporary forms of extreme tourism in which Euro-Americans pay thousands of dollars to participate in staged encounters with West Papuans. "Exclusive: First Contact!" screams the headlines on the cover of *Outside Magazine.* Michael Behar's (2005) essay "The Selling of the Last Savage" describes his travels through West Papua with an American tour operator who advertised an opportunity to meet "uncontacted native tribes who have never seen outsiders." Behar's expedition took video images of these rain forest encounters using a night vision camera that depicted everything in shades of green.[13] In the video, five or six West Papuan men suddenly appear and rush toward the tour members with their bows raised before backing off, only to return a few moments later to pose shyly for photographs, albeit with their backs to the cameras. They were extravagantly dressed for the encounter, wearing cassowary feather headdresses and palm-frond decorations more appropriate for a ritual or ceremony than hunting in the rain forest. The temporary shelter in which they were camping when the tourist party walked by was newly constructed from fresh palm fronds and leaves. Given the shaky camera work, the panic and confusion of the participants, and the disoriented moments of reflection during which the participants anxiously tried to make sense of their experiences, the video reminded me of the teenage horror film *The Blair Witch Project* (Sánchez and Myrick 1999).

The *New Yorker* also published an account of a similar expedition to West Papua the same year by the journalist Lawrence Osborne (2005). He interprets the distressed response of the Kombai people whom he met during his visit as evidence they had never encountered outsiders before. In contrast, anthropologist Rupert Stasch (2005), who has conducted research with the neighboring Korowai people, suggests that the Kombai reaction indicates that the tourists were being intrusive or were simply unwelcome.[14] Osborne claims to have found the encounter terrifying; and in response to my comments on the film, which were forwarded to him by a colleague, he wrote, "I went on the trip and it sure as hell wasn't *The Blair Witch Project.* I thought I was going to die!" (Deborah Gewertz, pers. comm., 2005). However, it is not especially surprising Behar and Osborne were frightened, as the sense of exhilaration and fear—like that experienced while riding a scary roller coaster—is precisely what these forms of adventure tourism are marketing.

As in other accounts of lost tribes in West Papua, the stereotypes of primitive violence reenacted in these tourist encounters obscure the violence of the state. It is telling that the first Korowai man whom Osborne meets has the nickname Brimob, the acronym for the Indonesian mobile defense forces, which he acquired when he allegedly shot a soldier in the eye with an arrow. Yet it is the journalists participating in these encounters who remain blind to the political implications of their work. These tales of terror in out-of-the-way places perpetuate rumors about the presence of uncontacted peoples who are inherently violent, reinforcing the rationale of the Indonesian state for appropriating their land and resources in the name of development and modernization. By keeping West Papuans in the "savage slot" (Trouillot 1991), and in particular by presenting them as dangerous and violent, these narratives legitimate the continued militarization of the Indonesian province.

These tourist accounts are also part of a larger pattern. In the post-Suharto era, media attention has concentrated on several remote areas of West Papua, and especially on the Korowai, Kombai, and Mek peoples. This includes articles written for the general public in the *Christian Science Monitor, National Geographic,* the *New Yorker, Outside Magazine,* and *Reader's Digest* (Stasch 2011). There have also been documentary films and television programs made about the same peoples produced by the Travel Channel, the Discovery Channel, and the Smithsonian Institution (Hoesterey 2012; Kirsch 1997a). As one Indonesian NGO recently observed in a report about a proposed oil palm project in West Papua: "The Korowai and Kombai [are] amongst the most well-known tribes in Papua because of their custom of living in treehouses high in the forest canopy. While the Korowai lifestyle is romanticized in magazine documentaries about 'exotic' indigenous peoples, for many of Indonesia's bureaucrats in Papua, they are a symbol of the need to bring development to the forest interior" (Franky and Morgan 2015, 38). The same report cites "former army general Bambang Darmono, who was appointed by President Susilo Bambam Yudhoyono to head the 'Unit for the Acceleration of Development in Papua and West Papua' program" as offering a "prime example of this attitude" following a visit to the Korowai: "I am honestly so sad I want to cry that after this country has existed for nearly 70 years there are still people who live naked" (Franky and Morgan 2015, 38).

Several anthropologists have offered insightful comments on these representations. Rupert Stasch (2011; 2016, 20) describes Euro-American desires for primitivist encounters, in contrast to Korowai interest in participating in "egalitarian transactionality." Danilyn Rutherford (2012) writes about the persistent association between West Papua and the "savage slot" in public imaginaries. And James B. Hoesterey (2012), who worked as a translator for several adventure-style television programs about West Papua, chides anthropologists for overreacting to the public's enjoyment of these interactions. But none of these anthropologists have asked what seems to be the most important question from a political perspective: Why, in a militarized province otherwise closed to journalists, where accredited human rights investigators are regularly denied access, where documentary filmmakers are routinely refused permission to film and jailed if they do so anyway, and where anthropologists rarely receive permission to conduct ethnographic research—why have these journalists, filmmakers, and the occasional anthropologist been granted permission to work with the same three groups of people?

The obvious answer is that the Indonesian state prefers to have West Papua represented to the world by these particular groups of people, rather than by West Papuans raising flags and staging protests in urban areas, by people ousted from their land to make room for oil palm plantations, or by the professional class of West Papuan teachers, lawyers, and journalists. The Indonesian military continues to restrict access to West Papua to ensure that the rest of the world views West Papuans in this tightly scripted fashion, denying their coevalness and carefully erasing all hints of political agency or resistance to the state. In this regard, it is unsurprising that the sensationalist Indonesian film *Lost in Papua* is set in a Korowai village. The images of the Korowai and their neighbors reinforce the Indonesian mandate to govern West Papua by continuing to frame the province and its people as a compelling target for modernization in the form of development, including the use of force as necessary.

FROM VIOLENCE TO HUMAN RIGHTS

Under Suharto, dissent in West Papua was violently suppressed. Lacking civil liberties, West Papuans had few channels for the expression of alternative political views. A movement based on cultural activism led by the West Papuan anthropologist Arnold Ap during the late 1970s and early 1980s included the performance of local songs, dances, and satirical skits. Ap also used his position as curator at Cenderawasih University to document West Papuan art, including carving, sculpture, and pottery (Glazebrook 2008, 36). Other contemporary artists were also involved (Glazebrook 2004). The West Papuan cultural renaissance ended after Ap's arrest and death at the hands of the state in April 1984, shortly after the protests in Jayapura and ensuing military crackdown that triggered the flood of political refugees into Papua New Guinea (Glazebrook 2008, 32–47; Rutherford 2002, 212–13; Zubrinich 1997).

Since the mid-1960s, however, the primary vehicle of West Papuan political resistance has been the Organisasi Papua Merdeka, or Free Papua Movement. Its paramilitary organization replicated the militarization of the state, and guerilla violence was central to its activities in West Papua. For example, the documentary film *One People, One Soul* included the performance of a song about their armed struggle: "Oh, the brave commandos / are willing to die / from a bullet on the battlefield / as a sign of loyalty to the flag of the morning star" (Burns 1987). The OPM also organized protests and symbolic flag-raisings in urban areas. A faction of the OPM was responsible for kidnapping several European university students in the highlands of West Papua in 1995, which backfired by alienating foreign supporters (Start 1997). Despite its reliance on violence, the OPM has maintained broad popular support across West Papua (Tebay 2005, 5), which the refugees in the border camps in Papua New Guinea expressed in their claim "We're all

OPM!" The primary objective of the organization has always been to obtain independence from Indonesia and establish a democratic state for the West Papuan people (Tebay 2005, 5; Ondawame 2010).

For a brief period after the fall of Suharto in 1998, new opportunities for political debate emerged (Chauvel 2005; King 2004; Kirksey 2012). Political dissent during the "Papuan Spring" included efforts to document and redress human rights abuses and environmental problems, including legal claims regarding pollution from Freeport-McMoRan's Grasburg mine. Formal participation in the political system also increased, although the pro-independence resolutions of the Papuan Congress provoked a harsh response from the state, including the assassination of the popular West Papuan politician Theys Eluay by members of the Indonesian Special Forces (Kopassus) and mass killings at a public demonstration in Biak (Chauvel 2005, 106; Rutherford 1999).

The West Papuan Institute for Human Rights Study and Advocacy (Elsham) was especially effective in promoting human rights as a means of transforming political possibilities in West Papua. One of its initiatives was to provide human rights training to rank-and-file Indonesian soldiers stationed in West Papua (John Rumbiak, pers. comm., 1999) and members of OPM paramilitary camps (Rutherford 2005, 163n40). Elsham also promoted the call to transform West Papua into a demilitarized "zone of peace" by withdrawing combat troops, eliminating independent militias, and banning Indonesian military participation in commercial activities (Tebay 2005, 26). However, efforts to engage the Indonesian military and state on these issues were not successful.

The political use of violence has largely been abandoned by the most recent generation of West Papuan activists. The change is in keeping with both the discourse of human rights and the reconceptualization of their struggle in religious terms (see Farhadian 2007), viewing self-determination and territorialized nations as manifestations of divine will (see Kirsch 2006, 185–86). The shift away from violence was also pragmatic in the context of the post-9/11 "War on Terror," given that West Papuan activists hoped to enlist support from, rather than alienate, the United States. The earlier militarism of West Papuan resistance, never very effective, would be anathema in the current political climate. The new strategy also makes clear how earlier forms of violent resistance were a historical reaction to Indonesian militarism rather than an expression of the "violent nature" of West Papuans suggested by the negative stereotype (Kirsch 2010a).

International efforts to enlist political support for the West Papuan cause have proliferated since the mid-1990s. The West Papuan situation has been debated by the European Union (Rumbiak 2003). The U.S. Congress has been asked to revisit the 1962 New York Agreement that facilitated the territory's transfer from the Netherlands to the United Nations and the contested 1969 UN Act of Free Choice, which ceded control over West New Guinea to Indonesia. The United Nations has also been asked to include West Papua on its list of decolonizing nations, and the UN Permanent Forum on Indigenous Issues adopted a resolution supporting the West Papuan political struggle. Despite objections from Australia and Indonesia, regional political forums in the Pacific increasingly include delegates from West Papua. The United Movement for the Liberation of West Papua was recently granted offical standing as an observer at the Melanesian Spearhead Group, which brings together the countries of the west Pacific, and in which Indonesia participates as an associate member (Maclellan 2015). This development led the secretary general of the organization, Octovianus Mote, to assert that the new status signals recognition of West Papua as a "nation in waiting" (cited in Maclellan 2015, 278).

It was during the shift from militarism to human rights activism that I began to interact with West Papuan activists and the NGOs collaborating with them. I first met John Rumbiak, a human rights activist from Biak, West Papua, in the late-1990s. The founding director of Elsham, Rumbiak became the leading spokesperson for West Papuans in the post-Suharto period, and continued his advocacy even after death threats in 2003 forced him to seek political asylum in the United States. Slender, articulate, and at ease in a sports coat and the spotlight, Rumbiak fit the image of a successful international diplomat. It was not difficult to imagine him receiving a Nobel Peace Prize one day had his work not been cut short by illness.

Rumbiak's activities were taken over by Octovianus Mote, a West Papuan journalist from the Me-speaking area of the highlands. Mote was the head of the Papuan bureau of *Kompas,* Indonesia's largest daily newspaper, until he, too, was forced to seek political asylum in the United States. Soft-spoken yet exuberant in his optimism and commitment to West Papuan nationalism, Mote wears glasses that contribute to his scholarly mien. He actively pursues support from anthropologists and historians working in the region, but recognizes the limits of their contributions. We overlapped for a year in

New Haven, including a memorable afternoon during which we took turns asking the Indonesian ambassador to the United States to explain his country's policies on West Papua, and which culminated in a cookout with an underground oven using heated cooking stones, Me-style, in his suburban backyard in nearby Hamden. With Rumbiak and later with Mote, I attended workshops and meetings with groups like the East Timor Action Network, Freedom Now, the Robert F. Kennedy Memorial Center for Human Rights, Survival International, and Tapol.

In 2011, I attended a series of meetings organized by Human Rights Watch at the United Nations in New York City and in Washington, DC, with Mote, Budi Hernawan, and J. Septer Manufandu, a West Papuan human rights advocate from the Dani area who has worked on youth issues and land rights. At the UN, we met with a representative for political affairs in the Asia-Pacific region and the Office of the Special Adviser on the Prevention of Genocide. We were instructed that the meetings were confidential and off the record, which prevented me from taking notes or reporting on their substance in any depth. Although I was invited to contribute to the conversation, I ended up listening to the presentations by Hernawan, Manufandu, and Mote.

The officials with whom we met possessed general knowledge about the political circumstances in West Papua, but were eager for updated information from a human rights perspective. Hernawan and Manufandu described the state's failure to implement the special autonomy package proposed as a partial solution to the problems in West Papua. Several of their interlocutors asked about the Indonesian government and military response to the infamous torture videos and the status of political prisoners in West Papuan jails. My colleagues explained that lower-level personnel had been tried and convicted, but that the state had failed to prosecute superior officers or institute reforms. Hernawan also briefed them on his research on torture as a public spectacle and mode of governance (Hernawan 2013, 2014). The staff members explained how their organizations process information and expressed interest in continuing to hear from unofficial (i.e., nonstate) sources on human rights issues.

We subsequently traveled to Washington, DC, to meet with Senate staff members on Capitol Hill, members of the National Security Council at the White House, and the country representatives for Indonesia from the U.S. Agency for International Development and the U.S. Department of State. Traveling between offices, we brainstormed about how to reach different

FIGURE 3. West Papuan activist J. Septer Manufandu and an advertisement for a television program on cannibalism in West Papua, in New York City. 2011. Photo: Stuart Kirsch.

audiences. To the staff members of a congressman who had sponsored legislation on reporting requirements for companies that purchase minerals from war-torn central Africa, I described the relationship between the Indonesian military and Freeport-McMoRan's Grasburg mine, asking whether the copper and gold produced by the American company should also be classified as conflict minerals. The aide scribbled notes and promised to consult with the congressman. The same congressman cosponsored legislation regarding British Petroleum's disastrous oil spill in the Gulf of Mexico, which we compared to Freeport's environmental impact on the Ajkwa River and Arafura Sea. To the staff members of a congressional committee concerned with religious freedom, my colleagues emphasized discrimination against Christians in West Papua. At meetings with a staff member from John Kerry's office, which represented the U.S. Senate Committee on Foreign Relations, they recommended using U.S. financial support to encourage Indonesia to reform its policies toward West Papua. However, when they pressed the director of the Indonesia desk at the State Department to make U.S. military support contingent on reform, he pushed back against their recommendation, arguing that it would reduce their influence with the Indonesian military. We were joined at several of these meetings by the American anthropologist Eben Kirksey, a veteran of many similar discussions (see Kirksey 2012, 143).

As Mote noted at the end of our meetings, the Indonesian state views the West Papuan conflict as a problem of development rather than a human rights issue. In contrast, West Papuans emphasize freedom and self-determination (see Kirsch 2010a, 14–15).[15] Their other concern is demographic, given that West Papuans have become a minority in their homeland, which they describe as "slow-motion genocide" (see Elmslie 2010). However, it is difficult for the U.S. government to criticize development initiatives or the freedom to move within the borders of the nation-state, even though these actions have negative consequences for West Papuans.

It is not uncommon for anthropologists or other scholars working in the region to accompany West Papuan activists to such meetings.[16] Although Eben Kirksey (2012), drawing on Danilyn Rutherford's insights from her research in Biak (2002), attributes these alliances to the West Papuan desire for things foreign, there are strong parallels to the practice of solidarity activism in other parts of the world. For example, there is a robust tradition of "solidarity work" joining progressive activists and organizations in the United States with their political counterparts in Central and Latin America, which seeks to counteract the negative consequences of U.S. interventions in the region (see Nelson 1999; Tate 2007, 2013; Theidon 2001, 2006).[17] The practice of solidarity activism also seems to have shaped one of the more influential definitions of activist anthropology, which Charles Hale (2007, 105) describes as the "decision to align oneself with an organized group in a struggle for rights, redress, and empowerment and a commitment to produce knowledge in collaboration and dialogue with members of that group."

In contrast to the legal cases in which I have provided informal advice and expert testimony, I was unable to contribute much of substance or even strategy at these meetings. My participation also differed from the disinterested testimony of a nonpartisan observer, a structural position that might have supplanted the speech of my counterparts. Instead of drawing on my ethnographic knowledge or scholarly authority, my involvement in these meetings might be compared to the role of solidarity activists in Central and Latin America. Nonetheless, the opportunity to support the activities of my counterparts in New York and Washington may have been the closest I have come to meeting the challenge posed by the refugees at the male initiation ceremony so many years ago.

BORDER CROSSING

After more than two decades spent working with West Papuan refugees and activists, I had become increasingly self-conscious about continuing to write about the political situation on the other side of the border without having been there.[18] In particular, I was concerned that my earlier work on political representations was one-dimensional, given that most of my interactions were with refugees and exiles. Consequently, in 2014 I crossed the border to Indonesia from the town of Vanimo on the north coast of Papua New Guinea. I felt a twinge of culture shock as I heard the Muslim call to prayer and again when I saw the tidy concrete houses and tile roofs of Indonesian migrants, in contrast to the raised wooden houses with thatched roofs I had just left behind. In their markets, they were selling fruits commonly found in Indonesia, like *rambutan, salak,* and star fruit, rather than the bananas, yams, and betel nut on display in markets across Papua New Guinea.

My West Papuan host generously offered to introduce me to her colleagues in Jayapura and Biak. The first office we visited belonged to the Commission for the Disappeared and the Victims of Violence (Kontras), a national organization in Indonesia. Because Kontras assists West Papuan activists, its employees are stigmatized for their work even though Indonesian law guarantees all of the nation's citizens the right to legal representation. Protests against corruption and other political issues are permitted in West Papua, the lawyer I interviewed told me, but not against human rights violations. If NGOs address human rights concerns in their work, they risk being arrested under article 106 of the Indonesian Criminal Code, which outlaws "rebellion" and is used to prosecute persons accused of advocating independence. The enforcement of article 106 in relation to human rights violations is unique to West Papua and criminalizes much of the work routinely undertaken by the lawyers at Kontras.[19]

FIGURE 4. *Politics* by West Papuan artist Donatus Moiwend. Photo: Rosa Moiwend.

I also met Donatus Moiwend, an artist who had been part of the West Papuan cultural renaissance with Arnold Ap during the late 1970s and early 1980s. He was supposed to have attended the meeting where Ap was arrested by the Indonesian police, but had been sick that evening and unable to attend. He continues to produce paintings and sculpture with political messages, although he never explicitly discusses politics. One of his paintings was inspired by a puddle teeming with tadpoles, all kicking and shoving each other out of the way. It reminded him of the friction and strife inherent in politics, and especially the way politicians behave, so he titled it *Politics*. He was working on a new series of paintings during my visit, including one that incorporated iconography from Asmat carvings, designs that he described as articulating a complete philosophy of life. Moiwend is also well known for painting biblical scenes with Melanesian figures and motifs on churches in West Papua (Cookson 2008, 309–20).

While in Jayapura, I also met with J. Septer Manufandu, with whom I had attended meetings in New York and Washington in 2011. Manufandu worked for the West Papuan NGO forum from 2005 to 2012, before setting up the People's Network for Ecological, Social, and Cultural Rights and Natural Resources in West Papua. The organization works with West Papuans living in rural areas to strengthen the ability of community organizations to manage their resources, protect customary land, and formulate alternative ideas for development. In particular, the organization uses digital mapping technology to promote new conversations about land use in West Papua. This entails cooperating with state officials to achieve the organization's goals. For example, NGO staff members regularly collaborate with the provincial department of planning. They also help rural communities document their resources, using these reports to educate other Indonesians about West Papuan land rights. I was surprised to learn that Manufandu, who was critical of the Indonesian state during our meetings at the UN and in Washington, DC, had established an NGO focused on building bridges with state officials.

I also met with the current director for the human rights organization Elsham, which was founded by John Rumbiak in 1998. Elsham conducts independent human rights investigations, reporting on violations committed by Indonesian security forces to the international human rights community. Like the lawyer I spoke with at Kontras, the director of Elsham complained of being stigmatized for his work with West Papuan political actors. When I asked him about the OPM, he explained that it was not only an organization but also a feeling or belief. This corresponded with what my host in Jayapura had told me, that the OPM continued to be a source of inspiration for West Papuans.

I also had the opportunity to interview a staff member of the organization Tiki ("Enough Is Enough"), which addresses women's rights. She was originally from Manokwari, the birthplace of the OPM, and her father and his brothers fought against the Indonesian state in the 1960s and 1970s. When she was a young girl, her father was arrested and her mother warned her to brace herself for his death. They beat and tortured him, leaving him paralyzed for a year. As a child, she did not understand the reason for her father's suffering. In telling me this story, she began to cry, and then apologized for becoming emotional, explaining that she rarely talks about her childhood experiences. As she grew older, she learned from the stories her father and other people told her about the New York Agreement, the transition from Dutch to Indonesian control, the manipulation of the Act of Free Choice, and the irony that these events were overseen by the same countries that were now promoting human rights. She also spoke about the need to address the problems of West Papua at the United Nations, asking rhetorically why the UN devotes so much time and energy to addressing the conflicts in Israel/Palestine and Syria but ignores the situation in West Papua. There is more than enough evidence to show that West Papua should not be part of Indonesia, she told me, but the powerful states at the United Nations refuse to discuss these issues with West Papuans. Until the UN is willing to address these issues, the human rights situation in West Papuan will never be resolved, she concluded.

I also conducted interviews with a pair of West Papuan journalists. One of them described how the military threatened her when she published a story about one of the torture videos. There was a security officer waiting outside her office when she finished work at 3:00 A.M., so she decided not to return home until the following day. Most of the time she wrote columns about daily life in West Papua on a range of topics, including environmental problems, protests, human rights, and other political issues. The other West Papuan journalist described his beat as writing about events in rural areas, especially protests, activism, and the actions of nongovernmental organizations. He found that most censorship came from within the media, out of fear of repression by the military. Although he had been followed by the Indonesian military, his editor had not forced him to change what he wrote about. When I asked about his views on the independence movement, he responded, "I'm a journalist; I should write the facts, not political opinion." As a West Papuan, he explained, he had his own opinions about the political situation, but he elected to work as a journalist rather than become an activist. The first journalist echoed his views, stating that journalists are required to remain independent. They explained that journalists working in West Papua have to be very careful when writing about political issues. Despite their commitment to objectivity, they still feel stigmatized as members of the sovereignty movement because they are West Papuan.[20]

Next I met with a lecturer from the university in Jayapura who was originally from Sumatra. He described the need to transform the political and historical consciousness of his students as the first step toward independence. I found him to be simultaneously charismatic and condescending, but my West Papuan host agreed with his prescription for change. I also met with a pastor from Biak who spoke about the political situation in terms of self-determination and nationhood being God's promise to all peoples, claims familiar to me from my conversations with West Papuan refugees living in Papua New Guinea (Kirsch 2006, 186; see Zocca 2008, 136).

In my conversations with West Papuan refugees and exiles, there was a clear emphasis on opposition to the Indonesian state and on the desire for independence. The people I interviewed in West Papua also expressed their commitment to independence. However, I felt another twinge of culture shock at the proliferation of political possibilities and attitudes toward these issues, perfectly summed up by Martin Slama and Jenny Munro's (2014, 2) observation that the situation in West Papua is "less straightforwardly 'separatist' or 'nationalist'" than one might assume. The people I met defended the victims of human rights abuses, expressed their political views through art, sought to educate the state about local land and resource use, investigated crime scenes, asserted their professional independence, tried to instill the proper political and historical consciousness in their students, and quoted scripture. In contrast to the relatively homogeneous political opinions of the refugees and exiles with whom I have worked, the people I interviewed in Jayapura and Biak were actively pursuing diverse political agendas. This recognition is an important corrective to the years I spent writing about West Papua from the other side the border. It also suggests the value of conducting comparative research on the dynamics of independence movements in repressive states both in their home countries and among refugees and political exiles.

CONCLUSION

Several years ago, I was a guest speaker at a workshop on engaged anthropology at which a postdoctoral fellow studying mining conflicts introduced herself by confessing that she had originally hoped to do engaged research but had not found ways to participate in or contribute to local political movements. Her comments made an impression on me, because even though my work on mining has segued relatively easily from one project to the next, my relationship to West Papuan politics has been much closer to her experience. The examples presented here suggest that it is not always possible for anthropologists to make a meaningful contribution to the political struggles of the people with whom they work.

I also ask whether engaged anthropology is possible where access is restricted or prohibited, as in the case of West Papua. My primary response to this dilemma has been to write about the politics of representation, which has proven to be fertile ground for discussion about rumor and political violence, including stories about "lost tribes" that undermine the political agency of West Papuans. Although the shift from paramilitary activities by the OPM to new political projects based on human rights created opportunities for collaboration, my contributions have been constrained by my lack of ethnographic experience in West Papua. Moreover, as I learned during my recent trip to West Papua, there are significant differences between the practices pursued by activists living in the Indonesian territory and their counterparts in exile, suggesting the limits of political engagement that is not based on firsthand ethnographic knowledge.

A final insight from these experiences is the value of persistence in building relationships and pursuing opportunities for participation as they arise, even if it is not immediately apparent how or whether these activities contribute to scholarly knowledge production or political goals. These activities resemble what anthropologists and others collaborating with activists in Central and Latin America call solidarity work. It is not a coincidence that the most significant locations for West Papuan activism have been in the Netherlands, the former colonial power; the United States, responsible for the 1962 New York Agreement that allowed Indonesia to assume control over West Papua; and Australia, which plays a significant role in regional politics. However, this trend has shifted in recent years as West Papuan activism has come to "rely less on solidarity from Westerners and more on the huge swell of support . . . from Pacific Islands communities from Melanesia and beyond" (Webb-Gannon 2017, 26–27), raising new questions about whether anthropologists can help West Papuans achieve their political aspirations.

THREE

The Search for Alternative Outcomes

CONSERVATION AND ENVIRONMENTAL DEGRADATION IN PAPUA NEW GUINEA

ENGAGED ANTHROPOLOGISTS CONCERNED ABOUT social and environmental problems may look to the activities of nongovernmental organizations for potential solutions. Hoping to identify alternatives to destructive forms of resource extraction like the Ok Tedi mine, I joined a team of conservation biologists working in the Lakekamu River basin in Papua New Guinea during the summer of 1994. In addition to conducting research on biodiversity, they had a mandate to establish a new kind of protected area, known as an integrated conservation and development program.[1] My goal was to establish whether such initiatives, which provide local communities with economic opportunities consistent with biodiversity conservation, could establish a bulwark against the proliferation of logging and mining projects in Melanesia.[2]

These projects became popular after the 1992 Earth Summit in Rio de Janeiro, which brought renewed attention and financial support for biodiversity conservation.[3] They were organized differently than conventional parks and protected areas, which typically exclude indigenous residents despite their historical contribution to shaping the landscapes these projects seek to preserve. As Michael Wells and others argued in 1992: "Successful long-term management of protected areas depends on the cooperation and support of local people, and . . . it is often neither politically feasible nor ethically justifiable to exclude the poor—who have limited access to resources—from parks and reserves without providing them alternative means of livelihood" (Wells et al. 1992, 2).[4] Thus, in contrast to the dominant model for biodiversity conservation, which seeks to separate "wilderness" from society (Cronon 1995), integrated conservation and development programs formally recognized indigenous land rights within protected areas and sought to collaborate with the people living there.[5]

Such "experiments" in conservation practice (Brown and Wyckoff-Baird 1992, xiii) seemed especially appropriate for Papua New Guinea, where the majority of land in rural areas continues to be controlled by traditional landowners whose property rights are enshrined in the constitution and afforded legal protection. Consequently, logging companies need to obtain permission from landowners before cutting down their forests (Lynch and Alcorn 1994), and communities are central stakeholders in negotiations with mining companies (Ballard and Banks 2003). Like the people living in rural areas of neighboring Indonesia that Tania Li (2007, 2014) describes in *The Will to Improve* and *Land's End,* most Papua New Guineans embrace the promises of development. People living in rural Papua New Guinea often feel that their economic needs and goals have been neglected by the state, which they view as responsible for promoting development (Schieffelin 1997). In contrast, logging and mining companies garner support by promising employment, business opportunities, improved transportation infrastructure, and support for basic services, as well as royalties and other direct economic benefits. When logging and mining represent the only tangible prospects for rural development, people living in these areas may come to see resource extraction companies as allies that can provide benefits the state has failed to deliver (Jackson 1992). Thus, rural communities in Papua New Guinea are often forced to choose between destructive forms of development and an unsatisfactory status quo. Integrated conservation and development programs were therefore intended to provide rural communities with alternatives to large-scale resource extraction.

The stakes of these initiatives are considerable. The population of Papua New Guinea has nearly doubled since political independence in 1975. More forests have been logged and ore mined in this time than during the previous century of colonial control. The resulting social and environmental problems include the military blockade and civil war in Bougainville (Connell 1991; Filer 1990), deforestation and pollution downstream from the Ok Tedi mine (Kirsch 2006, 2014), and a destructive logging boom during the 1990s that was fueled by Malaysian capital (Filer 1997b; Saulei 1997). Virtually the entire country has been carved up into overlapping concessions for logging, mining, oil, and natural gas projects. Consequently, the international conservation community funded a dozen integrated conservation and development projects in Papua New Guinea and the neighboring Solomon Islands during the early 1990s (McCallum and Sekhran 1997, 2).

This chapter is based on several weeks of ethnographic research at the project site in the Lakekamu River basin, which was directed by Conservation

International, an American NGO.[6] My study was designed to collect ethnographic data about the four sociolinguistic groups who previously lived on the margins of the river basin, including information about their land claims and attitudes toward conservation and development. I also observed interactions between the conservation biologists and the local communities. The conservationists were interested in my findings and provided logistical support, but did not impose any restrictions on my inquiries or activities. I spent part of my time working at the field camp operated by the biologists near the Sii River in the southeastern portion of the basin, where they conducted surveys of local bird populations and tree species with the goal of understanding the relationship between the two. However, I spent the majority of my time conducting interviews and facilitating group discussions in the villages near the administrative center of Kakoro, in the northern portion of the basin. Planning for the integrated conservation and development project was still in its preliminary phase, focused on discussions with local landowners. Although my overall assessment of the initiative was positive, my findings emphasized the difficulty in obtaining approval for the project from the four groups that claimed overlapping land rights in the basin (Kirsch 1997e).[7] I also sought to explain why the different communities possessed such radically different visions for the future of the region.[8]

I begin by describing the relationships between the four sociolinguistic groups in the Lakekamu River basin and their implications for the conservation project. Next, I review the major criticisms of integrated conservation and development projects in relation to my ethnographic findings. I then describe the eventual outcome of the initiative in the Lakekamu River basin and comparable projects in Melanesia. Finally, I consider how the search for alternative outcomes can influence the conclusions drawn by engaged anthropologists.

THE LAKEKAMU RIVER BASIN

Located at the intersection of Central, Gulf, and Morobe Provinces in Papua New Guinea, the Lakekamu River basin covers an area of approximately twenty-five hundred square kilometers, including the northern tributaries of the Lakekamu River, which drains into the Gulf of Papua (Sakulas 2012, 161).[9] The basin is composed of a large, relatively pristine tract of rain forest, approximately one hundred meters above sea level, surrounded by hills and moun-

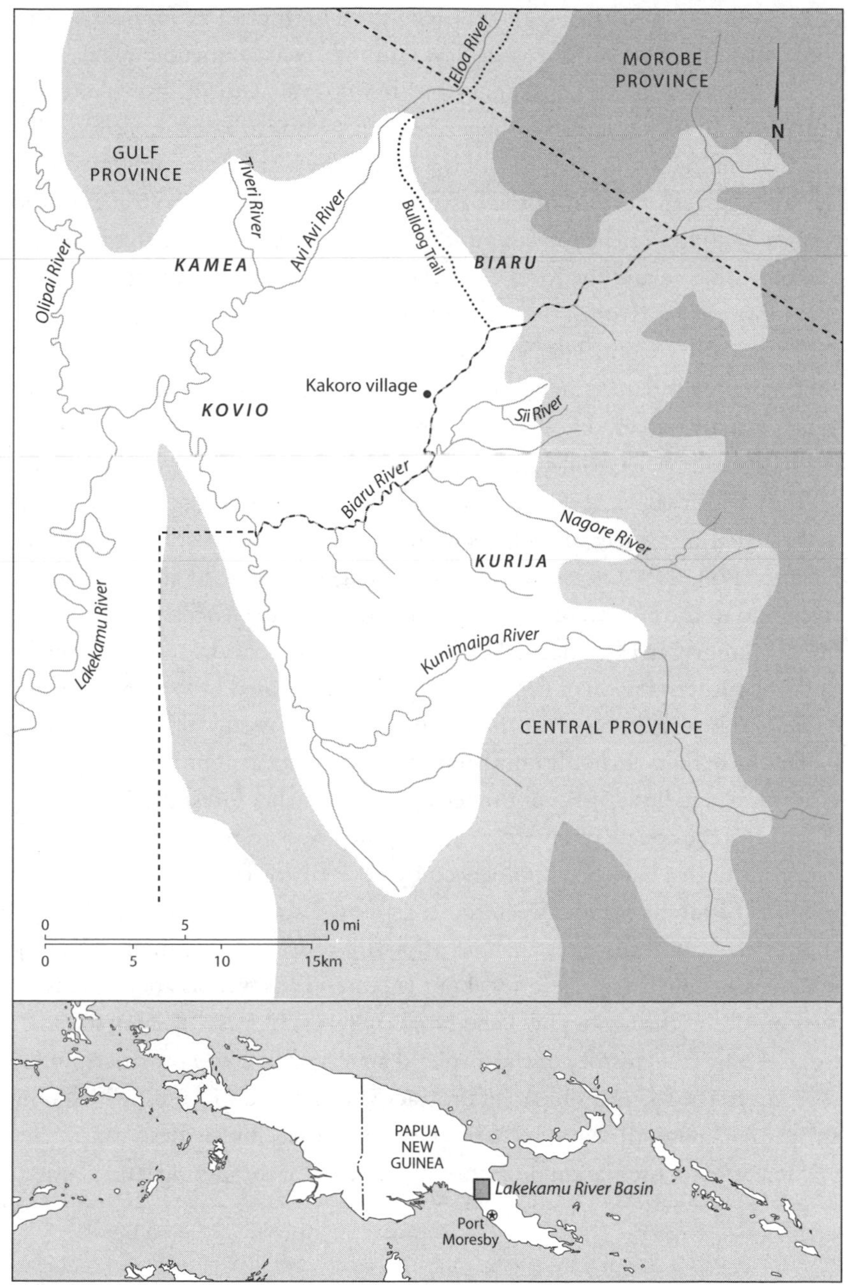

MAP 4. Sociolinguistic groups in the Lakekamu River basin, Papua New Guinea.

tains on three sides. The region was assigned a high priority for biodiversity conservation in a survey of Papua New Guinea (Swartzendruber 1993).

The resources in the Lakekamu River basin were historically exploited by four different sociolinguistic groups: the Biaru, who are based in the foothills and mountains to the northeast of the basin; the Kurija, who migrated into the southeastern portion of the basin from the mountains to the east; the Kamea, who live in the foothills and mountains along the northern perimeter of the basin; and the Kovio, a lowland group who lived along the southern rim of the basin until the early colonial period. In describing the region, anthropologists Colin Filer and Wari Iamo (1989, 17) point out: "Even by Melanesian standards, the . . . area exhibits a measure of cultural diversity which is truly remarkable, and the demarcation disputes which characterize the relationships between cultural groups have a long and complex history."

The majority of the two thousand residents of the Lakekamu River basin have settled in a string of villages located near an administrative center at Kakoro (PNG NSO 1991). Several other villages are located along the major rivers and in the mountains to the northeast. The name *Kakoro* means "dried up" or "hungry" in Hiri Motu, the trade language historically spoken throughout the southern region of Papua New Guinea. Founded in 1972, Kakoro has a school, a health center, a provincial office, and a grass airfield. The southern half of the basin is currently uninhabited, although local populations regularly visit the area to hunt, fish, cut timber, and gather other forest products.

During the course of my research, I learned how responses to the conservation initiative have been influenced by both historical and contemporary patterns of interaction between social groups. Land rights in the basin are subject to heated disputes that occasionally erupt into conflict, affecting what the people living there say about themselves as well as about the past. Writing about the region, Filer and Iamo (1989, 31) suggest "a search to establish the one 'true' history of the disputed area is unlikely to provide a simple solution to the social problem [of protracted territorial disputes] which now exists." Although this appears to be an extreme case, it provides a cautionary tale for other conservation projects where there are competing land claims.

THE BIARU

Three of the four groups that claim ownership of land and resources in the lowland portion of the Lakekamu River basin are members of larger sociolinguistic groups based in the nearby highlands fringe. Members of one of these groups, the Biaru, live in several villages to the north of Kakoro, on the west side of the Biaru River. According to my informants, there are four major Biaru descent groups, or patriclans; clan membership, however, is apparently no longer of primary importance to the Biaru, who say that such affiliations have become "all mixed up."

The Biaru own the land in the mountains northeast of Kakoro. They also claim the land from the east side of the Biaru River to the Avi Avi River, which they describe as the border separating them from the Kamea. In contrast, the Kamea assert ownership of all the land between the two rivers. The difference in perspective is related to the history of the basin. Before the imposition of colonial control, the Kamea used to raid Biaru settlements (Filer and Iamo 1989, 31), which prevented the latter from living in the disputed territory. The Biaru acknowledge being intimidated by the Kamea, whom they accuse of having practiced cannibalism.[10] Both groups probably made intermittent use of the resources in the area between the Avi Avi and Biaru Rivers, although neither group settled there.

The Biaru also claim that the land between the Sii and Nagore Rivers, south of Kakoro, belongs to them, although both the Kurija and the Kovio dispute this assertion. The Biaru deny that the Kurija have land rights in the area because the latter recently moved into the river basin from the headwaters of the Kunimaipa River, a distance of several days' walk. In contrast, the Kurija assert that they have lived there for multiple generations, and therefore, that the land belongs to them. The Biaru acknowledge the historical presence of the Kovio, however, with whom they have had long-standing trade relations.

Biaru leaders were reluctant to talk about the history of the area with me because of an ongoing dispute regarding small-scale gold mining at Nowi Creek. Mindful of the unsettled issues associated with land ownership in the basin, they told me the following myth, which describes their relationship to other Biaru speakers in the mountains of Morobe Province, where they are also known as the Gorua:

> Sankep is the name of the ancestor of the Biaru. He came to the Biaru River with his son Tie. Sankep did not know how to build a house, so they slept in the forest. Tie put his firstborn son, Paur, in a men's house and decorated him with shells used in exchange. Men came to the ceremony from all around.
>
> Moin came down from the headwaters of the Sii River. He killed a pig, removed its skin, and came down from Maoru Mountain. Along the way,

> he met a man called Maorarai, and the two men camped there overnight. Maorarai wanted to kill Moin, but someone warned him, and he ran away. Moin then sent a message: "When the river becomes dirty, Tie should climb to the mountaintop." When the time came, women in the mountains pissed into the river, fouling the water downstream. This told Tie that it was time for him to climb the mountain.
>
> Tie and his wife, Ruipispis, started walking to Maoru Mountain. Tie stopped to look for game in the forest, sending his wife ahead along the track. Ruipispis met Moin along the way, and they had sex together near a small bamboo stand.
>
> When Moin and Tie met, Moin showed Tie how to build the men's house, which they call *aniak*. Moin showed Tie how to make a knife from bamboo. He also taught Tie about exchange, and as a result, they became friends and trading partners.

The myth addresses history, social relations, and land rights and has a broad regional distribution (see Filer and Iamo 1989, appendix 3, 92–96). It describes the relationships between two Biaru groups; the main population in the mountains of Morobe Province, and a splinter group that moved into the foothills to the south, close to Kakoro. According to the narrator of the myth, the two groups share a common language but maintain separate descent groups.

Sankep and his son, Tie, represent the Biaru people living on the edge of the Lakekamu basin. The dispute between the two groups, represented by Moin's affair with Ruipispis, Tie's wife, is resolved through exchange. Moin gives Tie access to sacred knowledge, enculturating him through participation in male cult ritual. The two groups are also connected through an exchange relationship established by their joint participation in the ritual. The events depicted in the myth follow a common Melanesian scenario in which exchange transforms conflict into productive social relationships (Schieffelin 1976).

The myth also helps explain the dynamics of regional exchange in the Lakekamu basin. The lowland Biaru occupy an important position in this system. In the past, they had regular trade relations with the Kovio, who controlled exchange between the coast and the highlands. This was an important route for shell valuables central to the exchange economies of the highlands (see Hughes 1977). The shells were obtained from the coast and from lowland mangrove forests. They were traded from the south through the Lakekamu basin, becoming increasingly valuable with the distance from their source. In return for shells, the Biaru traded bird feathers, bark cloth, and spears to the Kovio. The lowland Biaru traded the shells to the mountain Biaru for pigs and quarried stone used for ax blades. Shells were central to Biaru exchange; they told to me they were used "like money" and in bridewealth payments.

THE KURIJA

The Kurija claim ownership over the southern portion of the Lakekamu River basin. They are the westernmost group of the Kunimaipa, who live in the mountains of the Goilala subdistrict in Central Province (Hallpike 1977). Their language has three major dialects, the first spoken in the mountains, the second near the headwaters of the Kunimaipa River, and the third by the Kurija. In the 1950s, the Australian anthropologist Margaret McArthur worked in the Kunimaipa Valley. What the Kurija told me about their social organization and ritual practices was consistent with what she described for the highland Kunimaipa (McArthur 1971).

The Kurija are patrilineal, with land held collectively by the lineage rather than divided among its individual members. People who are not members of the lineage must obtain permission to use the resources on that land, whether they wish to garden, fish in the rivers and streams, or hunt in the forests. If a person plants a tree on another person's land without permission, the landowner has the right to uproot it.

Kurija is known as the "big name" for their clan structure, which they describe as the "backbone" of their society. There were originally nine Kurija lineages, two of which are now defunct. Each lineage is named after its founder, and all are exclusively local. Every lineage has a headman, known as the *amip,* who directs its affairs. The position is ideally acquired through hereditary primogeniture. During feasts, the *amip* instructs the participants on proper behavior, exhorting them to refrain from stealing, fighting, or otherwise inciting conflict. However, the main role of the headman is to settle disputes that arise between lineages, leading the Kurija to compare his duties to those of a lawyer.

Kurija lineages are exogamous, and couples reside patrilocally after marriage. Relatives of the bride and groom are expected to exchange small gifts of dog teeth and bird-of-paradise feathers, but until recently they did not exchange bridewealth at marriage. By 1994, however, payments of five hundred to twelve hundred kina had become the norm.[11] The Kurija told me that their lineages had not fought among themselves in the past, because their numbers were so small. Instead, disputes were settled by paying compensation, the value of which was generally negotiated by the respective headmen of the two lineages. In the event of a dispute with members from another group, however, all of the Kurija would join together to fight if necessary.

The Kurija told me the following myth to explain how they came to live in the Lakekamu basin. They previously lived in the mountains east of Kakoro, at the headwaters of the Kunimaipa River, which they call the Kutkut. They were members of a clan called Komi Garoi, named after the senior man of the group. A dispute between two factions of the clan caused a permanent rift to emerge:

> The people known as the Komi Garoi took turns hunting and collecting firewood. When the people responsible for bringing firewood back to the village forgot to do so, it led to a quarrel. The dispute was settled by splitting into two groups, the Komi Garoi and the Kurija.
>
> The Kurija left the mountains and moved to the headwaters of the Nagore River. In all, seven brothers settled along the Nagore. Only men moved down from the mountains; there were no women.
>
> One evening, one of the men saw something odd and called the others to come see: there was a strange light coming from a stand of bamboo. From a distance, it looked like fire. "What is it?" they wondered. They decided to go closer and investigate. They also sent a message to Komi Garoi in the mountains, inviting him to come.
>
> When they reached the bamboo, they saw the light was made by women. One by one, the women stepped outside, and the men chose the women they preferred: "You take this one, I'll take that one," and so forth. Each man took one woman as they came forward.
>
> Komi Garoi came down from the headwaters of the Kutkut River. He told the men: "Now you are married, so it is time to have a marriage feast." Before they ate, however, Komi Garoi stood and spoke again: "Now, I'll divide the land among you." He designated a different plot of land for each brother. The brother named Lairao [from the narrator's clan] was to live on the land between the Sii and Nagore Rivers. The eldest brother, Kurija, was to live along the Kunimaipa River. The other brothers were told to live in different locations along the Sii, Nagore, and Kunimaipa Rivers.
>
> Now Komi Garoi is dead; his body is buried on the other side of the Kunimaipa River, at a place called Kuiki [Sharp Mountain].

Like all myths, this one has multiple meanings. It asserts that the Kurija have lived in the lowlands between the Sii, Nagore, and Kunimaipa Rivers for many years. One genealogy I recorded suggests that six generations of Kurija have lived in the Lakekamu basin over a period of about 150 years, although this is not necessarily an accurate means of making a chronological assessment, as genealogies are regularly telescoped or foreshortened. The myth also explains the relationships between the Kurija lineages and the distribution of land among them. There is more to the myth than a group of people staking out their land claims, however; like the Biaru myth presented here, it also explains the relationship between populations in the mountains and the lowlands.

Conflict between clan members may be resolved through fission, by separating the feuding parties into independent groups. The event that triggered the split between the two factions, the failure to collect firewood, is trivial in relation to its consequences, suggesting the need for an alternative interpretation. The alternation of tasks between the two lineages implies a society with a simple division of labor. Physical labor was reciprocated directly, in contrast to more prevalent systems of exchange in Papua New Guinea, in which the products of labor are exchanged directly through barter, or indirectly by means of mediating tokens of values, such as shells or money. The failure of the one group to fulfill its obligation to the other revealed the insufficiency of the economic system depicted in the myth.

Komoi Garoi is credited with instructing the Kurija to move from the mountains into the lowlands. This allowed the Kunimaipa people to establish trade relations with the Kovio for shells from the coast. In return for bows and arrows, tobacco, and dog teeth, the Kurija acquired shell valuables they later traded to the Kunimaipa living in the highlands. This permitted the Kunimaipa to establish a more complex economic system based on intergroup alliances, which were organized through the exchange of shells and other valued objects.

The second half of the myth is concerned with the social relations between the Kurija and other Kunimaipa who remained in the mountains. When the women emerge from the stand of bamboo, the resulting marriages are anomalous. Since the women have no relatives, the Kurija have no affines with whom they can form alliances. Komi Garoi approves the marriages anyway and apportions the land accordingly. The Kurija are no longer beholden to their relatives in the mountains for either land or marriage; this portion of the myth asserts their autonomy. The Kurija told me that they did not resume intermarriage with other Kunimaipa speakers from the mountains until recently. The myth describes the movement of the Kurija from the mountains into the Lakekamu basin, where they became an independent group that participated in the shell trade from the coast into the highlands.

The Kurija claim the land between the Biaru and Kunimaipa Rivers, including the territory between the Sii and Nagore Rivers. They confirm the

Biaru assertion that the two groups did not have contact until recent years, although they claim that the Biaru River is the border between the two groups. Like the Biaru, the Kurija deny having been in contact with the Kamea before the colonial period or having ventured into their territory. They only saw the footprints the Kamea left behind in the sand along the Biaru river. They traded regularly with the Kovio, and some of them learned to speak their language, although the two groups did not intermarry. In contrast, the Kurija do not speak or understand the languages of the Kamea or the Biaru.

In an interview about the future of the Lakekamu basin, several Kurija leaders expressed concerns about the potential negative impacts of large-scale resource extraction projects. They are opposed to large mining projects because of the chemicals (*marasin* in Melanesian Tok Pisin) that are released into local waterways, which can poison fish and other riverine life. They were concerned that the noise from generators and engines would scare off the wildlife and ruin their hunting. They also worried that people coming from outside the basin to work on these projects might cause trouble and disrupt their way of life (*bagarapim ples* in Tok Pisin). Although they were opposed to the presence of large mining or logging companies in the basin, they expressed support for smaller-scale development projects that would not harm the environment (*spoilim ples* in Tok Pisin).

THE KAMEA

Most of the Kamea who claim land rights in the lowland portion of the Lakekamu basin reside in the hills and the mountains to the north.[12] The Kamea are one of many Anga-speaking groups living in the eastern portion of Papua New Guinea's central mountain range, spanning Morobe, Gulf, and Eastern Highlands Provinces (Bamford 1997). In the past, Kamea living in the northern foothills regularly exploited the resources of the basin, trading lowland produce for pandanus nuts (*karuka* in Tok Pisin), which grow at higher altitudes.

Marriage exchange in this patrilineal society took the form of gifts of smoked game and garden produce (Filer and Iamo 1989, 54). After killing and smoking a large quantity of animals, a man interested in marriage would make a formal gift of meat to his prospective in-laws. If the prospective groom's offer was accepted, he would plant a new garden, build a new house, and invite his affines to attend a wedding feast. There were no bridewealth transactions involving shell valuables.[13] Given that this group of Kamea did not exchange shells, they had no need to participate in the regional exchange system to their south. Instead, they maintained exchange relations with other Kamea communities living at higher altitudes, with whom they traded lowland produce, including red pandanus (*marita* in Tok Pisin).

As a result, the Kamea did not have trade relations with the other groups living in the Lakekamu basin. Their relationships with these groups were shaped by conflict and intimidation. Kamea raids against the Biaru prevented them from settling in the northeast portion of the basin, in the area between the Avi Avi and Biaru Rivers (Filer and Iamo 1989, 31). The Kovio also recall violent interactions with the Kamea. The combative reputation of the Kamea, including allegations of cannibalism, kept their neighbors at a distance. While both the Kamea and the Biaru made intermittent use of resources from the area, it remained unoccupied until the colonial era. Current disputes over land ownership reflect this history.

There is one Kamea village near Kakoro. Iruki was established by the residents of Nukeva and Tekadu, located in the mountains to the north, after Kakoro was founded in 1972. Once primary schools had been built in the mountain villages, almost all of the Kamea living in Iruki returned home. To maintain their settlement at Iruki, and to protect their claims to nearby land and resources, the Kamea invited people from villages outside of the basin to settle there. When I was there in 1994, most of the residents in Iruki were from Kamena and Kaintiba in the mountains. In Iruki, in contrast to the other communities in the basin, village exogamy is the norm. This is not surprising given its transient population. Only one-quarter of the people in a sample of recent marriages in the village consider either Iruki or the two closest Kamea villages in the highlands to be their home. Although they all identify as Kamea and speak the language, they are placeholders for landowners living in Nukeva and Tekadu. They have permission to use the resources in the surrounding area but do not have the right to make decisions regarding development or conservation projects.

The territorial claims of the Biaru and the Kamea have substantial overlap, and both groups previously made intermittent use of the resources in the area. Neither group actually lived in the contested area until recently, however, as the Kamea resided in the foothills and the mountains, while raids by the Kamea forced the Biaru to locate their settlements to the east, out of harm's way.

THE KOVIO

The Kovio are the only lowland group living in the Lakekamu River basin and the only Austronesian language speakers. They have allies among several groups from the Gulf Coast, including the Mekeo, who speak a closely related language (Brown 1973, 284).[14] They also possess strong cultural continuities with the Mekeo, including their ritual face-painting style, which has become well known throughout Papua New Guinea from performances in urban areas.[15] The Kovio regularly intermarry with the Mekeo, providing the former with valuable social ties and regional connections. Their broad social network is particularly important, given that the total Kovio population is fewer than five hundred people (PNG NSO 1991).

The Kovio lived in the southern portion of the Lakekamu River basin along the lower Kunimaipa River until the 1950s, when they moved closer to the Lakekamu River.[16] The proximity of the three Kovio villages to the Lakekamu River facilitates travel to the towns and cities along the Gulf Coast. Unlike the other three groups living in the basin, the Kovio never relocated to villages closer to Kakoro, although several Kovio civil servants are employed at the government station there.[17]

The Kovio claim ownership of most of the land in the Lakekamu basin. Some of the Kovio say that their land rights extend north along the Tiveri River, past its junction with the Avi Avi River and into the mountains of Morobe Province, near the colonial border between the territories of Papua and New Guinea. Other Kovio deny that their land rights extend that far north. Given the friction between the Kovio and the Kamea in precolonial times, it is not surprising that the boundary between them remains undefined and contentious. The Kovio also claim land along the Sii and Nagore Rivers, challenging Kurija claims to the area. They argue that Kurija land rights are limited to the upper Kunimaipa River. According to one account, a Kovio man working with an expatriate pastor from the United Church invited the Kurija to settle in the Lakekamu basin, but did not transfer ownership of the land to them. If true, this would place their movement into the lowlands considerably later than the genealogical estimate by the Kurija.

Writing about their southern neighbors the Mekeo, the Tongan anthropologist Epeli Hau'ofa (1981, 17) notes that they were well positioned to manage the trade that moved through the region: "With the Kuni and Goilala, the Mekeo traded not only betelnut and coconut but also the shell ornaments they had received from the coast, in return for stone axes, flints, plumes and pandanus nuts. Being located strategically along a major waterway between the coast and the mountains, Mekeo acted as intermediaries through whom the products of the sea and the mountains passed both ways."

The Kovio, too, were strategically located in relation to their neighbors in the basin. The Kovio traded shells, along with bows and arrows, to the Kurija in return for dog teeth and pigs. They also established trade relations with the Biaru, who had a similar desire for the shells they controlled. In their analysis of social relations in the Middle Sepik River region, Deborah Gewertz and Frederick Errington (1991) show how one group may dominate even in a system of commensurate differences, in which all of the societies are interdependent and relatively equal, which also characterizes Kovio relationships with their neighbors. The historical ability of the Kovio to control the shell trade in the Lakekamu basin underwrites their sweeping land claims across the entire area.

The strategic location of the Kovio in the precolonial landscape is replicated in their contemporary political and economic position in the basin. The proximity of their villages to the Lakekamu River and their relationships with the Mekeo increase the access of the Kovio to urban resources. Given their proximity to the regional high school, which is located in Mekeo territory, they are the best educated group in the Lakekamu basin. They are actively involved in regional politics and more "fully integrated into the cash economy" than their neighbors (Filer and Iamo 1989, 54). A landowners association established by a lawyer from one of the Kovio villages is said to represent all of the Kovio, as well as other interested parties from the Lakekamu River basin. The association's support for large-scale development projects directly challenges the conservation initiative. The urban orientation of the Kovio leadership also means that they are more willing to develop the natural resources of the Lakekamu basin than its other residents, who depend on local rivers and forests for their subsistence practices.

ECONOMICS AND DEVELOPMENT

The Biaru, Kamea, and Kurija plant large, swidden gardens, usually along riverbanks, in which they grow bananas, sweet potatoes, and yams, among other crops. They also harvest seasonal tree crops, including betel nut, okari, breadfruit, and red pandanus. June and July are the months of the yam harvest, and the dry season extends from September to December, which are the best months for hunting. The Kovio make smaller gardens than their neighbors because they rely more heavily on sago (*Metroxylon sagu*), which is a common staple in the interior lowlands of New Guinea (Ruddle et al. 1978). In contrast, the other groups living in the basin process and consume sago only during lean times between harvests.

Economic opportunities for the residents of the Lakekamu River basin are currently limited. The climate and soil conditions in the basin are well suited for agriculture. Despite their success in growing coffee and cocoa, financial returns have been limited owing to the lack of transport for cash crops to urban markets (Filer and Iamo 1989, 51). A small market held twice weekly in Kakoro caters primarily to government personnel based there. Peanuts and betel nut are sold in Kerema and Port Moresby, along with seasonal forest products, meat from wild pigs, crocodile skins, and plumes from a number of wild bird species, including birds-of-paradise, sulfur-crested cockatoos, crowned pigeons, and cassowaries. Travel by river to the coast, and then to Port Moresby by road, is expensive, and travelers are vulnerable to thieves. People report that most of the money they earn on these trips is expended on travel, accommodations, and inexpensive goods like the kerosene lanterns they purchase. A few of the residents in the basin earn small sums of money selling colorful beetles and butterfly larvae to an insect-marketing program run by the Wau Ecology Institute (Orsak 1991).

Some of the Kamea, Kurija, and Biaru are involved in small-scale alluvial mining in the creeks that run through the hills to the northeast of Kakoro (Filer and Iamo 1989, 30). The Biaru have panned for gold in Nowi Creek since the 1980s. The residents of a settlement known as Bundi Camp, which is located just northeast of Kakoro on the Biaru River, migrated into the basin from Goroka in the Eastern Highlands to work local gold deposits. The Kurija residents of Mirimas village pan for gold in the eastern tributaries of the Oreba River (Filer and Iamo 1989, 30). Some of the residents of the Kamea village of Iruki migrated to the basin to work the gold at Omoi Creek. In the late 1980s, the Biaru invested in dredging equipment, but this angered the Kurija, who claim ownership of the land beside Nowi Creek. With support from the Kovio, the Kurija raided the Biaru mining camp, destroying their equipment and causing a number of injuries. However, the Biaru were backed up in the dispute by the coastal Moveave, who have their own territorial quarrels with the Kovio (Filer and Iamo 1989, 32). Both sides went to court in 1993, and a temporary injunction was placed on mining until the land disputes were settled, although small-scale gold panning continued without interruption.

More substantial gold reserves are located near the Olipai River, a western tributary of the Lakekamu River. A baseline planning study for the Lakekamu Gold Project was conducted in 1989 by anthropologists Colin Filer and Wari Iamo. It described operations supporting a single, large dredge capable of processing several million cubic meters of material a year during the estimated five-to-fifteen-year lifespan of the project (1989, 5–7). The study predicted that operating the dredge would have "very limited impact on the natural environment" (Filer and Iamo 1989, 15, emphasis removed). The project was expected to generate local employment and business opportunities, including contracts to supply food to the workers (Filer and Iamo 1989). With regular barge service from Port Moresby along the Lakekamu River and the construction of a new airstrip, the project would also have facilitated transport of cash crops and other goods to urban markets (Filer and Iamo 1989, 5–6). However, the mining project was never developed.

Timber is another resource in the Lakekamu River basin with significant economic value. At the time of my study, there were no active logging concessions in the basin, although a proposed project in Gulf Province would have encroached on its southwest corner (Tim Werner, pers. comm., 1995). Several Malaysian timber companies also expressed interest in obtaining logging rights for much of the remainder of the basin (Bruce Beehler, pers. comm., 1995). Logging in the Lakekamu basin was especially attractive to developers because of the large stands of primary forest. In addition, heavy machinery could be transported directly from Port Moresby by barge, and felled timber could be floated south to the coast via the Lakekamu River. However, the economic benefits provided by commercial logging projects in Papua New Guinea rarely meet local expectations (Bell, West, and Filer 2015). This is especially true in rural areas that lack the infrastructure to productively absorb cash payments (Burton 1998). When I interviewed them in 1994, landowners were divided about the prospect of logging in the Lakekamu basin. They subsequently vetoed a proposal to establish an oil palm plantation organized into a series of smallholdings, which would have required clear-cutting a significant portion of the forest (Sakulas 2012, 186–87, 199).

As part of the integrated conservation and development project in the Lakekamu River basin, Conservation International proposed setting up several ecotourism projects to generate revenue for the people living in the basin, including the development of a hiking trail through the mountains from Wau, along the historical Bulldog Trail constructed during World War II, a lodge for tourists interested in bird-watching and other naturalist activities, and a biodiversity research center that would attract scientists from abroad and train students from Papua New Guinea in biology and conservation (Sakulas 2012, 180). These proposed projects followed an "environmental custodian" model for conservation and development, in which communities are provided with financial incentives to protect natural resources. The income generated by such initiatives is intended to replace revenue that might otherwise be obtained from resource extraction or other forms of development. Such programs build on the experience of international conservation organizations in Africa that seek to protect wildlife from pastoralists and poachers (Brockington 2002).

Conservation International also proposed setting up programs to harvest and sell nontimber forest products from the Lakekamu River basin. The "rain forest marketing" model of conservation and development was formulated among forest peoples in the Amazon basin, although there are also precedents from Southeast Asia and Africa (Nepstad and Schwartzman 1992). Such projects are intended to provide an economic rationale for forest conservation by developing ways to profit from the sustainable use of renewable forest products. They may also strengthen local land claims by helping communities demonstrate productive stewardship of the forest and its resources.

LOCAL HISTORIES AND REGIONAL PLANNING

Attitudes toward development vary within and between the sociolinguistic groups in the Lakekamu River basin. Regardless of their opinions about logging and mining, most of the people living in the basin were receptive to opportunities to participate in small-scale, income-generating ventures consistent with continuing village residence. However, some individuals, including several vocal leaders in particular, expressed concern about the effects of these projects on their future economic plans. Very few of the people with whom I spoke referred to conservation as a goal in the abstract, despite their ongoing interactions with project members, although some mentioned the practical value of the forests and rivers to local livelihoods. In addition, the history, geographic position, and political power of the different groups in the basin influenced their attitudes toward the integrated conservation and development project.

Of the four groups, the Kurija expressed the strongest reservations about large-scale resource extraction in the basin. They are opposed to large-scale mining and logging projects because of their likely impacts on wildlife and the local river system. They also expressed concern about the potentially disruptive influence of workers affiliated with such projects. Cut off from their political allies in the mountains to the east, and unsuccessful in their ventures in the closest urban centers of Kerema and Port Moresby, the Kurija regard subsistence agriculture and hunting as an integral part of their future; and consequently, they recognize the need to protect the resources of the river basin. Their position differs from the narrow view of conservation as the protection of nature or biodiversity; instead, it is an example of what Joan Martinez-Alier (2003) calls "environmentalism of the poor." Practical reliance on local resources, rather than conservation in the abstract, fuels Kurija desires to protect the Lakekamu River basin. Consequently, many of them were outspoken proponents of the proposal to establish a conservation and development program in the basin. In addition, by presenting themselves as responsible guardians of the southern half of the Lakekamu River basin, they hoped to gain support from Conservation International in their territorial disputes with the Kovio.

The Kovio response to the initiatives sponsored by Conservation International differed significantly from the positions taken by their neighbors. Given their participation in the cash economy and their comparative political clout, they speak more favorably and confidently about the prospects of development. They organized their landowners association to take advantage of the economic potential of the basin, including the exploitation of minerals and timber. According to one Kovio leader, the goal of these undertakings is to raise the capital necessary for greater participation in the national economy. The Kovio make broad claims to much of the territory in the Lakekamu basin; and in the recapitulation of historical patterns of exchange, they regard the economic agenda for this territory as theirs to dominate.

The Biaru and Kamea responded positively to some of the economic initiatives proposed by Conservation International, including ecotourism. The major concern for the Biaru was that they continue to enjoy unimpeded access to their artisanal mining projects in the hills and mountains to the northeast of the basin. And while the Kamea had no objection to the projects proposed by Conservation International, they were equally interested in exploring other development options. The people living in the Kamea village near Kakoro are primarily migrants who serve as placeholders for landowners living in the foothills and mountains. The landowners living in the mountains act like absentee landlords, and their geographic location to the north of Lakekamu means that logging would not directly affect them. Consequently, most of the Kamea people I interviewed support logging in the basin, and many of them joined the landowner corporation established by the Kovio to develop its resources.

Not surprisingly, the Kovio reject proposals to divide the resources of the basin among the four groups who lay claim to them, or to have all of the groups living in the basin participate as equal partners or stakeholders in discussions about its future. Their leaders, many of whom are based in the provincial capital, are wary of initiatives that might deprive them of the opportunity to control the economic future of the area. Perched at the edge of the Lakekamu River basin, and oriented toward opportunities available only at the national level, many of the Kovio view the resources of the area as the means to fashion new roles for themselves in the rapidly expanding national economy.

CRITICISM AND CONTEXT

Anthropologists have generally been critical of conservation and development initiatives (e.g., Brockington 2002; Li 2002; West 2005). One concern is that development exposes isolated communities to exploitation by making their labor and resources available to global markets (Escobar 1995). Similarly, the task of cataloging regional biodiversity and identifying projects with commercial potential might be criticized for colonizing the natural world (Pratt 1992). Nature is reduced to commodity form, the value of which is determined by external markets rather than local use and exchange. This process may also result in symbolic violence to local cosmologies and systems of classification as Euro-American discourses of science and development are imposed on indigenous lifeworlds (Bamford 2002).

Conversely, it has been suggested that small-scale development projects promoted by conservation initiatives are problematic because of their economic marginality, and that the "butterfly farming" approach to rural development prevents indigenous peoples from competing as equals in the national and global economies (Howard 1993). Michael Dove (1993) argues that when rural development projects are economically successful, they are vulnerable to capture by actors with greater social capital. These projects also have the tendency to promote representations that essentialize indigenous peoples, taking for granted their treatment of nature as sacred and their reluctance to participate in the capitalist economy (Bamford 2002, 41–42; Conklin and Graham 1995).

Ethnographic research in the Lakekamu River basin helps set aside some of these criticisms and put the remaining concerns into perspective. The river basin is hardly a secluded enclave of gift relations independent of capitalist relations of production or the influence of the state. Settlement patterns in the basin have been driven by the state since the founding of Kakoro in the 1970s. The history of capitalist expansion into the Lakekamu River basin dates back even farther, to a small gold rush beginning in 1920. One of the first conflicts between the British and the Germans after the declaration of World War I occurred near the border between German New Guinea and the British territory of Papua in the alluvial goldfields of Lakekamu (Nelson 1976, 224–37). Furthermore, in contrast to societies of Southeast Asia that seek to avoid interaction with the state (Scott 2010), most of the people living in the Lakekamu basin aspire to greater participation in the larger economic system.

Even the risks posed to local ways of knowing need to be contextualized. It would be wrong to imagine these societies as either static or possessing closed systems of knowledge. One might ask, for example, how the mountain-dwelling Kurija applied their taxonomies to new flora and fauna after migrating to the lowland river basin. Moreover, the people living in the Lakekamu basin already draw on multiple and competing discourses about nature and the environment. Children learn Linnaean principles of classification in primary-school biology lessons, and Christians listen to biblical parables about the relationship between humans and nature in church, but these new perspectives do not necessarily replace or diminish the old. Nor is it necessary to treat science and ethnoscience as opposed rather than potentially complementary. Consider the following example: Although the director of the Lakekamu project is one of the world's leading scientific experts on the birds of New Guinea, he spent his evenings at the research camp interviewing people from the river basin to learn more about the behavior of the birds living there. Their interactions encourage us to think of conservation projects as sites for the exchange of information rather than a unidirectional effort to impose Euro-American categories, practices, and values on the people living there.

Although Michael Dove (1993) encourages conservationists to direct their attention to state policies in need of reform rather than to rural communities whose power and agency are limited, one should not overlook the ability of landowners in Papua New Guinea to exercise veto power over logging and mining projects. Given that integrated conservation and development projects attempt to diversify local economies rather than focus on a single cash crop or resource, they are less vulnerable to external capture. The projects proposed by Conservation International, moreover, were intended to supplement rather than replace existing economic opportunities in the Lakekamu River basin, which range from gold panning to raising cash crops like coffee and copra, and to selling betel nut and other produce in urban markets. The rationale for the conservation and development project in Lakekamu was to identify and facilitate economic development consistent with long-term conservation of biodiversity while meeting the needs and aspirations of local residents, providing them with alternatives to large-scale resource extraction projects, which often end up exacerbating local economic conditions (see Kirsch 2014). Recognition of the diverse attitudes of the people living in the basin toward conservation and development options also belies concerns about reproducing essentialized representations of indigenous peoples.

A final criticism of these initiatives is that they are incompatible with the attitudes of Papua New Guineans, who, it is sometimes said, are unconcerned with protecting the environment (see Macintyre and Foale 2004). This argument follows influential research by the anthropologist Roy A. Rappaport on the ritual cycle of the Maring people in the highlands of Papua New Guinea. Rappaport (1968, 9) was more interested in documenting the adaptive dimensions of human behavior than Maring agency, concluding that the management of natural resources was a "latent function" of their rituals rather than the outcome of conscious decision-making. His conclusions have been challenged by Gillian Gillison (2001, 298), who criticizes Rappaport for "driving higher reason and communal interest into the unconscious." Similarly, Aletta Biersack (1999, 15n3) criticizes Rappaport for neglecting women's understandings of how people compete with pigs for sweet potatoes when their herds become too large, the trigger for a new ritual cycle. Scholars influenced by Rappaport continue to emphasize the contribution of ritual and taboo to sustainable resource management, neglecting contemporary debate about these issues among Papua New Guineans, which has become increasingly common. The range of local perspectives on these issues is evident in the differences between Kamea and Kurija attitudes toward resource extraction projects. These examples suggest the need for ethnographic accounts of conservation and development projects that acknowledge local agency in decision-making and adequately represent the diversity of perspectives on these issues.

Although representatives from the conservation organization continued to live and work in the Lakekamu River basin for a number of years, disagreements over land rights effectively blocked implementation of the project. None of the large-scale threats to the biodiversity of the lowland rain forest—whether logging, large-scale mining, or oil palm plantations—materialized either. This has probably been a source of frustration for the pro-development factions of the Kovio and Kamea, but a relief to the Kurija and the conservation biologists conducting research in the Lakekamu basin (see Beehler 2008, 155–80).

Lakekamu was not the only integrated conservation and development project in Papua New Guinea to fail. In my original article on the subject, I cited a press release announcing that the Lak people in New Ireland decided to cancel a contract with a logging company that had already wreaked havoc on their forests, rivers, and marine resources, opting instead to participate in an integrated conservation and development program (Barry 1995, cited in Kirsch 1997e, 105–6). However, news of the logging project's demise was premature. Instead, it was the conservation and development project that was unable to compete with economic expectations raised by the logging company, leading to its cancellation after only two years (McCallum and Sekhran 1997).

The longest-running integrated conservation and development project in Papua New Guinea, at Crater Mountain, closed down in 2005 (West and Kale 2015, 155). It had a history of economic problems owing to the high cost of transporting supplies to the site and declining tourism in Papua New Guinea (Pearl 1994). However, Paige West (2005) attributes the demise of the project to the fundamental incommensurability between the goals of the conservationists, who wanted to forestall development, and the Gimi, who actively pursued it. Frustration with the failure of the conservationists to establish the kind of reciprocal social relations they desired ultimately led the Gimi and their neighbors to take their chances with a mining project that has already produced its first gold (West 2006; West and Kale 2015).

In their requiem for the conservation and development project among the Lak in New Ireland, Rob McCallum and Nikhil Sekhran (1997) argue that the establishment of protected areas is probably not the most appropriate strategy for biodiversity conservation in Papua New Guinea. They offer a number of reasons, including landowner desire for rapid economic development and the competitive advantage of developers who violate the law with impunity (McCallum and Sekhran 1997, 74). The primary exception appears to be projects initiated by communities seeking to safeguard their resources from development (McCallum and Sekhran 1997, 75; see also Regenvanu, Wyatt, and Tacconi 1997). One long-running conservation project receives vigorous support from the Maisin of Collingwood Bay in eastern Papua New Guinea, who have continuously rebuffed efforts to log their forests (Barker 2016).

My research on the proposed conservation and development project in the Lakekamu River basin provided an early snapshot of an important trend in conservation policy and practice. It also offers several lessons about conservation initiatives, most notably the need to understand the social history of project sites. Given the complexity of relationships between groups in Papua New Guinea, including conflict, exchange networks, and migration, the resulting disputes over land and resource ownership were central to the responses of the different groups living in the basin to the proposed conservation area. My study also shows how attitudes toward the environment and development are influenced by regional dynamics, including access to various political and economic resources. These factors influenced aspirations for the future, including whether or not they felt the need to protect local forests. For the Kurija, forest conservation was not only commensurate with but also essential to local livelihoods, whereas the Kovio placed a higher value on development than protecting the forest. Given the small scale and size of most political groups in Melanesia, such issues are likely to be consequential elsewhere in the region as well.[18] My research also showed that Papua New Guineans have diverse attitudes and opinions about the environment and conservation, and that their views may be influenced by a variety of factors, including history, political standing, and economic opportunity. Even where there is a desire to protect the lowland rain forest, it may be driven less by a conservation ethic than by materialist concern for preserving access to key resources.

In hindsight, I recognize that my search for alternatives to large-scale resource extraction resulted in unwarranted optimism regarding the prospects of integrated conservation and development initiatives in Papua New Guinea. Despite correctly diagnosing what eventually proved to be the project's fatal flaw—the complex social history of the Lakekamu River basin and the resulting disputes over land ownership and resource rights—I nonetheless wrote about its prospects in hopeful terms.[19] I concluded that these initiatives might help curtail more destructive forms of development wreaking havoc on rural landscapes and, consequently, offered a spirited defense of these experiments in conservation practice:

> Integrated conservation and development projects have only recently been introduced into the region. They are likely to progress slowly, for collective decision-making and community discussion about long-term patterns of resource use are time-consuming processes. Yet there are clear signs that such programs have been well received in many communities. On Makira Island in the Solomons, a program co-sponsored by Conservation International, which includes a *ngali* nut oil project [and] an ecotourism project . . . apparently inspired villagers to reject an offer to purchase their timber from a Malaysian logging firm. The Bahinemo of the upper Sepik River region of Papua New Guinea have asked the World Wide Fund for Nature (WWF) for help in managing their natural resources and in establishing a conservation area to keep loggers out of the Hunstein Mountain Range (Kirsch 1997e, 107; references omitted).

Ironically, the final positive example cited in this paragraph was the flawed announcement about the conservation project among the Lak in New Ireland, which had already failed by the time my article appeared in print. In my own defense, however, I also acknowledged the limits of my prognostication: "Although it is too early to ascertain whether or not Conservation International will be successful in implementing its plan for an integrated conservation and development program in the Lakekamu River basin, they clearly face a number of substantial challenges. Overlapping resource claims and conflicting political and economic agendas have complicated even their efforts to maintain a physical presence in the basin" (Kirsch 1997e, 107–8).

Nonetheless, my account represents a cautionary tale about engaged anthropology. It shows that the search for alternative outcomes can influence the resulting analysis. My desire to identify economic opportunities that could reduce support for destructive resource extraction projects like the Ok Tedi mine did not alter my ethnographic findings, confirming the validity of the underlying research. But its effect on my overall assessment of conservation initiatives suggests the need for greater attention to these issues by engaged anthropologists, whose conclusions may be influenced by their policy agendas and political objectives.

My experience studying the Lakekamu project also led me to undertake different kinds of engaged research, shifting from research on conservation projects that might limit the harmful impacts of mining, to becoming actively involved in the struggle against the mining industry (see chapter 1).

I came to doubt whether it is sufficient to protect a small percentage of the planet in the form of national parks and conservation areas while avoiding stronger regulations on the industries responsible for environmental degradation. This is especially true in the age of global climate change and given the mobility of industrial pollutants, which make it impossible to protect specific places from harm. Instead, we need to address the creation of environmental problems by raising standards and preventing harm from occurring in the first place. I also came to question the legitimacy of asking communities least responsible for environmental degradation to bear a disproportionate share of the costs of biodiversity conservation, an issue to which I return in more detail in chapter 7.

Consequently, my work on the Lakekamu project was a turning point for both my research and my political activism. From work as a consultant on social impact studies sponsored by a mining company and a conservation organization, I increasingly moved into spaces of political opposition against the mining industry, working with communities and nongovernmental organizations to challenge corporations responsible for causing harm.

FOUR

When the Intervention Fails, Does the Research Still Matter?

OVERTAKEN BY EVENTS IN SOLOMON ISLANDS

THE DAY AFTER I ARRIVED in Honiara, the capital of Solomon Islands, on October 26, 1998, the front page of the *Solomon Star* carried a story about a large, unexplained fish kill in the Tinahula River, downstream from the Gold Ridge mine (SS, Oct. 27, 1998).[1] The people from nearby Bemuta village found the dead fish and prawns on Sunday morning and alerted the newspaper, which dispatched a reporter and photographer the following day. The newspaper quoted one of the villagers as saying, "We were confused and surprise[d] to see the dead creatures." The article explained, "The dead fish and shrimps triggered . . . fear among the villagers because the river provided for all their needs." Another person identified as a "concerned villager" told the reporter: "We use the water for washing, swimming, cooking, and of course, drinking." The *Star* concluded, "No causes have been identified for the death of fish and other water creatures at Tinahula River in Central Guadalcanal last weekend" (SS, Oct. 27, 1998).[2]

I was visiting Honiara as a consultant for the Australian law firm Slater and Gordon, which was suing Ross Mining, the owner and operator of the Gold Ridge mine, in the High Court of Solomon Islands. The lawsuit addressed the environmental impacts of and potential risks from the mine. I had close ties to Slater and Gordon from our work on the lawsuit against the Ok Tedi mine in Papua New Guinea from 1994 to 1996, which was settled out of court for an estimated $500 million in compensation and commitments to tailings containment (Kirsch 2014). The lawyers asked me to assist with their case in the Solomons by investigating land tenure and property rights among the Ghaobata people living beside the Metepono River and its tributaries on the north coast of Guadalcanal. They also wanted me to document the social and environmental impacts of the project. They hoped

I might come to play a role in the Gold Ridge proceedings comparable to my participation in the Ok Tedi case. However, I was meeting their clients for the first time, in contrast to my long history of interaction with the Yonggom and their neighbors. I was sympathetic to the concerns of the people living downstream from the Gold Ridge mine and viewed my involvement in the case as an opportunity to gain comparative knowledge about the role of litigation in mining conflicts.

The day after the media reported on the fish kill, I drove to the Tinahula River to see the situation for myself. Littering both sides of the shallow but steadily flowing river were thousands upon thousands of dead fish and prawns. This nightmarish scene reminded me of the stories my Yonggom informants had told me about the effects of a cyanide spill on the Ok Tedi River in 1984 (see Hyndman 1988, 94). At the time, the Yonggom did not know what had killed the fish, prawns, and turtles in the river, which they gathered up and ate. They subsequently came to view the event as an early warning of the mine's eventual impact on their river and forests. To witness something comparable in Solomon Islands, albeit on a much smaller scale, was doubly resonant in terms of helping me understand the experiences of the people living on the Ok Tedi River, as well as the threat posed by the Gold Ridge mine to the people living downstream.

The defensive response by Ross Mining to the article published by the *Solomon Star* was instructive. The company denied any responsibility for the fish kill (SS, Oct. 30, 1998). Instead it insisted that the tailings retention system for the mine was completely sealed and therefore could not have released cyanide into the river system. This was confirmed, a spokesman for the mining company explained, by the project's electronic sensors, which showed no indication of a leak. The mining company also sought to deflect responsibility for the fish kill by seeking to naturalize the event, suggesting it may have been caused by the loss of oxygen in the river. Deoxygenation can occur along the bend of a slow-moving river or in a stagnant body of water, but is unlikely in a swiftly flowing river descending from the mountains into the lowlands. As the chairman of the Gold Ridge Landowner Council observed, "We have lived . . . along these rivers for years, but nothing such as that happened. These are running rivers and not swamps" (SS, Oct. 30, 1998).

After my visit to the Tinahula River, I sought out a reporter from the *Solomon Star* to discuss the similarities between the fish kill downstream from the Gold Ridge mine and the cyanide spill on the Ok Tedi River. Since I came to the Solomons directly from my field site in Papua New Guinea,

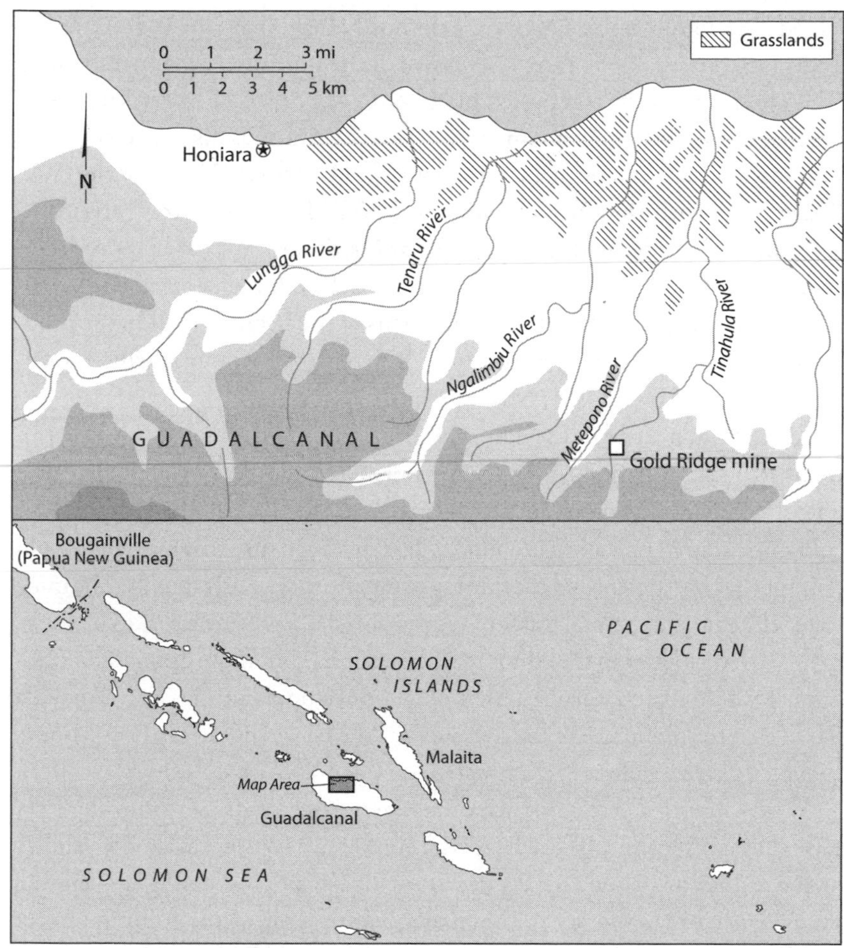

MAP 5. Gold Ridge mine and the surrounding area. Guadalcanal, Solomon Islands.

I asked the newspaper staff to develop a roll of black-and-white film still in my camera, which included images of deforestation on the banks of the Ok Tedi River. Following the publication of a story comparing the two mining projects—titled "Will Ok Tedi Repeat Itself?"—I was interviewed about the controversy on the national radio station. These activities were commensurate with my early involvement in the Ok Tedi case, during which I sought to raise awareness of the environmental impact of the mining project (Kirsch 2014, 57).

The public response to the controversy in the Solomons was sharply divided. The author of one letter to the editor observed, "I am a Solomon

Islander and grew up in PNG. . . . I do not believe that this is another Ok Tedi" (SS, Nov. 4, 1998). A representative of the mining company responded even more vigorously, as reported by the *Solomon Star:* "While acknowledging that unforeseen problems may arise, Ross Mining has dismissed comparisons made by an American anthropologist[,] Dr. Stuart Kirsch, of the Gold Ridge mine with the Ok Tedi mine in PNG: 'It is absolute[ly] absurd to compare Gold Ridge with Ok Tedi. What Dr. Stuart fails to see is the difference between how the two mines operate. . . . To tell the people of Solomon Islands that this is another Ok Tedi, or this is the beginning of many problems to come, is absolutely misleading.' 'Dr. Stuart is simply scaring the villagers', the official said" (SS, Nov. 4, 1998).

In contrast, a letter to the editor by Dr. Culwick Togamana, a lecturer in chemistry and environment at the University of the South Pacific in Suva, noted, "Similar incidents of this sort also occurred here in Fiji when Mount Kasi gold mine started operation in 1996. . . . It is my hope that this incident should prompt the government and the mining company to seriously monitor the mine water effluents and natural water resources on a daily routine basis" (SS, Nov. 5, 1998). Another letter to the editor reached a similar but more dramatic conclusion: "I would like to warn the users of the 'once-upon-a-time clean Tinahula River' that the usefulness of the river is over. Maybe we should ask Ross Mining to supply us with gallons of clean water every day" (SS, Oct. 24, 1998).

When scientific tests conducted on water samples drawn from the river several days after the spill—a delay that could have compromised the validity of the results, as cyanide breaks down rapidly in tropical sunlight—showed no evidence of the chemical, the managing director of the mining project once again "slammed recent comparisons of the Gold Ridge project with the Ok Tedi mine in Papua New Guinea. . . . 'Attempts to compare our project with the Ok Tedi mine can only be described as scaremongering,' he said. 'Comparisons with Ok Tedi are clearly designed to frighten and manipulate people into opposing the Gold Ridge project. . . . [I]f our investigations reveal any problems with the return water system, they will be rectified immediately" (SS, Nov. 6, 1998). An op-ed published in the *Solomon Star* asked whether it was a coincidence that an anthropologist happened to arrive in Honiara at the same time as the "dead fish mysteriously found in the Tinahula River," while suspiciously providing photographs of denuded forests downstream from the Ok Tedi mine to the local newspaper (SS, Dec. 8, 1998).

Three weeks after the original incident, however, the *Solomon Star* reported that a "discharge of waste water has occurred along the Gold Ridge water return line on Sunday when Ross Mining re-opened its system following the recent controversies over the dead fish discovered in the Tinahula River." Ross Mining characterized the spill as "minor" and claimed that it had "no detrimental effects" on the river. However, the minister of mines described the same spill as "quite large" and warned against drinking from the river (SS, Nov. 17, 1998).

For many people living in Honiara, the competing explanations for the fish kill—a cyanide spill or malfeasance on the part of critics of the mine—were equally plausible: "If the problem is caused by leakage from the mining operation, Ross Mining must be made to pay. However, if the problem [was] deliberately caused by opponents of the mining operation[,] . . . then Ross Mining must be cleared. The problem is highly sensitive and must not be left to drag on" (SS, Oct. 28, 1998).

When the managing director of the Gold Ridge mine, Dr. Bertus de Graf, complained to the *Solomon Star* (Dec. 8, 1998) that "it was unfortunate that a localized fish death occurrence in the river was alleged by some parties to be directly linked to the [Gold Ridge mine] despite the lack of any scientific evidence that this was the case," Nick Styant-Browne, the lead attorney in the case from Slater and Gordon, felt compelled to respond. On December 10, 1998, Styant-Browne published an op-ed in the *Solomon Star* in which he argued that the fish kill was "no mystery," and that "it does not take much more than common sense to link the mine's use of cyanide to the problems downstream" (SS, Dec. 10, 1998).[3] De Graf fired back, accusing the plaintiffs of "seeking to close down the mining operations" (SS, Dec. 10, 1998). He also pointed out that the legal action hurt the Solomon Islands government through "a reduced tax take from the Gold Ridge mine" (SS, Dec. 10, 1981).

Solomon Islanders concerned about the environmental impact from the mine variously referred to what became known as the "dead fish incident" as "a signal of problems," "the first evidence," and as having "already proven the point" about the contamination of local rivers. In addition to my déjà vu experience, the mining company's repeated denial of its responsibility for the fish kill and its attempt to naturalize the problem were patterns of behavior that have become familiar to me through research on the relationship between corporations and their critics (Kirsch 2014).

These interactions occurred during a period of rising tensions in Solomon Islands—between the people of Guadalcanal and migrants from the neighboring island of Malaita—that slowly morphed into civil conflict which paralyzed the country from 1998 to 2003. The ethnic tensions, as these events are now known, resulted in 150 to 200 deaths. Thousands more were assaulted and 35,000 people were displaced (Allen 2013; Bennett 2002; Fraenkel 2004; Kabutaulaka 2001; McDougall 2016; Moore 2004; TRC 2012).

The dismissal of the lawsuit against Ross Mining and the Gold Ridge mine in early 1999, for reasons I explain below, and the ensuing conflict prevented me from returning to the Solomons for many years. My research, which was limited to three short visits to Honiara and the surrounding area, remained incomplete and unpublished.

Consequently, I ask whether ethnographic data collected in the context of engaged research, which may begin with specific problems to investigate, still have value when circumstances change and the project loses its raison d'être. I returned to Solomon Islands in January 2014 to answer this question. While conducting research in the archives of the *Solomon Star,* the leading daily newspaper in Solomon Islands, I realized that my earlier work on Ghaobata land rights offers constructive insights into the relationship between the protagonists in the civil conflict, especially the structural contradictions engendered by the extension of land rights by landowners from Guadalcanal to Malaitan migrants. It also helps explain why Solomon Islanders overwhelmingly reject explanations of the conflict that focus on historical enmity between the two groups despite the mobilization of the protagonists along ethnic lines. Thus I show how ethnographic data obtained during the course of engaged research may have unexpected relevance in new contexts. Given my involvement in the court case, I also wanted to know whether the dispute over the Gold Ridge mine and the subsequent failure of the lawsuit were catalysts for the conflict, like the relationship between opposition to the Panguna copper mine and the ensuing civil war in neighboring Bougainville. Finally, given the passage of time since my original fieldwork, I assess the long-term environmental impacts of the project in relation to the original legal claims.

THE LAWSUIT

The Gold Ridge mine commenced operation in October 1997 and produced 210,000 ounces of gold during its first twenty-two months (Nanau 2014, 77–78).[4] By international standards, it was a small project, with initial capitalization costs of about U.S.$55 million dollars. The mine was conservatively projected to produce 100,000 ounces of gold per year during its ten-year life span. Given the limited scope of the country's formal economic sector, the project was expected to contribute 10 percent of its GDP.

According to Ross Mining, the project adhered to the standards of "best practice" for the mining industry. At an estimated cost of U.S.$12 million, the mine constructed a closed tailings system designed to contain the cyanide used to process gold. But given the high annual rainfall in the Solomons, water from the tailings pond would periodically have to be filtered and released into the Metepono River system, a process known as "dewatering." The tailings dam was also vulnerable to damage from the cyclones that regularly visit the coastline, including the risk of catastrophic failure, as a study commissioned by Slater and Gordon concluded (Dunkerley and Hallam 1997). The removal of overburden from the mine site had already shifted a significant quantity of waste rock, sediment, and other debris into local rivers. To make matters worse, the mining company refused to release the project's environmental impact assessment to the public, even though making such documents accessible is regarded as a best practice.

In 1996, Ross Mining announced a U.S.$3 million compensation agreement, equivalent to approximately 2.5 percent of the U.S.$122 million in profits the company anticipated earning over the life of the project (*Justinian* 2002). The funds were earmarked for the people relocated from the mine site and the adjacent tailings pond. The compensation agreement failed to address the environmental impacts of the project, including the risks posed to the people living downstream along the Tinahula and Metepono Rivers (Nanau 2014). This exclusion was a red flag for Slater and Gordon, whose case against Ok Tedi Mining and BHP included the company's refusal to provide adequate compensation to the people affected by pollution from the mine. The Gold Ridge compensation agreement also indemnified Ross Mining against all future claims arising from environmental impacts, which would be deducted from subsequent payments to the relocated communities, an accounting trick to limit economic liability that was also employed in the Ok Tedi case.

Slater and Gordon became involved in the legal action against the Gold Ridge mine in March 1997. The previous month, the neglected landowners had warned Ross Mining that the company "risked another Bougainville" if it failed to compensate the people living along the Metepono River, referring to the decade of civil war in nearby Papua New Guinea (Moore 2004, 86). The threat was especially chilling, given the large number of ex-combatants and refugees from the Bougainville conflict living in Honiara. Nick

Styant-Browne called on Ross Mining to settle the case and pointed out that his firm had "a proven capacity to negotiate reasonable resolutions to these sorts of claims," referring to the Ok Tedi case. But he also brashly threatened to "embark on lengthy and internecine litigation" against the mining company if it refused to negotiate a settlement, a comment that rankled many people living in Honiara, and which was frequently repeated by the media in the ensuing months. The lawsuit sought compensation for environmental damage during the construction phase and early operation of the mine, as well as the establishment of a trust fund to cover the costs of mitigating potential adverse effects from the mine, including problems associated with the tailings dam.

LIFE IN THE GRASSLANDS

Before visiting Solomon Islands, I turned to Ian Hogbin's (1964) classic work on the Kaoka people of the Guadalcanal Plains. Hogbin, a student of both A. R. Radcliffe-Browne and Bronislaw Malinowski, published monographs about several different societies in Solomon Islands and New Guinea. Based on fieldwork conducted in the early 1930s, he described the Kaoka as living in five dispersed matrilineal clans along fifty miles of coast and grasslands.[5] They were organized into villages of 175 to 200 persons, which were composed of a string of hamlets along a path, each located on clan land. "Land . . . appertains to the clan," not the village, Hogbin (1964, 6) wrote. The exception was fertile land along river deltas, which was held in common (Hogbin 1964, 6).

Kaoka village headmen were similar to other Melanesian big men in that positions of leadership were achieved rather than ascribed (Hogbin 1964, 62). One of the most important political responsibilities of the headman was to settle disputes, which often entailed consultation with an informal council of senior men (Hogbin 1964, 6). The headman was expected to use his personal wealth in organizing periodic feasts, the primary collective economic activity of the village (Hogbin 1964, 64–69). His power was subject to the classic limit of small-scale polities, in that "he can never impose his will against popular opinion" (Hogbin 1964, 63).

Avunculocal postmarital residence with delayed onset was the norm among the Kaoka, much as it was among the Trobriand Islanders (Malinowski 1935). Boys lived with their fathers until early adulthood, when they generally "migrate to the district of their own clan, where their rights cannot be contested" (Hogbin 1964, 17). "However, his father may also invite him to stay on land that belongs to his clan" (Hogbin 1964, 6). Although the son's use of his father's land is unlikely to be challenged, "he is permitted to be there as a favor and . . . to some degree [remains] an outsider" (Hogbin 1964, 6). Similar use rights were also extended to other kinsmen and affines (Hogbin 1964, 4).

The Kaoka grew yams, taro, and sweet potatoes, maintaining four to six gardens at a time, each at a different phase of production (Hogbin 1964, 41). They fished along local reefs and in the sea, especially for bonito (Hogbin 1964, 44). Each clan maintained three shrines, belonging to a shark spirit, a snake spirit, and a warrior spirit. Until the 1930s, they made regular sacrifices at these shrines: at the shark shrine before fishing, to ensure their safety; at the snake shrine, which was dedicated to a female spirit associated with gardens and fertility, at the time of first harvest; and at the warrior shrine before fighting, to ensure victory. These shrines resembled local dwellings, and each was occupied by a priest. They were also repositories for trophies and relics, including ancestral skulls. The Kaoka had already converted to Christianity by the time of Hogbin's research, so even though he was able to collect information about seventy-five shrines, only three were still in use (Hogbin 1964, 72–79). Despite their neglect, these shrines continue to have significance in contemporary land claims (Naitoro 1989).[6]

GHAOBATA LAND RIGHTS

During the course of my discussions with the Ghaobata on property rights, it became evident that one of the most contested issues was the status of secondary land rights. The subject was important to the legal proceedings because the plaintiffs in the case were people with land rights in the impacted areas. Like the neighboring Kaoka, the Ghaobata belong to five dispersed matrilineal clans. After marriage, a man who grew up on his father's land could move to the district of his own matriclan, but more often he ended up staying near his father, using land allocated for his use. The Ghaobata refer to the resulting access to land as "secondary rights."[7]

Other kin and affines may also acquire the right to live and make gardens on land belonging to another matrilineage. These rights are ordinarily restricted to the generation of people to whom the permission was initially granted. After the death of the person who originally acquired use rights, both the land and any improvements made to it revert back to the original owners. The owners of the land must compensate relatives of the deceased for these investments. But if someone with use rights makes sacrifices to the clan shrines of his hosts and contributes to their mortuary feasts, it is possible to transfer his usufruct rights to the members of the next generation. The resulting claims to land are also known as secondary rights.

When Ghaobata men started building permanent houses and settlements with running water and electricity, they wanted their sons to inherit these structures even though they were not members of their father's matrilineage. This was also the case for Ghaobata men who planted coconut palms, cocoa, and other cash crops that provide a return for many years. Such divided interests are not unusual in matrilineal kinship systems. Writing about the matrilineal Tolai in East New Britain, Papua New Guinea, Keir Martin (2013, 32) notes that there was a "common expectation that a man's children would be able to continue to live on or use his land, even after his death." But he also cites T.S. Epstein's (1968, 67) example of a Tolai man who "bought land in his sons' names and planted it with cocoa and coconuts so that they alone will inherit his perennial crops. At the same time, he continues to support matrilineage interests by association in . . . joint matrilineal land" (Martin 2013, 34). He maintains loyalties to both his lineage and his sons, but transactions that facilitate patrilineal inheritance promote exclusive forms of ownership, which can be divisive (Martin 2013, 34; see also Monson 2015). As Martin argues, the introduction of cash crops and permanent houses made "land something to be fought over" (Martin 2013, 31).

As in the example of the Tolai man who acquired land in his sons' names, Ghaobata men have devised strategies to transfer land to their sons. In some cases, they are able to purchase land for their sons to use. An alternative is to convert property held by the matrilineage from customary to registered land. Once it has been registered by the state, it is no longer subject to the rules of customary land tenure, which allows them to buy and sell land like any other commodity. This permits men to convert matriclan land into private property that can be permanently transferred to their sons. In effect, they use laws concerning land registration that date back to the colonial period to "launder" land that belongs to the matrilineage. Both of these practices increase the demand for and quantity of alienated land despite widespread opposition to the commodification of customary landholdings in Solomon Islands.

These developments accompany the shift to permanent settlements and the advent of commercial agriculture. Men seek to protect their personal investments in these new forms of immoveable property through the extension of secondary land rights, outright purchase of land, and registration of clan land with the state so that it can be transferred to their sons. Although land alienated from the Ghaobata for plantations and other purposes remains a source of powerful grievances against the state, as I discuss below, some of the men living in the grasslands nonetheless employ the rules responsible for their colonial dispossession to subvert customary practices of inheritance.

FROM BIG MEN TO CHIEFS

After my initial visit to Guadalcanal in 1998, I consulted Isireli Q. Lasaqa's (1972) monograph on the Ghaobata, whom he called the Tadhimboko. A human geographer from Fiji who studied with Harold Brookfield at Australian National University, Lasaqa sought to challenge prevailing assumptions about the incompatibility of "traditional social group[s], [and] the links based on marriage, co-residence and obligatory relationships," with economic development (Lasaqa 1972, 285). He argued that the "flexibility of land-usage rights" among the Ghaobata have, in fact, "facilitated economic growth" (Lasaqa 1972, 285; see also Kama 1979, 155).

Like Hogbin (1964), Lasaqa (1972) referred to political leaders in the grasslands of Guadalcanal as "big men."[8] One of the chapters in his monograph compares the careers of two local big men. Jacob Vouza's employment as a policeman for twenty-five years "in many parts of the Solomons made him a well-known and widely respected person" (Lasaqa 1972, 88). During World War II, Vouza volunteered to scout for the Allied Forces and was captured and held prisoner by the Japanese (Lasaqa 1972, 88). After the war, he became the leader of the anticolonial Marching Rule movement in Guadalcanal (Lasaqa 1972, 89). He subsequently became involved in local government, holding a series of elected offices over several decades. However, his authoritarian tendencies fostered resentment, which eventually led to his replacement by a younger man in 1964, events Lasaqa (1972, 90; see Akin 2013, 314–15) compares to the rise and fall of a big man.

The second big man profiled by Lasaqa was Samuel Saki, who later became the lead plaintiff in the lawsuit against the Gold Ridge mine. In contrast to Vouza's participation in electoral politics, Saki rose to power through his entrepreneurial prowess and generosity. Younger than Vouza, he nonetheless worked for the American forces during the war. Afterward, he returned to his matriclan land and worked in the scrap metal business, earning enough money to start his own transportation company. He subsequently parlayed these investments into a string of enterprises that made him "the most successful Melanesian businessman in Guadalcanal" (Lasaqa 1972, 91). He used his economic resources to employ members of his matrilineage and provide them with "assistance in times of difficulty" (Lasaqa 1972, 91), which are also activities Lasaqa identifies as being commensurate with the responsibilities and actions of a big man.

By the late 1990s, Samuel Saki's economic ventures were no longer generating significant revenues, although he was comfortable in his retirement and respected for his leadership and community support. When I first encountered Saki's name in the legal documents for the case against Ross Mining, I was surprised to see him identified as the "paramount chief" of the Ghaobata. When I asked my informants about this, they explained that the Ghaobata were organized into five ranked clans, each of which possesses its own chief. Samuel Saki was the chief of the highest-ranking clan and therefore recognized as the paramount chief.

Although the shift in terminology might be taken to imply a transformation in political organization, scholars working in the region have argued that there is more fluidity in the categories of big man and chief than implied by the classic anthropological types (White and Lindstrom 1997). Whereas the status of a big man is achieved and his career is ephemeral, in contrast to the ascribed status of a chief who occupies an existing office, anthropologists have historically invoked these categories in support of arguments about scale and political evolution (e.g., Sahlins 1963) that are not applicable to Solomon Islands (Lindstrom and White 1997, 6, 9). The new vocabulary does not imply that the Ghaobata replaced their big men with chiefs, but rather that the category of chief possesses sufficient flexibility to encompass the former. Although the term *big man* has always been more popular among anthropologists than among Solomon Islanders (Lindstrom and White 1997, 6, 9), the title of chief acquired additional political significance during the postwar period.

Much of the anticolonial discourse of the 1950s and 1960s blamed colonial dispossession on the absence of strong chiefs. Consequently, the major political movements of the period emphasized the role of chiefs in defending local land rights. The leader of the postwar Moro movement in Guadalcanal instructed his followers: "Everything in this land and sea belongs to you. . . . All the things that are yours should be used, not allowed to stand unused or to be exploited by others. Your people own it and control it" (Davenport and Çoker 1967, 141). A creation myth transcribed by members of the Moro movement asserts that all of the plants, animals, food, stones, and metal ore in Guadalcanal belong to their chiefs (Davenport and Çoker 1967, 144). William H. Davenport and Gülbün Çoker (1967, 145) argue that the Moro movement sought to establish the "role of local chief as a centre for economic transactions, as defender of customary law, and as preserver of district boundaries."

The emphasis on local chiefs intensified after the country's independence from Great Britain in 1978.[9] As one government minister opined the following year: "Chiefs and elders acting under the authority of the tribe, line[age], and clan names can confirm and advise the true rights to land. [Only] they can transfer land. . . . Members can use any part of tribal land as they wish, but the chiefs' and elders' consent must first be sought" (Zoleveke 1979, 3). He also fought back against the commodification of land by invoking the authority of the chiefs: "I do not wish us to continue with the capitalist principle that land is a marketable commodity and I wish to return the authority over land from the law back to chiefs and elders" (Zoleveke 1979, 7). This perspective was consolidated in the passage of an amendment to the Local Courts Act in 1985 "to ensure that 'chiefs' heard land cases before they were taken into the court system" (White 1997, 240). The law reinforced the role of the chief as the proper authority over land regardless of whether such institutions had local historical precedent. This included the High Court's recognition of the clan chiefs and the paramount chief as the appropriate representatives of the Ghaobata.

COLONIAL LEGACIES

Solomon Islands was named after King Solomon's mines in 1568 by Álvaro de Mendaña y Neira, the nephew of the viceroy of Peru, who hoped to attract future Spanish settlers with the lure of gold. Two centuries elapsed between Mendaña's visit and the arrival of the British.[10] The British protectorate was established in 1893, primarily to keep the territory from falling into the hands of the French (Hookey 1973, 229). European planters had already begun to acquire land along the coastal plain of northern Guadalcanal for copra plantations. They wanted secure land tenure to protect their investments, as coconut palms take up to ten years to bear fruit and have productive lifespans of 50 to 80 years. Colonial regulations facilitated alienation of land declared vacant or undeveloped, known in legal parlance as "waste land," akin to terra nullius (Lasaqa 1972, 32). Once registered as Crown land, these plots could be leased to planters for periods of 99 to 999 years.

By 1905, 5 percent of the land in Guadalcanal had been alienated from its customary landowners, including much of the territory along the north coast suitable for plantation agriculture (Moore 2004, 74–75). Levers Pacific Plantation was the primary beneficiary of these policies, which allowed the company to acquire nearly three hundred thousand acres of land by 1914 (TRC 2012, 37).[11] This land, which previously belonged to the Ghaobata and their neighbors, became the basis of the company's copra plantation at Tenaru on the coast.

Solomon Islanders criticized these policies and practices from their inception. As Lasaqa (1972, 32) notes, "To the [Ghaobata], waste land as such did not exist. Any piece of unoccupied or uncultivated land always had claims of ownership attached to it, and custom provided for the transfer of ownership rights when the land-owning group died out." In response to local objections, the colonial administration ended land acquisitions by private parties in 1914. However, sales to the state continued, which then offered long-term leases to commercial developers (McDougall 2016, 165). From 1919 to 1923, the Phillips Commission addressed the complaints of customary landowners who stated that their land had been improperly expropriated (Ruthven 1979). The commission overturned fifty-five land transfers, proving that much of the land classified as vacant or "waste land" was actually customary land (Ruthven 1979). Almost a century later, however, colonial expropriation of land in the Solomons remained an incendiary issue for customary landowners, especially in northern Guadalcanal, where the extent of dispossession was greatest.[12]

Overseas recruitment of labor from Solomon Islands ended in Queensland in 1904 and in 1911 in Fiji, resulting in lower wages for plantation workers in Guadalcanal owing to the absence of competition (Lasaqa 1972, 1; see Akin 2013). British concerns about securing sufficient labor to work in the plantations during the 1920s led to the imposition of a head tax on men aged sixteen to sixty that had to be paid in cash (TRC 2012, 38; Akin 2013, 44). Given the high population density and the shortage of wage labor opportunities in the neighboring island of Malaita, many of the people living there were forced to seek paid employment elsewhere, with the result that as many as one in ten adult males from Malaita was involved in plantation labor at any given time (Bennett 1987, 165). By 1931, 68 percent of the protectorate's formal labor force was from Malaita (Bennett 1987, 165; see Akin 2013).

During World War II, there was intense fighting in Guadalcanal between Japanese forces and the U.S. military, which later made the plains their base of operations. Malaitans also fought in the defense forces and subsequently taunted people from Guadalcanal about their respective roles in the war, telling them: "We risked our lives to save your land!" (David Akin, pers. comm., 1999). As the fighting in Guadalcanal wound down, the Allies recruited a labor force of several thousand men, many of whom were from Malaita. People living in the grasslands still point to features in the landscape from the wartime period, including roads, wells, and even grass planted by the Allies. The capital of Solomon Islands was later moved to Honiara to take advantage of the infrastructure built by the Americans.

After the war, Malaitans continued to migrate to Guadalcanal to work in the plantation sector. They formed a large, landless population that worked initially on copra plantations and later on oil palm plantations. Although copra contributed one-quarter of the export earnings of the state at independence, the industry ceased being profitable by 1990 (Moore 2004, 72). In 1972, Solomon Islands Plantation established an oil palm plantation on an initial 1,478 hectares of land between the Ngalimbiu and Metepono Rivers (Moore 2004, 73). It subsequently expanded to 6,000 hectares and two hundred thousand oil palm trees. Landowners received an initial payment of five hundred Solomon Island dollars per hectare and one hundred Solomon Island dollars in annual rent (Kabutaulaka 2001).[13]

The division of labor in the plantation economy led to the emergence of class distinctions between the people of Malaita and Guadalcanal. For decades, Malaitans toiled at the bottom of the economy as a landless proletariat engaged in wage labor. Although they came to dominate the supply of garden produce to urban markets in Honiara by the late 1960s, their inability to secure local land tenure prevented them from investing in longer-term cash crops, including copra and cocoa (Lasaqa 1972, 162–63). In contrast, people from the grasslands planted coconuts and processed copra on their own land rather than accept wage labor in the plantations (Lasaqa 1972, 165–92). They also grew cocoa and raised cattle (Lasaqa 1972, 193–217). Some of the Ghaobata and their neighbors also received rent and royalties from the oil palm plantations on their land. According to my informants, however, Malaitans who had access to education moved into government posts more quickly than the people from Guadalcanal and eventually came to dominate the civil service, one of the largest sectors of the economy in Solomon Islands.

There are parallels between the plantation economy in Guadalcanal and the British colony of Fiji, where indentured laborers brought from India to work in the sugarcane fields subsequently came to play a prominent role in the retail sector and the economy more generally (Howard 1991; Lal 1992; Lasaqa 1984). In both cases, local populations came to resent labor migrants who were seen as "getting ahead" at the expense of the original inhabitants and landowners. Throughout much of contemporary Melanesia, the view that wealth is derived from place (Ballard 1997), in contrast to modern understandings of money and wealth as independent of place or tradition (Simmel 1978), has contributed to conflicts over resource extraction. The people from Guadalcanal were especially frustrated and angry that outsiders making use of their land and resources had become more successful than local landowners, reversing traditional expectations. Malaitans were the most frequent targets of resentment.

LANDOWNERS AND MIGRANTS

These relationships were especially prominent along the Guadalcanal plains, where the density of Malaitan settlers was the greatest. A remarkable study by the late Thomas Kama (1979), conducted while he was a law student from Guadalcanal at the University of Papua New Guinea, indicates that the number of migrants living on public and customary land in Guadalcanal rapidly increased during the 1970s.[14] Kama observed that many of these migrants had informal agreements with local landowners, usually with the head of the landholding group. Others gained access to land through intermarriage. The majority of the traditional landowners did not receive financial compensation from outsiders for using their land (Kama 1979, 150).

Migrant workers from Malaita were expected to find accommodation for their families, but the shortage of housing and the high rents forced working-class laborers to build houses in nearby squatter settlements (Kama 1979, 151). At the time of Kama's research, there were more Malaitans living in Guadalcanal than any other ethnic group, and Malaitans occupied most of the informal housing on the outskirts of Honiara. The living conditions and health standards in these areas were very low (Kama 1979, 151).

To escape these settlements, migrant workers often formed friendships with members of local landowning groups (Kama 1979, 152). These relationships developed further when migrants gave landowners gifts of money and store-bought foods. In return, landowners might offer the migrants access to land. In this way, migrants obtained permission from local landowners to build houses and make gardens on their land. After settling down, migrants would bring their immediate family members and sometimes invite other relatives to live with them (Kama 1979, 152). These arrangements followed established principles of extending use rights to guests in many parts of the Solomons (McDougall 2016), resulting in what the Ghaobata and others also call secondary land rights.[15]

Both parties viewed these arrangements as temporary and "did their best not to disrupt the agreements" (Kama 1979, 152). Although the settlers were permitted to make gardens for their own use, they needed to ask permission before planting cash crops or buying building materials to improve their houses. To maintain their relationships with the landowners, migrants contributed to customary feasts, marriage exchanges, and community work (Kama 1979, 152). By being cooperative neighbors, they hoped to be able to continue living on their hosts' land (Kama 1979, 152).[16]

In other cases, migrants paid cash for access to land from customary landowners, although the amount of money involved in these transactions was rather modest, well short of the market value of the land (Kama 1979, 155). These transactions were not treated as outright purchases or registered with the state (Kama 1979, 153). Instead they operated more like secondary land rights. Migrants did not have the right to sell the property. When they moved on, any improvements made to the property were assumed by the original owner (Kama 1979, 153). The legal status of these transactions was ambiguous, but they were treated as legitimate as long as the migrants continued to reside there.

Agreements between landowners and migrants were verbal (Kama 1979, 152). They were also "not always secure" (Kama 1979, 152). The head of the landholding group usually chose to settle disagreements among the parties rather than take the matter to court. When one of the parties to an agreement died, the other members of the landholding group might challenge its continuation, especially if there had been disputes between them (Kama 1979, 152). Commitments made by a landowner were not considered binding on his descendants after his death (Kama 1979, 152).

Some migrants planted cash crops, including cocoa and coconut trees (Kama 1979, 152). They could undertake these projects only after receiving permission from the landowner, who sometimes sought payments in return. However, members of the two groups rarely collaborated economically unless there was intermarriage, as both parties feared being exploited by the other (Kama 1979, 152, 153). In some cases, conflict was the result of ownership rights being "claimed over land where only usage rights previously existed" (Lasaqa 1972, 121). Other conflicts were caused by competing claims to the ownership of improvements (Lasaqa 1972, 112).

Such arrangements between landowners and migrants, although undertaken voluntarily and on an individual basis, nonetheless occurred at a significant scale, contributing to the friction between the two groups. Cultural differences between hosts and settlers were also a source of tension. The migrants had their own customs and practices, which sometimes conflicted with the values of their hosts. In some instances, this included misunderstandings about the status of their land transactions (TRC 2012). The hosts occasionally felt that the migrants failed to respect their customs (Kama 1979, 153).

Other conflicts occurred when the migrants invited guests from the outside who caused problems, including theft from the landowners. There were also concerns about the safety of local women and children, especially when they were working in their gardens (Kama 1979, 153). These sentiments intensified after a murder in 1975, leading people from Guadalcanal to feel "they [had] been deprived of their own rights in their own land" (Kama 1979, 153).[17] Anger about other murders allegedly committed by Malaitans in Honiara became a prominent rallying cry among the people from Guadalcanal in the period leading up to the ethnic tensions.

LEGAL SHORT-CIRCUIT

The lawsuit against the Gold Ridge mine was flawed from the outset. The original plaintiffs were Willie Roni, the paramount chief of the people from Gold Ridge who were relocated from the mine site, and David Thuguvoda from the Ghaobata, representing the downstream landowners. Both men had ties to an Australian journalist turned businessman named Denis Reinhardt.[18] Reinhardt represented a syndicate seeking a contract to build the Lungga hydropower project, which was intended to supply the capital city of Honiara with additional electrical capacity. The scheme included plans to lease two used high-capacity diesel generators to the Solomon Islands Electrical Authority until the hydropower plant was operational, but at a total cost later determined to be two or three times that of purchasing brand new equipment (SS, June 10, 1997). Reinhardt also informed the state electrical authority that the Lungga project would not be economically viable unless Ross Mining was a customer.

Ross Mining, however, insisted on controlling the eight- to ten-megawatt power supply needed to operate the Gold Ridge mine, although it also expressed its willingness to consider purchasing power from the Lungga hydropower plant once it became operational. When the power commissioner, Gordon Billy Gatu, refused to release Ross Mining from its legal obligation to purchase electricity from the state, the prime minister dismissed the entire commission, including Gatu. Reinhardt then turned to Slater and Gordon because of their previous interactions during the Ok Tedi case, when his position as a government adviser helped the firm gain access to politicians and confidential documents. The legal firm was keen to capitalize on the successful out-of-court settlement of the Ok Tedi case two years earlier and began to investigate the merits of legal proceedings against Ross Mining. Slater and Gordon also agreed to represent Gatu in a separate case against the state, claiming that his dismissal was a breach of procedure. They argued that Ross Mining put pressure on the government to take this action to ensure approval of its application to generate its own electric power.

In their review of the legal agreements between Ross Mining and the state, Slater and Gordon noted the absence of compensation for the people living downstream from the Gold Ridge mine and the limit on corporate liability for future environmental impacts. They filed suit on behalf of Roni and Thuguvoda in March 1997. Seven months later, the case was "fatally compromised" when the two plaintiffs accepted payments from Ross Mining, including shares in the mine, cash, a house, a car, and the promise of employment in return for withdrawing their claims (SS, October 1997).

Slater and Gordon promptly filed another pair of writs on behalf of the people affected by the mine. The first plaintiff was the Ghaobata paramount chief, Samuel Saki, who represented one thousand people living in the grasslands near the Metepono River. The other lead plaintiff was John Manigela, who represented the two hundred people relocated from the mine lease area, who sought to challenge the original compensation agreement. Justice Palmer of the High Court of Solomon Islands dismissed both of their claims on December 19, 1997, finding that the environmental claims were largely speculative in nature, and that Manigela's claim was illegitimate because the compensation agreement had been negotiated on their behalf by the state. He also ruled that the claims were frivolous, vexatious, and an abuse of process. However, the Saki writ was subsequently reinstated on appeal (*Justinian* 2002).

In the meantime, Thuguvoda and Roni switched sides again, claiming that Ross Mining pressured them into withdrawing their initial claims. Slater and Gordon felt compelled to refile claims on their behalf, which were subsequently dismissed in April 1998 by Justice Palmer, who awarded costs to Ross Mining (*Justinian* 2002).

In December 1998, Ross Mining went on the offensive against Slater and Gordon, as well as Reinhardt, claiming they used the landowners as a bargaining chip in negotiations with the power company. Lawyers representing the mining company also alleged that Slater and Gordon had committed the tort of champerty and maintenance, referring to their encouragement and support of the plaintiffs, in bringing vexatious litigation against a third party by paying for multiple flights from Solomon Islands to Australia and several weeks' worth of food and lodging for Roni and Thuguvoda. Ross Mining argued that Slater and Gordon sought to destroy its business by means of a media campaign, improper pressure to negotiate a settlement, and false and defamatory statements made to the Australian Stock Exchange about the legal proceedings.

The case against the Australian law firm was filed in late December, after the Christmas holiday, and Slater and Gordon failed to respond with their defense, asserting that the court lacked jurisdiction to hear the matter. The High Court of Solomon Islands disagreed and, on March 23, 1999, issued a default judgment against Slater and Gordon, finding that the firm had engaged in a civil conspiracy, abuse of process, and champerty, which resulted in a multimillion-dollar settlement of the claims by Ross Mining. The law firm memorably concluded the litigation by announcing that "Slater & Gordon regrets ever having become involved in the proceedings against Ross Mining in respect of its mining operations in the Solomon Islands and acknowledges that such proceedings harmed Ross Mining" (*Justinian* 2002).

Slater and Gordon's relationship to Reinhardt and his dubious business ventures; the general support for mining by the state and the business community; the differences between tactics that had previously been successful in Port Moresby, where aggressive rhetoric is often the only way to have one's voice heard, in contrast to the face-to-face relationships that characterize interaction in the much-smaller capital city of Honiara; and finally, the questionable behavior of the initial plaintiffs, which seemed to confirm public skepticism about the case, combined to doom the lawsuit to failure despite the legitimacy of the claims made by the people affected by the Gold Ridge mine.

During a discussion that took place in the initial phase of the conflict in Honiara in February 1999, one of my informants told me that he did not believe the acts of violence were the result of a unified opposition movement. Instead, he thought several different groups of people had taken the law into their own hands out of frustration with the state's failure to respond to their demands. He explained that they objected to agreements made by a previous generation of landowners that allowed migrants to settle among the people living in the grasslands.

There is widespread agreement among Solomon Islanders on what they refer to as the root causes of the conflict (Pania 2000). In 1988, Gordon Billy Gatu, who subsequently became a client of Slater and Gordon after being dismissed from his position as chairman of the Solomon Islands Electrical Authority, presented a petition from "the indigenous people of Guadalcanal" to Prime Minister Ezekiel Alebua (Fraenkel 2004, app. 2; see TRC 2012, 55–56). The petition decried the expropriation of land under colonial rule and the resulting long-term leases of their land to foreigners. It also complained about the problems caused by the large population of migrants living in Guadalcanal, including a number of unsolved murders attributed to outsiders. Among other demands, the petition called for relocating the national capital away from Guadalcanal, decentralized government, and most interestingly, increased investment in development projects in *other* provinces to reverse the flow of migrants to Guadalcanal. Many observers from the Solomons attribute the primary motivation for the conflict to "frustrations [over] the failure of successive governments to address" these demands (Pania 2000, 47).

During the conflict, militants from Guadalcanal harassed, assaulted, and sometimes killed migrants living in rural areas, especially people identified as Malaitan (TRC 2012). In some cases, the victims of these attacks were also tortured. Women were humiliated, sexually assaulted, and raped. Many of the victims from Malaita had been living in close proximity to the people from the grasslands area, sometimes for their whole lives. People from Guadalcanal who were married to Malaitans or were the descendants of mixed marriages were often accused of being a "spear," or spy, for the opposing side and, consequently, targeted for abuse. The perpetrators and supporters of these actions eventually became known as the Isatabu Freedom Movement, invoking the name for Guadalcanal associated with the Moro movement in the 1950s and 1960s (Nanau 2014, 79–80).

FIGURE 5. Members of the Isatabu Freedom Movement with homemade shotguns prepare to patrol on the outskirts of Honiara, Solomon Islands. 2000. Photo: Ben Bohane / wakaphotos.com

Driven from their homes in rural Guadalcanal by the violence, Malaitans subsequently formed their own paramilitary organization, the Malaita Eagle Force (Nanau 2014, 79–80). The conflict escalated, resulting in armed skirmishes between the two sides in and around Honiara. Several efforts to promote reconciliation and pay compensation to both sides failed to achieve a sustainable peace. The Townsville Peace Agreement of 2000 brought an end to overt combat, although conflicts between and within the various factions continued for several years. The militias ceased operations only after an intervention by the Pacific Islands Forum states and the arrival of peacekeeping forces led by the Australians, which began in July 2003 and lasted until 2014 (Nanau 2014, 79–80; McDougall 2016, 228–35).

MINING CONFLICT

Given that the lawsuit against the Gold Ridge mine and its subsequent dismissal overlapped with the beginning of violence in Guadalcanal, it is reasonable to ask whether either of these events was a significant catalyst in the ethnic tensions in Solomon Islands. Considering the prevalence of resource conflicts in Melanesia (Kirsch 2014) and elsewhere (Peluso and Watts 2001), there is also a related question about the role of mining projects in these events. Matthew G. Allen (2013, 114–15) notes the criticism of foreign mining interests in Guadalcanal since the Moro movement in the early 1960s (see Davenport and Çoker 1967, 144), which he attributes to widespread rejection by Solomon Islanders of the colonial and postcolonial states' claim to own subsurface minerals.[19] Allen (2013, 116) also points to the displacement of artisanal miners from the Gold Ridge mine site, depriving them of access to an important source of revenue. He concludes, "The Gold Ridge mine site was a recurring flash point[,] . . . and ideology was an important motive in targeting the mine" (Allen 2013, 115).[20] Similarly, McDougall (2016, 224) argues that the mine was a powerful symbol of both the "hidden wealth of the island" and its exploitation by foreigners.[21]

Two months before filing the original lawsuit against Ross Mining in 1997, David Thuguvoda issued a statement criticizing the project, noting, "The [rights of the] people of Guadalcanal have been given away so many times in the name of national development without getting anything in return," suggesting that the Gold Ridge mine was only the most recent example of how resources from Guadalcanal have been used to benefit the state at the expense of local landowners (SS, Jan. 31, 1997). He also objected to the environmental impact of the project: "We are not against development as long as it benefits everyone, but [what] we are concerned about is the damage the mining will cause to our rivers" (SS, Jan. 31, 1997). The majority of land in the grasslands suitable for plantation agriculture has long since been alienated from its original owners. The people living in the grasslands were already forced to compete with migrant laborers for access to the remaining land for cash crops and subsistence production, and were concerned that the mine would further deplete their limited resources.

Similarly, Allen (2013, 116) quotes an ex-combatant who referred to the mining project as an example of the "sort of development" the militants sought to "stop." Two of the witnesses testifying at the public hearings of the Truth and Reconciliation Commission hearings held in Honiara after the civil war made comparable observations. The first testified, "We have never benefited from CDC Oil Palm plantation and the Australian Ross mining company at Gold Ridge. We [stood by and] watched as millions of dollars were extracted from our lands into the hands of the very rich foreigners; and the ashes were thrown to us as if we have never owned these resources" (TRC 2012, 1120).

A second witness testified: "Now I would like [to] openly tell everyone and the Commissioners why I was involved in the area. Since the national Government failed to recognize us [as] the indigenous people of this island. Most of the major companies were operating on north Guadalcanal, for instance, SIPL [Solomon Islands Plantations, Ltd.,] and the likes of Gold Ridge Mining. . . . Unfortunately, when we submitted our demands, concerns and wishes to the Government they failed to listen to us" (TRC 2012, 1101).

However, another witness from the Gold Ridge area testified that his community remained neutral at the start of the conflict (TRC 2012, 1087). Reporting by the *Solomon Star* suggests that the mining project was gradually caught up in the larger conflict rather than singled out as an ideological target from the outset:

- In May 1999, armed men wearing traditional dress intruded into the compound at the Gold Ridge mine while firing gunshots, although they were there to obtain supplies rather than attack the mine (SS, May 28, 1999).
- In June 1999, a mining company spokesman denied a rumor circulating in Honiara that the rebels had stolen containers of sodium cyanide in order to poison the town water supply (SS, June 14, 1999).
- In July 1999, the police recovered a company vehicle that had been stolen by the militants (SS, July 1, 1999).
- Later in July 1999, the management of the mine commented on the situation: "We are determined to weather the storm but are concerned at all times not to place any employees at risk" (SS, July 22, 1999).
- In August 1999, a roadblock affected operations at the mine, and concerns were raised about another shooting in the area (SS, Aug. 12, 1999 and Aug. 16, 1999).
- In September 1999, another vehicle was reported stolen (SS, Sept. 1, 1999).
- In October 1999, the company acknowledged that the growing civil unrest had become a major concern (SS, Oct. 12, 1999).

The Gold Ridge mine continued to operate for another eight months, until the Malaita Eagle Force attempted to overthrow the elected government of Prime Minister Bartholomew Ulufa'alu on June 5, 2000. The Isatabu Freedom Movement raided the Gold Ridge mine on the same day, stealing weapons and vehicles, which led to the closure of the mine. The mining facility subsequently became a base of operations for supporters of the Isatabu Freedom Movement in northern Guadalcanal.

In contrast to the situation in Bougainville, in which the civil war was triggered by opposition to the Panguna mine (Connell 1991; Filer 1990) and began with the shooting of an Australian mine worker, the dispute over the Gold Ridge mine was but one of many grievances harbored by the people of Guadalcanal against the state. The lawsuit and its failure do not seem to have played a significant role in the conflict, although it is possible that a more favorable outcome in the case, acknowledging the rights and interests of local landowners, might have relieved some of the underlying tensions.

SECONDARY LAND RIGHTS AND CONFLICT

Scholarly accounts of the conflict in Solomon Islands reject a primordialist understanding of ethnicity in the sense of perduring differences and historical enmity between groups (Kabutaulaka 2001). McDougall (2016, 23, 222) points to the relatively low number of casualties and subsequent reconciliation between the protagonists as evidence of this. As I suggested above, the general consensus in both scholarly and public accounts is that colonial dispossession and subsequent frustration with the postcolonial state's failure to address landowner concerns were the root causes of the conflict.[22] But explaining why the conflict took the form of violence between landowners from Guadalcanal and Malaitan migrants requires us to return to questions about secondary land rights, including structural contradictions between ideology and practice.[23]

Relationships between landowners and migrants were mediated in part through practices associated with customary land tenure. Many of the migrants gained access to land through the extension of secondary land rights. This practice exhibits the traditional flexibility of Ghaobata land rights to which Lasaqa (1972) attributed their economic success during the late colonial period. However, transactions between landowners and migrants were also beset by contradictions, much like the proliferation of secondary rights to address new forms of immoveable property and other transactions that promote exclusive forms of ownership. As I have noted, these practices contravene ideological commitment to the protection of customary land tenure and widespread opposition to the commodification of land, positions that have been valorized since the anticolonial movements of the postwar period.

The extension of secondary land rights to Malaitan migrants resulted in comparable structural contradictions. Although these practices brought migrants into close relations with landowners, the resulting relationships were fundamentally insecure (Kama 1974). In particular, the unsettled status of secondary land rights contributed to misunderstandings between landowners and migrants in northern Guadalcanal. The temporary and informal nature of these arrangements promoted short-term responses to the needs of individual migrants at the expense of long-term solutions to the problems associated with labor migration to Guadalcanal. The resulting interactions also provided everyday and intimate reminders of the contradiction between the consensual nature of these transactions and ideological opposition to the presence of the migrant population in Guadalcanal. The failure to resolve the resulting double bind seems to have driven the violent response of people from Guadalcanal against the Malaitan migrants.

Despite the violence, broadly shared understandings of the situation—that they were on opposite sides of a problem to which everyone objected—made it possible for both sides to "empathize with their enemies" (McDougal 2016, 228).[24] The Truth and Reconciliation Commission report noted the frequency of statements that "indicate a good *personal* relationship between Guadalcanal people and Malaitan settlers on the village level" (2012, 62, emphasis in the original). The report also indicated: "The problem of coming to terms with the contradiction between the Malaitan as the down-to-earth individual who lived next door, and the Malaitan as an aggressive and land-grabbing *stereotype* was perceivable in quite a number of testimonies given by Guadalcanal witnesses" (TRC 2012, 62–63, emphasis in the original). In many instances, migrants were "warned by friends from Guadalcanal or even the landowners they had bought land from; they informed them about the imminent uprising and advised them to leave" (TRC 2012, 62). Some Malaitans who were married to partners from Guadalcanal were given the opportunity to buy their way out of the conflict as well (TRC 2012, 63). Such crosscutting allegiances have been noted in the literature on Melanesia as having the potential to mitigate violence (Schieffelin 1976, 80–87).

However, the prevalence of interethnic ties also led to the intensification of other forms of violence. A significant proportion of the aggression was directed against people from Guadalcanal by members of their own militias, especially against persons accused of spying on behalf of the Malaitans. Suspicion of divided loyalties turned ethnic violence inward against the members of their own group. The frequency and intensity of intra-ethnic violence may help explain why the people from Guadalcanal and Malaita have been able to coexist relatively peacefully since the resolution of the tensions. It also helps account for their confidence in dismissing the threat of reemergent hostilities between the two groups.

Relationships between landowners and migrants had a significant impact on the civil conflict in Solomon Islands. In particular, the extension of secondary land rights to migrants contributed to structural problems that could not easily be resolved.[25] Petitions that called on the state to address their concerns also failed to bring about the desired changes. These interactions bear resemblance to the events described by Mike McGovern (2011) in his analysis of conflict in Côte d'Ivoire, where the recurring need for agricultural labor also resulted in tensions between landowners and migrants. In addition, politicians in both countries exploited what McGovern (2011, 85–99) calls the "politics of resentment" for their own purposes (see Fraenkel 2004). The underlying structural similarities between the two cases suggests the need to pay closer attention to the role played by customary land tenure, including secondary rights, in conflict and civil war.

CONCLUSION

After spending a week reading through the newspaper archives in January 2014, I understood enough about the events that occurred during the intervening years to venture out of Honiara into the surrounding area. I arranged for a taxi driver to take me into the grasslands on my final day in the Solomons. We stopped briefly at a village beside the Metepono River and I spoke with someone there. He told me that the river alternates between clear days and muddy days depending on the rainfall in the mountains; the children from the village continue to swim in the river even though it irritates their skin. People from the village wash their clothes in the river when it runs clear, but are reluctant to use the water for any other purpose. His comments reminded me of the letter to the editor published after the controversial fish kill in the Tinahula River in 1998, which warned "the users of the 'once-upon-a-time clean Tinahula River' that the usefulness of the river is over."

I had hoped to find my friend Chief John Salea, with whom I had worked closely during the lawsuit, but was saddened to learn that he had died a few years earlier. I thought briefly about visiting Samuel Saki's family compound, where I had attended a number of meetings with the plaintiffs. However, when reading through the newspaper archives, I learned about the fate of his son Selwyn, who became a leader of one of the political factions during the civil war. After the Townsville Peace Agreement was signed in August 2000, the violence continued in other forms, including internal conflict within the factions (TRC 2012, 93, 239). On September 22, 2001, Selwyn Saki was kidnapped from his village in the grasslands. In early October, Samuel Saki told the *Solomon Star* that hired assassins had killed his son (SS October 8, 2001, 1). Samuel Saki died of a heart attack shortly after the body of his murdered son was recovered. Under the circumstances, I was unable to imagine a rationale for visiting the family that outweighed my intrusion. Given the failure of the lawsuit and the losses suffered by the Saki family during the conflict, I concluded that my arrival would inevitably stir up unwelcome memories.

I also learned what happened to the Gold Ridge mine since the project was closed in June 2002. That December, political risk insurance paid off Ross Mining's policy and the insurer took possession of the mine (Nanau 2014, 82). An international tender was held in September 2003, and Australian Solomons Gold acquired the Gold Ridge mine in 2004 (Nanau 2014, 82). The mine remained closed until Allied Gold acquired the project in 2009 and restarted production later the same year (Nanau 2014, 84). The Australian company St. Barbara, which operates several small mines in Papua New Guinea and Australia, acquired Allied Gold in 2012 and continued production at the Gold Ridge mine.

In April 2014, three months after my return visit to the Solomons, a devastating tropical cyclone struck the coast near Honiara, killing more than twenty people and leaving thousands homeless. The storm also destroyed the bridge leading to the mine. Thought by some observers to be grateful for an opportunity to escape from an unprofitable investment, St. Barbara evacuated most of its expatriate employees. Heavy rainfall during the cyclone filled the tailings dam to capacity, raising concerns about its structural integrity. Even though the collapse of the dam would result in catastrophic flooding, the state refused to allow St. Barbara's employees to return to the country and discharge untreated water from the tailings dam.[26] These events reminded me of the original goal of the lawsuit against Ross Mining and the Gold Ridge mine, which was to address the effects of pollution on the communities downstream, including the risk posed to the tailings dam by cyclones. Even though the lawsuit against the mining company was unsuccessful, the concerns raised by the case about the environmental impact of the mine have proven to be valid.[27]

What began as a short consulting project on property and pollution for a court case has become a much more complicated account about secondary land rights and civil conflict. In the course of writing about these issues, I turned to other ethnographic accounts and historical sources to supplement my original field notes.[28] This is not to say that my earlier ethnographic research—despite being overtaken by events—was without value. The analysis of secondary land rights among the Ghaobata—and of comparable rights that were extended to migrants from Malaita, which resulted in double binds that shaped the violence between the two groups—complements the existing literature on the ethnic tensions in the Solomons, including works by Allen (2013), Fraenkel (2004), Kabutaulaka (2001), McDougal (2016), Moore (2004), and others cited here. It may also provide a useful starting point for scholars studying violence and civil war in other contexts.

This suggests that the value of engaged anthropology may extend beyond the immediate goals of a project, making it possible to contribute to larger debates. It also demonstrates that ethnographic data produced in the context of engaged research projects may find new relevance in changed circumstances.

FIVE

How Analysis of Local Contexts Can Have Global Significance

DOUBLE EXPOSURE IN THE MARSHALL ISLANDS

IN 1954, THE UNITED STATES MILITARY detonated a hydrogen bomb at Bikini atoll in the Marshall Islands. The weapon was designed to maximize radioactive fallout, and the people living downwind of ground zero on Rongelap atoll were "intentionally left on their islands to provide scientists with more data about the effects of radiation exposure" (Kahn 2009, 204). The people from Rongelap were subsequently relocated, and they and their descendants continue to live in exile because it remains unsafe for them to return home. In 1999, I joined two other anthropologists in the Marshall Islands for preliminary research in support of a case representing the people of Rongelap Atoll before the Nuclear Claims Tribunal (Kirsch 2001; Johnston and Barker 2008). The tribunal was established to adjudicate compensation for loss and damage to persons and property resulting from exposure to radiation and other negative consequences of nuclear weapons testing by the United States during the 1940s and 1950s (Smith-Norris 2016). The rationale for the consultation was presented as follows:

> In this unique and unusual quest for assessing the value of land in a nonmarket environment, for the purposes of awarding just compensation, claimants are not suggesting that the Tribunal ignore the transactional indicators that do exist. They are suggesting, however, that other factors such as tradition and custom must also be given due consideration to ensure that justice is done. It is therefore the intent of the claimants to involve knowledgeable anthropologists, sociologists, and others understanding of the importance of land in the Marshalls throughout the appraisal process to ensure that the valuations ultimately reached are truly relevant. (Graham and Lowe 1998, 1)

During an advisory committee meeting with representatives from Rongelap, we were told, "Land gives you the meaning of life and the role of each individual in society" (Mike Kabua, cited in Johnston and Barker 2008, 63). Another participant at the meeting told us: "You cannot put enough value on land. . . . How do you put a value on something that people consider as a living thing that is part of your soul?" (Wilfred Kendall, cited in Johnston and Barker 2008, 63). Several committee members framed their concerns with reference to loss, especially the loss of culture, including the observation "When the bomb exploded, the culture was gone, too. It is impossible for people to act in their proper roles" (Mike Kabua, cited in Johnston and Barker 2008, 186). Another person we interviewed explained, "We have lost our knowledge, our ability, our moral standing and self-esteem in the community. What we were taught is no longer practical. . . . A lot has been lost, not just our land" (Ken Kedi, cited in Johnston and Barker 2008, 189).

Previous awards for compensation by the tribunal were based on land values derived from a record of lease payments in the Marshall Islands. In contrast, we argued that commercial transactions do not necessarily take the social and cultural value of land into account. Conventional land values may also exclude the marine resources that sustain the Marshallese way of life. My colleagues went on to document these claims in greater detail in their submission to the Nuclear Claims Tribunal (Johnston and Barker 2008). Their emphasis on "the loss of access . . . to a healthy ecosystem . . . [and the resulting] inability to interact in a healthy land and seascape in ways that allow the transmission of knowledge and the ability to sustain a healthy way of life" offered a more holistic way to assess the consequences of nuclear weapons testing for the people of Rongelap (Johnston and Barker 2008, 88).

In my contribution to the Rongelap case, I focused on the question of loss, especially the concept of culture loss. This included comparative research on claims about loss by other indigenous peoples, as well as analysis of differing perspectives on these issues by the anthropologists who testified at previous hearings of the Nuclear Claims Tribunal.[1] I argued that contemporary discussion about cultural property rights offers a constructive way to help conceptualize these losses. My goal was to assist the people from Rongelap in making their claims legible to the tribunal. I subsequently published this work in an article that examines how indigenous claims about culture and loss have been shaped by legal proceedings from Alaska to Australia (Kirsch 2001).

In the intervening years, questions about culture loss have acquired new salience in the context of global climate change. This is especially true for the Marshall Islands. As a nation of low-lying coral atolls, the Marshalls are ground zero for another environmental catastrophe: the threat of rising sea levels, as the average elevation in the Marshalls is only one meter above sea level, and the highest point in the island chain is only ten meters above sea level (Rudiak-Gould 2013, 2). Like the claims about loss and damage from nuclear weapons testing adjudicated by the Nuclear Claims Tribunal, the risk of inundation raises questions about the assessment of values that are not adequately measured by the market. Climate change is already affecting peoples and populations vulnerable to melting ice caps and glaciers, rising sea levels, and altered weather patterns. Concerns about accounting for the "noneconomic loss and damage" associated with global climate change are consequently being addressed by the United Nations and international NGOs (Warner and van der Geest 2013; Serdeczny et al. 2016). These debates overlap with and explicitly draw on earlier discussions of cultural property and culture loss (Morrissey and Oliver-Smith 2013; Barnett et al. 2016). The novel application of previous work on the consequences of nuclear weapons testing to the potential impacts of climate change shows how the analysis of local contexts can have global significance.

INDIGENOUS PEOPLES AND THE DISCOURSE OF CULTURE LOSS

A significant counterpoint to claims made about the benefits of globalization are indigenous peoples' expressions of loss associated with the transformation of their societies, including relocation from traditional lands, threats to the continuity of their languages, and the erosion of their political autonomy. Their sense of loss is especially pronounced in the wake of environmental disasters that damage land and resources, including oil spills, exposure to nuclear radiation, deforestation, and the toxic impacts of mining.[2] But similar reactions are also found where indigenous peoples have been displaced from their land for other reasons. For example, Deborah Rose (1996, 20–21) describes the Aboriginal characterization of land that is no longer being managed by its caretakers as "a loss of life, a loss of life support systems, and a loss of relationships among living things and their country. For many Aboriginal people, this 'wild' [i.e., land that is no longer maintained through fire] has a quality of deep loneliness." Richard Baker (1999, 179), also writing about Aboriginal Australia, quotes an informant as saying, "We have lost all our everything." Looking out across a changing landscape, the Fuyuge of Papua New Guinea anticipate the growing impacts of mining, including new social boundaries and the potential "loss of culture" (Hirsch 2001, 308). Verena Keck (1998) considers the various threats posed to traditional knowledge in the Pacific, especially the loss of information about the natural world.

A distinctive feature of indigenous responses to dispossession and environmental degradation is the claim of culture loss. The notion of culture loss poses a problem of analysis for anthropologists, given contemporary definitions of culture as a process that continually undergoes change, rather than as something that can be damaged or lost. Marshall Sahlins (1993, 4) points out that defining culture in this way "has the effect of erasing the logical and ontological continuities involved in the different ways that societies interpret and respond to the imperialist conjuncture. If culture must be conceived as always and only changing, lest one commit the mortal sin of essentialism, there can be no such thing as identity . . . let alone continuity." To completely naturalize change also obscures what is lost or forgotten. In contrast, I argue that the notion of cultural property rights can be used to address this critical blind spot of the culture concept, in which loss is unseen or undervalued.

In particular, recognition of cultural property rights can help identify the referents of discourse about culture loss. Cultural property rights, as Marilyn Strathern (1999, 177) observes, imply new forms of integration and new ways of organizing persons and collectivities. These rights are intended to prevent the loss of property, knowledge, bodily integrity, and creativity itself, as well as the value of the things they may beget. Cultural property rights offer potential resources as ideas and things move into new contexts, orders of signification, and economic regimes of commodification. They can also make visible the losses experienced by indigenous communities.

Simon Harrison (1999, 11) argues that concerns about cultural appropriation—the desire to protect "cultural practices and symbols against unauthorised use or reproduction by outsiders"—are a form of boundary maintenance parallel to defensive efforts that seek to minimize the intrusion of foreign ideas or practices. Michael Brown (1998, 2003) raises concerns about the use of legal regimes to limit acts of cultural appropriation, most notably the implications of these restrictions for the unrestricted flow of information central to liberal democratic societies. Brown also wonders whether the extension of legal restrictions to cultural property might facilitate its commodification and thereby limit innovation and creation. Balanced against Brown's objections to recognizing cultural property rights, however, are the political resources they might provide indigenous communities, including enhanced control over what circulates, for property rights can restrict as well as facilitate distribution.

The examples of indigenous discourse considered here suggest that loss has recently become a critical site for the objectification of culture, raising questions that are distinct from the dilemmas of cultural appropriation. While there is a long history of discussion about culture loss within anthropology, including the allegory of Ishi, the last of the Yahi Indians (Kroeber 1976), and Ruth Benedict's (1960, 34) metaphor of a broken cup signifying "the loss of something that had value equal to that of life itself, the whole fabric of . . . [a] people's standards and beliefs," my argument addresses the disappearance not of entire societies or ways of life but of particular things—knowledge, ideas, and practices of value. Local vocabularies are often inadequate to account for these experiences, which have therefore found expression in terms of culture. This suggests that the concept of cultural property rights can provide a means to identify these losses, which might otherwise be obscured or ignored. While the problems associated with culture loss are especially salient with respect to indigenous communities because of their experience of colonial dispossession, they are by no means limited to them.

THE NATURE OF LOSS

If property is a manifestation of social relations (Hann 1998; Hohfeld 1913; C. Rose 1994, 227), then so is loss. What are the kinds of things or relations that can be lost, and what are the contexts in which loss is implicated? The notion of loss appears to have two primary registers. It may refer to possession, to the objects or other forms of property that one might claim rights to or ownership of. Loss in this guise implies value and property relations; it may therefore be possible to gain new understandings of property by examining responses to loss. In other contexts, however, such as the intimate losses associated with grief, loss may be improperly associated with property, as the rights to persons are not necessarily comparable to the rights to things. Here it is possible to speak of loss in relation to kinship and identity rather than ownership. This suggests that the relationship invoked by cultural property rights may be a form of belonging. The case before us requires that we take as an empirical question the relationships the Marshallese have with their land: Are they understood in terms of kinship and identity, property, or both?

Any discussion of loss must also acknowledge its productive possibilities. In order to form relationships, people must separate themselves from one another (see Strathern 1988), although differentiation in the social realm is not ordinarily conceptualized in terms of loss. In marriage, for example, people move into other categories of kin, other lineages. This is simultaneously a loss to their natal clan and the precondition for new kinds of social relations, for productive as well as reproductive relations of exchange. Consequently, marriage exchange may be understood as compensation for the loss of labor and claims to future offspring as members of one's kin group. Similarly, the dynamics of memory and forgetting, the entropic tendencies of ritual knowledge, and the incompleteness of the intergenerational transmission of knowledge all pose questions about the possibility of loss. Yet loss may be integral to these systems in that it permits innovation and improvisation.

In the case before us, however, it is difficult to conceptualize the losses experienced by the people affected by nuclear testing as productive. Their land was not transformed into something of value; rather, it was destroyed because it was of value to the U.S. government only in its potential loss.[3] This is negative reciprocity writ large across the landscape: the wholesale destruction of things (property, land, memory) and social relations organized through land, including the capacity for reproducing these relationships in place.

It might be argued that through compensation claims, people seek to establish relationships with the parties responsible for loss or damage and acquire a replacement for what has been lost. Yet in the Marshall Islands there is a fundamental incommensurability between what was taken and what might be given back in the form of compensation. When an exact equivalent is unavailable, the substitute is always inferior to the original, perpetuating the original sense of loss (see Schieffelin 1976, 109–12). The issue arises in both the payment of monetary compensation and attempts to imagine the possibilities of compensation in kind.

It is also important to consider the response that narratives of loss can evoke in an audience, given the proliferation of environmental and other disasters in the past century and our increased exposure to these events through the media. The phenomenon of compassion fatigue is one potential consequence; the politics of resignation (Benson and Kirsch 2010), the prevailing assumption that one is unable to do anything productive about one's concerns, is another. But by focusing on the problem of loss and re-embedding these events in social contexts and relations, it may be possible to carry out the analysis needed to understand these events.

NUCLEAR WASTELAND

Between 1946 and 1958, the United States tested sixty-seven nuclear weapons in the Marshall Islands. The most powerful of these tests was Bravo, a fifteen-megaton device—a thousand times more powerful than the bomb exploded over Hiroshima—detonated on March 1, 1954, at Bikini Atoll.[4] A second sun rose in the western sky that morning, followed by the roar of thunder, winds at tornado strength, and powerful earthquakes (Toyosaki 1986, 49). Radioactive fallout from the blast was carried by the wind to the east, where it reached the inhabited atoll of Rongelap several hours later (Alcalay 1992, 48).[5] People brushed the powder from their food and ate; they cleared it from their water cisterns and drank; children swimming in the lagoon put it in their hair and pretended it was soap. Shortly thereafter, the sixty-four people on Rongelap that day began to suffer the ill effects of acute radiation exposure: their hair fell out, their skin was burned, they began to vomit, and they suffered from a thirst water could not quench (Lijon Eknilang, interview by Holly Barker, Barbara Rose Johnston, and Stuart Kirsch, 1999).

Two days later, the U.S. Navy evacuated the people of Rongelap; they were subsequently resettled on Ejit Island in Majuro Atoll, at the center of the Marshall Islands (Weisgall 1994, 303).[6] In 1957, three years after Bravo, the people of Rongelap returned home (Kiste 1974, 194). They were assured that the background levels of radiation were within the parameters of safety. A medical team from the Brookhaven National Laboratory in Upton, New York, visited the island annually to monitor the long-term consequences of their exposure to radiation. Yet the people of Rongelap were not informed about their increased risk from the contaminated food and water they consumed for many years (Johnston and Barker 2008, 121), which resulted in their elevated rates of certain types of cancer (Johnston and Barker 2008, 22) and unusual numbers of miscarriages and birth defects (Pollock 2016). These health problems, combined with the release of additional information about their exposure to radiation, prompted the community to leave its atoll again in 1985, thirty-one years after the original event (Johnston and Barker 2008, 20). Most of the people from Rongelap currently reside in Ebeye, adjacent to the proving grounds for the U.S. missile defense system in Kwajalein Lagoon;

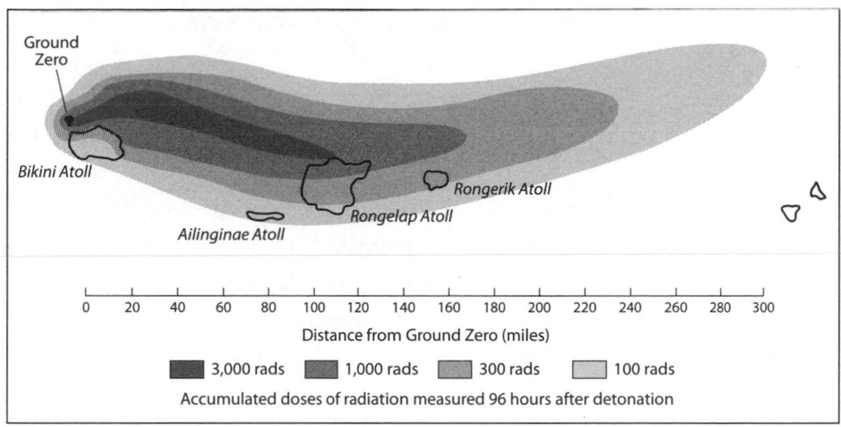

MAP 6. Nuclear fallout on Rongelap Atoll after the 1954 Bravo test, Marshall Islands.

in Mejatto; and in the capital city, Majuro. Funds have been set aside by the United States government to rehabilitate their home atoll, although there is disagreement over the appropriate level of risk: the more relaxed standard employed by the U.S. Department of Energy and the Nuclear Regulatory Commission or the more cautious standard of the Environmental Protection Agency, which might delay resettlement for many years.

Legal action taken by the Marshall Islands against the U.S. government was settled in 1983, with the United States formally accepting responsibility for loss and damage to persons and property resulting from its nuclear testing program. As part of a negotiated compact between the United States and the Republic of the Marshall Islands, a tribunal with the jurisdiction to "render determination upon all claims, past and future," was established in 1987 (Smith-Norris 2016, 144). The tribunal pays compensation for the health effects of radiation in addition to adjudicating class action cases for property damage, loss, and suffering brought on behalf of the people from Enewetak and Bikini, the two sites for weapons testing, as well as on behalf of the people from Utrik and Rongelap who were exposed to radiation.

In the following discussion, I draw on research for the Rongelap case and an earlier claim presented to the tribunal by the people of Enewetak, who lived in exile for thirty-three years as a result of nuclear testing. Central to the hearings on Enewetak were written reports and oral testimony provided by the anthropologists Laurence Carucci and Nancy Pollock, acting on behalf of the Office of the Public Advocate, and the Defender of the Fund for the Nuclear Claims Tribunal, respectively.[7]

THE CONTEXT OF CLAIMS FOR LOSS

Indigenous claims about culture loss are often influenced by the political and legal contexts in which communities seek reparations for past injustices. The sociologist John Torpey (2001) describes the recent efflorescence of forums that address different kinds of claims, including acts of violence and injustice committed during World War II, the transition to democracy in countries that have suffered from state terrorism and other authoritarian practices, and claims made by indigenous communities against states dominated by the descendants of European settlers. Restitution is sought in the form of monetary compensation and the return of property, policies of rehabilitation, and/or the negotiation of novel accommodations between local sovereignty and the state. Both the institutionalization of these forums and the legal statutes through which they are organized—including tribunals, truth commissions, land rights hearings, and heritage legislation—influence the form and content of the claims that are advanced.

James Weiner (1999) addresses this issue in his analysis of the Hindmarsh Island controversy in southern Australia. He describes the legislative processes governing Aboriginal heritage claims as a form of elicitation that shapes the representation of the practices they seek to protect. The dispute in question concerned a claim regarding Aboriginal women's rituals (or "business") associated with a proposed site for commercial development. The courts did not recognize culture as a contemporary process of valuation, relying instead on the more restricted criteria of historical significance and continuity. When the Aboriginal women elected to protect their claims to secret ritual knowledge by refusing to testify in court, the developers were granted permission to construct a bridge on the disputed site.[8] The participants in the debate failed to recognize how heritage legislation evoked a response that focused on secret ritual knowledge rather than contemporary political rights. Whereas Australian heritage protection requires Aboriginal communities to demonstrate the continuity of local traditions, the process is reversed in the Marshall Islands: the Nuclear Claims Tribunal, which provides compensation for damage and loss, obligates communities to demonstrate a break from the past. Much as Aboriginal culture is elicited in part through the Australian courts, Marshallese claims about culture loss are influenced by the legal processes through which they are adjudicated. As Laurence Carucci (2004, 448–49) argues, an important "message of cultural vitality is obscured in the story of destruction and abuse that must be told in front of the Nuclear Claims Tribunal."

The issue of culture loss also figured significantly in courtroom debates about the impact of the 1989 *Exxon Valdez* oil spill in Alaska, which released over 11 million gallons of crude oil into Prince William Sound. According to an analysis of that case by the anthropologist Joseph Jorgensen (1995), social scientists testifying on behalf of the indigenous plaintiffs used a definition of culture that was later challenged by both the opposing anthropologist and the court. They argued, "Damage to any core element [of a society] (e.g., natural resource base or kinship system) damages the culture and the people.... Because subsistence is the basis of modern Alutiiq culture, the oil spill ... damaged that culture in a multitude of ways.... [And] to the extent that Alutiiq people's subsistence, the most fundamental basis of their culture and life, remains disrupted, they and their culture have been damaged" (cited in Jorgensen 1995, 2).

Judge Holland rejected the reification of culture implied by this argument, determining instead that "villagers cannot collect damages for harm that was alleged to have been suffered by native culture" (Jorgensen 1995, 2). He based his opinion on the view that culture is "deeply embedded in the mind and heart" and is therefore undiminished by external events such as environmental disaster (cited in Jorgensen 1995, 5). While acknowledging "the *Exxon Valdez* was a disaster of major proportions," the judge concluded that "it did not deprive Alaska natives of their culture" (cited in Jorgensen 1995, 5). According to Jorgensen, his position was influenced by the testimony of the distinguished American cultural anthropologist Paul Bohannan, who had been engaged by Exxon. In his deposition to the court, Bohannan defined culture as a strategy for adaptation, "[a] basic device for surviving and prospering—a set of ideas and artifacts by means of which human beings adapt to the environment, including the social environment" (cited in Jorgensen 1995, 9). He argued that Alutiiq culture and its core meanings were not substantially affected by the oil spill. Finally, Bohannon concluded that the impact of the natural disaster was equivalent for all of those persons affected, regardless of ethnic or cultural identity, declaring, "I believe the Alaska natives are no different from anybody else in the matter" (cited in Jorgensen 1995, 11).[9] Judge Holland similarly concluded that there was no basis for distinguishing between the claims for loss by native and nonnative fishermen with respect to the impact of the oil spill: "All Alaskans have the right to lead subsistence lifestyles, not just Alaska natives," Holland (1996, 167) later explained.[10] The court ruled that the Alutiiq people had been deprived of access to resources, like all other people who depended on those waters for their livelihood, prompting a negotiated settlement with Exxon for U.S.$20 million.

LEGAL DETERMINATION OF LOSS

The analytic challenge in the cases before the Nuclear Claims Tribunal was how to make visible the referents of claims about culture loss, while the political challenge was how to do so with reference to existing legal categories. On one side was the view expressed by Philip Okney (1999, 17), the Defender of the Fund, who argued against the Enewetak claim for consequential damages resulting from their relocation, including hunger, deprivation, isolation, and physical distress. He was equally dismissive of claims for what he described as the "rather attenuated and ethereal injuries of 'mental suffering,' 'loss of cultural heritage and a customary and traditional way of life' and the 'loss of homeland.'" Okney asserted that such claims are "uncertain, speculative and disallowed" by the tribunal because they are not sufficiently associated with property. Instead, the claims "affix to the individual who makes up part of the whole which is claimed to have suffered the injury." He concluded: "The human being is not property such as one makes claim for in eminent domain or in the case of inverse condemnation."[11]

Okney's position on appropriate recompense for the people of Enewetak was governed by the application of the strictest possible test for determining the market value of property: "Only that which is capable of sale to a willing buyer can be properly considered for an award of damage." He presented the following fictional model of the "willing seller" and the "willing buyer":

> The willing seller is found, as held in J. O. Powel et al. v. Shelby County, 130 So 2d 170 (1961) to be a seller not forced to sell (to disallow reduced values) and the willing buyer is a buyer not required to buy (to disallow inflated values). Under the reasoning in Powel the willing seller is conceived to be a seller who would not be influenced by sentimental attachments to property and the willing buyer is also considered to be immune to the sentimental attributes of property. It is the fiction of the prudent buyer and the prudent seller that the courts employ and not the sentimental seller and the sentimental buyer. This rationale, as applied in Powel, dictate[s] that the sentimental value of the homestead [is] not allowed as an element of damage. (Okney 1999, 21)

Okney (1999, 2) acknowledged "that ethics demand that within the confines of negotiations for leaseholds that the government recognize the unique place of land rights in the life and law of the Marshall Islands. . . . The attendant changes in the lives of the lessors are obviously considered and taken into consideration when fixing the amount of compensation to be received by the lessors."

As Defender of the Fund, Okney has the responsibility to set appropriate limits on the compensation paid by the Nuclear Claims Tribunal. Yet it is not clear that the market provides an adequate measure of the value of land in the Marshall Islands. An alternative perspective on the potential scope of property claims was articulated in the case of *Eisenring v. Kansas Turnpike Authority,* cited in a property assessment for Bikini Atoll:

> The absence of market value, in the sense that there is a lack of evidence of comparable sales, does not prevent recovery by the owner in the event of condemnation. It occasionally happens that a parcel of real estate or a leasehold interest taken by eminent domain is of such a nature, or is held or has been improved in such a manner, that, while it serves a useful purpose to its owner, he would be unable to sell it at anything like its real value. Where the usual means of ascertaining market value are lacking, or other means must from necessity of the case be resorted to, it is proper to determine the market value by considering the intrinsic value of the property, and *its value to the owners for their special purposes.* The owner of the property taken is not required under such circumstances to make any pecuniary sacrifices. He is entitled to whatever the property is worth to him, or anyone else, for any purpose to which it is adapted. These special uses, or purposes to which the property is adapted must be real—founded upon facts capable of proof—and not merely speculative or imaginary. If the owner has adopted a peculiar mode of using the land by which he derives profit, and he is to be deprived of that use, justice requires that he be compensated for the loss to himself. *It is the value which he has, and of which he is deprived, which must be made good by compensation.* (Eisenring v. Kansas Turnpike Authority, 183 Kan. 774, 332 P [2nd] 539 [1958], emphasis added)

The ruling creates an opening for determinations of value that exist beyond the scope of the market, including cultural property rights. In his testimony before the Nuclear Claims Tribunal, the anthropologist and Enewetak ethnographer Carucci contrasted the values that Americans and Europeans "hold for their land" with the values the Marshallese hold "about, with, and for their land" (Nuclear Claims Tribunal 1999a).[12] He noted that Americans move, on average, six times during their lives and treat land as a commodity, "something that is used, purchased, and sold." Relationships to place are temporary, and land is "something that one can buy, utilize for a short period of time, and pass on." In Carucci's estimation, American attachments to place are "quite modest." In contrast, the Marshallese regard land as a "different kind of entity," an element "of one's very person" and an "integral part of who people are and how they situate themselves in the world." Their "sense of self, both personal and cultural, is deeply embedded in a piece of land," their *weto,* or land parcel.[13]

Carucci explained that land in the Marshall Islands is highly valued both because it is so limited in quantity[14] and because it "represents the collective labor of generation[s] . . . of human activity": "Living persons are but a minor piece of those generations of time that link people to their land and through that land to an extended history. . . . Living in a place, working in a place, changing that land into a piece of one's own being makes [a person] one with that land. Equally, consuming the products of that land continues and completes the cycle through which one comes to take on a total identity as person and place that will exist not only momentarily . . . but in perpetuity." Carucci's testimony suggests that in contrast to Euro-American understandings of land as a commodity, the value of which is determined by the market, the people of Enewetak rely on the idioms of kinship and identity to describe their relationship to their land.

PROPERTY AS A WAY OF KNOWING

David Anderson (1998, 69) suggests that for reindeer herders in Siberia, "property is a way of knowing," and that "knowing the land properly . . . is what legitimated their right to take wood, water and animals from the land, whilst at the same time explaining their capacity to do so." The nature of indigenous or local knowledge has been the subject of debate in anthropology. For example, Paul Sillitoe (1998) argues that the transition from capital-intensive technology to an information economy, and the emphasis on participation in development, have created new demands for local knowledge, especially in relation to the environment. Consequently, he recommends that anthropologists position themselves as knowledge brokers in this process. However, his respondents suggest that it may prove more difficult than Sillitoe envisions to convert indigenous understandings into other forms of knowledge, in part because they tend to be contingent and local rather than systematized and universal. Nonetheless, both Anderson and Sillitoe agree that alternative forms of knowledge have value even if they are not fully translatable. The most important dimension of local knowledge may not even be specific information per se but, rather, strategies for learning about the natural world and applying the resulting insights—practices that may differentiate indigenous from scientific knowledge (Ellen 1998).[15] Different ways of knowing may not necessarily be more or less accurate but more or less appropriate according to the context, participants, and objectives (Forsyth 1998). In other words, indigenous knowledge may be local knowledge in the sense that it is closely linked to specific places and the people who make use of it.

The people of Enewetak suffered greatly on Ujelang, a remote, uninhabited, and largely desolate atoll. In his testimony before the tribunal, Carucci noted the absence of the species of pandanus used by women to weave mats and mature breadfruit trees needed to build canoes: "Group organized tasks like building canoes fell apart. . . . This was an atoll that [lacked] the products that it was supposed to have." Absence from their home atolls posed a challenge to the continuity of the knowledge needed to build and sail canoes. Judge James Plasman asked Carucci for clarification: "The question of sailing canoes and the loss of the means to traditionally maintain and operate and build these canoes[:] . . . was [that] a loss of culture that people have suffered?" Carucci responded, "[The] real loss was the whole generation of young men who have grown up without the ability to practice under the most skilled of these men who knew how to shape a canoe properly. . . . Enewetak canoes are quite unique. I don't [know] . . . if there is a possibility of re-developing those skills."

The anthropologist Nancy Pollock, testifying for the Defender of the Fund, challenged Carucci's claims about the fragility of this knowledge during cross-examination by Davor Pevec, attorney for the people of Enewetak:

PEVEC: [If these resources] are not in existence or [can]not . . . be imported, people would not be able to maintain the traditional knowledge which you have described.

POLLOCK: It does not disappear.

PEVEC: It does not disappear, but they are not able to actually practice it.

POLLOCK: What is happening with canoe culture at the moment is that there is a lot of old knowledge which is being resurrected around the Pacific because of interest in canoes.

PEVEC: Unless you have the resources on your atoll . . . [He is cut off by Pollock].

> POLLOCK: No. People are very innovative. . . . Everywhere I go in the Pacific, I see small children, one of the things they love to do is . . . build little canoes, out of paper or whatever they've got. . . . It doesn't die, it remains. It is not easily replicated in the full size, but in the children's representations, the toy, that knowledge can be seen.

Marshallese canoes include the long-distance sailing vessel known as *walap,* which measures up to thirty meters in length, can transport forty passengers, and is built for travel on the open sea between atolls; the midsized *tipnol,* which carries up to ten passengers and is used for rapid transport and fishing in the lagoons and the open sea; and the small rowing canoe known as the *korkor,* which may also have sails and carries one or two people for fishing and traveling within the lagoon (Spennemann 1998). In the past, every family owned at least one midsized canoe and a small rowing canoe. Construction of these vessels required mature breadfruit trees for the hull and outrigger and a variety of other woods. People planted and tended trees that decades later would be used to build canoes. The complex requirements of canoe building, only hinted at here, raise questions about the effective intergenerational transmission of knowledge. In the absence of a robust tradition of literacy, such knowledge is reproduced through concrete acts of teaching and use; and the loss of access to the resources necessary for canoe building has significant consequences for the communication of these practices across generational lines.

Property can be a way of knowing, and local knowledge may depend on continued access to land and resources. Women on Enewetak no longer teach their daughters how to weave the mat sails for outrigger canoes because the necessary varieties of pandanus are unavailable, and men no longer teach their sons and nephews how to build sailing canoes because they lack access to the tall, straight breadfruit trees used in fashioning canoe hulls. The knowledge of how to construct and maintain the long-distance sailing canoes of Enewetak, unique in design, may already have been forgotten (Nuclear Claims Tribunal 1999a). On Rongelap, the consequences of nuclear testing and relocation have also "terminated the transmission of navigational knowledge" (Genz 2011, 12) needed for interisland sailing, including the ability to maintain course by tracking the rising and setting of the stars, and by interpreting "changes in wave action occurring when sea swells strike the islands of the chain" (Davenport 1960, 20), known as wave piloting.[16] Such knowledge is cultural property, and its vulnerability in the sense of being local should not diminish its value in the courts. It is neither imaginary nor speculative.

FIGURE 6. Long-distance sailing canoe *(walap)* at Jaliut, Marshall Islands. 1884. Photo: Herman Stolpe, Vanadis expedition / Bishop Museum.

THE VALUE OF SUBSISTENCE PRODUCTION

During interviews on Majuro, informants described how they had become dependent on the cash economy since their relocation from Rongelap. Contemporary replacements for traditional subsistence practices require capital investment. For example, whereas fishing grounds in Rongelap were accessible to all without restriction, in Majuro and Ebeye only people with boats and fuel are able to fish (Johnsay Riklon, interview by Holly Barker, Barbara Rose Johnston, and Stuart Kirsch, 1999). A man from Rongelap explained the transformation in terms of restrictions on his personal autonomy: "If you live in town, you are like a guest in someone's house, [whereas] on your own land, you feel freedom" (Ken Kedi, interview by Holly Barker, Barbara Rose Johnston, and Stuart Kirsch, 1999). The transformations of their subsistence economy have altered local relations of production and generated new forms of economic inequality in contrast to prior forms of hierarchy based on rank, in which chiefs have responsibilities to commoners.[17]

In Australia, the courts recognized the losses associated with damage to subsistence economies in hearings about the environmental impact of the Ok Tedi mine (Kirsch 2014, 94–97). That case did not address damage to property because the courts were unable to hear claims about property disputes in another jurisdiction (Gordon 1997, 153). Alternatively, lawyers for the plaintiffs made the novel argument that people living downstream from the mine had suffered a loss owing to its impact on their subsistence economy. Justice David Byrne (Rex Dagi v. BHP and OTML 1995, 16, emphasis added) endorsed the underlying principle, determining:

> To restrict the duty of care to cases of pure economic loss would be to deny a remedy to those whose life is substantially, if not entirely, outside an economic system which uses money as a medium of exchange. It was put that, *in the case of subsistence dwellers, loss of the things necessary for subsistence may be seen as akin to economic loss.* If the plaintiffs are unable or less able to have or enjoy those things which are necessary for their subsistence as a result of the defendants' negligent conduct of the mine, they must look elsewhere for them, perhaps to obtain them by purchase or barter or perhaps to obtain some substitute.

The case against the Ok Tedi mine established a precedent for the right to engage in subsistence production. In the negotiated settlement of the case, a commercial fisherman was awarded financial compensation for lost revenues. In contrast to the *Exxon Valdez* case, cultural difference was taken into consideration with respect to the reliance of subsistence economies on natural resources. The Australian courts recognized that subsistence production should be viewed as a set of economic rights, relations, and values comparable to the ownership of property in capitalist societies.

Anthropologists have observed that land and kinship are often "mutually implicated" in subsistence economies (Hirsch 1995, 9).[18] These practices often persist into the present in spite of widespread economic and political change. Writing about northern hunters, Marshall Sahlins (1999, xvii) observes, "Their long, intensive and varied engagements with the international market economy have not fundamentally altered their customary organizations of production, modes of ownership and resource control, division of labor, or patterns of distribution and consumption; nor have their extended kinship and community bonds been dissolved or the economic and social obligations thereof fallen off; neither have social (cum 'spiritual') relations to nature disappeared; and they have not lost their cultural identities, not even when they live in white folks' towns."

Hunters and gatherers still actively engage in these pursuits, Sahlins (1999) points out, and these practices have become central to their identities while remaining essential for their social relationships. In what he describes as the "indigenization of modernity," these communities have put capitalism in service of their subsistence practices. Yet these activities are contingent upon their continued access to land and resources, which elsewhere have been jeopardized or impaired by dispossession and development (see Brody 1988). The division of people into social categories through their relationships to land and resources is the basis of relations of production in many indigenous societies and an important means through which these relationships are reproduced; a community's capacity to support itself through subsistence production is simultaneously a matter of belonging and a matter of possession.

PLACE AND COMMUNITY

The anthropologist Roger Keesing (1989, 19) once argued that Pacific interest in land rights was a postcolonial invention, part of a broader creation of "myths of ancestral ways of life that serve as powerful political symbols." He claimed that "land, and spiritual connection to it, could not have, other than in a context of invasion and displacement and alienation, the ideological significance that it acquires in such a context" (Keesing 1989, 33). While land has gained new significance throughout the Pacific, comparable to the changes in Aboriginal valuation of their own traditions described by Weiner (1999), Keesing has been criticized for ignoring the value of land in the past (Trask 1991), especially in island communities where land is limited and population densities approach local carrying capacities.

In their testimony to the Nuclear Claims Tribunal, Carucci and Pollock offered contrasting interpretations of the relationships between people and land in Enewetak. As in the dialogue between Keesing and his critics, Carucci argued that the relationship between past and present was the most salient issue for the people of Enewetak. When they returned to their home atoll thirty years after it had been used to test nuclear weapons, they were stunned by its transformation: "All the markers of [their] sense of place and history, and their sense of their own person [were] transformed." Carucci also described the disjunction between the "new" and the "old" Enewetak, which now exists only in their memories: The "sacred landscapes ha[ve] been destroyed. . . . [A]ll of the embedded stories . . . [of] their own past [and] the activities of their ancestors going back to the first moment in time [are] no longer attached . . . to the physical locations with which they are associated in people's minds." The resulting "dissonance between what once existed and what [now] exists . . . presents people with a problem in terms of establishing a meaningful Enewetak identity."

While Pollock acknowledged Carucci's claim that "land anchors people in place . . . and gives them identity," she disagreed with him on the character of this relationship, arguing that "identity and . . . land exist beyond the economic, beyond the surface layer, beyond the map that we see here [in the courtroom]. It is a spiritual tie to land and it is a tie to land that can never be broken." Relations to land have a "very important continuing factor that was not severed as Dr. Carucci argued[,] . . . because the spiritual tie persists over time and over space, no matter where you are." Pollock supported her claim to the spiritual primacy of ties to land in two ways. She referred to her conversations with people in Majuro: "[When I] asked 'Where are you from?' . . . they would [name their home atoll]. They . . . may not have ever been there, but they still have very strong ties to land." Pollock also argued that the "Marshallese people are very proud of their history of movement. . . . They move constantly and the resurrection of the canoe and current interest in canoe building is all part of that. They've always moved freely using sailing canoes and linking up with the lands where they have kin relations."[19] The debate between the two anthropologists hinges on competing views of place, although they do not make their positions on the subject explicit.

To clarify these issues, I suggest a lateral shift to an alternative set of definitions. Arjun Appadurai (1995, 209) posits a distinction between neighborhood, which he defines as a "context, or set of contexts within which meaningful social action can be both generated and interpreted," and "ethnoscape," his neologism for collective identities that transcend place, as in the case of diasporic cultures. While an ethnoscape is independent of place, a neighborhood is a thing that can, of course, be destroyed. The dissolution of a neighborhood—a historical accumulation of experience and identity—not only represents a concrete loss but also affects the production of local subjects. A spiritual attachment to place is not the same as living on one's home atoll, nor is travel the same as forced migration; before the bomb, Marshallese sailors had homes to which they could return at will.

The distinction between ethnoscape and neighborhood must be qualified, however. Research on diaspora communities emphasizes the costs of disrupting local relations to place (e.g., Lovell 1998; Olwig and Hastrup 1997). Diasporic experience is always suffused with nostalgia, itself an awareness of loss, and accompanied by new strategies to preserve memory and identity. The severing of tangible connections between people and place always entails loss.

PROPERTY AND ALIENABILITY

In the debates before the Nuclear Claims Tribunal, the question of cultural difference emerged most significantly in relation to property. The legal scholar Carol Rose (1994, 296) has argued that "seeing property is an act of imagination—and seeing property also reflects some of the cultural limitations on imagination." She describes how the concept of property is constrained by assumptions about economic value and governed by commodity logic that assumes the detachability of persons and things. This limitation of Anglo-American property regimes is particularly telling in the Marshall Islands case. Largely concealed from view at the Nuclear Claims Tribunal, albeit implicit in Carucci's arguments about Enewetak relationships to land and place, is the assumption of alienability—the view that all forms of property have commodity potential (see Kopytoff 1986). In contrast, Annette Weiner (1992, 4) has emphasized the significance of inalienable possessions in Pacific societies, arguing that certain forms of property provide continuity to social relations by presenting an alternative to the ephemeral nature of human existence. The importance of these objects transcends their exchange value, and their loss poses a threat not only to their owners but also to the group in which they are members, because their historicity preserves memories of the past (Weiner 1992, 6).

Margaret Radin identifies alienability as the central paradox of Anglo-American property theory. On the one hand, "property is necessary to give people 'roots,' stable surroundings, a context of control over the environment, [and] a context of stable expectations that fosters autonomy and personality" (Radin 1993, 197). On the other, economic considerations require that property be subject to market forces. To resolve the contradiction, Radin (1993, 197) proposes the disaggregation of the concept of property, arguing that "some categories of property rights do justifiably become bound up with persons and then ought not to be prima facie subject to rearrangement by market forces." Like the legal precedent in *Eisenring v. Kansas Turnpike*

Authority discussed above, Radin's view provides an opening for the consideration of cultural property rights, because the designation of what is and what is not properly alienable is a cultural rather than an analytical matter. This observation is pertinent to the Marshall Islands case. In her testimony before the Nuclear Claims Tribunal, Pollock asserted that material conditions (including market forces) do not affect the relationship between persons and land in the Marshall Islands. Her position is comparable to the opinion expressed by Judge Holland in the *Exxon Valdez* case, that culture is located in our minds and hearts and therefore unaffected by external events. Furthermore, Pollock ignored the problem of alienability in the Marshalls: whereas individual blocks of land may, subject to local restrictions, be leased to others, there is no historical precedent for the alienation of an entire atoll (Zorn 1993, 126–29). When inalienable possessions are treated as alienable property, as occurred during nuclear testing in the Marshall Islands, the resulting loss is social as well as material and thus inadequately represented by its market value alone.

The alienation of land is a general concern for indigenous peoples; as I suggested earlier, the loss of otherwise inalienable homelands can jeopardize not only the material conditions of existence and the identities associated with subsistence practices, but also their capacity for social reproduction. Local knowledge and relations to place may be affected as well. The concept of loss, with its dual registers of belonging and possession, provides an alternative understanding of property, helping bridge what Rose (1994, 5) describes as "the peculiar gap between property-as-thing and property-as-relationship."

It is worth asking why the discussion of loss in the Marshall Islands should be framed in terms of property models at all. One might propose alternative strategies to analyze their losses. For example, Carucci and Maifeld (1999, 3–4) describe Enewetak experiences of anomie, as expressed by the Marshallese idiom of *jebw we,* a term that means "to drift at sea" and which is used to describe the "conceptually and emotionally disconcerting state of 'having no direction.'"[20] This idiom clearly expresses some of the pain and suffering experienced as a result of nuclear testing and relocation. Yet the Nuclear Claims Tribunal requires an interpretation that corresponds to Western models of property and loss.[21] Even judges sympathetic to the claims of people from Rongelap and Enewetak will find their options limited—and their analogies wanting—unless anthropologists provide them with the tools of analysis necessary to rule on these issues.

Consider another image, of a tribunal hearing in the High Court of the Republic of the Marshall Islands, the back benches crowded with interested plaintiffs from Enewetak, the front of the room occupied by three justices (one Marshallese and two American) and the opposing lawyers seated beside the anthropologists whom they have engaged as expert witnesses. I quote Judge Plasman, who addresses the implications of Carucci's testimony (Nuclear Claims Tribunal 1999a):

> When we talk about culture loss ... are we to some extent faced with a Humpty Dumpty situation where the pieces are broken and in some respects [it will not] be possible to put Humpty Dumpty back together again? ... The tribunal obviously has to struggle with this question. To the extent that the claim is that there has been a loss of culture, to what extent is the cure going to be worse than the sickness? People don't want to go back to the primeval garden of Eden.... Culture changes and accommodation has to be made between the old and the new. Where do you see that balance? Perhaps [Carucci's] comment that [this] needs to be done by the people of Enewetak themselves ... [is the right answer].

Culture has a new set of interlocutors and contexts for its deliberation as judges, juries, and expert witnesses deploy alternative definitions: something that can be lost or damaged, something embedded in our minds and hearts, a mode of adaptation, a process of change. In the *Exxon Valdez* case, Bohannan's emphasis on the human capacity for adaptation prevented him from recognizing important cultural differences between natives and settlers in Alaska. By arguing that culture is largely independent of the material world, Pollock presented an attenuated view of Marshallese culture. Carucci persuasively argued the case for cultural relativism, identifying fundamental differences between Enewetak and American conceptions of property. There is no anthropological consensus on how best to describe the complex histories of indigenous communities under colonialism and the associated problem of culture loss.

In one of the most widely read accounts of how the concept of culture is deployed in the courtroom, James Clifford's (1988, 277–346) analysis of the unsuccessful application for federal recognition by the Mashpee Indians of Cape Cod, metaphors of holism and continuity prevented the courts from appreciating their history of accommodation, political negotiation, and cultural innovation. Anthropological arguments about culture must be able to account for the contradictory demands the courts place on the Mashpee and the people of Rongelap with respect to culture: the requirement that the Mashpee emphasize continuity while downplaying loss, in contrast to Marshallese claims for compensation in the Nuclear Claims Tribunal, in which their culture appears as the object of loss. This points to the need for alternative conceptions that can transcend this figure-ground reversal (see Merlan 2001).

The proliferation of legal proceedings that invoke culture also raises other important issues for anthropologists to consider. Legal forums that adjudicate claims of loss might be seen to further emphasize commodification by establishing monetary values for cultural property that previously existed outside of economic domains. Money is hardly an ideal substitute, although it can be used as a means to other ends—to decontaminate Rongelap Atoll, for example—that cannot otherwise be achieved. Legal activism can provide important political and economic resources for indigenous peoples, as the examples in this book suggest, particularly when the terms of the debate are otherwise set and the mechanisms of justice controlled by nonindigenous bodies. Nonetheless, not all losses are compensable or even judicable. The acknowledgment of loss, however—along with appropriate acts of commemoration, historical documentation, and, where relevant, acceptance of responsibility, in addition to the implementation of reforms designed to prevent past wrongs from recurring—is a partial but valuable response to the experience of culture loss.

The problem of culture loss also invites questions about agency and responsibility. What distinguishes between human-made disasters and their natural counterparts, such as the seasonal cyclones that can inflict heavy damage on fragile Marshallese atolls and force temporary relocation? Carucci's answer to this question during the tribunal was that the Marshallese are well adapted to the risks and challenges of atoll life (Nuclear Claims Tribunal 1999a). The scale and scope of transformations wrought by the weather in contrast to nuclear weapons differ tremendously. Yet claims about culture loss may arise more frequently in the context of assigning social responsibility for negative events.

Why privilege the Rongelap claim or indigenous claims more generally if their experiences are not unique? Claims of culture loss may be a diagnostic feature of our time, given the unprecedented pace of technological change and its social consequences. The shift to a postindustrial economy in Europe and America, for example, has greatly reduced or even eliminated entire economic sectors, including small-scale farming and coal mining, often at considerable cost to the associated communities, including impoverishment, displacement, and a profound sense of loss (Read 1996; Charlesworth 2000). However, claims of loss are especially salient for indigenous communities, which frequently have ties to lands and territories that are essential to how these societies organize and reproduce themselves (Kirsch 2006). Consequently, analysis of the contemporary predicaments of indigeneity may provide the impetus for a general rethinking of the theoretical challenges associated with culture change, cultural property rights, and loss.

For the most part, anthropological debates on cultural property rights have focused on issues of cultural appropriation, commodification, and potential restrictions on the circulation of knowledge and creative processes (e.g., Brown 1998, Brush 1996, Coombe 1998, Dove 1996). I have chosen an alternative starting point, suggesting that ethnographic studies of loss may enrich our understandings of property, and conversely, that the concept of cultural property rights can inform ongoing debates—legal, indigenous, and anthropological—about the problem of culture loss.

DECISION

On April 17, 2007, the Nuclear Claims Tribunal issued its decision in the Rongelap case, "calling for payment of just over $1 billion in compensation to the claimants, a figure reflecting the costs for remediation and restoration of Rongelap (and associated islands/atolls), future lost property value and compensation for damages from nuclear testing" (Nuti 2007, 42). The award was substantially greater than prior judgments by the Nuclear Claims Tribunal for Enewetak ($323 million in 2000), Bikini ($563 million in 2001), and the smaller atoll of Utrik ($307 million in 2005). Each successive award incorporated and expanded upon previous determinations in calculating the appropriate level of compensation (Barbara Rose Johnston, cited in Nuti 2007, 43).

The tribunal weighed two methodologies for assessing the value of land. The "residential/agricultural use approach" calculated the "damage to natural resources; damage to real or personal property; subsistence use, revenues, and profits and earning capacities" (Plasman and Danz 2007, 11). The second methodology, which relied on real estate values of property that had been rented or sold, actually yielded the higher value. However, the tribunal previously established that compensation rates should be set with reference to the "highest and best use" of land, which they identified as residential and agricultural use rather than government purchase or rental. Consequently, the award to the people from Rongelap was based on lost use-values rather than real estate transactions (Plasman and Danz 2007, 12–13).

In making its determination, the tribunal disputed Johnston and Barker's (2008, 47) assertion that lost use-values assessed by the appraisers are incomplete in that they fail to address marine resources, including loss of access to "lagoon, reef heads, clam beds, reef fisheries, [and] turtle and bird nesting grounds." Instead, the tribunal argued that the assessment of agricultural and residential use "explicitly includes these values" because in most cases access to marine resources was directly linked to the ownership of land (Plasman and Danz 2007, 14, n. 32). Similar reasoning was applied to the symbolic or cultural value of resources, including "damage and loss of access to family cemeteries, burial sites of *iroij* [chiefs], sacred sites and sanctuaries, and *morjinkot* land," which is given by chiefs to commoners for bravery in battle (Plasman and Danz 2007, 14n32). The tribunal even argued that land that was culturally significant, but which had no discernable economic value—providing the example of an uninhabited and unused outer island in an atoll—was implicitly included in their analysis (Plasman and Danz 2007, 14n32). According to the tribunal, all of these specific cultural values were taken into account by the accounting procedures for residential and agricultural use.

The claims made by the people of Rongelap about the problems resulting from their "inability to interact in a healthy land and seascape in ways that allow the transmission of knowledge" were not explicitly recognized as a separate category of compensation by the Nuclear Claims Tribunal. The tribunal did not challenge or dispute arguments about the "loss of a way of life" or "culture loss," but concluded they were adequately addressed by the award for the loss of use (Plasman and Danz 2007, 19n41).[22] Based on the larger value of the award for Rongelap in comparison to previous judgments by the tribunal, these claims were implicitly folded into their assessment of land values. The decision expanded prior valuation of land in the Marshall Islands by taking the cultural significance of loss into account.[23] This outcome raises important questions about the role of convention and innovation in both legal claims and engaged anthropology, to which I return in the conclusion to this chapter.

Not only are the people living in the Marshall Islands still grappling with the radioactive legacy of nuclear weapons testing, but they also face potential inundation from rising sea levels. The low coral islands where they reside have been described as sentinels for global climate change (Lazarus 2012, 287). In both cases, the environmental threats experienced by the people living in the Marshall Islands are examples of slow violence, the consequences of which have historically been neglected in comparison to sudden, catastrophic events like an oil spill or a tsunami, which remain the archetype for disaster and intervention (Nixon 2011; Kirsch 2014, 28).[24] Whereas exposure to radiation forced the residents of several atolls to relocate, rising sea levels may imperil the social and cultural reproduction of the entire population of the Marshall Islands.

Questions about the impacts of global climate change that are not adequately measured by the market have recently become the subject of international attention under the rubric of "noneconomic loss and damage." The primary forum for discussion of these issues is the Warsaw International Mechanism for Loss and Damage associated with climate change impacts, which reports to the UN Framework Convention on Climate Change. Among the concerns being addressed by this body are impacts from global climate change on biodiversity, cultural heritage, ecosystems services, food security, human life, identity, livelihood, social cohesion and reproduction, and traditional knowledge. Given the transboundary character of both the causes and the consequences of global climate change, these impacts cannot be adequately addressed by individual states (Serdeczny et al. 2016, 3).

Noneconomic loss and damage are difficult to quantify or monetize. Consequently, there is a need to move beyond economic measures of what people are willing to accept or willing to pay to change when calculating the value of losses from global climate change, or cost-benefit analysis of these impacts, both of which are biased in favor of individuals and societies with greater economic resources. Noneconomic loss and damage also includes losses that cannot or should not be assigned a monetary price. Questions of equity also arise, as those populations with the least capacity to respond are often the least responsible for causing the problem. Ethnographic understanding of the context of these losses is essential to their evaluation, as the example of breadfruit trees, sailing canoes, and navigational knowledge in the Marshall Islands suggests, yet universal standards are required to incorporate these losses into an international framework for addressing the impacts of climate change.

Because these discussions reveal the full extent of harm associated with global climate change, they have been critical for making the case for faster and deeper reductions in the consumption of carbon-based energy sources. Representatives from the Marshall Islands, including Foreign Minister Tony de Brum, and other small island nations vulnerable to sea-level rise, played a pivotal role in rallying larger states to set more stringent standards in the meetings leading up to the 2015 Paris Agreement on climate change. Discussions about noneconomic damage can also contribute to planning for adaptation to climate-induced change, focusing mitigation efforts on specific vulnerabilities. They can help ensure that climate-change impacts that might otherwise have gone unnoticed or unaddressed by policy makers are incorporated into risk management practices (Serdeczny et al. 2016). Adequate assessment of these impacts is also needed to attract appropriate levels of support from national and international funds dedicated to adaptation and mitigation.

In August 2015, I participated in a workshop on noneconomic loss and damage in Bonn, Germany, that was organized by the Deutsche Institut für Entwicklungspolitik (German Development Institute), in which these issues were discussed. Many of the questions raised by my work in the Marshall Islands, including the relationship between ownership and belonging, the significance of inalienable possessions, and how environmental change can affect knowledge and identity, were central concerns. Other important insights included the recognition that livelihoods cannot be reduced to labor costs, that biodiversity loss increases social vulnerability, that there is an inverse relationship between precarity and the responsibility to remedy, and that the difference between acceptable and unacceptable losses may be culturally determined. Most of all, the participants in the workshop stressed the need to develop new frameworks and tools to evaluate noneconomic loss and damage caused by climate change, drawing in part on some of the concepts developed in my work for the Nuclear Claims Tribunal (see Morrissey and Oliver-Smith 2013; Barnett et al. 2016).

CONCLUSION

The relationship between the decision of the Nuclear Claims Tribunal in the Rongelap case and the emergence of new discourses and politics on noneconomic loss and damage associated with global climate change points to the tension between convention and innovation in engaged anthropology. Academic research ordinarily valorizes novel findings. Yet legal proceedings may favor conservative interpretations, leaving engaged anthropologists to choose between originality and precedent. In legal contexts, decisions about how to frame the argument presented in an affidavit may be influenced by whether one views the law as an open or a closed system. My experience suggests that legal proceedings can be understood as a set of practices for interpreting existing laws in which lawyers and judges may be open to new ideas and ways to fashion arguments and render decisions. The extent to which they are constrained by precedent depends on the forum as well as ideological factors; but in hearings concerning indigenous peoples whose cultures, economies, and histories differ significantly from the contexts in which the relevant legal principles were originally articulated, there may be greater receptivity to novel arguments.

This was evident in the unprecedented ruling about subsistence rights and property claims in the Ok Tedi case. That decision supports the counterhegemonic view of legal proceedings as potentially valuable weapons of the weak. In contrast, the Nuclear Claims Tribunal renders its judgments in the shadow of the American Congress—on which it depends to allocate the funds to pay compensation—and consequently, may be more conservative than comparable legal forums. This may account for the tribunal's reluctance to separately acknowledge a category of damage associated with the loss of a way of life (or culture loss) and thereby establish a precedent that might temper support for its decisions. Nonetheless, the tribunal was clearly concerned with the question of culture loss in its deliberations and appears to have taken evidence regarding these losses into account when rendering its final judgment.

In navigating the tension between convention and innovation, engaged anthropologists who serve as expert witnesses must choose between framing their arguments in ways that complement the understandings of the court and framing them in ways that challenge their assumptions. The examples discussed here illustrate both strategies. They use the language of property despite its awkward fit with ideas about belonging and identity, while encouraging the tribunal to recognize alternative conceptualizations of the value and meaning of land. This can be seen, for example, in Laurence Carucci's asking members of the tribunal not to assume that their personal views on the inherent alienability of land are universal. Similarly, consideration of cultural property rights was intended to help make local discourse about culture loss—including forms of knowledge and patterns of sociality that are contingent on living in a particular place—visible to the courts.

Straightening out the intercultural debates on these issues, as Arturo Escobar (2001) suggests, is both a worthy academic project and politically compelling. What is at stake in the cases examined here—in addition to the interests of the claimants themselves—is not only getting it right anthropologically, or even fashioning an academy that is continually challenged by rather than isolated from the world, but also, ultimately, a politics that acknowledges a wider range of analytic possibilities. Even though the introduction of the concept of culture loss to the Nuclear Claims Tribunal was only partly successful, its subsequent uptake in debates about noneconomic loss and damage suggests that engaged anthropologists should continue to pursue the kinds of innovative analyses that have the capacity to influence debates beyond the immediate context of their work.

SIX

The Risks of Intervention

CAMPUS DEBATES ON REPATRIATION

IN THE WINTER OF 2010, I was asked to say a few words at a meeting between a group of anthropology and archaeology graduate students and the Native American graduate student caucus at my university. The subject of the meeting was the long-standing conflict over the repatriation of Native American human remains from the university's museum of anthropological archaeology. To help break the ice, I acknowledged the strong feelings engendered by such debates. I subsequently learned that the archaeology graduate students had interpreted my (admittedly awkward) effort to stimulate discussion as a political provocation. Taken out of context and rephrased in an incendiary fashion, my comments were criticized in a letter by the archaeology graduate students that was circulated among my colleagues at the museum. Much like the main character in Milan Kundera's (1983) celebrated novel about Czechoslovakia under Soviet rule, whose joking comments scrawled on the back of a postcard attracted the scrutiny of the Communist Party, I later discovered that the letter had been posted on a university website by the Office of the Vice President for Research. Because of my frankness in acknowledging the tension in the room, I had been singled out and blamed for the friction between the Native American graduate student caucus and the museum of archaeology despite years of contentious debate about the disposition of Native American human remains and funerary objects in the collections of the museum.

My participation in these events had come about because I was the faculty sponsor of an interdisciplinary graduate student workshop concerned with the relationship between ethnography and activism (see Kirsch 2010b). In their collectively authored manifesto, the members of the group described the goals of the organization as follows:

> The workshop on ethnography-as-activism was set up to explore the challenges and benefits of ethnography that both studies and engages in activism. Through discussions of our specific field situations, the group considers the epistemic and ethical dilemmas presented by action or inaction in field research. Because ethnography entails long-term and often complex relationships between researchers and collaborators/informants, ethnographic research highlights important questions about the politics of knowledge production. This group attends to the implications of these questions within and beyond the communities where we study, the discipline, and the academy. (Ethnography-as-Activism Workshop 2010)

The members of the workshop discussed how the

> ethical and practical dilemmas [of activism] ... go beyond the widely explored questions of establishing trust and collaborations in ethnographic practice. For instance, how might one align with activists with whose agenda one does not fully agree? What are our responsibilities in producing and disseminating knowledge, and how do we gauge the consequences of our research? How do researchers manage demands placed on them by the community members with whom they are working? How should anthropologists formulate research agendas so that they are responsive to community needs? What kinds of interventions—within communities and the academy—are we seeking by being engaged in activist research? (Ethnography-as-Activism Workshop 2010)

The students also explained their desire to

> do more than raise ethical and methodological questions for collaborative research by pointing to the ways in which these questions may generate wider discussions on the meaning of scholar-activism. How can we bring together issues of social justice and social theory in order to create a more praxis-oriented, socially responsible disciplinary practice? How can we bring the insights we learn in the field to bear on our own institutions and the communities in which we live and work? Finally, how can we make ethnographic insight and theoretical understanding relevant to struggles for social justice, and simultaneously make lessons learned from struggles for social justice relevant for the development of ethnographic theory? (Ethnography-as-Activism Workshop 2010)

After discussing these issues for several years, the members of the group decided to undertake a collaborative project. They also wanted to demonstrate that engagement is something anthropologists do at home as well as in our fieldwork projects. The topic that generated the most interest among the students was the campus debate on repatriation. Despite my interest in indigenous politics and cultural property rights, I attempted to steer the graduate students toward a less controversial project. I was concerned that their interventions would generate friction among my colleagues in the anthropology department and archaeology museum, and that the students might suffer from the resulting backlash.

But the graduate students were insistent. They spoke passionately about the need to "break the taboo" against discussing the repatriation controversy in the department. Despite the administrative separation between the anthropology department and the museum of archaeology, the faculty and graduate students in the anthropology program were often treated as though they were responsible for decisions made by the faculty curators in the archaeology museum. The members of the group also felt that the silence of the anthropology graduate students on these issues made them complicit in the museum's handling of these issues. Given these concerns, they elected to pursue a project on repatriation.

About the same time, the Office of the Vice President for Research established an internal advisory committee to review the policies and practices of the archaeology museum regarding its stewardship of the North American collections. The committee was also charged with responding to pending rule changes in the Native American Graves and Repatriation Act (NAGPRA). The committee quickly came to recognize that progress in addressing these issues was needed to develop "more cordial and productive relations between American Indian tribes and the University of Michigan" (Advisory Committee 2010, 4).

During the course of their investigations, the committee learned "there was a great deal of negative feeling among members of the Native American community about how the University of Michigan has handled NAGPRA claims in the past" (Advisory Committee 2010, 12). In particular, there was disagreement with the way archaeologists labeled human remains and funerary objects as "culturally unaffiliated" and, therefore, not associated with any federally recognized tribe or lineal descendant for the purposes of repatriation. This included concerns that the curators might have strategically exploited uncertainty in the identification of Native American human remains to forestall their return. In this matter, the archaeology museum at my university was not unique; similar questions about tribal affiliation had held up repatriation claims across the country and contributed to the revised NAGPRA regulations (see Silverman and Sinopoli 2011, 35). Consequently, many of the archaeology faculty and graduate students felt they were being unfairly criticized for following federal regulations and fulfilling the responsibilities of the museum toward its collections.

The graduate students interested in promoting discussion of these issues began by forming a working group that included several Native American doctoral students from the Departments of Anthropology, History, and American Culture. The students read publications by anthropologists, archaeologists, and lawyers, including both Native and non-Native scholars, as well as work by activists. They collected information on the history of relationships between the museum of archaeology and the Native American tribes and nations in Michigan and the upper Midwest, including Canada. They invited several speakers to campus. They also convened the meeting between anthropology and archaeology graduate students with the Native American graduate student caucus, the group that had regularly expressed criticism of the archaeology museum.

These graduate student events overlapped with the meetings of the advisory committee established by the Office of the Vice President for Research. The advisory committee invited a number of individuals and groups to make presentations, including representatives of the Native American community from the surrounding region, the chair of the anthropology department, a delegation of Native American studies faculty, the museum curator in charge of NAGPRA claims, and the director of the archaeology museum. Several student groups were also invited to meet with the committee, including the Native American student association, the more radical Native American graduate student caucus, the workshop on ethnography-as-activism, and the archaeology graduate students.

On March 15, 2010, the U.S. Department of Interior issued an updated rule regarding the disposition of Native American human remains and funerary objects that were previously classified as culturally unidentifiable.[1] The new regulations require public museums and federal agencies to repatriate Native American human remains in their possession provided they were originally removed from what is currently tribal land or land in the possession of those tribes at the time of removal. Tribes that are not federally recognized are now permitted to make requests as well. The regulations also recommend repatriation of culturally unaffiliated funerary objects on the same basis as human remains. The government ruling expedited the work of the university's advisory committee, which subsequently interpreted the new NAGPRA regulations as a legal mandate to return the majority of the "culturally unaffiliated" human remains and funerary objects in the collections of the archaeology museum to Native American communities.

In April 2010, the graduate student workshop on ethnography-as-activism sponsored its final public event of the academic year, a roundtable discussion of repatriation issues. It was scheduled to coincide with the annual powwow in Ann Arbor, which had been held off campus for several years owing to the ongoing friction over repatriation. The audience at the roundtable discussion consisted of people attending the powwow, students, and faculty from a number of departments, including several archaeology professors. The invited speakers at the meeting were the chair of the university's advisory committee on repatriation, a Native American law professor from the Indigenous Law and Policy Center at nearby Michigan State University, and one of the graduate students from the workshop on ethnography-as-activism. The organizers of the event also asked me to address the forum, which occurred several months after the inauspicious meeting of the anthropology and archaeology graduate students with the Native American graduate student caucus. In an email message sent to all of the faculty and graduate students in the Department of Anthropology, the museum curator responsible for overseeing NAGPRA compliance declined to contribute to the roundtable discussion. The reason he gave for not participating was the poor treatment of the archaeology graduate students by the other members of the graduate student workshop on ethnography-as-activism.

In my own presentation to the roundtable discussion, I sought to make a pedagogical point, that anthropologists could analyze the different discourses invoked by the participants in politically contentious situations without taking sides. I also wanted to produce a text that members of opposing constituencies would recognize as an adequate representation of their positions while simultaneously presenting alternative perspectives on the issue.[2]

A valuable resource for me in thinking about how to write about political debates that divide communities was Faye Ginsburg's (1998) *Contested Lives,* which examines both sides of the abortion debates in North Dakota. Rather than treat competing views as irreconcilable, she focused on the middle ground for discussion. In the introduction to the revised edition of the book, Ginsburg (1998, xxviii) describes her role in the following terms:

> As an anthropologist, my task in studying this movement and the activists in it has been ... to give more visibility to those aspects of the movement that are least well known: the work of cultural activists on both sides of the

debate who are trying to create new forms of social intervention that rely on relations of trust and dialogue. In a shared desire to reduce both violence and the need for abortion, they are finding ways to make a common set of goals despite differences on the abortion issue itself.

Ginsburg's work suggests one strategy for writing about contentious debates, which is to focus on the work of cultural activists who seek to identify shared objectives. I hoped my presentation would help facilitate comparable discussion about repatriation.[3]

In the following section of the chapter, I share an expanded version of my presentation to the roundtable discussion before returning to my comment at the graduate student meeting and the unexpected response it provoked. These events show how anthropologists caught in the middle of campus debates may be subject to political backlash even when trying to identify the common ground among the participants.

SCIENCE, PROPERTY, AND KINSHIP IN REPATRIATION DEBATES

A striking feature of debates concerning the disposition of Native American human remains is their invocation of the conventional domains of science, property, and kinship. Strong political claims about repatriation tend to assert the primacy of one of these domains over the others: archaeologists emphasize the scientific value of the objects in their collections, including human remains; universities focus on their legal responsibilities to administer museum collections, which are their property; and members of the Native American community stress kinship ties to the remains of their ancestors. Yet in other contemporary American social contexts, the domains of science, property, and kinship have heterarchical relations in which no single perspective dominates, rather than hierarchical relations organized by a fixed ranking system.* My comments were intended to show how the selective invocation of claims about these three domains shapes debates on repatriation.

I began by discussing the domain of science, which offers the primary rationale for preserving Native American human remains in museum collec-

*A classic example of heterarchy is the children's game of rock, paper, scissors, in which paper covers rock (thus defeating it), but scissors cut paper, and rock breaks scissors. There is dominance without hierarchy.

tions. In its modern form, science combines knowledge production with particular social roles or professions. It is based on a relatively homogenous social process in which participation is restricted and hierarchical. Science and society are treated as separate domains (Nowotny et al. 2001). The normative status of this model is evident in claims that the science of global climate change has become politicized. Scientists value the pursuit of knowledge above most other values and support the principle of open access to information. This is also a core tenet of liberal, democratic societies. As the Russian physicist and political dissident Andrei Sakharov (1968) opined, a society that impedes the free exchange of ideas is doomed to failure. The contemporary academy is based on these understandings of science and how it should be practiced.

Recent discussions of science and society point to a transformation in how scientific knowledge is produced (Nowotny et al. 2001; Ziman 2000). Knowledge production is increasingly dispersed across a variety of institutions and settings. It is more heterogeneous, socially accountable, and reflexive. An example is the way museums and communities undertake collaborations neither could complete on their own. This entails mutual recognition of complementary forms of expertise. Science and society are no longer treated as separate domains; Nowotny and others (2001) argue that such arrangements produce more socially robust forms of scientific knowledge.

Rules and practices that restrict access to scientific information are seen to contradict the core values of liberal society. However, values associated with other domains regularly override this principle. For example, under certain conditions property rights trump access to information. We make exceptions to rules concerning open access to facilitate commerce: authors copyright their work and scientists patent their inventions for limited periods of time. These protections are intended to stimulate innovation and reward the investment of resources. They represent a compromise between the ideals of open access and information sharing and the desire to promote creativity (Lessig 2001; M. Rose 1993).

Similarly, the academy and the archive have not always fulfilled the ideal of open access to information. For example, Native Hawaiians once had difficulty in gaining access to the major repository of mele, the poetic verses that accompany hula performances (Stillman 2009). More generally, historians of science and empire have documented the relationship between scientific knowledge production and exclusionary practices of racism, colonialism, and imperialism (Pratt 1992).

The second domain referenced by debates about repatriation is property, which is also a foundational concept of liberal society and, in the form of private property, the cornerstone of capitalism. The ownership of property is closely associated with the prevailing form of modern personhood, the possessive individual (Macpherson 1964; Radin 1993). However, there are legal limits on ownership (Kirsch 2004b; C. Rose 1994; Sax 2001). An important example of restrictions on property rights was established by the Thirteenth Amendment to the U.S. Constitution, which abolished slavery; the law no longer recognizes property interests in human bodies. People are still "viewed as having control over their bodies and bodily integrity, but not as the result of the laws of property" (Greely 1998, 488).

Consequently, scientists who propose to carry out research on human tissue or DNA must obtain the permission of their subjects (Rabinow 1996). Individuals regularly agree to participate in clinical research in the altruistic hope that such studies will lead to scientific breakthroughs that will benefit others; the critical issue is consent. A legal settlement in 2010 addressed these issues. From 1990 to 1994, the Havasupai Indians granted scientists at Arizona State University permission to use their DNA for research on diabetes. However, the scientists later used the DNA samples for projects unrelated to Havasupai health concerns. The university's decision to settle with the Havasupai plaintiffs who objected to the new studies is considered significant, because it suggests that the "rights of research subjects can be violated when they are not fully informed about how their DNA might be used" (Harmon 2010).

Anthropologists have studied property since the beginning of the discipline (e.g., Maine [1861] 1986; Malinowski 1935). Whereas Euro-American law emphasizes private property, the dominant form of ownership in other societies may be collective. However, most societies recognize a variety of individual and collective property rights, as Malinowski (1935, 380) argues in relation to the Trobriand Islands. Colonial history can be characterized in part by the inability or refusal of the colonizers to recognize indigenous property rights (McLaren et al. 2005; Pocock 1992), resulting in the doctrine of terra nullius. These debates continue today, as indigenous peoples struggle to make collective claims to cultural property through legal systems that privilege individual rights (Brown 2003; Coombe 1998; Hirsch and Strathern 2004). More generally, contemporary understandings of property are being challenged by the implications of new technologies, including whether and how to assign ownership of genes (Kirsch 2004b; Pálsson 2007) and human embryos (Strathern 1999).

A brief aside regarding the domain of human rights is warranted here, as the participants in repatriation debates also frame their arguments in these terms (see Trope and Echo-Hawk 2000, 140). These principles articulate the fundamental rights of all human beings. However, legal systems generally lag behind the recognition of human rights, making them difficult to enforce. Consequently human rights claims often remain aspirational (see Goodale 2009). An important dimension of human rights is that legal standing is not required to make a claim; one can object to the desecration of a cemetery, for example, regardless of whether one has relatives buried there. Although NAGPRA regulations were originally presented as a response to human rights concerns (Erikson 2008), the legislation is written in the language of property rights.

The third domain invoked by debates about repatriation is kinship. Although Americans say that blood is thicker than water (Schneider 1980, 49), anthropologists recognize that kinship claims are more than just blood: they are also social relations (Carsten 2003). Kinship relations may also be legal relationships; the responsibilities of parents are both defined by law and considered to be matters of proper conduct and affect. It is not a coincidence that many of the founders of the anthropological study of kinship were lawyers by training, including John F. McLennan (1865) and Lewis Henry Morgan (1870).

The courts are also increasingly called upon to adjudicate kinship disputes in the era of DNA testing (Strathern 1999, 2005). For example, judges have been asked to determine whether someone who acted as a social father to a child by making child support payments is legally obligated to continue making those payments even when paternity tests indicate that he is not the biological father (Strathern 1999, 74). The affirmative response follows a social rather than exclusively biological view of kinship relations. In this case, the social definition of kinship trumps scientific information about genetic relationships.

Although kinship and the law are closely intertwined, the prevailing assumption is that in family matters the courts should defer to kin except under extenuating circumstances (Strathern 2005, 16). This is most clearly seen in the restraint exercised by the state with regard to interference with parental care of children. One instance in which this principle was ignored was the placement of Native American children into boarding schools, separating them from their family members and preventing them from speaking their own languages; these interventions were subsequently addressed by the Indian Child Welfare Act of 1978 (Smith 2005).

Possession is commonly said to be nine-tenths of the law, but anthropologists recognize that kinship dominates ownership through inheritance and succession. Kinship guides many forms of property distribution, including real property in land and moveable objects, as well as titles, social roles, and, in some cases, occupational status. But kinship and ownership belong to different domains. A husband and wife have certain legal rights vis-à-vis one another, but this does not include ownership. Kinship is better understood in terms of responsibility: I may or may not be my brother's keeper, but I am certainly not his owner. To invoke ownership with respect to kin is a category error. Similarly, many Native Americans reject the invocation of property rights with respect to human remains, which they view as kin rather than property.

Kinship claims regarding the disposition of human remains might be compared to how people take responsibility for relatives who are unable to communicate their intentions because they are minors or adults compromised by illness. In the United States, the next of kin have the right to arrange for the burial of the deceased (Greely 1998, 488). In the context of repatriation, Native Americans may also see themselves as protecting the interests of their relatives. These may be more than secular duties, however, as caring for one's ancestors is often understood as a religious obligation. The extended care and concern with which such responsibilities toward human remains are discharged is well documented for many other societies, too (e.g., Feeley-Harnik 1991; Richards 2010), and sometimes regarded as a hallmark of humanity.

Societies vary in how broadly they define the scope of kinship ties. Nuclear families in the United States often maintain relatively shallow genealogies. In other societies, however, even remote ancestors may be regarded as members of one's family; there is no parting of the ways with kin at death. In some cases, including among Trobriand Islanders, the members of future generations are already considered members of one's lineage (Weiner 1976). But it would be a mistake to treat these differences as oppositions. Americans can and do recognize lengthy genealogies, especially when they are associated with property and privilege, which explains why until recently a Ford still ran Ford Motor Company. Kinship relations are always subject to telescoping and collapse for various purposes; such flexibility is one of the features of kinship rather than an anomaly.

Given the racialized history of kinship in the United States (Dominguez 1986), it is not surprising that Native American claims about kinship and relatedness may be retrospectively extended beyond contemporary tribal boundaries in claims regarding the disposition of culturally unaffiliated human remains. Nor can these identifications be separated from historical contexts in which native peoples have lost land, cultural knowledge, and, in many cases, their languages through historical policies and practices of genocide, dispossession, and forced assimilation (Fine-Dare 2002). Shared histories of oppression have become de facto components of indigenous identity in many contexts (Niezen 2003). Repatriation is important to Native Americans both in terms of the proper treatment of their relatives (writ large) and as partial reparation for past injustices (Fine-Dare 2002; Mihesuah 2000). Gaining federal recognition, reclaiming tribal lands, revitalizing endangered languages, and repatriating the remains of fellow Native Americans are political responses to the colonial legacy with which Native Americans continue to struggle (Riding In 2000).

As I have indicated, the participants in these debates regularly make reference to all three domains. The pursuit of knowledge and understanding is not limited to scientific research by professors and students. All members of the state seek protection of their property under the law. All people value their families and kin. North Americans regularly invoke more than one of these domains at a time to establish priorities and settle disputes. These interactions must be carefully negotiated, for there is no stable hierarchy of values through which claims about the primacy of one domain over the others can be made. Given the heterarchical relations of these domains, invoking principles from multiple domains may result in complex and contested interactions, as when scientific knowledge about wetlands affects how landowners are permitted to make use of private property, or when parents refuse to have their children vaccinated.

However, the participants in debates concerning repatriation often restrict their claims to a single domain. As scientists, archaeologists may treat human remains primarily in terms of the research questions they can help answer.[4] As institutions chartered by law, universities and museums may view the same human remains primarily in terms of their responsibilities regarding property under their control, including compliance with the provisions of NAGPRA. Native Americans tend to view these human remains as ancestors and kin to whom they have important and even sacred responsibilities, although they also value repatriation as a political act of decolonization. The participants in these debates may be looking at the same material artifacts but seeing something entirely different (Henare et al. 2006).[5]

Writing about the domains of gender, kinship, and science, Marilyn Strathern (1992, 3) observes that "if a culture consists in established ways of bringing ideas from different domains together, then new combinations—deliberate or not—will not just extend the meanings of the domains so juxtaposed; one may expect a ricochet effect, that shifts of emphasis, dissolutions and anticipations will bounce off one area of life onto another." However, she acknowledges that culture "has its constraints and its effects on how people act, react and conceptualize what is going on around them: it is the way people imagine things really are" (Strathern 1992, 3). Thus it is not unexpected that debates about repatriation bequeath us both impasses and opportunities. By recognizing how political claims may emphasize hierarchy when invoking domains that ordinarily have heterarchical relationships, we can treat the resulting interactions as a source of information about the structure and organization of political disagreement. Resolving conflicts in heterarchical systems entails negotiation across domains rather than privileging a single domain, which requires the participants in these debates to understand how and why competing claims are fashioned.

AFTERMATH

The roundtable meeting organized by the graduate student workshop on ethnography-as-activism was well received by the audience, including participants from the Native American community, some of whom expressed frustration that despite repeated objections, the remains of their ancestors were still being stored in cardboard boxes in a warehouse near the football stadium. Their views were reinforced by several faculty and staff members who were critical of university policies. The representative of the university advisory committee, who had initially been reluctant to speak at the event, sought to reassure the audience that the university was committed to improving transparency and accelerating the process of repatriation. This included hiring an independent coordinator for implementing NAGPRA regulations who would report directly to the Office of the Vice President for Research rather than the museum of archaeology. Indeed, over the next few years, the university fulfilled these commitments to the Native American community. When the vice president for research stepped down from his position, his office sponsored an event celebrating the return of human remains and mortuary artifacts taken from eleven different sites. The event was attended by many of the members of the Native American community who had previously been outspoken in their criticism of the university. There was a widely shared recognition that a major impasse had been overcome, and that relations between the university and the Native American communities in Michigan and the upper Midwest were much stronger than anyone could remember.

In the interim, however, I found myself the target of criticism for my participation in these events, even though the policy changes implemented by the university advisory committee on repatriation eventually acknowledged all of the concerns expressed by the Native American graduate student caucus and the workshop on ethnography-as-activism. The criticism first appeared in the letter signed by three archaeology graduate students who had been scheduled to speak to the university advisory committee in March, but who had canceled their meeting after the announcement of the new NAGPRA regulations. Even though the advisory committee's discussions with eight individuals, one faculty delegation, and three student groups were treated as confidential apart from brief summaries of one to three sentences each, the two-page letter submitted by the archaeology students was appended to the committee's annual report in its entirety. It was the only section of the thirteen-page document submitted by the advisory committee to the Office of the Vice President for Research that was not written by the committee, which refrained from commenting on the contents of the letter.

The central focus of the letter was the interaction of the three archaeology students with the other participants at the meeting with the Native American graduate student caucus:

> We had hoped for productive dialogue and, indeed, we achieved productive and mutually informative dialogue at some of these meetings. *But when the faculty sponsor for this student group, in his introductory remarks prior to meeting with the Native Student Caucus, joked about "burning down the museum," the dynamic changed.* From there the meeting devolved into personal, not professional attacks on each archaeology graduate student in the room, as our anthropology graduate student colleagues, including the faculty sponsor of this group, quickly moved to distance themselves from us. Surely such actions are at least a disservice to our academic community, the goals of the Ethnography as Activism student group, and the goals of this committee, if not a threat to our well-being. We are deeply troubled and saddened that even in a group of our peers explicitly dedicated to a productive dialogue about repatriation, no such dialogue could be found. Rather, out of this swirl of distrust and misinformation comes an anger that is directed at the

archaeology graduate students on a regular basis simply because of our affiliation with the [archaeology museum]. Truly, this is a heavy burden to bear. (Advisory Committee 2010, appendix D, 10, emphasis added)

In the process of telling their story, the graduate students misrepresented my contribution to the meeting.[6] I arrived several minutes after the meeting had already started. The students from the Native American graduate student caucus were sitting on one side of the room, while the members of the workshop on ethnography-as-activism, including the three archaeology graduate students, were seated on the other. The participants were saying very little, especially the members of the Native American caucus. I tried to bring them into the conversation by acknowledging the long-standing conflict between the two groups, saying, "We're not here to burn down the museum," or words to that effect, "even if some of us would like to see that happen. Rather, we're here to find common ground." I left for another meeting a few minutes later.

I subsequently learned that the archaeology graduate students had been offended by my remarks. They attributed the hostility of the Native American community toward archaeology and archaeologists to my comments rather than several centuries of excavating Native American cemeteries without permission and more than a decade of conflict over repatriation between the archaeology museum and the Native American graduate student caucus. Rather than recognize that my brief remarks were intended to acknowledge the different points of view represented in the room, they accused me of turning the ensuing conversation against them. The archaeology students expected the Native American students to accept their good intentions as sufficient, without first acknowledging the validity of Native American criticism of past archaeological practices (see Povinelli 2002, 155).

The archaeology graduate students first reported their indignation to the curator in charge of the North American collections. Their letter was then circulated among the other curators in the museum of archaeology and forwarded to the advisory committee on repatriation established by the Office of the Vice President for Research. None of my archaeologist colleagues asked to hear my account of the meeting. Nor did the vice president for research provide me with an opportunity to respond before posting the student letter online. When I finally learned about the letter, which had been circulating without my knowledge for months, I contacted the vice president for research. I told him that his decision to make these comments public without discussing them with me first violated standards of collegiality. Such conduct might be understandable from others embroiled in heated conflicts, but I had higher expectations for the Office of the Vice President for Research. When I asked him to either take down the letter or append my response, he refused, suggesting that I write a letter to the student newspaper if I was unhappy with his decision. After being turned away by the faculty ombud's office as well, I decided to let the matter drop. I had no interest in being singled out as either the hero or the victim in the story—after all, it was not my ancestors whose remains were stored in cardboard boxes in a warehouse on campus. I was also concerned that negative publicity about the review process might harden the hearts of the advisory committee on repatriation—which had yet to issue its final recommendations—against the Native American community.

In my contribution to campus debates on repatriation, I sought to facilitate mutual understanding among the protagonists. But when political debates are polarized, showing how different points of view are constructed may engender resistance. In the midst of these events, I became concerned about being identified with the conflict, given my forthcoming promotion review, and asked the department chair to insert a note in my personnel file explaining my role as the faculty sponsor of the graduate student workshop on ethnography-as-activism. I was right to be concerned, because the only negative votes in my promotion review reportedly came from several of the archaeologists in the department. As a result, the department's cover letter to the dean about the vote began by explaining their failure to support my case. At the end of the day, there were more than enough votes to make up for the abstentions, but the implications of the story are chilling. It is not difficult to imagine a different outcome for a sociocultural anthropologist in a department dominated by archaeologists, a university in which democratic decision-making on tenure cases is not the norm, or simply a borderline dossier for which a few additional objections would be enough to sway the outcome. Anthropologists are often discouraged from taking sides in politically contentious debates, but the events described here show that there may also be risks involved even when seeking to identify common ground.

SEVEN

Dilemmas of an Expert Witness

INDIGENOUS LAND RIGHTS IN SURINAME AND GUYANA

IN AUGUST 2014, I VISITED Isseneru village on the Middle Mazaruni River in Guyana. Their lawyer asked me to conduct research and write an expert report for the Inter-American Commission on Human Rights on the problems associated with the land title granted to them by the state in 2007. During a preliminary meeting to discuss the project, I explained that the state claimed Isseneru was "not a traditional Akawaio community," because its members intermarried with outsiders, spoke English in the village, were engaged in artisanal gold mining, and received a percentage of the gold extracted by nonindigenous miners working on their land (Government of Guyana 2013, 11, 22). The state also disputed their claim to be the traditional landowners of Isseneru, because they relocated there from the Upper Mazaruni River in the 1970s (Government of Guyana 2013, 22).[1]

Not surprisingly, people at the meeting in Isseneru reacted very strongly to these claims, saying that they were "extremely upsetting to hear." They also objected to being asked to explain themselves to me, saying, "Yet another visitor who would like to know who we are" and noting they have already been interrogated about "how we live, where we come from, who we got our land title from." They added, "We know this land is ours, and that's why we live here," and "our grandparents [and ancestors] lived, farmed, and hunted on all of these lands." Feeling somewhat chagrined by their response, I acknowledged the validity of their concerns and reiterated that I was there to help document their legal claim, not to judge their decisions.

This chapter presents two affidavits I wrote for the Inter-American Commission on and Court of Human Rights, institutions responsible for monitoring the thirty-five independent nations that are members of the Organization of the American States and ensuring their compliance with human rights guarantees.[2] The first case was concerned with the detrimental consequences of Suriname's refusal to recognize indigenous land rights despite its international obligations to do so.[3] The second addressed problems with indigenous land titles in Guyana granted under the country's Amerindian Act of 2006. The invitation to visit Suriname and Guyana, investigate these questions, and provide affidavits supporting their claims came from Fergus MacKay, senior counsel for the Forest Peoples Programme in the United Kingdom, who represented the indigenous complainants in both cases. MacKay had previously asked me to contribute to an independent review of a proposed bauxite mine in the Bakhuis Mountains in west Suriname (Goodland 2009; Kirsch 2009a). Before agreeing to participate, I had the opportunity to read through various reports, affidavits, and preliminary rulings and to discuss the legal proceedings with MacKay. He did not provide instructions about the form or content of the affidavits, although he suggested questions to ask and provided comments on several drafts.

To illustrate what affidavits prepared by anthropologists look like, I present both of these documents as submitted, apart from minor editorial changes. I also discuss the hearings on the Suriname case and the final judgment; the results in the Guyana case are still pending. Comparing the two cases allows me to reflect on the dynamics of short-term ethnographic research conducted for expert-witness reports. I describe the need to make these affidavits legible to three different audiences, each of which possesses its own frame of reference: not only to the lawyers and the legal system but also to the communities seeking recognition of their rights and to the discipline of anthropology (Paine 1996, 63). I also discuss the narrative choices that I considered in writing these affidavits, the political dilemmas associated with being an expert witness, and the compromises and value of short-term ethnography.

AFFIDAVIT I: INDIGENOUS LAND RIGHTS IN SURINAME

In November 2008 I was invited by the counsel for the petitioners in Case 12.639, *Kaliña and Lokono Indigenous Peoples (Suriname),* to prepare an expert report concerning the territorial rights and situation of the indigenous peoples and communities of the Lower Marowijne River. Their petition submitted to the Inter-American Commission on Human Rights alleges both

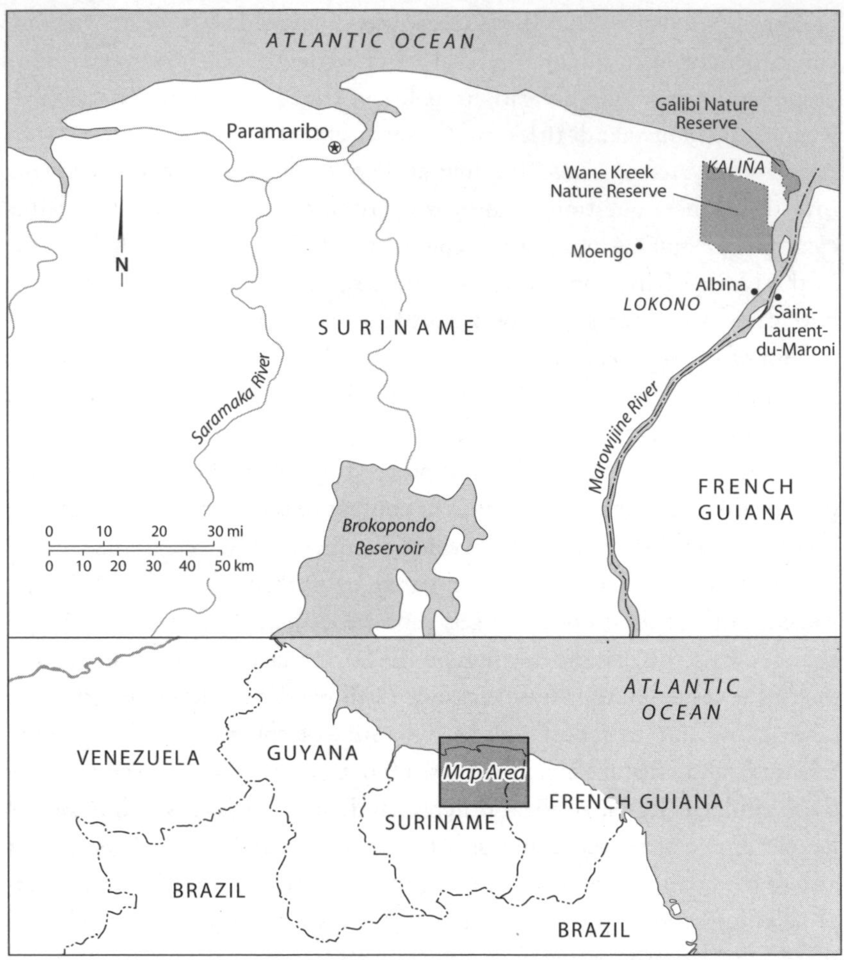

MAP 7. Lower Marowijne River, including the Galibi and Wane Kreek Nature Reserves, Suriname.

the failure of the government of Suriname to recognize their territorial rights and the active violation of those rights caused by the establishment of protected areas, grants of individual titles, bauxite mining, and other unwelcome intrusions. I conducted the research for this report in January 2009.

Encroachment on Kaliña and Lokono Territories

The gradual dispossession of the Kaliña and Lokono indigenous peoples in the Lower Marowijne region predates the establishment of the Republic of

Suriname. The indigenous peoples of Suriname supported the country's independence from the Dutch colonial administration in 1975 in part because they hoped the new government would recognize their land rights. In 1976, the indigenous peoples of the Lower Marowijne River organized a march to the capital city, Paramaribo, to deliver a petition to Johan Ferrier, the first president of Suriname (VIDS 2009, 27). They asked the state to recognize indigenous land rights. They protested the expropriation of indigenous lands for the Galibi Nature Reserve, and the nonconsensual allotment (subdivision of land rights into individual titles) of the four villages closest to the town of Albina on the Marowijne River, but did not succeed in either effort. Progress on these issues was subsequently delayed by the Interior War from 1986 to 1992.[4] One of the most important articles of the 1992 Lelydorp Peace Accord refers to the fact that negotiations over land rights have not been completed, and it stresses that this issue must be addressed. It is notable that, to date, the state has failed to comply with this provision of the peace accord.

Government intransigence toward recognition of indigenous land rights continues. In 2008, the former president of Suriname reportedly told one of the captains, or elected village heads, from the Lower Marowijne that he would do everything in his power to prevent indigenous peoples from gaining land rights. He told Captain Ricardo Pané, a representative of the Kaliña, that it will take many more years to address the question of land rights for indigenous peoples in Suriname, although the current rate of development and other incursions on Amerindian land suggest that there may be very little land or resources to protect by the time the state takes appropriate action on its own. The state's refusal to revise its policies and laws pertaining to indigenous land matters persists despite its binding international obligations and commitments to do so, including two recent judgments of the Inter-American Court of Human Rights that directly address this issue (Moiwana Community v. Suriname 2005; Saramaka People v. Suriname 2007).

The indigenous peoples of Suriname, especially those from the Lower Marowijne, have remained active in their pursuit of land rights, organizing a variety of protests against the imposition of nature reserves and other takings of their land. For example, in 1997 they held a public vigil next to the High Court of Justice in Paramaribo for several days to protest a legal claim filed by a nonindigenous titleholder against the captain of Wan Shi Sha (Marijkedorp) village.[5] They have established new organizations to represent their rights, including the Association of Indigenous Village Leaders in Suriname (VIDS), which coordinates indigenous political action across the country, and regional associations such as the Organization of Kaliña and Lokono in Marowijne (KLIM).[6] Although they have submitted numerous constitutional claims and other petitions, and held multiple meetings with the minister of physical planning, land and forestry management, they have never received a written response from the government to their requests for change. They have also collaborated with international NGOs that have provided organizational and human rights training, resources, and legal assistance. In addition, the indigenous peoples of Suriname have begun to document and map their own territories and patterns of resource use (see CLIM 2006). They learned a great deal by following the case *Saramaka People v. Suriname* (2008), in which a Maroon group in Suriname successfully sued for recognition of its land rights in the Inter-American Court of Human Rights. In sum, since the late 1970s the Kaliña and Lokono indigenous peoples have used all of the tools of civil society available to them—from protest and petition, to better organization and documentation of their claims—without a productive or conclusive response from the state regarding recognition of their land and other rights.

Problems Caused by the Galibi Nature Reserve

The Galibi Nature Reserve was established by the Dutch colonial administration in 1969, six years before independence (Kambel and MacKay 1999, 111; VIDS 2009, 42–43). According to the current captains of the Galibi villages, Dutch authorities instructed their predecessors to sign papers relating to the Galibi Nature Reserve. Neither of the captains was able to read these documents and both thought they were being asked for permission to conduct research on sea turtles, not to establish a nature reserve. Some of their agricultural plots and houses were located inside the nature reserve, forcing them to relocate. There were many disputes between the two indigenous communities on the coast and the Galibi Nature Reserve authorities during its establishment. However, neither the captains at the time nor the people from the two nearby villages knew how or where to protest the taking of their lands. The current captains of Galibi believe that the Dutch colonial administration took advantage of the fact that the Kaliña were unfamiliar with their rights. Consequently, the community members and their captains consider the process through which the Galibi Nature Reserve was established to be fraudulent and therefore a violation of their rights.

The Kaliña living in Galibi face economic and other problems in coping with restrictions on their use of resources imposed by the nature reserve, and they remain aggrieved that an integral part of their territory was taken from them by the state. While some community members have established a successful ecotourism business that operates during the sea turtles' egg-laying season, the communities do not see this as adequate compensation for the taking of their land for the Galibi Nature Reserve. Since the 1970s, they have consistently demanded complete restitution of all of their lands incorporated into the reserve.

The captains of the Galibi villages also believe the nature reserve is not adequately protecting sea turtle populations, some of which are in decline. They assert that the most significant threat to sea turtles is not from the Kaliña but from commercial fishing boats using long drift nets in the Marowijne River estuary, which kill the animals when they become entangled in the nets and drown. Most of these boats are from Paramaribo. Apparently, the state exerts little control over the fishing boats responsible for killing turtles in nets (Kambel 2002, 143).[7] However, the Galibi Nature Reserve continues to impose strict conservation rules on the Kaliña, who have a traditional taboo against eating sea turtles, although in the past they harvested turtle eggs for consumption and sale.[8] Captain Pané of Galibi observes, "We don't need a nature reserve to protect the animals, because we have traditional knowledge that is very old to protect them. Although the government has not succeeded in protecting biodiversity[,] . . . indigenous peoples have been protecting biodiversity since before the Spanish conquistadores came to South America." Captain Pané also asks why sea turtles have land rights, whereas the indigenous peoples of Suriname do not.

Problems Caused by the Wane Kreek Nature Reserve

Another significant taking of indigenous lands occurred with the establishment of the Wane Kreek Nature Reserve in 1986 (VIDS 2009, 49). This action has had more destructive consequences for the environment than the establishment of the Galibi Nature Reserve, which protects land from development. In contrast, the Wane Kreek Nature Reserve has become an industrial zone for resource extraction, including a bauxite mine operated by Suralco and BHP Billiton.

In the late 1970s, the government of Suriname conducted an ecosystem inventory of the country's coastal plains. Because of extensive development along much of the coast and the comparatively intact ecosystem of Wane Kreek, this area was chosen for a nature reserve. The protected area was established despite preexisting mining and logging rights granted by the Dutch colonial administration of Suriname. The irony that the state established a conservation area in Wane Kreek precisely *because* indigenous communities have sustainably managed the resources there, but then opened the area to resource extraction, is not lost on the Kaliña and Lokono.

I was told that Wane Kreek was "home to a large number of plant and animal species," which is "why the government made a nature reserve there." The indigenous peoples of the Lower Marowijne had been able to protect this area while actively making use of its resources: "We are people of nature; we live with it and by it. But the people who [established the nature reserve] don't live in nature; they work in offices, and they made the decisions without us. They are using the knowledge of indigenous peoples [which has protected the forest] against indigenous peoples [by setting up a nature reserve and permitting resource extraction]."

The people living in the Lower Marowijne area first learned about the Wane Kreek Nature Reserve in 1997, eleven years after it was established. Similarly, the people in Galibi discovered the plans to mine for bauxite in Wane Kreek only when one of their hunters inadvertently came across a road being built by Suralco in the reserve. The people of the Lower Marowijne area oppose the establishment of conservation areas on indigenous land because these decisions have been made without consulting the people who live in the area and use these resources. By converting their land into state property, these projects violate indigenous rights. They also negatively affect their economic standing, traditional practices, and well-being.

Mining in the Wane Kreek Nature Reserve

Bauxite was discovered in Suriname in the early 1900s. In 1916, the Suriname subsidiary of the Aluminum Company of America (Alcoa), now called Suralco, began to mine bauxite in the Cottica region. In 1958, the government issued a concession of 123,000 hectares to the company for a period of sixty years. The town of Moengo grew up around the project (CLIM 2006, 10). It was not until 1997, however, that Suralco partnered with Billiton (later, BHP Billiton) to exploit the bauxite deposits at Wane Hills inside the Wane Kreek Nature Reserve. Despite the global norm of conducting environmental and social impact studies before undertaking projects of this magnitude

(Goldman 2000), BHP Billiton and Suralco failed to do so because there "is no formal requirement under Suriname legislation for an [environmental impact study]" (Ian Wood, vice president for sustainable development, BHP Billiton, pers. comm., 2009). A report produced by SRK Consulting for BHP Billiton acknowledges: "Considerable damage has already been done to Wane [Hills] 1 and 2 by bauxite mining" (SRK 2005, iv, 20). As one of the indigenous people from the area told me about the mining company: "Within the concession, they do whatever they want."

When Suralco began to mine bauxite in the Wane Hills in the mid-1990s, explosions from dynamite blasts shook Alfonsdorp village six to eight times per day. The resulting noise and vibrations caused wildlife to flee, which has made hunting in Wane Kreek very difficult. Villagers also told me that while it is still possible to find small animals there, it is difficult to find larger game animals. One must spend several days in the forest hunting to find larger animals, whereas before they were plentiful. Knowledgeable local informants also report that the mine polluted Wane Kreek: "Although the water looks clear, there aren't as many fish in the river and creeks as before."[9] A hunter from Pierrekondre was even more negative: "For four years it has been useless to go into Wane Kreek, because there are no animals or fish."[10]

As one of the indigenous people from the area told me: "Mining was very destructive. Everything came down; there is no forest any more. What they are leaving behind is a pile of junk; there is nothing [of value] left." Another indigenous person told me: "Before, when the indigenous peoples heard about development, we were happy. But now, when you look at what the mining company has done, they haven't brought [the kind of] development [we were expecting] to the village."

Bauxite deposits are generally shallow and located close to the surface, so extracting the ore typically requires strip-mining large areas for processing. Consequently, significant areas of the Wane Kreek Nature Reserve have been cleared of forest covering. The red laterite that remains after strip-mining bauxite is inimical to forest regrowth, and rehabilitation efforts by BHP Billiton and Suralco have had very limited effectiveness.[11] Visual inspection of the reclamation areas managed by BHP Billiton and Suralco suggests that relatively little effort or expenditure has been invested in reforestation. In the areas I examined, one could see a small sprinkling of topsoil on the ground, holes dug into the laterite, and the planting of small fast-growing trees from the genus *Cecropia,* which are common pioneer species in cleared areas. However, their growth remains stunted even ten years after being planted. In most of the reclamation area, there is little evidence of other trees, plants, or even weeds taking root in the barren red rock.

In addition, the construction of mining roads has made it easier for legal and illegal loggers to enter the area and clear the forest. Other companies extract sand and gravel from the area. It is not unusual to find a layer of kaolin beneath bauxite, which is now being extracted for sale. Kaolin is an important, traditionally used resource of the indigenous peoples of the Lower Marowijne. These activities have further degraded the Wane Kreek Nature Reserve, which has become a de facto open access zone for resource extraction.

It is unclear why these projects have been granted license to operate in a nature reserve. It is also important to note the double standard here: mining companies retain control over their concessions at Wane Kreek and elsewhere in Suriname, but the preexisting land rights of indigenous peoples are not protected. The state favors its commitments to transnational corporations over its obligations to indigenous peoples.

Social and Cultural Consequences of the Encroachment on Indigenous Territories

The forests are of great value to the Kaliña and Lokono: "The forest, the creek, and the river is where we get our food; it is our pharmacy. We don't have to pay for it; we get everything we need from it." "Our knowledge of the forest is great; we know which plant is poisonous and which is not, and when a child is injured or sick, we take a leaf for a wound, or sap for an illness." Central to their identity as indigenous peoples is their relationship to their land and resources, their knowledge of local flora and fauna, their taboos and limits on consumption that help them protect the environment, and their subsistence practices. Although the Kaliña and Lokono also value Western education and development, maintaining their relationship to the forests and rivers is of vital importance to them. Hunting, fishing, and the use of non-timber forest products not only are the historical basis of their livelihood but also continue to be a way of life for the Kaliña and Lokono.

However, encroachment on indigenous territories has compromised the relationship of the Kaliña and Lokono to the forest in significant ways. As I have described, they must contend with the state's expropriation of their land for nature reserves. The state has also granted logging concessions on indigenous land to numerous individuals and companies. Illegal logging operations in the

Lower Marowijne are rampant and generally ignored by the state. Nonindigenous people cut down trees, build homes, make gardens, and operate businesses on indigenous lands without permission from the state or the indigenous landowners. In particular, the villages closest to the town of Albina, especially Pierrekondre, Wan Shi Sha (Marijkedorp), and Erowarte, regularly contend with nonindigenous people making use of their land and resources without permission. Sometimes these infringements on their property end up in the courts, but the indigenous peoples of the Lower Marowijne lack the resources to adjudicate every violation of their land rights. Moreover, their experiences with the courts have led them to conclude that the laws in Suriname are biased against indigenous peoples and provide no protection or support for their rights—a conclusion also reached by four different international human-rights bodies (Moiwana Community v. Suriname 2005; Saramaka People v. Suriname 2007; CERD 2009; HRC 2004; SRIP 2003, para. 21).

These encroachments on their territories mean that the indigenous peoples of the Lower Marowijne hunt and fish less often. One man from Alfonsdorp told me how he previously went hunting in Wane Kreek several times a week. He explained that when hunting there, "you knew you would get meat." He would give his family some of the meat and sell the rest. Sometimes he did not even have to walk very far from the village, because the game was so abundant. Now he no longer goes there to hunt; he must drive for several hours from the village to find reliable hunting grounds. Several people told me stories from the past about entire families camping out in Wane Kreek, living on food from the forest for days at a time. One woman told me how she used to take cassava bread and very little else with her into the forest, apart from salt, sugar, and pepper. She found everything she needed in the forest. But another person commented that now it would be difficult for a family to stay in Wane Kreek, given the limited food supply.

In most of the villages in the Lower Marowijne, people have to travel farther to hunt, and hunting yields diminished returns. As one person told me: "There is logging everywhere, making it difficult to hunt. All of the hunting tracks are being destroyed. The creeks are being destroyed. The animals are going away. It is more difficult to make a living [from the forest]." Even though they are less able to rely on hunting to earn their living, men who do not have jobs must continue hunting to feed their families.

Local diets are changing in other ways as well. They continue to eat cassava, but not daily: "Today we mainly eat rice and bread, although when there is cassava, we will eat it. Children like to eat cassava, but they also like to eat rice and bread." As people have to purchase a greater share of their food, they become more dependent on money and the cash economy. One person told me: "Before it was okay if you didn't have money, but now we need money [to survive]." In Galibi, they told me that participation in the monetary economy was fine for the individuals who succeed, but they realize that not everyone in the community will be successful. Moreover, they share food when hunting and fishing, but not their monetary earnings. Their incorporation into the cash economy poses unprecedented challenges. For the most part, their societies continue to be egalitarian, but the new forms of inequality have already begun to affect social relations. The only effective buffer against these problems is greater control over their territories, so that everyone has access to the resources needed for survival.

In addition, because the Kaliña and Lokono are "going less often into the forest or to the river, they are also losing traditional knowledge" (CLIM 2006, 108). When I asked young people whether they are still interested in hunting and fishing, the response was almost always positive. However, one hunter told me that it is difficult for young people to hunt and fish very often because the closest hunting grounds are several hours away. Consequently, they are restricted to the very limited hunting and fishing available in the vicinity of the village. None of the young men I interviewed expected to pursue hunting and fishing as their primary economic livelihood. For the most part, young men choose to hunt and fish together as a group rather than learning from more experienced hunters. In many of the villages, hunting is gradually becoming more of a recreational pastime and source of identity than a regular source of food and income. Many of these changes are the consequence of encroachment on indigenous territories rather than choices made by the Kaliña and Lokono. Their opportunities to pursue traditional subsistence practices are being reduced or, in some cases, eliminated altogether by the destruction of the forest.

One positive development has been the emergence of markets for agricultural, forest, and riverine goods produced by the Kaliña and Lokono. In particular, there is strong demand for cassava bread and *kasiri,* an alcoholic beverage made from fermented cassava. People also want to buy *atyupo* (*peprewatra,* or hot soup, also made from cassava), a variety of fruits from their gardens and the forest, and other goods. Indigenous peoples from the villages on the Marowijne River regularly travel across the river by boat to the twice-weekly market in Saint-Laurent-du-Maroni in French Guiana. They sell fresh, dry, and salted fish in the markets of St. Laurent and Albina,

FIGURE 7. Selling indigenous produce from Galibi at the market in Saint-Laurent-du-Maroni, French Guiana. 2009. Photo: Stuart Kirsch.

although some of the larger and more valuable fish species have become quite rare (CLIM 2006, 17, 62). There is also a strong demand for seasonal forest products (CLIM 2006, 67–68), including several varieties of palm fruits (*awara, podosiri,* and *kumbu*) and forest apples (*busi apra*). They also sell fruits grown in their gardens, including pineapple, avocado, and mango. On occasion, they buy these goods from other villages to sell at the markets in Saint-Laurent-du-Maroni, where the prices are higher. The demand for cassava and *kasiri* has also stimulated a market for *matapi* (cassava sieves or squeezers).[12] The new markets for cassava, cassava beer, and other forest products provide the indigenous peoples from the Lower Marowijne with an important opportunity to earn money from traditional practices. A recent meeting of indigenous leaders from the Lower Marowijne with the mayor of St. Laurent confirmed the continued interest in the products they market.

However, the material conditions of these practices are changing. For example, they sometimes teach young women to weave the *matapi,* even though traditionally this was a task performed by men. Many of the practical skills associated with subsistence production are no longer regularly taught by fathers to their sons and mothers to their daughters: "Today, the young people have to want to learn, you cannot force them. In some families, there are no elders to teach them these things. And even to get the materials needed[,] . . . you can no longer find them locally because of logging but have to travel long distances." Young men and women often want to learn these skills but lack opportunities to do so. Consequently, community leaders want their organizations to address this problem by creating a training program to help teach traditional skills and knowledge.

This proposal reveals their recognition of how much their lives have changed—that the reproduction of key skills and knowledge is no longer feasible following traditional models for teaching and learning. However, it also shows the positive value these practices continue to have for the Kaliña and Lokono, as well as their efforts to adapt to changing circumstances. At present, no one really questions whether they will be able to pass on these skills and other forms of traditional knowledge, or whether they will be able to find the necessary raw materials from the forest to do so. But it is precisely the continued viability of these traditions that is at stake in their petition for land rights.

In many ways, their circumstances are similar to those faced by other indigenous peoples under intense economic and environmental pressure (see Kirsch 2006). The Kaliña and Lokono must balance the pressures of modernity with their strong desire to maintain their own culture and identity. But it is clear that many of the challenges they face are the result of encroachments on their territories: government taking of their land for faux conservation projects like the Wane Kreek Nature Reserve, mining projects, both government licensed timber projects and illegal logging, and a variety of individual incursions onto indigenous territories. If they lose much more of their land, they may not be able to hunt or harvest important forest products at all. Even if the government or the courts could compel more robust rehabilitation measures at the closed Wane Hills bauxite mine, it would take generations for that land to be returned to productive use.[13] Meanwhile, the mining of kaolin, sand, and gravel continues to further damage the surrounding landscape. Logging and mining not only destroy the forest but also cause erosion and sedimentation of local waterways.

The Kaliña and Lokono are at a crossroads: if they do not regain control over their lands and territories soon, many of their successful adaptations to the cash economy will probably fail as the environment is progressively degraded. At that point, they will be vulnerable to both extreme poverty and pressure to move outside of their own territories, as without land rights and therefore control over their forests and rivers, they will lack the means to support themselves. Many of the problems faced by the Kaliña and Lokono could have been averted had the newly independent government of Suriname recognized their land rights in 1975. The Kaliña and Lokono may well have reached a tipping point in which the continued viability of their villages as functioning units, and all that this entails, is now at risk. Their *cultural survival* as indigenous peoples depends in large measure on the continuity of these villages and their individual and collective control over traditional resources, land, and territories, including the kinds of social relations this fosters and their contribution to the reproduction of their shared culture and values.

In the long run, societies continuously change and adapt to new circumstances. This was true for pre-Columbian times as well as the present, and has certainly been the case for the Kaliña and Lokono since extensive contact with outside societies began in the late 1800s (CLIM 2006). But it is also the case that the Kaliña and Lokono have maintained their own identities and cultures for centuries and continue to do so. They are committed to protecting their culture and passing it on to future generations. The fact that the four villages closest to the town of Albina experience the *most* pressure on their land does not mean they are any less committed to protecting their own indigenous way of life, preserving their own distinctive worldview, and maintaining strong social relations among community members. Rather than view these villages as more assimilated, they should be seen as more vulnerable and, therefore, in need of greater protection.

State Failure

A group of young men from Alfonsdorp whom I interviewed were especially articulate and compelling on the subject of indigenous land rights. One young man said the Suriname government "does not see the Amerindians or take them into account." Another said the government does not "let us participate in decision-making. Especially when it comes to land rights, the government doesn't want to listen to us. They don't want to give indigenous peoples their land rights." Yet another young man said, "We are rich in natural resources, but because we do not have land rights, we cannot protect our own land." So, they wonder, "What will be left for future generations?"

When I asked them whether land rights were important to them, they all emphatically said yes. I asked them why, and one replied, "You have nothing when you don't have a place to stay." This is not an abstract issue for them;

many members of their generation had to flee their land during the Interior War. Some of them were forced to stay away for years, and not all of them have returned. They also expressed the desire to stay in the village after they finish school; this is where they want to spend the rest of their lives. To continue their education or get a paying job, they have to move elsewhere. But they prefer to live in Lower Marowijne rather than move to Paramaribo or elsewhere in Suriname. They said they would like to see additional development in Lower Marowijne—more infrastructure, educational opportunities, rural electrification—so they can remain in their village.

The Kaliña and Lokono are critical of the government for its failure to take indigenous rights into account. They feel powerless in relation to a government that makes decisions without consulting them. Because the government does not recognize their land rights, a stranger can show up with a piece of paper and claim to be the legal owner of their land: "It can happen like this, and it has." They tell stories of walking through the forest and seeing a new logging operation on their land. If the loggers have a government permit, there is nothing they can do about it. And they say this will continue to happen until indigenous land rights are recognized.

The people of Wan Shi Sha village shared the following example of how they have been disenfranchised by the government's refusal to recognize their land rights. In the past, they traveled by canoe and caught fish in the Marowijne River. However, the government transferred land rights along the Marowijne River to wealthy outsiders from Paramaribo, who built vacation homes and posted "trespassing forbidden" signs. This prevented the people from Wan Shi Sha from leaving their canoes along the riverbank. They could still reach the Marowijne River by canoe via a creek that ran by their village. But when the government turned the creek into a concrete sluice canal, they were no longer able to paddle their canoes to the river. Today, the people from Wan Shi Sha have no access to the Marowijne River at all.

Another example of the problems caused by the state's refusal to recognize indigenous land rights is related to the environmental impact of the Wane Hills bauxite mine. When the Lower Marowijne Indigenous Land Rights Commission (CLIM) approached Suralco about their concerns, they were told to direct their comments to the government. When CLIM made their objections to the government via a number of formal complaints, they did not receive an answer from state officials, either. Not having legally recognized land rights meant no one responded to their concerns about the environmental impacts of the bauxite mine.

The people I spoke with attributed most of the problems they face to the government's refusal to recognize their territorial rights and respect their right to free, prior, and informed consent. The current proceedings before the Inter-American Commission on Human Rights are intended to help redress this concern. As the case *Saramaka People v. Suriname* (2008, 10) demonstrates, land rights are needed to "preserve, protect and guarantee the special relationship" that the Kaliña and Lokono have with their territories, so that "they may continue living their traditional way of life, and that their distinct cultural identity, social structure, economic system, customs, beliefs and traditions are respected, guaranteed and protected." The continued viability of these village communities, the cultural survival of the Kaliña and Lokono indigenous peoples, and the exercise and enjoyment of their right to freely pursue their own economic, social, and cultural development all depend on recognition of their resource, land, and territorial rights.

Freedom

When the noted economist Amartya Sen (1999, 38) redefined development in terms of freedom, he argued that political freedom is required along with security, opportunity, and transparency to realize economic development. Central to his perspective is the claim that the goal of development is to enhance human freedom, including a people's ability to shape its own destiny. Sen's work promotes the values and institutions of the liberal democratic state. But the historian Dipesh Chakrabarty (2000, 44–45) has argued against the identification of the modern state with freedom, as the state achieves its goals through projects of reform, progress, and development that may be coercive or violent. Also at risk in development projects are other understandings of freedom that may not be acknowledged or protected by liberal states (Povinelli 2002).

The notion of freedom is central to indigenous land rights in Suriname. The Kaliña and Lokono say they feel free only on their own land, where they can do as they please. One person told me: "We love this place. We want our own place where we can live." Without land rights, they emphasize, the land is not yours, and consequently you are not free. Without land rights, you have to seek permission from the government to make improvements or develop your land and resources. Without land rights, outsiders can gain title to your land. Without control over your land, you are unable to pursue opportunities for development (see Kambel 2002, 150–59).[14]

Other indigenous peoples I have interviewed in Suriname describe their ability to travel into the rain forest to hunt, fish, and gather forest products as a fundamental form of freedom (Kirsch 2009b). This is equally true for the indigenous peoples of the Lower Marowijne, one of whom told me: "Indigenous peoples love their freedom. . . . Indigenous peoples like to go hunting and fishing. We don't want someone to come and tell us we can't hunt." Today, however, they are "not free enough, [because] other people are coming into our territory." They felt that their territory is "becoming smaller because of other people" using their land. They also pointed out that they are a growing community and need enough land to continue living there alongside their children and grandchildren.

In addition, they recounted numerous examples of how their freedom was impinged upon. One man described the establishment of a nature reserve on their territory as a "loss of freedom." He explained, "Before we were free to go there, but now someone is imposing rules on us." Many people told stories about the "trespassing forbidden" signs along the Marowijne River, which they saw as an infringement on their fundamental freedom to move throughout their territory and make use of the resources found there. Their concerns about freedom were perhaps best summed up by the Lower Marowijne Indigenous Land Rights Commission: "We are losing control over the areas we occupy as the government creates nature reserves and issues licenses for logging and mining without consulting us and without our consent. As a result *we can no longer live freely in our own territories*" (CLIM 2006, 113, emphasis added). From the perspective of the indigenous peoples of the Lower Marowijne, their pursuit of collective land rights is at its most fundamental level the pursuit of freedom.

Conclusion (to the Affidavit)

In no sense did I find the Kaliña and Lokono to be antidevelopment, anticonservation, or antimining. Instead, what they want is collective control over their territories and resources, to be free in their own land, and to protect and preserve their culture and communities. They see themselves as part of the modern, developing world in which young men and women look forward to village life with improved infrastructure, including electricity, vocational training, and economic opportunities. But in contrast to many of their nonindigenous neighbors, they imagine a future on their own territories instead of migrating to the capital or other urban areas to seek their fortune.

They speak of their love of place and of the fundamental freedom to go hunting and fishing on their own territories, and how these practices are central to their identities as indigenous peoples. But only when the state recognizes indigenous land rights, including the right to free, prior, and informed consent in relation to development projects, will the Kaliña and Lokono be able to achieve these goals.

The state's conservation policies are also deeply flawed because they do not respect indigenous peoples' rights to land, including ownership and use of the resources on that land. In the first case examined here, the nature reserve at Galibi has not been as effective at protecting sea turtle populations as it could be, because it focuses exclusively on land-based threats to turtle populations and ignores evidence that the nets used by fishing boats on the coast and in the Marowijne estuary are hazardous to sea turtles. The state treats indigenous peoples as the primary threat to the resource instead of recognizing that they make a positive contribution to the protection of the ecosystems in which the turtles lay their eggs.

Another example of the state's failed conservation strategy is the Wane Kreek Nature Reserve, which is affected by mining for bauxite, kaolin, sand, and gravel, as well as legal and illegal logging. The decision by BHP Billiton and Suralco not to conduct an environmental impact assessment for the Wane Hills bauxite mine in the 1990s resulted in a project with substantial environmental impacts and concomitant social impacts for the indigenous communities that previously used this area to hunt, fish, and camp. Without state recognition of their land rights, the indigenous peoples of Suriname have no legal recourse or influence over BHP Billiton and Suralco regarding the need for higher standards in the cleanup and rehabilitation of the Wane Hill mine site.

Forest and wildlife protection as historically practiced by the indigenous peoples of the Lower Marowijne offers a valuable starting point for rethinking resource use and conservation in the area. In recent years, the communities have begun to document these unwritten rules and laws (CLIM 2006). These practices should ideally be coupled with new government policies and laws. All of the logging permits in the nature reserve and throughout all indigenous territories should be reviewed, and a crackdown on illegal logging throughout the region is urgently needed. Effort should be made to close the roads entering the Wane Kreek Nature Reserve and limit other forms of resource extraction.

At a more fundamental level, environmental degradation has had a detrimental impact on indigenous practices, forcing more indigenous people into wage labor and the cash economy. It also imposes significant limits on alternative-livelihood strategies. As people spend less time in the forests, they may lose important traditional knowledge. For the Lokono, this is compounded by widespread language loss. These problems should be seen not as natural or inevitable but as the direct consequence of the state's steadfast refusal to recognize indigenous land rights and protect indigenous resources.

This report has two major findings and recommendations. First, the state's refusal to recognize indigenous land and territorial rights has had deleterious consequences for the Kaliña and Lokono indigenous peoples and threatens their cultural survival. Consequently, the report calls for state recognition of indigenous land rights. To implement this policy change, the Kaliña and Lokono require resources to demarcate their collective territories. Second, the state's conservation policies are not only flawed but also prejudicial toward indigenous peoples. Consequently, the report recommends that the state should return control over the nature reserves discussed here to their indigenous owners and establish mutually agreed-upon mechanisms for their comanagement. It should cease using nature reserves as a form of accumulation through dispossession (Harvey 2003), in which indigenous lands and resources are expropriated by the state and converted into private business ventures in the form of logging and mining concessions. The African Commission (2010) recently made a similar determination with respect to the rights of the Endorois of Kenya, whose land and territories were wrongly expropriated by the state in the establishment of a nature reserve.

HEARINGS IN SAN JOSE, COSTA RICA

In February 2015, I attended the hearings of the Inter-American Court on the Kaliña and Lokono case in San Jose, Costa Rica. Captains Ricardo Pané and Jona Gunther testified about the state's refusal to recognize indigenous land rights. Captain Pané explained to the court: "We are here to continue our struggle in a just way, to have legal recognition of our land rights." In response to a question from the state, he answered that they had experienced physical and emotional suffering that amounted to trauma. When Judge Vio Grossi asked him: "Do you feel like a Surinamese national?" Captain Pané responded, "I do not feel like that as long as my rights have not been recognized." When the judge asked him: "Do you feel like a citizen?" Captain Pané replied, "No."

Jérémie Gilbert, a professor of law at the University of East London and an expert on indigenous rights, testified that indigenous land rights are fully compatible with the objectives of conservation (see Colchester 2004). Best practice in circumstances in which indigenous peoples have been displaced by nature reserves, he observed, involves restitution of their land and subsequent negotiation of comanagement plans for protecting threatened environments and endangered species (see African Commission 2010).[15] The UN special rapporteur on the rights of indigenous peoples, Victoria Tauli-Corpuz, also provided testimony on the contributions of indigenous peoples to biodiversity conservation.[16] In his final summation, the lawyer for the complainants, Fergus MacKay, argued that the state's failure to recognize the "legal personality" of indigenous peoples, or to establish a legal framework for granting land title to indigenous peoples, violated their human rights and contravened the obligations of the state under various treaties and international agreements.

The state's response to these allegations was that it was not ready to implement new laws recognizing indigenous rights, as this might exacerbate political tensions between ethnic groups in Suriname. During a break in the proceedings, one of the lawyers for the state told me that he expected to lose the case but was hoping they could "buy more time" for the state to address these issues. The judges on the Inter-American Court, however, expressed frustration with Suriname's failure to implement its decision in the Saramaka case eight years earlier, in which it instructed the state to formally recognize the land rights of the Saramaka Maroons (Saramaka People v. Suriname 2007, 2008).[17] The court carried out a site visit to Suriname in August 2015 before issuing its ruling.

JUDGMENT

On November 25, 2015, the Inter-American Court of Human Rights ruled that Suriname's refusal to recognize the legal personality and territorial rights of the Kaliña and Lokono peoples, including their rights to collective property, political rights, and judicial protection, violated the American Convention of Human Rights (Kaliña and Lokono Peoples v. Suriname 2015; Forest Peoples Programme 2016). The court directed the state to grant the Kaliña and Lokono collective title to their traditional territories along with the resources necessary for their demarcation. This includes restitution of lands improperly granted to nonindigenous parties. The court also instructed the state to undertake the steps necessary to ensure that the Kaliña and Lokono have access to and use of their lands within the Galibi Nature Reserve and the Wane Kreek Nature Reserve, as well as participate in the management of those lands, and to ensure that activities within these areas do not negatively affect them. The court also found active violations of their rights in relation to bauxite mining carried out by the subsidiaries of Alcoa and BHP Billiton without the participation of the Kaliña and Lokono, and which occurred on land that was both an indigenous territory and a nature reserve. Consequently, the court instructed the state to rehabilitate the mine-affected areas within the Wane Kreek Nature Reserve (Kaliña and Lokono Peoples v. Suriname 2015; Forest Peoples Programme 2016).

The judge also sought to ensure nonrepetition of these events by ruling that these decisions apply to all indigenous and tribal peoples throughout Suriname and not only to the people of the Lower Marowijne (Kaliña and Lokono Peoples v. Suriname 2015; MacKay 2016). More broadly, it recognizes the compatibility of indigenous rights and biodiversity conservation. This means that indigenous peoples should have access to and use of traditional territories that are part of nature reserves. These rights should be protected by agreements to collaboratively manage such areas, including the integration of "indigenous peoples' knowledge, institutions, practices, strategies and management plans related to conservation" (cited in MacKay 2016). The judgment affirms the claims and requests of the complainants, and the arguments put forward in my affidavit, in almost every instance. But given the state's failure to implement the Inter-American Court's decision in *Saramaka People v. Suriname* (2007, 2008), it remains to be seen how robustly the new judgment will be implemented.

AFFIDAVIT II: INDIGENOUS LAND RIGHTS IN GUYANA

In August 2007, the State of Guyana issued title to approximately 260 square miles of land in the Middle Mazaruni River region to the Akawaio people living in the village of Isseneru. The decision followed the community's unsuccessful requests for title to their lands in 1987 and 1994, both of which the state ignored. Concerned about the intrusion of gold miners operating dredges on the Mazaruni River, Isseneru made another formal request for

MAP 8. Middle and Upper Mazaruni River, including Isseneru village, Guyana.

land title in 2003. After Guyana passed the Amerindian Act of 2006, the minister of Amerindian affairs invited the Akawaio to apply for title to their land. As I describe below, the minister arbitrarily reduced the size of their land title to one-quarter of the original request. Moreover, the title excludes a large number of areas that had previously been allotted to mining permits. When the people of Isseneru sought to appeal the minister's decision, their efforts were ignored. After years of frustration, and with no other hope of domestic redress, the people of Isseneru filed a petition and an application for precautionary measures at the Inter-American Commission on Human Rights.

In June 2014, I was invited by the counsel for the petitioners in Petition 1424-13, *Akawaio Indigenous Community of Isseneru,* to conduct research in Guyana for an expert report concerning the territorial rights and the situation of the indigenous community of Isseneru on the Middle Mazaruni River. Their petition to the Inter-American Commission on Human Rights alleges that the State of Guyana has "violated Isseneru's right to property in relation to its failure to adequately delimit, demarcate and title its traditionally owned land and its active violation of those rights through the issuance of numerous mining concessions on those lands, all of which threaten its survival as an indigenous community." In November 2014, I conducted the research for this report.

History of the Akawaio People at Isseneru

The Akawaio are an indigenous people living on the Lower, Middle, and Upper Mazaruni River and elsewhere in Guyana; other Akawaio speakers live across the border in Venezuela and Brazil (Butt Colson 2009; Carrico 2007). They are one of nine indigenous peoples in Guyana. In the Akawaio language, they refer to themselves as Kapong, which means "Sky people." The Akawaio people living in the Middle and Upper Mazaruni River regions are united by their shared history and culture, by intermarriage, and by their communal land tenure system. They have their own religion, known as Alleluia, which combines Christianity with traditional religious beliefs and practices (Staats 1996), although they are also members of several other churches. Their oral histories indicate that they have lived along the Mazaruni River since time immemorial.[18] Interaction between the communities living in the middle and upper portions of the river has been continuous throughout this period, both to take advantage of different resources in the two regions (such as the larger fish found in the Middle Mazaruni River, including the *aimara*), and for the purpose of intermarriage, which remains common today.

In the communal land tenure system of the Akawaio, land is owned by the community as a whole.[19] If a man or woman wants to clear a plot of land for agriculture, he or she is free to do so as long as it is not already in use. If there is an existing farm nearby, they first ask the people working there whether they have plans to use the land. The Akawaio are free to hunt and fish anywhere on their communal lands. They can build houses anywhere on their territory. If they wish to cut down a tree in the forest, they are free to do so and may mark the tree in advance so that no one else will use it. If a stranger wants to use their land and resources, they must ask permission from the community to do so.

FIGURE 8. Akawaio cassava farm near Isseneru village, Guyana. 2014. Photo: Stuart Kirsch.

When it is time to clear a new garden in the forest for cassava, which provides their staple food and beverage, married couples work together: the man cuts down the tall trees while his wife clears the underbrush. A communal work party from the village is then assembled to finish preparing the land for planting: chopping up felled trees and stacking the wood along with the branches and other plants to be burned. The resulting ash fertilizes the soil. The owners of the new farm feed the workers with cassava bread and fish and provide cassiri (cassava beer) to drink before and during their labor. They also begin plowing the soil by hand and planting cassava stems. After work in one family's plot is complete, the work party moves to the next one. This process continues over a period of several weeks until all of the new gardens for the village have been planted. Cassava is planted twice yearly—in October or November, and again in March or April—and takes six months to mature.

The collective labor of the Akawaio is an expression of their communal system of land tenure. As one man told me while we were clearing brush from a cassava plot: "When I work by myself, I feel selfish. But when I work with others, I feel like I am doing something worthwhile." His assertion that the highest value of labor is achieved through collective undertakings differs from understandings in capitalist societies about the creation of private property through the application of individual labor to nature (Locke [1689] 1947). Among the Akawaio, labor is valued most for its contribution to society, rather than as a means for individual accumulation or consumption. Their practices of communal labor continue as strongly today as in the past (Griffiths 2003, 26). They can be contrasted the individualism of wage labor that dominates urban life in Guyana.

Land is very important to the Akawaio people: they describe the forest as their grocery store, their doctor's office, and their university. They teach their children to how to catch fish from the river and creeks that run through their territory, which plants to eat or use for medicinal purposes, how to plant and take care of their cassava gardens, and today, how to mine for gold. In addition to cassava, they grow potatoes, bananas, sugarcane, and greens, as well as other crops. "Their traditional land base and its natural resources are essential for making a living and maintaining their individual, family, and collective well-being, and their sense of a distinct cultural identity" (Griffiths 2003, 35). The Akawaio regard detailed knowledge of their territory, in both its practical and its spiritual dimensions, as attributes of ownership and demonstrations of their land claims (Griffiths 2003, 21). This includes their knowledge of place names, or toponyms (Griffiths 2003, 21; see also Bulkan 2008, 440).

To continue to live as Akawaio, they require land. Consequently they need to have their land rights fully recognized by the government of Guyana. They do not want to live anywhere else; they want to continue living on the land of their grandparents and ancestors. They also need secure land tenure to prevent outsiders, including miners, from using their land.

The people from the Middle Mazaruni River were living not far from the contemporary village of Isseneru, and close to their current cassava gardens, in the 1950s when gold and diamond miners from the coastal area of Guyana and Brazil began to operate large river dredges on their land. To avoid potential conflicts with the miners, about half of the community relocated to the Upper Mazaruni to live with their relatives. They were encouraged to do so by the British colonial administration, which established schools and a health clinic near Kamarang (Griffiths 2003, 15). Other members of the community continued to reside in the Middle Mazaruni.

In the early 1970s, however, the state proposed building a dam and a large hydroelectric power plant on the Upper Mazaruni River (Colchester 2005).[20] Flooding from the dam would have forced the Akawaio to relocate.[21] Consequently, the Akawaio who previously moved to the Upper Mazaruni decided to return to their land in the Middle Mazaruni, where they established the current village of Isseneru. But as the people living in Isseneru made clear in multiple interviews, they were not moving to unknown or unclaimed land; this was where their parents, grandparents, and ancestors previously had resided.[22] This was not a place that was unfamiliar to them; the older people remembered the place names and the old village sites, the location of earlier gardens, and where all the resources they needed could be found.

It is important to note that both migrations occurred in direct response to the policies of the colonial administration and postcolonial state, initially to avoid the influx of miners from the coast and Brazil, and subsequently to avoid flooding from the proposed dam on the Upper Mazaruni River, which would have left them with nowhere to live. The years they resided in the Upper Mazaruni did not extinguish their land rights in the Middle Mazaruni, and the people who remained behind continued to live in these areas and maintain their land rights as well.

Isseneru Responses to Claims by the State

In response to the state's claim that Isseneru was "not a traditional Akawaio community" (Government of Guyana 2013, 22), the people living in the village acknowledged that there have been changes: "Today, yes, [the village] is changing." One person commented, "In the early days, we did not live in fancy houses, like you see today. [But] I had a rich childhood." Another observed, "There are churches, permanent buildings, and we have established a permanent village." One person explained, "Before, . . . we lived in different houses [made from forest timber with thatched roofs], but we were told that they had a negative connotation." The *toshao,* or elected village head, asked rhetorically: "Have we done something wrong to build these [new] houses?" They blamed the government for some of these changes: "For the government to claim we are not Akawaios, when they introduced the schools, which do not teach our history or language" is hypocritical. Others acknowledged, "Sometimes, we are embarrassed that our children don't speak our language" and "We know that we are losing our culture by only teaching them English. With development comes a lot of changes."

In contrast, others asserted, "We are not forgetting our traditions." One man said, "We live here as Kapong." Several people pointed out: "We still make cassava" and "drink cassiri." Another said, "We farm, we hunt, and we fish," like their grandparents and ancestors. However, one man acknowledged: "It is a challenge to keep our stories and histories; I'm afraid it will be lost."

Regarding development, one man nostalgically described his childhood: "We learned how to fish. We had dugout canoes and bark canoes. We lived a good life." He concluded by pointing out: "We ate organic all the time," which prompted laughter. Another explained why people in Akawaio became involved in mining: "Because we want to be independent as a people, we want to grow our own food, and we are growing our own food. But there is also a need for money. After searching for alternatives, we turned to mining for our own development. But what we find is that the government is coming in with their laws and making it difficult for us. Now the government is upset that we are doing mining. The plan was to be self-sufficient. So our people have gone into mining."

Several other people, too, explained the decision to mine for gold. One said, "With this many people in the village, we have to mine." Another noted, "We are planning our own development and have to plan it ourselves. The government didn't tell us how to do it, but we are doing it ourselves." Another said, "When it comes to mining, many outsiders are mining on our land. It came to the point that we decided to use these resources for ourselves."

They acknowledged that there was ethnic diversity in the village, including intermarriage with Arawaks, Wapichans, and Patamonas, but denied its significance: "It is true that we Akawaio . . . are mixed with other tribes, but we are Akawaio." Such intermarriage is common among Amerindian communities in Guyana (see Griffiths 2003, 20). "This is the land our ancestors made," even though "we are mixed today." Another added, "People who we knew followed us here." One speaker challenged the state's claim about their identities: "We are the true Akawaios and this is true wherever we go. We have our own indigenous religion, Alleluia, which was handed down from our parents. We don't want it to die away. We are connected to the other Akawaio in Guyana, two villages in Lower Mazaruni, and also connected to the Upper Maz [Mazaruni River]." She also pointed out: "The place-names here are in our language. For instance, what is called Apikwa [a Brazilian mining outpost] is really Abak Ekwa [in Akawaio language]. [The place-name] Haimara Ekwa comes from the aimara fish in the creek."[23] Such toponyms confirm the antiquity of their land claims.

They also criticized the state: "The government is intent on telling us how to live. They tell us that these are not our lands. All those lands [given to the miners] belong to Isseneru." "We want to say to the government: 'Leave us alone, this is our land. We will not go anywhere, we live here.'" They conveyed their reluctance to challenge the state through their complaint to the Inter-American Commission: "We are upset that we have to send a petition." However, they acknowledged, "we are fed up with the government. The government has not responded. So we are supporting what [the lawyers] are doing with our case. There is nowhere [else] we can go for satisfaction; that is a reality. The government is not respecting international standards [for indigenous land rights]. We are raising concerns about the land situation: We own everything here. The government gave [land title to the Akawaio] with one hand and undermines the title with another." They vowed, "We will fight for justice. We are a threat to the government because we are becoming self-sufficient. If the Amerindian Act can't represent us, we have to represent ourselves. We are not afraid of the government." "All we want is our land and rights to be recognized."

Finally, they observed, "The state claims that the Amerindian Act reflects international standards—but it doesn't reflect the living conditions of Amerindian people." They also asserted that their petition to the Inter-American Commission represents not only the interests of the Akawaio people but also the "entire Amerindian brotherhood. [Other Amerindian peoples in Guyana] are facing the same problems with land title. We are [just] the first village to fight."

Mining in the Middle Mazaruni River

Gold and diamond mining in the Middle Mazaruni began in 1904 or 1905, in an area adjacent to where the people from Isseneru currently mine and have their cassava farms. The miners used hand tools and drills and sent divers underwater to scour the gravel banks for minerals and gems. In the 1950s, people from the coast and Brazil began mining with large dredges along the banks of the Middle Mazaruni River.

Since the 1990s, the people from Isseneru have operated their own small-scale, or artisanal, mines near their cassava farms. They do not see a contradiction between mining and farming, as both involve "making use of [their] resources for the benefit of the community," although they acknowledge that the two activities may compete for the same land. To initiate a mining project, villagers apply to the village council for a concession. Work crews combine people from the village and laborers from the coast, all of whom stay at the mining camp throughout the process. They speak a mixture of Akawaio

FIGURE 9. Hydraulic mining by Akawaio near Isseneru village, Guyana. 2014. Photo: Stuart Kirsch.

and English in the camps. Some of the outsiders who came to work in the mining camps later settled in the village and married women from the community.

They begin each project beside a creek, using diesel pumps and pressure hoses to expose the gold-bearing gravel, a process known as hydraulic, or jet, mining. They follow deposits of gravel that contain gold. They explained that the first pit might produce an ounce or two of gold and subsequent pits might contain as much as ten or even twenty ounces of gold, but eventually the yield comes down to a pennyweight or two of gold, at which point they stop mining. They work for periods of five or six days to two weeks at a time, progressively moving from square to square and backfilling the excavated pits as they advance. The ore-bearing gravel is pumped through a shaker box, or sluice, which uses gravity and water to isolate the heavier minerals.

After the mining is finished, the crew opens the shaker box. Everyone witnesses the opening of the box, as crew members are paid a percentage of the final take. This step is crucial, since mutual verification is what maintains trust among the members of the ethnically mixed workforce.[24] Mercury is then used to separate the gold via amalgamation, after which the crew monitors the weighing of the final product. The government requires artisanal miners to use a retort to capture most of the mercury vapor released when the amalgam is heated, as well as other safety equipment. The miners from Isseneru assert that they are careful to follow the rules established by the state to protect their health and the environment when mining gold.

Local rangers also witness the opening of the shaker box and the weighing of the gold, taking a portion for state taxes. Twelve percent of the gold from indigenous mining projects is given to the village, the same percentage paid by outsiders granted concessions within their titled lands. If the amount of gold is substantial, they may travel to the capital city, Georgetown, to sell it to the government gold board; for smaller amounts, they sell to licensed gold buyers, who do not normally pay the full price. Before selling their gold, they check the international price on the Internet. Gold buyers test their finds with chemicals, and it is usually about 90 percent pure. When traveling to Georgetown by air, miners are required to show their production book and worksheet at the airport, which prevents them from selling their gold on the black market.

The people from Isseneru reject the state's criticism of their participation in gold mining, as they use the revenue to enhance development in their community, which, they point out, the state promotes everywhere else in Guyana. Their 12 percent share of gold mined on their land allows the village to support the elderly, families with young children, and children attending school. They also use these funds to pay for public works that benefit the entire village, including the building where we held our meetings and the guesthouse where I stayed.

There have been concerns about mercury levels in the Middle Mazaruni since the 1980s, before the people from Isseneru began mining. Some of the mercury may have originated from mining projects in the Upper Mazaruni, which have been in operation since the mid-1880s (Hennessy 2014, 11). Given their exposure to mercury, they have been advised not to consume too much fish, although they lack an alternative source of protein in their diets. They were also told to avoid carnivorous fish, which have higher levels of mercury, but very few of them follow this advice. Some people say that they have tried to "ease up a bit" on fish consumption because of health concerns. Pregnant women in particular have been discouraged from eating too much fish, although one woman asked me: "What's the alternative?"

The people in Isseneru told me that they would welcome ways to reduce or eliminate the use of mercury in gold mining. However, the primary option would require them to process their gold using expensive equipment based at a central location. When asked about this option, they expressed reluctance to transport the unprocessed gold elsewhere for two reasons. First, they were not sure whether they could trust the operators of the equipment to give them full credit for the gold they produced. Second, the current labor system relies on the ability of the entire crew to observe the opening of the sluice box and the amalgamation of the ore, and this oversight ensures the fairness of the process. Thus finding an alternative to mercury use would require not only a technical solution but also a social one.

The people from Isseneru report that there is not much difference between villagers' and outsiders' mining methods, although while the villagers make sure to backfill their mining pits, some of the outsiders do not.[25] In general, the practices in the Isseneru area are described as better than farther down the Mazaruni River, where "it is easy to see mass destruction." Indeed, these sites are readily visible from the air when flying from Georgetown to Olive Creek in the Middle Mazaruni. The people from Isseneru do not know whether outsiders comply with state rules regarding mercury use, including the use of retorts to reduce mercury emissions during the amalgamation process.

The village has issued twenty-five permits for mining within its titled land, although only about seven of them were active during my visit. The toshao expressed concern that continuing to mine on a regular basis might have detrimental consequences for their health. He also noted that the gold deposits will not last forever, so the community plans to develop alternative sources of revenue.

The Isseneru Land Title

Before submitting their petition for land title to the minister of Amerindian affairs, the toshao and village council prepared a map of their traditional territory following the natural boundaries of the mountains, rivers, and streams. These boundaries were drawn to include the full range of resources needed to maintain the community and its way of life. Their crops do not grow in the mountains where the soil is rocky. Nor do they grow on swampy ground. Only some of their land is suitable for growing cassava; and because of their practice of shifting cultivation, they need to move to new fields after two or three consecutive harvests. This is an ecologically sustainable way to farm in tropical ecosystems, as the long fallow period after use allows the forest and soil to regenerate, and burning the new growth adds nutrients to the soil. Other resources are available only in certain parts of their territory, such as purple heart trees (*Peltogyne* sp.), the bark of which was traditionally used to make canoes, and which grow only south of the village. *Mucru* plants used to make the long, narrow cassava sieves for processing bitter manioc grow only at higher altitudes to the north. The jasper or flint used to make cassava graters is available only in the mountains. Large fish like the aimara can be caught only downstream from the village. The village council took care to include access to these important resources when formulating its original request for land title; however, many of these essential resources were eventually excluded from the title granted by the state. Given the restricted size of the land title allotted by the state, the toshao from Isseneru is also concerned about whether they will have enough land suitable for growing cassava in the future.

In contrast to capitalist economies, where people meet their needs by selling their labor in order to purchase commodities produced by others, the Akawaio require access to different types of land to acquire the different resources they need. Consequently, the people living in Georgetown and other coastal areas of Guyana do not necessarily understand the needs of the Akawaio and other Amerindian peoples. As a senior lawyer from Georgetown explained to me, people living in urban areas tend to view their claims as a "massive land grab" (Nigel Hughes, pers. comm., 2014). These views are also shaped by the relatively high levels of poverty in the country as well as the legacy of its socialist tradition, which has difficulty accommodating special rights for indigenous peoples (Hennessy 2014).

When the people from Isseneru presented their land claim to the state, the minister of Amerindian affairs informed them they had asked for too much land: "More than the land mass of Barbados," which is 166 square miles. She told them to reduce the size of their request and sent them back to the village to redraw their map. Their need for a formal land title was urgent because of the intrusion of mining dredges on their territory, so the people of Isseneru submitted a smaller claim. The state calculated the size of their initial claim as 1,000 square miles. When Isseneru submitted the revised claim, the minister told them that she "already knew" that their request would not be approved by parliament, so she reduced the size of the requested territory yet again, leaving a land mass of 260 square miles. She made this decision without conducting a lands investigation, which is a statutory requirement under the Amerindian Act of 2006. She told the Akawaio it was the largest land title for any indigenous people in Guyana, although this is not true: the Wai Wai have title to 2,300 square miles for a population comparable in size to that of Isseneru, and there are other indigenous peoples in Guyana with more land per capita than that of the people of Isseneru. The people living in Isseneru assert that the state "give[s] us what they feel like giving." They concluded that the state "refused what was rightly ours and we had to accept it."

The minister also failed to inform the delegation from Isseneru that a number of large blocks within the titled area had previously been allotted to mining concessions. When they received their land title, they expected the state to force the miners to relinquish their claims, but this did not occur. The mining claims were protected by a clause in the title deed that allotted land to indigenous communities "save and except" those lands included in concessions previously granted to miners. As their petition to the Inter-American Commission on Human Rights argues, this contravenes international principles, which recognize that indigenous land rights preexist the state. The Akawaio should not be deprived of their property as a result of the state's long delay in recognizing their land rights. Title to their land should have been granted by the state without restrictions or encumbrances. The mining claims may predate the official land title, but Akawaio land rights preexist the mining claims by centuries. This is why several people from Isseneru told me that the "Amerindian Act betrays us."

What this means in practice is that the people from Isseneru lack the ability to prevent others from using their land. Miners from Georgetown and Brazil operate river dredges and uproot their forests in order to mine using pressure hoses. They do not follow government regulations that require them to maintain a buffer zone around the titled lands, and they violate government regulations that restrict dredging along river banks. They regularly mine inside the titled area. Some of the miners do not request permission from the toshao to mine on titled land, and some do not pay the 12 percent fee requested by the Isseneru village council for mining on their land. They ignore these obligations with impunity.

When efforts by the Isseneru council to amicably resolve these disputes were unsuccessful, they tried to stop the miners from entering their land. The miners sued them for access and were successful. When the people of Isseneru turned to the courts for protection against unauthorized mining on their titled land, their claim languished in court. This continues to be the case, and there is no mechanism available to the people of Isseneru to stop outsiders

FIGURE 10. Dredge mining near Isseneru village, Guyana. 2016. Photo: Oda Almås / Forest Peoples Programme.

from mining on their titled land. The people of Isseneru have shown patience and resolve in fighting for the integrity of their titled lands, but their faith in the judiciary system of Guyana has not been rewarded. Consequently, they have been forced to turn to the Inter-American Commission on Human Rights to seek protection of their rights.

In response to their petition to the Inter-American Commission, the state has sought to punish and penalize the people of Isseneru. The state falsely claims that Isseneru is "not a traditional Akawaio community," given its mixed residence and the fact that people from the village mine for gold and collect fees from outsiders mining on their land.[26] The implication is that such activities are incompatible with their status as indigenous people, and more importantly, that these practices invalidate their land rights. Neither conclusion is warranted. The state also asserts that the people living in Isseneru are not the traditional landowners of the Middle Mazaruni, which is contradicted by the history presented here. In addition, the state has harassed mining crews from Isseneru, revoking their mining permits even though their operations have been found to be in compliance with the relevant regulations. In contrast, the state defends the rights of outside miners under the "save and except" clause in Isseneru's title deed and at the expense of the people from Isseneru.

Mercury, Fish Consumption, and Secure Land Title

One of the most significant environmental impacts in the Middle Mazaruni results from the use of mercury in artisanal gold mining. Mercury is a potent toxin that poses special risks to pregnant women and young children. Documents produced by the state already recommend that the Akawaio and other people living in the Middle Mazaruni restrict their dietary intake of fish (Government of Guyana 2014). However, fish are the primary source of protein in Akawaio diets, and it is unlikely that these warnings will be heeded in full.

At present, the people of Isseneru have limited influence on the level of mercury use in the Middle Mazaruni. The "save and except" clause in their title deed not only interferes with the ability of the Akawaio to control their territory but also encourages all of the actors in the region to treat the Middle Mazaruni as a de facto open access zone. Research on common property has shown that participants in open access systems lack sufficient incentive to conserve resources or protect the environment (Feeny et al. 1990; Ostrom 1990), which can result in a "tragedy of the commons" (Hardin 1968). In contrast, individual or collective property rights that include the power to exclude other users are more likely to result in behavior that reduces negative environmental impacts. As long as outsiders continue to have open access to their land, the Akawaio are unable to limit the harmful effects of gold mining and mercury use. This provides them with little or no incentive to restrict their own mining activities despite concerns about the impact of mercury on their environment and health. The state has given no indication that it will reduce access to the area in the future and continues to grant new mining concessions despite its awareness of the problems caused by the release of mercury into the environment.[27] In the absence of new measures by the state, recognition of indigenous land rights may be the only way to achieve better management of mercury use, even if it does not completely eliminate the problem. Legal protection for indigenous land rights may help control mercury use in the Middle Mazaruni and reduce its potentially catastrophic effects on humans and the environment.

Conclusion (to the Affidavit)

In 2006, the government of Guyana amended existing legislation to establish procedures setting out how indigenous peoples could request land title.

However, the state controls the implementation of these laws and does so without reference to indigenous peoples' rights, and in a discriminatory fashion. This is achieved in part by making assertions about who is indigenous and who is not. Such determinations seem to rest on the degree to which they have allegedly assimilated into mainstream society, including references to intermarriage, church affiliation, language use, and participation in the national economy, including mining for gold. In contrast, the people of Isseneru argue that none of these changes affect their identity as Akawaio or invalidate their land rights. There are also fundamental differences in how the state and the Akawaio view the rights to land: In contrast to the emphasis on private property in common and civil law systems, Akawaio land is collectively owned. This is reflected in their collective management of use rights as well as their communal labor. The people of Isseneru also require access to different resources distributed across the Middle Mazaruni. When they asked the state to recognize their claim to a territory large enough to include all of the resources essential to their cultural and physical survival, people living in Georgetown viewed their request, ironically, as part of a "massive land grab" by the some of the poorest members of society. Indigenous participation in the mining industry is also seen to compete with the economic interests of people living in coastal areas (Hilson and Laing 2017a), which results in their assertion that 10 percent of the country's population claims more than its share of the nation's land and resources.

The mistakes made by the state can be rectified only by reevaluating Isseneru's land claim, whether on the basis of their initial request or a government sponsored lands investigation, as required under the Amerindian Act of 2006. Accommodating their needs as an indigenous people requires expansion of their existing land title. It also requires invalidation of permits improperly granted to miners working within the boundaries of Isseneru's current land claim, perhaps by compensating permit holders for their losses or by providing them with licenses to mine elsewhere in the country. Such changes may have the additional salutary effect of better management and reduced use of mercury in the Middle Mazaruni.

CONCLUSION

As noted earlier, both affidavits needed to be legible not only to lawyers and the legal system but also to the communities involved and to the discipline of anthropology (Paine 1996, 63). In the first instance, this required the use of concepts like "cultural survival," which is recognized as a fundamental right deserving of protection by the Inter-American Court, even though anthropologists rarely make reference to the concept except in the context of advocacy.[28] An example of meeting the second criterion is my reference to the Akawaio claim to have occupied their territory since "time immemorial," which is a perfectly legitimate way to refer to the distant past, before archaeological or historical evidence, although not a concept ordinarily employed by anthropologists. With regard to the third criterion, these affidavits are not necessarily the place to review anthropological debates on the subject at hand, such as the complicated relationship between conservation organizations and indigenous peoples, although it may be useful to draw selectively from these discussions.

To meet the expectations of all three audiences, I chose to emphasize a prominent theme that emerged in the course of conducting ethnographic research, much like the subject of "culture loss" in the Marshall Islands case (see chapter 5). Focusing on a topic of importance to community members, such as freedom or collective property rights, enhanced the legitimacy of the affidavit for them. By developing a narrative that was greater than a summary of the facts, I also sought to make the affidavits compelling and persuasive, which anthropologists routinely strive for in ethnographic writing. In addition, I hoped the internal coherence of the argument would help ensure that even if a particular detail were questioned or challenged, it would not significantly affect the overall evaluation of the affidavit. The focus on a specific theme also had the advantage of making the project relevant to larger anthropological debates.

For the affidavit on land rights in Suriname, the people's discourse on freedom was an obvious choice. The significance of this issue was independently confirmed by the Surinamese legal scholar Ellen-Rose Kambel (2002, 144–50), who identifies three discourses used by Amerindians in Suriname to challenge the state's refusal to recognize indigenous rights: (1) the argument that land cannot be owned, which appears to be an older discourse now on the wane, given its incompatibility with contemporary political objectives, (2) the reference to historical precedent, that they were the original inhabitants and therefore have the right to exclude others, and (3) the importance of land rights for preserving their freedom. She notes that only the first two rationales for indigenous land rights have thus far been taken up in national debates (Kambel 2002, 154).

In addition to their references to the freedom to hunt and fish in the rain forest, and the need for land rights to secure their freedom, the Kaliña and Lokono also mentioned their freedom to be indigenous, to possess their own culture and way of life. Kambel (2002) explains that the Kaliña and Lokono are familiar with the provisions of the UN Declaration on the Rights of Indigenous Peoples, including the "collective right to live in freedom, peace, and security as distinct peoples" and the freedom to express "indigenous cultural diversity" without prejudice. In this sense, the freedom to be indigenous implies the right to determine and reproduce important cultural knowledge and values.

The concept of freedom has political resonance across Suriname, a Dutch colony from 1667 to 1975. The majority of the people living in Suriname are descendants of slaves or indentured laborers. Creoles make up 16 percent of the population but are the strongest political faction. Maroons, the descendants of escaped slaves who settled in the rain forest, constitute 22 percent of the population. The largest group of people in the country is composed of Hindi-speaking Indians brought to Suriname as indentured laborers after the abolition of slavery, who comprise 27 percent of the population. Another 14 percent of the population is made up of the descendants of indentured laborers from Java. About 20 percent identify as mixed or other. Given the historical significance of forced and coerced labor in Suriname, freedom is a powerful unifying discourse among its citizens, including the Amerindian communities, which comprise between 1.5 and 2 percent of the country's population.

In these examples, freedom is a multivalent concept that simultaneously references traditional ideas about persons and social relations; the freedom to hunt and fish in the rain forest; the UN Declaration on the Rights of Indigenous Peoples, which supports the freedom to be indigenous; and freedom in a recently independent country comprised largely of the descendants of former slaves and indentured laborers. Concerns about freedom are neither exclusively indigenous nor modern, and they are simultaneously a shared concern of the members of the state as well as the basis of claims to difference.

The central theme of the second affidavit, about the Akawaio people living in Isseneru village in Guyana, was the significance of their collective land rights as what distinguishes them from other parties seeking to mine for gold and diamonds in the Mazaruni River. My attention to this question was in part the fortuitous result of being present during the cassava-planting season to observe and participate in a collective labor party. The comment about these practices—"When I work by myself, I feel selfish. But when I work with others, I feel like I am doing something worthwhile"—and the way it differs from assertions about the creation of private property through the application of individual labor to nature, helped draw my attention to the importance of collective land rights.

My focus on land rights was also influenced by the contrast between the Amazon and Melanesia, where I have conducted the majority of my ethnographic research (Kirsch 2006). Since the publication of Bronislaw Malinowski's (1935, 280) pioneering study *Coral Gardens and Their Magic,* which he undertook in the Trobriand Islands, anthropologists have recognized that land tenure in Melanesia is "not the either-or" of collective ownership versus private property "but the relation of collective and personal claims." As I describe in chapter 1, land rights along the Ok Tedi and Fly Rivers in Papua New Guinea are held by individual members of a lineage, and no one has the authority to make decisions about another person's land. The difference between what was familiar to me from Melanesia and the emphasis on collective ownership among the Akawaio also heightened my attention to this issue.

Another key difference between the two culture areas is the Akawaio expectation that their territory should include all of the resources they need for their survival. In contrast, as I describe in chapter 3 about the Lakekamu River basin, people in Melanesia do not expect to have access to all of the resources they need on their own land. Instead, they value relationships formed through exchange, even to the point of having taboos against consuming the products of one's own labor, compelling the exchange of identical items (Malinowski 1935; Rubel and Rosman 1978). Interdependency through exchange relationships is as important to people in Melanesia as the autonomous collective emphasized by the Akawaio.

The communal ethos and practices of the Akawaio influenced my research methods as well. For similar projects, I have generally conducted interviews with individuals and small groups of people, such as village leaders, women, or young men. Focus groups like this worked especially well in Suriname, and my expectation was that this would also be the case in Guyana. But the people of Isseneru determined the format of our interactions. Instead of allowing me to explain my goals to several key individuals who could then help me arrange for interviews, the village council scheduled a general meeting of the entire community. I unexpectedly found myself explaining the purpose of my research to an audience of forty to fifty adults, who subsequently took turns standing up and sharing their views for the rest of the day. I had no choice but to accept the forum in which they chose to interact with me: in the presence of other community members rather than as individuals speaking to me in private, where others could not hear or challenge what they told me. It is not an exaggeration to say that from the moment I arrived in Isseneru, their collective orientation had already begun to influence what I would write about them.

I also elected not to discuss one potentially significant topic in my affidavit for the Guyana case. In our preliminary conversations, the lawyer for the case referred to a ritual system that connects the people living in the Middle and Upper Mazaruni. He suggested that these practices might have significance for their land claim, as the state denied that Isseneru was part of traditional Akawaio territory. However, my reading of the existing literature on the Akawaio suggested that their ritual system is no longer as significant as it was in the past, and that ethnographic information about these practices relied on the historical memories of elders rather than contemporary observations and experiences (Griffiths 2003). Nor did anyone in Isseneru mention the ritual system to me in response to my questions about religion or the ties between the communities in the Middle and Upper Mazaruni River. Although the protection of sacred sites and religious practices has been an important component of indigenous land claims in almost every part of the world, the intrusion of states and their legal systems into matters indigenous peoples prefer to keep private can result in unanticipated problems (Brown 2003; Niezen 2003; Povinelli 2002; Weiner 1999). All of these factors contributed to my decision not to discuss these ritual systems in my affidavit.

The short-term ethnography on which these affidavits were based posed several challenges. On the one hand, shared political goals may facilitate participation in research, yielding "information which might otherwise take years of patient effort and trust to gain" (Macdonald 2002, 101). On the other, even though anthropologists recognize that there is a gap between what people say and do, rapid appraisal must rely heavily on reported speech. During the course of long-term fieldwork, it is generally possible to make the appropriate corrections through direct observation or independent confirmation by other members of the community. In contrast, I was unable to document claims about encroachments on indigenous lands, for example, even though I heard similar reports from multiple parties. Nor did I have the opportunity to supplement oral histories with archival research, as I did in the Solomon Islands case. Directly reporting on what people told me accorded their comments approximately the same weight as established facts, even though the two are not always equivalent.

Another compromise of short-term research is the difficulty in establishing the kind of rapport with informants that ordinarily develops over the course of extended fieldwork. One indicator of the quality of my relationships with people in Suriname and Guyana was that all of our meetings were conducted in public spaces, as I was never invited into anyone's home. In some cases, we even forgot each other's names after several years elapsed between my visits to Suriname. Although there were opportunities to "hang out" (see Geertz 1998) at night in the town of Albina in Suriname, or drink Banks beer and dance to Brazilian techno-pop at high volume in a small mining outpost on the Mazaruni River, most of our time together was highly structured. Nonetheless, in both cases I sufficiently earned their trust, so that they consented to my request to continue writing about the situation beyond the affidavit, despite their criticism of anthropologists who have written about them in the past.

Writing affidavits in support of legal claims may also pose political dilemmas for anthropologists.[29] One concern is that the arguments in these affidavits could influence the response to future claims about indigenous rights. As Charles Hale (2006, 11) asks, "How does one formulate indigenous land claims and represent them in a language necessary to achieve legal recognition, without portraying them in terms that would reinforce internal rigidities or create criteria that other subaltern communities would be unable to meet?" It is possible, for example, that arguments about collective land rights could be applied as a litmus test for indigenous rights in Guyana or elsewhere, despite the diversity of indigenous property regimes and their flexibility in response to political and economic change. I nonetheless chose to focus on collective property rights because it was an issue that people from Isseneru felt defined and differentiated them from other groups in Guyana, in contrast to ritual knowledge they might have wanted to exclude from the public domain, or its diminishing significance, which might be used to discredit their land claim.

There is also a risk of political backlash when reproducing essentialized representations of indigenous attitudes toward the environment (Conklin 1997; Redford 1991). In the Suriname case, Captain Pané emphasized the contribution of traditional knowledge and practices to the protection of sea turtles in Galibi despite their previous participation in the commercial sale of turtle eggs. Similarly, Gilbert and Tauli-Corpuz attested to the compatibility of indigenous land rights and biodiversity conservation despite what anthropologists know about the diverse attitudes of indigenous peoples toward the environment and development (see chapter 3). The backlash against these stereotypes is evident in the Guyana case, where the Akawaio are criticized for their participation in artisanal gold mining, which has significant environmental impacts. Similarly, the assertion that Amerindians in Guyana seek to expand their land rights only where there are proven gold reserves (see Hilson and Laing 2017a, 180) cynically reduces the question of indigenous rights to a political strategy in a contest over access to mining concessions.[30] However, the people living in Isseneru sought to protect their land rights for a variety of reasons, including the importance of collective labor for social relations. They mined for gold, but they also needed land to plant cassava and obtain other important resources.

I also needed to reconcile my support for their land rights and my concerns about the mercury used in artisanal mining, which generates environmental hazards that pose significant risks to human health. When I was in Georgetown, I interviewed a fishery biologist at the University of Guyana whose first career assignment was to study the impact of the infamous cyanide spill at the Omai gold mine in 1995, which temporarily extinguished all organic life in the Omai River, a tributary of the Essequibo, the country's largest river. When I asked him whether he was more concerned about the impact of cyanide or mercury, both used in processing gold, his answer surprised me. He explained that cyanide breaks down in a relatively short period of time in the tropics, and consequently the rivers were replenished with fish and plants from adjacent waterways more quickly than anyone had anticipated.[31] In contrast, mercury accumulates within the food chain, and the process of methylation through which it becomes bioavailable readily occurs in the lowland rivers of Guyana, which frequently flood their banks, stranding shallow pools of water that facilitate these reactions. The fishery biologist was far more concerned about the long-term impacts of mercury use in artisanal gold mining despite having been an eyewitness to one of the worst cyanide spills in the history of industrial mining.

I initially assumed that I would have to suspend my personal judgment on the question of mercury pollution to compose an affidavit supporting Akawaio land rights. But in the process of talking with people in Isseneru about these issues, I learned that they shared my concerns about the impact of mercury on their environment, health, and well-being. I subsequently recognized that only by gaining control over their territory, including the ability to exclude other miners, will the Akawaio people living in Isseneru village be able to limit future environmental impacts from mercury.

Finally, it is reasonable to ask whether these affidavits qualify as "good enough" ethnography (Scheper-Hughes 1989, 28). Gaynor Macdonald (2002, 107) argues that instrumental research conducted in support of legal claims is incompatible with the disciplinary ideal of ethnographic texts that are open-ended and capable of supporting competing interpretations. However, engaged research projects are probably closer to the problem-oriented focus of most contemporary ethnography than either is to the kind of "thick description" (Geertz 1973) that previously dominated the discipline. Nonetheless, the ethnographic findings of these short-term projects cannot be separated from the circumstances in which they were produced. What I learned from interviews and group discussions was inevitably influenced by the framing of the legal proceedings. For example, my informants in Suriname and Guyana emphasized the negative consequences of their inability to exclude others from their land because that was the focus of their legal claims. Consequently, the ethnographic information in the two affidavits is not sufficiently robust that it can be presented on its own, independent of the context in which it was elicited (see Macdonald 2002). Nonetheless, the two cases offer valuable comparative insight into the way claims about indigenous land rights are formulated and contested, as well as into the forms of adjudication that address such claims, including how discourses like freedom or collective land rights are mobilized by actors in different national contexts.

Conclusion

ENGAGED ANTHROPOLOGY BUILDS ON ethnographic knowledge, not just on prior political commitments. This information can come from a site where the anthropologist has previously conducted ethnographic research, such as my participation in the campaign against the Ok Tedi mine. In other cases, the anthropologist may move laterally from one context to another, either elsewhere within the region as I did when studying a conservation and development project in Papua New Guinea, or by following a particular phenomenon across regions, as when I worked on mining and indigenous land rights in Suriname. All of the projects discussed in this book were based on prior ethnographic knowledge, albeit in different ways.

Engaged anthropology is open-ended and experimental. It involves taking risks. There is no guarantee an intervention will be successful. It requires moving beyond familiar contexts and working with new interlocutors. Participation in engaged research may lead anthropologists to become identified with the project, which can limit opportunities to investigate other topics or incur responsibility for the shortcomings of the intervention. Engaged projects have independent and unpredictable timelines, sometimes necessitating short-term interventions that increase reliance on reported speech, and other times lasting for years, frustrating compliance with the demands of tenure clocks and audit regimes for academic outputs and impacts. There is no playbook for engaged anthropology, which requires flexibility and innovation. These activities are unlikely to receive institutional recognition or rewards, and can result in criticism. However, avoiding bureaucratization prevents engaged anthropology from being routinized and preserves opportunities for unexpected outcomes and novel contributions to the field.

Engaged anthropology also creates new opportunities for participation. In addition to reading legal briefs and attending court hearings, this might include attendance during witness preparation, vetting confidential proposals for settling a dispute, or contributing to legal strategy. For example, the most important precedent established by the Ok Tedi case was set into motion during a taxi ride to the airport in Port Moresby. Lawyers representing the mining company had filed a motion seeking to throw the case out of court by invoking a nineteenth-century common law rule that prohibited the recovery of damages to property in another jurisdiction. My response to the dilemma was that the majority of the plaintiffs were not actually landowners but held use rights for subsistence purposes. The resulting intervention led the court to recognize the validity of subsistence rights when addressing losses caused by environmental damage (see Kirsch 2014, 94–97). Engaged anthropology may also result in invitations to new field sites where the barriers to entry would otherwise have proven insurmountable, enhancing comparative knowledge.

Engaged anthropologists gain access to their interlocutors through their contribution to these projects rather than by remaining neutral, which can limit opportunities for interaction. In my work, this included access not only to people living in rural areas but also to lawyers, corporate executives, government officials, NGO workers, experts on freshwater fish and tropical rain forests, and so forth. Consequently, this work has more in common with that of colleagues doing legal anthropology, studying corporations, or working in science and technology studies than might be expected, given its practical orientation, not to mention its relatively traditional focus on indigenous peoples.

Engaged anthropology may also require innovative methods, especially when accelerating ethnographic research in rapid appraisals and short-term assessments. Engaged anthropologists may also influence the context in which they work more than other ethnographers, as I described in relation to the summit meeting in Kiunga that I helped organize. Conversely, the people with whom engaged anthropologists collaborate may determine the methods anthropologists use, as when I had to abandon my plan to conduct individual interviews and focus groups in Guyana because the Akawaio decided to respond to my questions in a public forum. My experience as an engaged anthropologist has taught me that even though not all methods yield the same information, there are multiple ways of doing ethnography, and even short-term research has the potential to offer valuable insights.

Engaged anthropology also reveals new topics for consideration, such as the multivalent discourse of freedom in Suriname. In short-term research, I often seek to identify a key theme on which to focus, such as the importance of collective land ownership for the Akawaio in Guyana. In that case, my attention was drawn by their preference for communal labor in contrast to the Lockean emphasis on the individual application of labor to nature, which results in private property. The resulting themes often resonate across contexts, offering opportunities for comparison. For example, concerns about culture loss expressed by people living in the Marshall Islands were also prevalent in comments made by the Kaliña and Lokono in Suriname, as well as by my Yonggom informants in Papua New Guinea (Kirsch 2006). Similarly, indigenous peoples' concerns about restrictions on their freedom are also common in many of the places where I have worked.

The experiments in engaged anthropology discussed here suggest caution on a number of fronts. In my research on conservation and development in the Lakekamu River basin in Papua New Guinea, my attention to overlapping land claims and incommensurate goals among the different groups led to the recognition of a crucial vulnerability of these initiatives. However, the desire to identify an alternative to destructive forms of resource extraction influenced my evaluation of the project, illustrating the risk that the findings of engaged anthropologists may be overly optimistic. These projects also suggest caution when writing from a distance, as I learned when visiting West Papua, Indonesia, where political strategies differ from those of the refugee and exile community. Engaged anthropologists may also encounter negative reactions to their inquiries, as I experienced in Guyana when the people from Isseneru expressed frustration with having to explain themselves and justify their choices, even though they appreciated my contribution to their case. In some instances, foreign anthropologists may be discouraged from participating in local politics, as I was counseled by a law professor from Papua New Guinea, although the people living in rural communities affected by the mine felt otherwise, demanding that I remain involved. Anthropologists who work in contentious contexts may also face political backlash, as I learned from the project on repatriation at my university, despite my effort to identify common ground among the participants and despite the implementation of policies that addressed the concerns raised by the initiative.

Moreover, it is not always apparent how one might contribute to an ongoing political struggle, as I learned in my interactions with political leaders and refugees from West Papua. Such impasses are seldom, if ever, addressed in the literature on engaged anthropology. Even though my contribution to their goals has thus far been limited to participation in various forms of solidarity politics, I have been able to address some of their concerns in publications about the refugees living along the border and the politics of representation in West Papua.

As suggested by the examples presented here, engaged anthropology has the capacity to yield findings of general significance. This challenges the high-low distinction between purely academic and engaged forms of research, including the view that the former is innovative and creative, while the latter is conventional and conservative. For example, my work in the Marshall Islands explains how material losses can have significant consequences for the reproduction of local knowledge. The absence of breadfruit and pandanus trees on the atolls where the people from Rongelap were relocated prevented them from teaching subsequent generations how to build their distinctive sailing canoes, contributing to the decline of long-distance voyaging and the loss of knowledge about navigating by the stars and wave patterns. Recent discussion about noneconomic loss and damage caused by global climate change draws on this earlier work on the consequences of nuclear weapons testing, demonstrating that the findings of engaged research projects may be of value beyond the immediate context.

One of the questions that arose while preparing materials for the Nuclear Claims Tribunal was how to strike an appropriate balance between innovation and convention. Although the law is sometimes conceived as a closed set of texts, my experience has been that lawyers and judges are often receptive to alternative interpretive frameworks. This is especially true when addressing unfamiliar contexts and questions, such as indigenous rights, even when these ideas are not formally acknowledged in the final judgment. This leads me to encourage engaged anthropologists to help expand existing legal frameworks by promoting novel concepts like subsistence rights and culture loss.

The project in Solomon Islands suggests that data collected for one purpose may be of value when answering other questions. Ethnographic research on property rights helped explain the subsequent civil conflict in Honiara. It also generated hypotheses about the role of customary land tenure in conflict and civil war that could be investigated elsewhere. Similarly, my trip to West Papua in 2014 revealed the different dynamics of political activism inside and outside of repressive states, a topic worthy of future comparative examination.

The analysis of claims made about the repatriation of Native American human remains also produced generalizable findings. That work shows how the participants in those debates make hierarchical assertions about domains that ordinarily have heterarchical relationships, offering insight into how political claims are fashioned and the structure and organization of political disputes. It also shows how competing arguments may draw on shared domains.

Finally, I would like to revisit the three questions raised at the outset of this book: whether engaged research produces "good enough" ethnography, whether it contributes to desirable political outcomes, and whether it is good for the discipline of anthropology. Ethnography produced through engaged research is more vulnerable to omissions associated with ethnographic refusal, even though this may be the result of ethical obligations to protect research subjects. These commitments may be intensified by access to confidential information, especially when the political stakes are high. Nonetheless, it is possible to revisit these issues after political circumstances change.

The information gathered during short-term inquiries differs from the results of long-term ethnographic research in several ways. It may not be sufficiently robust to support alternative interpretations. It may be overly dependent on reported speech, given the researcher's inability to verify information through observation, additional interviews, or archival research. Consequently, there are constraints on how the resulting materials can be used. Nonetheless, shorter interventions can provide valuable insight into how political claims are formulated and their interactions with legal systems, corporations, and the state. Comparing the findings of short-term research against the disciplinary ideal of "thick description" ignores the constraints under which these projects operate and is probably unwarranted, given its similarities to the multisited, problem-oriented focus of most contemporary ethnography. In addition, these projects offer valuable comparative perspectives that benefit ethnographic research, as the contrast between land claims in Melanesia and the Amazon suggests. Short-term projects can also be expanded through historical and archival research, as illustrated by the chapter on Solomon Islands.

The findings of these projects are inseparable from the political context of the research, such as the myths told to me by the people living in the Lakekamu River basin because of their reluctance to speak directly about contested land claims, or the responses focused on loss that were elicited by the Nuclear Claims Tribunal. What we learn from these projects is how people in these societies mobilize their culture, history, and identities in relation to political challenges and aspirations. Thus the answer to whether engaged anthropology produces "good enough" ethnography depends on the goals of the project and the context of the research.

The second question is whether engaged anthropology contributes to productive outcomes. Let me consider each of the projects discussed here. The Ok Tedi case cost the mining company $2 billion in profit when the company was forced to transfer its shares in the project to a development trust; however, the mine continues to pollute the river system. No one, including the mining company, disputes the fact that the project is an environmental disaster, a recognition that was far from settled when I began working on these issues in earnest. The case has also influenced international discourse about mining and its environmental impacts, including the responsibilities of mining companies to indigenous communities, although thus far the industry's commitments to reform remain largely symbolic (Kirsch 2014).

My contribution to the West Papuan independence movement warrants an incomplete grade, given its restriction to solidarity politics and academic writing. In recent years, a new cohort of scholars has been able to conduct ethnographic research in West Papua, resulting in more nuanced accounts of the political situation (see Slama and Munro 2014). However, academic research on West Papua has helped raise the international profile of the independence movement.

My work in the Lakekamu River basin in Papua New Guinea enabled me to evaluate a new conservation strategy with the goal of limiting destructive forms of resource extraction. Ethnographic investigation revealed the presence of overlapping land claims, alternative perspectives on the environment, and competing aspirations for the future, all of which contributed to the project's failure. The avoidance of development initiatives with negative environmental impacts in the intervening years might have been influenced by discussions with conservation biologists, although it may also be a source of frustration for some of the people living there. Attention to these issues can help to identify the circumstances in which conservation projects are likely to succeed or fail. They also suggest the need to focus on the environmental problems affecting the entire planet rather than efforts to protect a small portion of it.

My work in Solomon Islands was derailed by the failure of the lawsuit against Ross Mining, although subsequent environmental problems associated with the Gold Ridge mine indicate that the concerns addressed by the case were warranted. Although the lawsuit does not seem to have exacerbated the civil conflict, a more successful resolution of the dispute might have alleviated some of the underlying tensions. Nonetheless, my research on property rights helps to explain why the conflict took the form of violence between landowners from Guadalcanal and Malaitan migrants.

In the Marshall Islands, my colleagues working on the case helped secure the largest award from the Nuclear Claims Tribunal to date for the people of Rongelap (Johnston and Barker 2008), although payment is contingent on additional appropriations from the U.S. Senate. My work on culture loss and property rights has also influenced larger discussions about noneconomic loss and damages caused by global climate change, which will affect millions of people living in many different areas of the world.

On campus, the repatriation debate contributed to significant policy changes by the university that were facilitated by new federal rules, resolving the conflict to the mutual satisfaction of the larger Native American community and the Office of the Vice President for Research, although not to the satisfaction of all of the archaeologists at the museum.

Finally, with respect to the two land rights cases in the Amazon, only the first has been decided. The ruling in the Lower Marowijne case in Suriname paralleled the arguments in my submission, although this owes more to the strength of their claims than to my contribution to the proceedings. Nonetheless, I was able to play a constructive role in helping bring about this outcome, even though the state has yet to fully implement the judgment of the court. These cases can also help set important precedents for indigenous communities seeking to protect their land rights in other jurisdictions (see Gilbert 2016; MacKay 2013–14).

The legal claims discussed in this book have a direct bearing on the debate between hegemony and counterhegemony theorists with respect to whether the law favors the interests of the powerful or can be successfully mobilized to promote constructive political change. Mark Goodale (2016) argues that the juridification of indigenous politics is more likely to result in soft forms of political recognition rather than in tangible forms of redistribution.[1] A comparative study of strategic litigation on the land rights of indigenous peoples reached a similar conclusion (Gilbert 2017). Although the legal claims analyzed in this book are unable to settle the debate between hegemony and counterhegemony theorists, they shed light on both the risks and the benefits of legal activism. Moreover, engaged anthropologists can help resolve these debates by contributing to legal efforts intended to bring about political change.

Thus the political interventions described in this book are neither accounts of unqualified success nor complete failures. Instead, they offer a realistic assessment of the kinds of contributions anthropologists can make to political change in the process of conducting engaged research. Counting political victories and losses may not be the best measure of these efforts, as constructive political change is hard to come by, and all of these projects have the potential to influence future events.

The final question is whether engaged research is good for anthropology. I began these conclusions by asserting that engaged anthropology is based on ethnographic knowledge. I am equally committed to the corresponding argument that engaged anthropology should contribute back to the discipline. This may not be the primary goal of engagement. But in my experience, engaged anthropology has the capacity to reveal aspects of the world that might not otherwise be apparent in the course of more conventional research projects. It is a valuable proving ground for anthropological concepts and an exciting stimulus that leads to the formulation of new ideas and theories. Anthropologists also have skills and knowledge that can help their informants work toward achieving their political goals, as befits a discipline based on reciprocity. The relationship between research and politics may be awkward at times, but they have much to offer each other. Given that a diversity of approaches is one of the strengths of anthropology, engaged research has the capacity to expand the possibilities and contributions of the field.

Engaged anthropology, anthropology as advocacy, activist anthropology, collaborative anthropology, public anthropology: these are worthy experiments in anthropological practice, and this book is meant to enhance recognition of their potential. My recommendation that anthropologists pay greater attention to reflexivity and politics beyond the text is intended to facilitate these initiatives. Engaged anthropology responds to questions about the responsibilities of anthropologists to their informants and the desire to address contemporary problems in our work. It differs from other anthropological projects in its recognition that anthropologists have more to contribute to the solution of these problems than just their texts. Amid disciplinary conversations about shifting anthropology's attention from the "suffering subject" to questions about ethics and the "good life" (Robbins 2013; Ortner 2016), this book suggests an alternative path. Rather than just another discursive turn, engaged anthropology offers an opportunity to mobilize the discipline to work toward achieving a more ethical world.

NOTES

INTRODUCTION

1. Ginsburg (1997, 140) encourages anthropologists to "identify how new social imaginaries are emerging out of peoples' daily lives, map points of potential innovation and activism, and ... build on these findings to enhance the possibilities for positive change."

2. Today it is the so-called STEM fields—science, technology, engineering, and mathematics—that are experiencing a crisis. There are serious questions about whether statistical tests produce valid results. There is widespread evidence of the manipulation of scientific results for economic returns in industries as disparate as tobacco, mining, and pharmaceuticals (Kirsch 2014). The manufactured crisis of uncertainty surrounding global climate change inhibits adequate political response. For the most part, scientists have been reluctant or unable to develop mechanisms capable of analyzing and addressing these issues. Sociocultural anthropology, which was once seen as the antithesis of science—or even "antiscience"—because it called for greater reflexivity in recognizing the partial and situated character of knowledge production, may, ironically, possess the intellectual resources needed to help the STEM fields navigate these political and commercial challenges.

3. However, these affiliations pose new risks to ethnographers when nongovernmental organizations act as gatekeepers in what might be called "en*caged* anthropology" (Andrew Shryock, pers. comm., 2012).

4. Egyptologists describe the effects of museum displays in recovering the forgotten histories of the dead and preserving their names as helping ancient Egyptians achieve their goal of immortality (Richards and Wilfong 1995, 10).

5. As Roy A. Rappaport (1993, 295) notes, "The application of anthropology to the solution of real world problems" has "never been valued very highly in our discipline."

6. Alcida Ramos (1999, 172) argues, "In Brazil, as elsewhere in Latin America, to do anthropology is a political act."

7. As Marilyn Strathern and Eric Hirsch (2004, 7) observe, "Property . . . travels along with NGOs, human rights discourse, multinational companies and the expanding universe of the life sciences to broker all kinds of relationships between people and the products of people's enterprises. It has international currency as a ubiquitous fact of life. But it also has its own life within the politics of the nation-state, the industrial revolution, and the economies of empire, in addition to disciplinary histories within the sciences of human behavior, including social anthropology."

8. The label *activist* may also have political consequences, as critics may seek to discredit social movements by suggesting they are organized by outsiders and, thus, do not express the views and commitments of the participants.

9. Nancy Scheper-Hughes (1995) mixes her metaphors in referring to both "barefoot" and "militant" anthropology, with the former echoing liberation theology's attention to the poor and marginalized (Brice 2017), while the latter suggests the need to forcefully respond to violence and oppression (Scheper-Hughes 1995, 417). However, it is not apparent what either term contributes to an understanding of engaged anthropology apart from their dramatic self-positioning.

1. HOW POLITICAL COMMITMENTS INFLUENCE RESEARCH

1. More than two thousand square kilometers of lowland rain forest have been affected by tailings from the mine, and an additional one thousand square kilometers will eventually be underwater for several months a year (Tingay 2007).

2. In contrast, there was no conflict within landowning groups or intergenerational strife in the Ok Tedi case, and participation in the lawsuit gave rise to new forms of political leadership (Kirsch 1997c, 121).

3. Filer, Banks, and Burton (2008, 191) argue that "indigenous political and intellectual leaders are very adept at complaining to a global English-speaking audience about anything that they regard as a violation of their rights and customs," putting mining companies at a disadvantage when it comes to public relations.

4. The recognition of past mistakes can be a source of insight for anthropologists, as Emrys Peters (1972) argued in an article reconsidering his earlier views on rank and power in a Lebanese village (Peters 1963)

5. In 1989 the PNG government "told BHP to do something about compensating these people for the damage being caused to their natural environment, and the company then set up a programme of research to monitor the social impact of the compensation package" (Filer, Banks, and Burton 2008, 184–85).

6. This provision of the American Anthropological Association code of ethics has been modified to allow anthropologists to conduct confidential research on behalf of corporate clients (Plemmons and Barker 2016). It encourages anthropologists to "consider all reasonable requests" for access to their findings and to make the results of their research "appropriately available" to others (American

Anthropological Association 2009, 3), which may protect corporate interests at the expense of the people with whom anthropologists conduct their research.

7. One of the footnotes added to my article concerned BHP's relationship to the PNG Compensation (Prohibition of Foreign Legal Proceedings) Act of 1995, which criminalized Papua New Guinean participation in foreign legal proceedings against mining companies operating in Papua New Guinea. The act made it a crime punishable by substantial fines and/or incarceration for the plaintiffs in the lawsuit against the Ok Tedi mine to continue with their legal action against BHP in the Supreme Court of Victoria in Australia. Despite the threat of imprisonment, the lead plaintiffs elected to continue with the case. A constitutional challenge to the act was pending before the High Court of Papua New Guinea when the case was settled out of court in 1996. The footnote submitted by BHP and appended to my article in *Anthropology Today* asserted that the legislation was "enacted without consultation with BHP or the mining company" (Kirsch 1996a, 15–16), but the Supreme Court of Victoria concluded that BHP's lawyers drafted the bill (Gordon 1997, 144).

8. Catherine Coumans (2011, S33) compares anthropologists who consult for mining companies to journalists embedded in the U.S. military during the second Iraq war, including the restrictions imposed on what the journalists saw and how they were permitted to report on it.

9. There is no word for *village* in the Yonggom language, hence loan words like *kampong* in Bahasa Malayu, *ples* in Melanesian Tok Pisin, and the English *village* are used to refer to these settlements.

10. Other affidavits I submitted in the Ok Tedi case were more straightforward—for example, when I was asked to comment on the adequacy of the methods used by the lawyers to communicate information about the legal proceedings to the plaintiffs. The judge presiding over the case was critical of BHP's efforts, noting with disapproval its attempt to deny the plaintiffs access to legal relief because of the challenges of communication in rural areas where multiple languages are spoken: "There is a certain irony that the defendant's solicitors appear to be much more concerned about the fulfillment of the democratic process than Slater & Gordon [representing the plaintiffs]" (Gabia Gagarimabu v. BHP and Ok Tedi Mining 2001, 68).

11. As a system that reconciles evidence from multiple points of view, the law has always recognized the partial and situated character of both witness claims and expert knowledge.

12. The relationship between lawyers and their clients after the conclusion of a lawsuit might be compared to the way real estate agents stop taking calls once they hand over the keys. In contrast, Slater and Gordon dedicated considerable time and resources to the implementation of the first settlement and, despite their misgivings about its prospects in court, felt compelled to file a second suit accusing BHP of abrogating the terms of the original settlement agreement.

13. The Eighth Supplemental Agreement between the mining company and the state established a general compensation fund of PNG K110 million before the settlement of the lawsuit in 1995; the Ninth Supplemental Agreement legally executed a series of agreements—between Ok Tedi Mining and the affected communities—

known as the Community Mine Continuation Agreements. The Ninth Supplemental Agreement also approved BHP Billiton's exit from Ok Tedi Mining and the transfer of its shares to the Papua New Guinea Sustainable Development Program in Singapore. The fund has long-term reserves of about U.S.$1.4 billion.

14. This decision also facilitated the governor's ability to take credit for the process rather than ceding political authority to the organizers of the meetings.

15. This was made explicit during a meeting with a recently appointed managing director of the Ok Tedi mine, who told me that he asked an employee from the mine impact area to read one of my papers and report back to him. He consented to meet with me only after the employee confirmed the accuracy of my account.

2. WHEN CONTRIBUTIONS ARE ELUSIVE

1. The western half of the island of New Guinea has been known by many names over the years, including Dutch New Guinea, West Irian, and Irian Jaya. In 2003, the Indonesian government divided the territory into the provinces of Papua and West Papua. I use the name *West Papua* to refer to the entire area in deference to the wishes of the people living there.

2. The acronym used by the Indonesian government for the OPM and other groups that resist or challenge state power is GPK (Gerombolan Pengacau Keamanan), their Orwellian designation for "Security Disruption Group" (Daley 2000).

3. Authorship was attributed solely to my coauthor because of a government ban on research with the refugees at the time.

4. A slight adjustment to the southern portion of the border was made in order to compensate for the loss of territory caused by following the western curve of the Fly River across the 141st parallel (Veur 1966, 66–68).

5. West Papua has figured prominently in the territorial aspirations of Indonesian nationalists since the incarceration of political prisoners in Boven Digoel, in Muyu territory, during World War II (Osborne 1985, 34).

6. Ninety-four refugee families from the resettlement center in East Awin were voluntarily repatriated to West Papua in 1993, and another 632 refugees returned in 2000 (Glazebrook 2008, 10).

7. However, Zocca (2008, 143) notes that after more than twenty years in exile, many of the refugees no longer anticipate returning to West Papua.

8. The problem remains as true today as when I first wrote about it in 1996, as confirmed by an op-ed published by the *New York Times* (2015) titled "Lost Voices of the World's Refugees," which argues, in part: "In the many conference and diplomatic discussions about refugees, their own voices are rarely heard."

9. The Indonesian state has long impeded the flow of virtually *all* information about West Papua, as John MacDougall (1987, 103, emphasis in the original) observed in 1987: "The official blackout is *more* effective than the one for East Timor. The Indonesian press remains under tight strictures not to become curious

about, much less report, anything about armed conflict, casualties, or even detentions in [West Papua]. Consequently, the low-level war in [West Papua] is as unknown to most Indonesians as it is to most foreigners."

10. Anthropologists who managed to conduct ethnographic research in West Papua under Suharto were justifiably concerned that publishing accounts of political violence could endanger the subjects of their research. Speaking out against political violence in West Papua might also have jeopardized access to Indonesia for individual scholars and other members of the institutions with which they were affiliated. Consequently, relatively few anthropologists were willing to write about state-sponsored violence during Suharto's rule, especially in the outer islands.

11. The story is reminiscent of the broad humor and pathos of Yonggom accounts about the early colonial period (Kirsch 2006, 45–46).

12. Karma was the focus of an international campaign by the organization Freedom Now, which works to free political prisoners. He was released in November 2015 after serving ten years of his fifteen-year sentence for raising the "morning star" flag.

13. Behar describes the skeptical reactions of the anthropologists he interviewed about the possibility of finding people who remain unaware of the outside world. He also reports the tour operator's dismissive response that his academic critics "are just lecturers at nice universities who have tenure and cushy jobs.... If they think I've staged this[,] ... I give them an open invitation to see for themselves" (quoted in Behar 2005, 112–13).

14. According to Rupert Stasch (2017, 17–19, 23), the Korowai refer to foreign tourists as "zombies."

15. In West Papua, the notion of *merdeka,* which is usually translated as "freedom" or "liberation," has commonly had millenarian overtones associated with both Christian theology and autochthonous religious movements. In keeping with recent emphasis on human rights and more robust efforts at international diplomacy, activists have also invoked *merdeka* in relation to concerns about social justice (Golden 2003; see also Webb-Gannon 2014).

16. For example, Eben Kirksey (2012, 138–72) has spent months in Washington, DC, lobbying on West Papuan affairs, especially in relation to the shooting deaths of several Americans on the road to Freeport's Grasburg mine in West Papua, which he vividly describes in *Freedom in Entangled Worlds.* Danilyn Rutherford was a member of a fact-finding committee on West Papua at the Asia-Pacific Institute in Washington, DC, for several years. Other scholars have played comparable roles in Australia and the Netherlands.

17. I gained firsthand knowledge of the workings of solidarity politics in El Salvador while collaborating on a study of a foundation established by a mining company that was suing the state for changing its mining regulations (Kirsch and Moore 2016).

18. My only previous experience in West Papua was a clandestine visit with some Yonggom friends to their hunting grounds (see Kirsch 2010a, 3).

19. Raising the "morning star" flag can be prosecuted under article 106 of Indonesian law, which resulted in Filep Karma's lengthy jail term.

20. Ross Tapsell (2015) reached similar conclusions based on his interviews with journalists and newspaper editors working in West Papua: that self-censorship among journalists is common, especially among non-Papuan journalists (2015, 330); that journalists working in West Papua are committed to objective reporting (2015, 332), and that West Papuan journalists feel stigmatized and are more likely to be harassed (2015, 330, 331).

3. THE SEARCH FOR ALTERNATIVE OUTCOMES

1. As Bruce Beehler (pers. comm., 2016), the project director, notes, "The project was not much more complicated than asking the question 'What would be the best way to ensure that the Lakekamu Basin and its forests, and especially its bird life, would still be there in ten, twenty, or even one hundred years?' The forests of Papua New Guinea are clearly under threat in so many areas; what could be done about this particular, very special place for biodiversity?"

2. Elsewhere I have referred to actions that seek to prevent environmental damage from occurring, rather than responding after the fact, as examples of the "politics of time" (Kirsch 2014, 188–223).

3. Funding for the new conservation projects came from the Global Environment Facility, established in the preparations for the 1992 Rio Earth Summit; Conservation International, which cosponsored the Lakekamu project, was one of the original partners (see Sakulas 2012, 181–83, 198).

4. Similarly, Daniel Brockington (2002, 8) notes, "It is widely suggested that if protected areas are to have a long-term future, they must enlist support from their immediate neighbours. Only if they exist with local approval can they exist at all."

5. This chapter is based on research conducted in 1994 and published three years later (Kirsch 1997e). While the interdisciplinary literature on conservation initiatives has subsequently burgeoned, I have not systematically incorporated these debates into this chapter.

6. Conservation International was established in 1987 and initially based in Washington, DC. By 1997, it had field projects in twenty-two countries. Conservation International's local partner in the Lakekamu project was the Foundation of the Peoples of the South Pacific, which was founded in 1968 and is based in Port Moresby.

7. Political disputes over responsibility for the Lakekamu River basin at the provincial level also interfered with the implementation of the project (Beehler 2008; Sakulas 2012).

8. I also contributed a technical report on the social history of the area to a rapid biological assessment of the river basin (Mack 1998). The Rapid Assessment Program was created by Conservation International in 1990 to compile "biological information needed to make quick but sound conservation decisions in the developing world" (Alonso et al. 2011, 18). From 1990 to 2010, there were seventy-four such assessments (Alonso et al. 2011, 92–93).

9. See Bruce Beehler's (1991, 191–205; 2008, 155–80) description of several expeditions to conduct ornithological research in the Lakekamu basin.

10. The attribution of cannibalism to one's neighbors is not uncommon in New Guinea and may be a metaphor for hostile social relations rather than a literal statement about consumption practices.

11. One Papua New Guinea kina was worth approximately one U.S. dollar at the time.

12. Their language is known as Kapau (Bamford 1997). The colonial-era exonym for the Anga was Kukukuku.

13. However, Kamea living in the mountains near Kaintiba used shells called *nuwa* in marriage exchange (Bamford 1997, 158).

14. The Mekeo are divided into two groups, the so-called Bush Mekeo, who live in the swampy areas south of the Lakekamu basin (Mosko 1985), and the central Mekeo, who live to the southeast (Hau'ofa 1981; Stephen 1995).

15. The Kovio refer to the Mekeo using the Melanesian Tok Pisin term *wantok,* which literally means "one language" but is a fractal term indicating shared identity.

16. The Kovio lived in the flat, swampy lowlands along the southern tributaries of the Kunimaipa River until they moved north to the junction of the Kunimaipa and Biaru Rivers in the 1950s. After this settlement was flooded, the Kovio moved farther west to land adjacent to the Kunimaipa and Lakekamu Rivers.

17. At the time of the 1990 census, the main Kovio village of Okavai had twenty-six households and 175 residents (PNG NSO 1991). The people in the village belong to five exogamous patrilineages. In the past, each lineage had a pair of authority figures: a political leader or headman, referred to as a "man of kindness" and a sorcerer, known as a "man of sorrow" (see Stephen 1995). Today only the headman of each lineage is recognized.

18. McCallum and Sekhran (1997, 9) independently reached a similar conclusion, arguing that "social indicators, not political and biological criteria, must guide the choice of project site" for conservation initiatives.

19. I was also influenced by colleagues at Conservation International who were still trying to make the project work and consequently beseeched me not to prematurely concede failure.

4. WHEN THE INTERVENTION FAILS, DOES THE RESEARCH STILL MATTER?

1. A tributary of the Metepono River, which extends north to the coast, the west branch of the Tinahula River runs through the mine lease area adjacent to the tailings dam for the Gold Ridge mine.

2. In the same issue of the *Solomon Star* that described the original Tinahula River fish kill, another letter to the editor expressed concern after the author saw ten dead ducks floating in the tailings pond for the Gold Ridge mine (Nov. 10, 1998).

3. Years later I met the man who had been responsible for environmental management at the Gold Ridge mine. When I asked him what happened to the Tinahula River that October, he shrugged his shoulders and replied, "It's a mystery." He continued to promote doubt and uncertainty, even though he no longer worked at the mine and the project had undergone a change in ownership (Kirsch 2014, 149).

4. Ross Mining acquired the lease to the mine from Amoco Minerals in 1995 for U.S.$15 million. In anticipation of the development of the project, Solomon Islands passed the Mines and Minerals Act in 1990, which identifies subsurface minerals as the property of "the people of the Solomon Islands" rather than of customary landowners (Moore 2004, 84).

5. Hogbin (1964, 2) visited Guadalcanal several times between 1927 and 1945, although his monograph is based primarily on research conducted in 1933.

6. Solomon Islands anthropologist John Naitoro (1989, 53) observes, "Land tenure is demarcated by . . . sacrificial sites or shrines." These "shrines are . . . 'pegs' or 'points of reference'" for identifying land rights (Naitoro 1989, 49). On the same subject, Thomas Kama (1979, 158, emphasis added) notes, "Sacred shrines (now abandoned but still preserved) were an important *proof* to ownership of land" in the grasslands, the same language used by my informants in 1998.

7. References to "primary" and "secondary" land rights are commonly employed by Solomon Islanders, especially in multiethnic and multilingual contexts like Honiara, to gloss a range of locally salient distinctions between ownership and use rights (see McDougall 2016, 130).

8. In 1979, Thomas Kama (1979, 156) also noted the absence of a chiefly system in this area.

9. The entry for Solomon Islands in the U.S. Central Intelligence Agency's *World Factbook* (2014) rather appropriately describes the country's system of government as a "parliamentary democracy tending towards anarchy."

10. This review draws extensively on materials assembled by the suspended Solomon Islands Inquiry into Land Dealings and Abandoned Properties in Guadalcanal (Brunton et al. n.d.).

11. Three hundred thousand acres is approximately 469 square miles.

12. As Lasaqa (1972, 34) presciently observed, "Thus did the Government sow the seeds of future disputes with the Melanesian [land]owners."

13. In 1995, the exchange rate was approximately SI$0.28 to U.S.$1.

14. Thomas Kama was a researcher in a study for the Ministry of Agriculture and Lands in Solomon Islands directed by Ian Heath, a doctoral student of Alan Ward, who had been influential in debates about land reform in Papua New Guinea (Clive Moore and Peter Larmour, pers. comm., 2015).

15. Lasaqa (1972, 117) also compares land rights extended to Malaitan migrants and affines to secondary land rights among the Ghaobata: "Malaitans who have married into [the Ghaobata] or are closely associated with the local big-man have obtained land-usage rights which differ little, if at all, from those enjoyed by local men who do not belong to the land-owning unit. . . . They are permanent residents

of the village and participate fully in the community's activities and consciously, if not conscientiously, enter into its network of reciprocal obligations."

16. Debra McDougall (2016, 13) describes how similar transactions elsewhere in the Solomons are commonly prefaced by speeches in which settlers explicitly acknowledge that their gifts do not imply the purchase of land.

17. Lasaqa (1972, 118) makes a similar claim about people from Malaita living in Guadalcanal, whom he describes as "strangers in a not-so-strange land."

18. Reinhardt was declared persona non grata in Papua New Guinea for his role in the dispute over the 1998 Mount Kare gold rush, in which he purportedly sought to acquire the concession to a valuable gold prospect at the expense of the license holder, and for his controversial role as adviser to the PNG minister of finance in relation to the development of the Lihir gold mine (Filer and Imbun 2009, 93–95).

19. The insurgency included people from Guadalcanal's Weather Coast who had land claims in the Gold Ridge area and were among the rebellion's strongest supporters (Evans 2010, 124; McDougall 2016, 224).

20. Daniel Evans (2010, 121–22) is even more emphatic on this point, arguing, "The mine was both a cause and a target of the fighting that took place there and the Guadalcanal uprising more broadly."

21. Gordon Leua Nanau (2017, 208) disputes the claim that gold was a "central factor contributing to the tensions," characterizing it as a "highly questionable proposition."

22. Both McDougall (2016) and Allen (2013) emphasize the corrosive effects of resource extraction on the national economy, including the failure of the state to equitably distribute its benefits to local landowners and the lack of development benefiting local landowners.

23. McDougall (2016, 217n3) argues that Honiara was the locus of the conflict because "the centralization of development in Honiara after 1960 intensified population pressures . . . in a way that [it] did not" elsewhere in the Solomons, although the conflict spilled into neighboring areas.

24. McDougall (2016, 220) notes, "Perhaps the most surprising thing about the so-called Ethnic Tension is the fact that the victims of Guale [people from Guadalcanal] violence largely accepted the legitimacy of the Guale grievances. Many settlers from the island of Malaita who suffered from Tension-related violence, and even some who later took up arms against the Guale militants, accepted that their hosts had the moral right to evict them."

25. Other land conflicts may also have contributed to the tensions. Allen (2013, 308) describes disputes within landowning groups concerning the distribution of rents and royalties from palm oil plantations and the Gold Ridge mine. Rebecca Monson (2015, 446) describes how the courts often interpret land rights in a hierarchical fashion, excluding legitimate claimants to land. She also argues that the sale and rent of land increasingly came to resemble commodity transactions, in which economic benefits are captured by a few individuals, in contrast to gift exchanges, which ensure that the proceeds are more broadly distributed (Monson 2015, 448; see Martin 2013, 34).

26. Flash floods in April 2016 resulted in the news headline "Major Tailings Dam Spill at Solomon Islands 'Disaster' Gold Mine" and a government warning to the eight thousand people living downstream "not to use river water for drinking, washing, bathing, swimming, or fishing" (*SBS Australia* 2016).

27. As this book was going into production, the local landowning group that acquired the Gold Ridge mine from St. Barbara in return for a token payment of one hundred dollars in 2015 was negotiating with a Chinese property developer to restart operations (Radio New Zealand 2017).

28. Although the Truth and Reconciliation Commission (2012, 27) expressed regret that much of the literature on the Solomons was written by foreigners, I have emphasized important contributions to these debates by scholars from Solomon Islands and the Pacific, including Thomas Kama and Isireli Lasaqa.

5. HOW ANALYSIS OF LOCAL CONTEXTS CAN HAVE GLOBAL SIGNIFICANCE

1. In her written submission to the Nuclear Claims Tribunal, Pollock (1999, 1) described the historical and institutional dimensions of claims about culture loss in the following terms: "The issue of 'cultural loss' is currently a subject of much debate in international fields as indigenous people assert their claims against uninvited disruptions to their lives. Reparations sought include claims for loss of land and all its cultural meanings, loss of a way of life that had been passed down from ancestors, loss of social interactions leading to the ongoing viability of society, loss of the basis of indigenous belief systems and loss of the right to self-determination. The assumption [of the anthropologist] is that these elements of culture are not static but continually readjust to current and past contexts. But the contexts being highlighted in this debate are all ones where the loss was derived from impositions by major powers, colonial powers, that exerted their power over minority states to achieve . . . [their] goals, both economic and strategic."

2. Such sentiments have a deeper history than I am able to describe here. For example, the distinguished North American historian William Cronon (1983, 107) characterizes the environmental transformations wrought by settler colonialism at the end of the eighteenth-century as a "loss of a world of ecological relationships." In support of this claim, he presents an excerpt from a Mohegan petition in 1789, which describes the situation in the following terms: "The times are Exceedingly Alter'd, Yea the times have turned everything upside down" (cited in Cronon 1983, 107).

3. This attitude is epitomized by Henry Kissinger's infamous assertion "There are only ninety thousand people out there, who gives a damn?" (cited in Kiste 1974, 198).

4. Commenting on the naming of women's two-piece bathing suits after Bikini Atoll, Teresia Teaiwa (1994, 87) argues, "The sexist dynamic that the bikini performs—the objectification through excessive visibility—inverts the colonial dynamics that have occurred during nuclear testing in the Pacific, objectification by rendering invisible."

5. In addition to the sixty-four persons on Rongelap at the time of the Bravo test, another eighteen people were on the nearby atoll of Ailinginae, including four pregnant women who gave birth during the period of relocation. Thus the total number of exposed persons, according to the U.S. government, including the four in utero, was eighty-six (Bill Graham, pers. comm., 2000). Radiation also affected the crew of the *Lucky Dragon,* a Japanese fishing boat downwind of Bikini atoll (Makhijani 2010; Higuchi 2008).

6. As Arjun Makhijani (2010, 201–2; see also Higuchi 2008) notes, "The severe radiation suffered by the Rongelapese and the Japanese fishing crew of the *Lucky Dragon* sparked a worldwide movement to ban nuclear weapons testing that was, at the time, the leading edge of a demand for nuclear disarmament. . . . The fallout from Bravo was perhaps the most consequential single event that mobilized leaders of countries and grassroots activists to call for disarmament, eventually leading to the atmospheric nuclear test ban treaty."

7. Pollock (1992) is the author of *These Roots Remain,* a comparative study of foodways in the central and eastern Pacific, which draws on fifteen months of fieldwork in the Marshall Islands from 1967 to 1969. Carucci (1997) is the author of *Nuclear Nativity,* an ethnography of ritual and exchange on Enewetak, which draws on more than three years of field research between 1976 and 1996.

8. Consider Deborah Bird Rose's (1996, 2) comments on this subject: "During the course of my work in New South Wales, Aboriginal people have told me time and again that because they have lost so much, they are not prepared to speak publicly about their knowledge in any detail. They fear that they will lose control of that which remains."

9. In contrast, Jorgensen (1995) argues that there are substantive differences between the two communities, native and nonnative. He makes the following observation about native choices post–*Exxon Valdez*: "Packing up and leaving . . . is not the native solution to adversity. . . . Native cultural traditions, as instanced by the nexus of kinship and friendship obligations, facilitate remaining in place, while sentiments and ideas about place and space influence a person's resolve to stay" (1995, 20). Jorgensen (1995, 4) also argues that natives are "very different from nonnatives" in terms of the "ethics that they express and practice, . . . in the ways and extent to which they participate in their communities, in the networks and activities in which they engage, . . . in their family household organizations, and, if class is an issue, in their education, occupations, incomes, political knowledge and participation in political affairs." He shows that there are substantial differences between the two communities in terms of "subsistence activities, knowledge of the environment, ideas about the environment, sentiment about the environment, and sharing activities," all of which are relevant to the consequences of the oil spill (1995, 56).

10. Judge Holland (1996, 169), however, denied that Bohannan's testimony influenced his judgment.

11. *Eminent domain* refers to "the inherent power of a governmental entity to take privately owned property, esp. land, and convert it to public use, subject to reasonable compensation for the taking," whereas *inverse condemnation* refers to "an

action brought by a property owner for compensation from a governmental entity that has taken the owner's property without bringing formal condemnation proceedings" (Garner 1999, 287, 541).

12. Unless otherwise indicated, all quotations from Carucci are taken from his oral testimony (Nuclear Claims Tribunal 1999a).

13. Annette Weiner (1992, 104) argues that "taking a possession that so completely represents a group's social identity as well as an individual owner's identity and giving it to someone outside the group is a powerful transfer of one's own and one's group's very substance."

14. As Holly Barker (1997, 293) notes, "In a nation with just 70 square miles of land, land is by no means expendable."

15. In contrast, Arjun Agrawal (1995) argues against efforts to distinguish indigenous knowledge from science, which reify them as different things. Paul Nadasdy (2005) shows how the categories of the state influence indigenous knowledge.

16. The knowledge required for long-distance navigation, including navigation by the rising and setting of the stars and wave piloting, survived in the Caroline Islands and has been undergoing revitalization across the Pacific during the past few decades (Finney 1994; Low 2013).

17. Exposure to radiation creates an additional paradox of place for the people from Rongelap. The risk of visiting the lagoons or islands affected by nuclear testing is minimal; Bikini Atoll, ground zero for many of the tests, now markets itself as an ecotourism destination for scuba-diving (see www.bikiniatoll.com). The primary radiation risk is from consuming local foodstuffs over an extended period of time. Radiation thus inverts the notion of property: whereas in the past the people's relationship to land implied exclusive use of its resources, today the risks of cumulative exposure to radiation prevent them from exploiting these resources, even though strangers who lack historical connections to Rongelap, including fishing boats from Southeast Asia, are not prevented from doing so (Ken Kedi, interview by Holly Barker, Barbara Rose Johnston, and Stuart Kirsch, 1999).

18. For Aboriginal Australians, "the relationships between people and their country are intense, intimate, full of responsibility, and, when all is well, friendly. It is a kinship relationship, and like relations among kin, there are obligations of nurturance. People and country take care of each other" (Rose 1996, 49).

19. Pollock also suggests that relocation has a cultural precedent in the Marshall Islands: "[The] Iroij or chief of the Marshalls . . . had the power to [order people] to relocate. Relocation, as I understand it, is a part of Marshallese culture" (Nuclear Claims Tribunal 1999b). Here she conflates two very different processes: the authority to ostracize individual members of the community by forcing them to relocate, which is an effective form of punishment precisely because these individuals are separated from their social group, and the power to remove the entire community from its home atoll, which has no local precedent.

20. Pollock disputes Carucci's reference to anomie, which she describes as being "very much taken from Western ideas and trying to account for [the] response to the cash economy." She argues that the concept is inapplicable in the Enewetak case:

"People felt that [their relocation] was beyond their control, but they tried their best to adjust. That does not mean that they suffered any anomie" as a result (Nuclear Claims Tribunal 1999b).

21. Lawrence Rosen (2001) and Madhavi Sunder (2001) adopt opposing positions on whether claims about culture loss are best argued as property claims or tort law. Sunder agrees that property claims may provide significant opportunities for addressing the subjective evaluation of loss, including culture. Rosen argues that tort law is the more promising avenue for redress, suggesting that harm to "cultural integrity" may be compensable. But given broad differences in forum and historical circumstances, and depending on whether statutory authorities are primarily concerned with the valuation of loss or the demonstration of continuity, having recourse to more than one legal remedy seems desirable rather than problematic.

22. Additional compensation was provided for the pain and suffering caused by inadequate and unhealthy living conditions, and by subjecting people from Rongelap to unnecessary medical procedures (Plasman and Danz 2007).

23. The hearings provided the people of Rongelap with an opportunity to challenge the state's claim to moral authority by offering testimony about their experiences (Johnston and Barker 2008, 225).

24. As I argued in *Mining Capitalism* (Kirsch 2014, 28), "Such slow-motion disasters are more difficult for us to perceive than catastrophes caused by earthquakes, hurricanes, or tsunamis. Sudden events also form the template for industrial disaster in the public imagination: the explosion that released a cloud of poisonous gas in Bhopal, the nuclear meltdown in Chernobyl, or the *Exxon Valdez* shipwreck that spilled eleven million gallons of crude oil in Alaska. It requires a different sense of time to adequately perceive the impact of slow-motion disasters as they are happening."

6. THE RISKS OF INTERVENTION

1. The rule went into effect sixty days later, on May 14, 2010 (U.S. Government 2010).

2. In addition, I wanted to encourage the graduate students to write about their experiences as engaged anthropologists by setting an example (see Kirsch 2011).

3. The resulting article (Kirsch 2011) has been taught in archaeology classes as well as courses on kinship and property.

4. This has led some archaeologists to accuse Native Americans who invoke other domains in relation to repatriation—including decolonization, human rights, or kinship—of being "antiscience" (Erikson 2008, 66). Some museum curators report feeling "besieged" by the public debates on repatriation, although they also acknowledge their educational value (Silverman and Sinopoli 2011, 34–36).

5. However, there are other ways to think about these issues. Archaeologists increasingly draw on collaborative models of science when working with Native

American communities (Colwell-Chanthaphonh and Ferguson 2008; Thomas 2000). New rules concerning the disposition of culturally unaffiliated human remains (U.S. Government 2010) have resolved many outstanding claims, although some archaeologists feel the new regulations do not sufficiently value historical knowledge or research about the past (Sinopoli 2010).

6. Notes taken by one of the organizers of the event omitted the controversial comment but summarized my remarks as follows: "Stuart: 'We're all here because none of us is happy with the status quo. Interest in breaking taboo [against talking about the conflict over repatriation] in [the] anthropology [department]. We don't just want to talk amongst ourselves. We are interested in collaboration'" (Nathansohn 2009).

7. DILEMMAS OF AN EXPERT WITNESS

1. The state also denied that the Akawaio possess an "indigenous spiritual relationship" with the land, because "Isseneru's spirituality is rooted in Christianity . . . as well as the [Alleluia] movement, an indigenous interpretation of Christianity" (Government of Guyana 2013, 20).

2. Decisions of the court are binding on member states; but with the exception of compensation payments, its rulings are not enforceable.

3. The case against Suriname was initially presented to the Inter-American Commission in February 2007. After the state failed to implement recommendations made by the commission in July 2013, the case was transferred to the Inter-American Court in January 2014.

4. The Interior War in Suriname was fought by factions representing the country's Maroon population and the national army. It was triggered by the mass murder of thirty-five people in Moiwana village by the army (Moiwana Community v. Suriname 2005; Price 2011, 83–103).

5. See Tjang A. Sjin v. Zaalman and Others, Cantonal Court, First Canton, Paramaribo, May 21, 1998. The claim was based on an alleged act of interference with property rights. The court found for the plaintiff on the basis that a real title issued by the state will always take precedence over traditional rights held by indigenous peoples. The court also dismissed a counterclaim brought by all of the indigenous village leaders of the Lower Marowijne, which argued that their property rights arise from traditional occupation and use and, thus, supersede the laws of the state.

6. KLIM was formerly known as CLIM, the Lower Marowijne Indigenous Land Rights Commission.

7. According to a conservation official in Suriname, it is politically easier to blame indigenous peoples for the decline in sea turtle populations than to challenge the fishing industry (cited in Kambel 2002, 144).

8. There is a long history of commercial harvests of turtles for meat and turtle eggs from this region (Kambel 2002, 138–40).

9. Within the nature reserve, Wane Kreek splits into Wane and Moiwana Creeks, tributaries of the Cottica and Marowijne Rivers, respectively, and pollution from the mine may also affect these rivers.

10. BHP Billiton declined to provide information about the environmental impacts of the mining project in Wane Hills.

11. In these environments, there is only a thin layer of topsoil between the forest and the underlying bauxite and laterite; without this organic layer, nothing can grow. Removal of the bauxite layer also destroys the shallow aquifer, which "acts like a sponge that takes up water during the rainy season and slowly releases water to streams during the dry season" (Maest 2009, 68). As a result, the area is much dryer than it was before it was mined for bauxite. An independent scientist described the resulting landscape as "one of the most impossible environments to rehabilitate."

12. It is impossible to process bitter cassava without a *matapi,* which lasts only three months when used intensively. One woman told me she gets her *matapi* from her nephew, who makes good ones. She says that it is possible to make a living from this kind of basketry work.

13. The original plateau was covered by slow-growing hardwoods that thrive only in mature forests. The ecological requirements of these trees cannot be met in an open area. Instead of planting hardwood trees to rehabilitate the area, BHP Billiton and Suralco must begin by planting fast-growing trees from the genus *Cecropia*, such as the bush papaya, which are common pioneer species in cleared areas. They can cope with the high temperatures and dry environments created by clearing the original forest. Once these trees mature and the canopy closes, other softwood species can grow in the shaded areas underneath, gradually replacing the *Cecropias*. Only several decades later, in the mature phase of the forest, will hardwood trees begin to take root and grow underneath the softwood trees.

14. Indigenous land rights do not expire, unlike the forty-year leases issued by the government of Suriname. Consequently, recognizing indigenous land rights could encourage long-term planning and sustainable use of resources.

15. Comanagement, also known as collaborative or joint management, promises "democratic local governance and social justice" (Tsing, Brosius, and Zerner 2005, 31). It is intended to "capitalize on the local knowledge and long-term self-interest of users, while providing for coordination with relevant uses and users . . . at potentially lower transaction" costs (Feeny et al. 1990, 14). Comanagement policies are sometimes seen to infringe on local property rights (see chapter 3), although in this case it would be an improvement over the status quo. It might also result in improved conservation outcomes.

16. My report was submitted as a written affidavit.

17. One argument against a universal concept of indigenous peoples rights (e.g., Bowen 2000; Li 2000) is that the definition of indigeneity excludes other marginalized peoples and minorities. However, in the Saramaka case and similar judgments, including the Endorois case in Kenya (African Commission 2010), the previously recognized rights of indigenous peoples have been extended to other groups of people who are similarly situated.

18. Carrico (2007, 16) notes archaeological and linguistic evidence indicating that the Akawaio were living on Middle Mazaruni River near Issano in 80 B.C. The Akawaio are first mentioned in European historical records in 1596, the year after Raleigh's voyage to Orinoco (Carrico 2007, 31), and subsequently became known for their role in the trade of annatto, used to produce red dye (Carrico 2007, 32). Colonial records are replete with references to the Akawaio people and their presence along the Lower, Middle, and Upper Mazaruni River, including their role in the Akawaio-Carib War of the 1670s and 1680s (Carrico 2007, 36; see also Butt Colson 2009).

19. Actual land management practices may differ slightly from the structural account presented in my affidavit. Writing about the Upper Mazaruni, the anthropologist Tom Griffiths (2003, 6) notes, "Extensive oral and empirical findings confirm that . . . the collectivity holds superior ownership rights over the total territory . . . whilst village communities, families and individuals possess different levels of subsidiary tenurial and use rights to portions of that territory." It is also likely that their historical experience of insecurity over their land rights has contributed to the reification of their communal land tenure system.

20. Colchester et al. (2002, 23) suggest that the threat of forced relocation from the hydro project further consolidated Akawaio notions of tribal or ethnic identity and their shared connection to particular territories.

21. The dam ultimately did not proceed, owing to a lack of funding, although see Dooley and Griffiths (2014, 53–59) for discussion of a recent proposal to revive the project.

22. As anthropologist Tom Griffiths (2003, 12, 13) notes, "According to Akawaio . . . tradition, families normally retain recognized proprietary interests in land formerly occupied by their ancestors." Moreover, "it was common for Akawaio . . . people to move to the sites of former settlements previously occupied by their ancestors many years before." The Akawaio also "say they return to ancestral sites because they feel a strong emotional attachment to sites where foreparents lived and worked and where they remain buried" (Griffiths 2003, 13).

23. *Abak Ekwa* means "the land of many avocado trees"; *Haimara Ekwa* means "the land of many aimara fish" (*Hoplias aimara*).

24. This is standard practice among gold miners in Guyana, even when working on river dredges.

25. Gavin Hilson and Tim Laing (2017b) argue that the government of Guyana encourages small-scale gold mining as a way to avoid the problems of the "resource curse" associated with large-scale corporate mines, although the policy results in other problems, including corruption and the higher transaction costs of monitoring thousands of mining projects.

26. The Akawaio people living in the Upper Mazaruni also supplement their hunting, fishing, and farming activities with income earned from artisanal gold mining.

27. The state has developed programs to reduce mercury use and contamination (Hennessy 2014, 14), including partnerships with several international organizations.

28. Cultural "survival" is defined by the Inter-American Court as the ability of indigenous peoples to "preserve, protect and guarantee the special relationships that they have with their territory," so that "they may continue living their traditional way of life, and that their distinct cultural identity, social structure, economic system, customs, beliefs and traditions are respected, guaranteed and protected" (Saramaka People v. Suriname 2008, paragraphs 37-39).

29. In his discussion of *Saramaka People v. Suriname* (2008), Richard Price (2011, 238-239) describes the "fundamental tension" between the reification of culture and tradition in international human rights law and contemporary anthropological discourse.

30. Hilson and Laing (2017a, 177) argue that efforts to justify Amerindian land claims in Guyana by making reference to the desire to "continue leading traditional ways of life" tend to backfire when gold is involved, because mining can alter consumption patterns at the expense of traditional economic activities.

31. However, cyanide breaks down into compounds that may continue to be harmful to aquatic organisms and persist in the environment for extended periods of time (Moran n.d.).

CONCLUSION

1. Goodale (2016) also warns of increased risk of dispossession as a consequence of the formalization and consolidation of indigenous land titles, which can reduce the transaction costs of "land grabs."

REFERENCES

ARCHIVAL SOURCES

SS Solomon Star (Honiara).

TRC Truth and Reconciliation Commission, Solomon Islands. 2012. *Confronting the Truth for a Better Solomon Islands.* Final Report. February. Vols. 1–5. Honiara, Solomon Islands: Truth and Reconciliation Commission.

SECONDARY SOURCES

Abu-Lughod, Lila. 1990. "The Romance of Resistance: Tracing Transformations of Power through Bedouin Women." *American Ethnologist* 17 (1): 41–55.

Advisory Committee on Culturally Unidentifiable Human Remains under NAGPRA, University of Michigan. 2010. "Report and Recommendations, Year-End Report."

African Commission. 2010. "Centre for Minority Rights Development (Kenya) and Minority Rights Group (on Behalf of Endorois Welfare Council) versus Kenya." African Commission on Human and Peoples' Rights. Document no. 276/2003. www.achpr.org/files/sessions/46th/comunications/276.03/achpr46_276_03_eng.pdf.

Agence France-Presse. 1999. "Indonesia to Probe Report of Irian Jaya Amazon Cannibal Tribe." Jakarta, April 21.

Agrawal, Arun. 1995. "Dismantling the Divide between Indigenous and Scientific Knowledge." *Development and Change* 26:413–39.

Agrawal, Arun, and Clark C. Gibson. 1999. "Enchantment and Disenchantment: The Role of Community in Natural Resources Conservation." *World Development* 27:629–49.

Akin, David. 2013. *Colonialism, Maasina Rule, and the Origins of Malaitan Kastom.* Honolulu: University of Hawai'i Press.

Alcalay, Glenn. 1992. "Pax Americana in the Pacific." *Covert Action* 40:47–51.

Allen, Matthew G. 2013. *Greed and Grievance: Ex-Militants' Perspectives on the Conflict in Solomon Islands, 1998–2003.* Honolulu: University of Hawai'i Press.

Alonso, Leeanne E., Jessica L. Deichmann, Sheila A. McKenna, Piotr Naskrecki, and Stephen J. Richards, eds. 2011. *Still Counting . . . Biodiversity Exploration for Conservation. The First 20 Years of the Rapid Assessment Program.* Arlington, VA: Conservation International.

American Anthropological Association. 1971. "Statement on Ethics Principles of Professional Responsibility." Adopted May 1971. http://ethics.iit.edu/ecodes/node/3162.

———. 2009. "Code of Ethics of the American Anthropological Association." Approved February 2009. http://s3.amazonaws.com/rdcms-aaa/files/production/public/FileDownloads/pdfs/issues/policy-advocacy/upload/AAA-Ethics-Code-2009.pdf.

Anaya, S. James. 2004. *Indigenous Peoples in International Law.* 2nd ed. Oxford: Oxford University Press.

Anderson, Benedict. 1995. *Imagined Communities: Reflections on the Origin and Spread of Nationalism.* Revised and expanded ed. New York: Verso.

———. 1999. "Indonesian Nationalism Today and in the Future." *Indonesia* 67:1–11.

Anderson, David G. 1998. "Property as a Way of Knowing on Evenki Lands in Arctic Siberia." In *Property Relations: Renewing the Anthropological Tradition,* edited by C. M. Hann, 64–84. Cambridge: Cambridge University Press.

Anti-Slavery Society. 1990. *West Papua: Plunder in Paradise.* Indigenous Peoples and Development Series report no. 6. London: Anti-Slavery Society.

Appadurai, Arjun. 1995. "The Production of Locality." In *Counterworks: Managing the Diversity of Knowledge,* edited by Richard Fardon, 204–25. London: Routledge.

Bahtiar, Irham Acho, dir. 2011. *Lost in Papua.* Jakarta: Nayakom Mediatama; Merauke: Merauke Entertainment. DVD.

Baker, Richard. 1999. *Land Is Life: From Bush to Town—the Story of the Yanyuwa People.* Sydney: Allen and Unwin.

Ballard, Chris. 1997. "'It's the Land Stupid!' The Moral Economy of Resource Ownership in Papua New Guinea." In *The Governance of Common Property in the Pacific Region,* edited by Peter Larmour, 47–65. Pacific Policy Paper 19. Canberra: National Centre for Development Studies, Australian National University.

Ballard, Chris, and Glenn Banks. 2003. "Resource Wars: The Anthropology of Mining." *Annual Review of Anthropology* 32:287–313.

Bamford, Sandra. 1997. "The Containment of Gender: Embodied Sociality among a South Angan People." PhD diss., University of Virginia, Charlottesville.

———. 2002. "On Being 'Natural' in the Rainforest Marketplace: Science, Capitalism and the Commodification of Biodiversity." *Social Analysis* 46 (1): 35–50.

Barker, Holly. 1997. "Fighting Back: Justice, the Marshall Islands, and Neglected Radiation Communities." In *Life and Death Matters: Human Rights and the Environment at the End of the Millennium,* edited by Barbara Rose Johnston, 290–306. London: AltaMira.

———. 2004. *Bravo for the Marshallese: Regaining Control in a Post-nuclear, Post-colonial World.* Belmont, CA: Wadsworth.

Barker, John. 2016. *Ancestral Lines: The Maisin of Papua New Guinea and the Fate of the Rainforest.* 2nd ed. Toronto: University of Toronto Press.

Barker, Geoffrey, and Stewart Oldfield. 1999. "BHP Admits Mine Is a Mess, but Downer Says Dig In." *Australian Financial Review,* August 12.

Barnett, Jon, Petra Tschakert, Lesley Head, and W. Neil Adger. 2016. "A Science of Loss." *Nature Climate Change* 6:976–78.

Barry, Glen. 1995. "PNG: Sustainability and Logger's Threats." PNG Rainforest Campaign News, August 7.

Bateson, Gregory. 1972. *Steps to an Ecology of Mind.* New York: Ballantine.

Beehler, Bruce M. 1991. *A Naturalist in New Guinea.* Austin: University of Texas Press.

———. 2008. *Lost Worlds: Adventures in the Tropical Rainforest.* New Haven, CT: Yale University Press.

Behar, Michael. 2005. "The Selling of the Last Savage." *Outside* (February): 96–113. www.outsideonline.com/1823241/selling-last-savage.

Behar, Ruth. 1993. *Translated Woman: Crossing the Border with Esperanza's Story.* Boston: Beacon.

Bell, Diane. 2002. "Writing in the Eye of a Storm." Response to Gaynor Macdonald's review essay on *Ngarrindjeri Wurruwarrin. Australian Journal of Anthropology* 13 (2): 219–23.

Bell, Ian, Herb Feith, and Ron Hatley. 1986. "The West Papuan Challenge to Indonesian Authority in Irian Jaya: Old Problems, New Possibilities." *Asian Survey* 26 (5): 539–56.

Bell, Joshua A., Paige West, and Colin Filer, eds. 2015. *Tropical Forests of Oceania: Anthropological Perspectives.* Canberra: Australian National University Press.

Benedict, Ruth. 1960. *Patterns of Culture.* New York: Mentor.

Bennett, Judith. 1987. *Wealth of the Solomons: A History of a Pacific Archipelago, 1800–1978.* Honolulu: University of Hawai'i Press.

———. 2002. "Roots of Conflict in Solomon Islands—Though Much Is Taken, Much Abides: Legacies of Tradition and Colonialism." State, Society and Governance in Melanesia Discussion. Paper no. 5. Canberra: Research School of Pacific and Asian Studies, Australian National University. https://digitalcollections.anu.edu.au/handle/1885/41835.

Benson, Peter, and Stuart Kirsch. 2010. "Capitalism and the Politics of Resignation." *Current Anthropology* 51 (4): 459–86.

Bertrand, Jacques. 2004. *Nationalism and Ethnic Conflict in Indonesia.* Cambridge: Cambridge University Press.

Besteman, Catherine, and Angelique Haugerud. 2013. "The Desire for Relevance." *Anthropology Today* 29 (6): 1–2.

Biersack, Aletta. 1999. "Introduction: From the 'New Ecology' to the New Ecologies." *American Anthropologist* 101 (1): 5–18.

Bowen, John. 2000. "Should We Have a Universal Concept of 'Indigenous Peoples' Rights'?" *Anthropology Today* 16 (4): 12–16.

Brice, Anne. 2017. "Celebrating 'Barefoot Anthropology'—a Q&A with Nancy Scheper-Hughes." *Berkeley News.* April 28. http://news.berkeley.edu/2017/04/28/celebrating-barefoot-anthropology-nancy-scheper-hughes/.

Brockington, Dan D. 2002. *Fortress Conservation: The Preservation of the Mkomazi Game Reserve, Tanzania.* Bloomington: University of Indiana Press.

Brody, Hugh. 1988. *Maps and Dreams: Indians and the British Columbia Frontier.* Toronto: Douglas and McIntyre.

Brown, Herbert A. 1973. "The Eleman Language Family." In *The Linguistic Situation in the Gulf District and Adjacent Areas, Papua New Guinea,* edited by Karl J. Franklin, 280–376. Canberra: Pacific Linguistics C-26, Australian National University.

Brown, Michael, and Barbara Wyckoff-Baird. 1992. *Designing Integrated Conservation and Development Projects.* Washington, DC: Biodiversity Support Program, USAID.

Brown, Michael F. 1998. "Can Culture Be Copyrighted?" *Current Anthropology* 39 (2): 193–222.

———. 2003. *Who Owns Native Culture?* Cambridge, MA: Harvard University Press.

———. 2014. *Upriver: The Turbulent Life and Times of an Amazonian People.* Cambridge, MA: Harvard University Press.

Brundige, Elizabeth, Winter King, Priyneha Vahali, Stephen Vladeck, and Xiang Yuan. 2004. "Indonesian Human Rights Abuses in West Papua: Application of the Law of Genocide to the History of Indonesian Control." Allard K. Lowenstein International Human Rights Clinic, Yale Law School. https://law.yale.edu/system/files/documents/pdf/news/westpapuahrights.pdf

Brunton, Brian, Steven Tahi, Manoa Rabuka, Ruth Townsend, and Chris Waiwori. N.d. "A Review of the Literature: Commission of Inquiry into the Land Dealings and Abandoned Properties on Guadalcanal." http://www.comofinquiry.gov.sb/articles/Articles.htm.

Brush, Stephen B. 1996. "Whose Knowledge, Whose Genes, Whose Rights?" In *Valuing Local Knowledge: Indigenous People and Intellectual Property Rights,* edited by Stephen B. Brush and Doreen Stabinsky, 1–21. Washington, DC: Island Press.

Budiardjo, Carmel, and Liem Soei Liong. 1988. *West Papua: The Obliteration of a People.* 3rd ed. London: TAPOL.

Bulkan, Christopher Arif. 2008. "The Land Rights of Guyana's Indigenous Peoples." PhD diss., York University.

Burns, Bob, dir. 1987. *One People, One Soul.* Darling: Australian Film Commission. Video.

Burton, John. 1998. "Mining and Maladministration in Papua New Guinea." In *Governance and Reform in the South Pacific,* edited by Peter Larmour, 154–82. Canberra: Australian National University Press.

Butt, Leslie. 2013. "'Lipstick Girls' and 'Fallen Women': AIDS and Conspiratorial Thinking in Papua, Indonesia." *Cultural Anthropology* 20 (3): 412–42.

Butt, Leslie, Gerdha Numbery, and Jake Morin. 2002. "The Smokescreen of Culture: AIDS and the Indigenous in Papua, Indonesia." *Pacific Health Dialog* 9 (2): 283–89.

Butt Colson, Audrey J. 2009. *Land: Its Occupation, Management, Use and Conceptualization. The Case of the Akawaio and Arekuna of the Upper Mazaruni Distinct, Guyana.* Panborough, U.K.: Last Refuge.

Carr, Frances. 1998. "Mamberamo Madness." *Inside Indonesia* 55 (July–September). www.insideindonesia.org/mamberamo-madness?highlight=WyJtYW1iZXJhbW8iLCJtYW1iZXJhbW8ncyIsIm1hZG5lc3MiLCJtYWRuZXNzJyIsIm1hbW-JlcmFtbyBtYWRuZXNzIl0%3D.

Carrico, Christopher Robert. 2007. "Changing Forms of Identity and Political Leadership among the Akawaio Kapong." PhD diss., Temple University.

Carsten, Janet. 2003. *After Kinship.* Cambridge: Cambridge University Press.

Carucci, Laurence Marshall. 1997. *Nuclear Nativity: Rituals of Renewal and Empowerment in the Marshall Islands.* DeKalb: Northern Illinois University Press.

———. 2004. Review of *Bravo for the Marshallese,* by Holly Barker. *Contemporary Pacific* 16 (2): 445–49.

Carucci, Laurence Marshall, and Mary H. Maifeld. 1999. "*Ien e Taan im Jerata,* Times of Suffering and Ill Fortune: An Overview of Daily Life on Ujelang and Enewetak since 1946." Report submitted to the Public Advocate's Office, Nuclear Claims Tribunal, Majuro, Republic of the Marshall Islands.

Cavadini, Fabio, and Amanda King. 2010. *Colour Change.* Sydney: Frontyard Films. DVD.

Central Intelligence Agency. 2014. "Solomon Islands." *The World Factbook.* www.cia.gov/library/publications/the-world-factbook/geos/bp.html.

CERD (Committee on the Elimination of Racial Discrimination). 2009. "Concluding Observations of the Committee on the Elimination of Racial Discrimination: Suriname." UN Doc. CERD/C/SUR/CO/12, March 13. http://tbinternet.ohchr.org/_layouts/treatybodyexternal/Download.aspx?symbolno=CERD/C/SUR/CO/12.

Cernea, Michael, ed. 1985. *Putting People First: Sociological Variables and Rural Development.* New York: Oxford University Press.

Chakrabarty, Dipesh. 2000. *Provincializing Europe: Postcolonial Thought and Historical Difference.* Princeton, NJ: Princeton University Press.

Charlesworth, Simon. 2000. *A Phenomenology of Working-Class Experience.* Cambridge: Cambridge University Press.

Chatterton, Paul. 1996. "Conservation as Development." Networked as "PNG: Conservation thru Community Development." PNG Rainforest Campaign News, March 25.

Chauvel, Richard. 2005. *Constructing Papuan Nationalism: History, Ethnicity, and Adaption.* Policy Studies 14. Washington, DC: East-West Center.

Checker, Melissa. 2005. *Polluted Promises: Environmental Racism and the Search for Justice in a Southern Town.* New York: New York University Press.

Clark, Jeffrey. 1997. "State of Desire: Transformations in Huli Sexuality." In *Sites of Desire/Economies of Pleasure: Sexualities in Asia and the Pacific,* edited by Lenore Manderson and Margaret Jolly, 191–211. Chicago: University of Chicago Press.

Clifford, James. 1988. *The Predicament of Culture: Twentieth-Century Ethnography, Literature and Art.* Cambridge, MA: Harvard University Press.

———. 2015. "Feeling Historical." In *Writing Culture and the Life of Anthropology,* edited by Orin Starn, 25–34. Durham, NC: Duke University Press.

Clifford, James, and George Marcus. 1986. *Writing Culture: The Poetics and Politics of Ethnography.* Berkeley: University of California Press.

CLIM (Commissie Landrechten Inheemsen Beneden-Marowijne). 2006. "*Marauny Na'na Emandobo Lokono Shikwabana* (Marowijne—Our Territory). Traditional Use and Management of the Lower Marowijne Area by the Kaliña and Lokono: A Surinamese Case Study in the Context of Article 10(c) of the Convention on Biological Diversity." Paramaribo, Suriname: VIDS and Forest Peoples Programme.

Colchester, Marcus. 2004. "Conservation Policy and Indigenous Peoples." *Environmental Science and Policy* 7:145–53.

———. 2005. "Maps, Power, and the Defense of Territory: The Upper Mazaruni Land Claim in Guyana." In *Communities and Conservation: Histories and Politics of Community-Based Natural Resource Management,* edited by J. Peter Brosius, Anna Lowenhaupt Tsing, and Charles Zerner, 271–303. New York: AltaMira.

Colchester, Marcus, Jean La Rose, and Kid James. 2002. *Mining and Amerindians in Guyana.* Ottawa: North-South Institute.

Colwell-Chanthaphonh, Chip, and T.J. Ferguson, eds. 2008. *Collaboration in Archaeological Practice: Engaging Descendant Communities.* Lanham, MD: AltaMira.

Comaroff, John L., and Jean Comaroff, eds. 2006. *Law and Disorder in the Postcolony.* Chicago: University of Chicago Press.

———. 2009. *Ethnicity, Inc.* Chicago: University of Chicago Press.

Conklin, Beth. 1997. "Body Paint, Feathers, and VCRs: Aesthetics in Authenticity in Amazonian Activism." *American Ethnologist* 24 (4): 711–37.

Conklin, Beth A., and Laura R. Graham. 1995. "The Shifting Middle Ground: Amazonian Indians and Eco-Politics." *American Anthropologist* 97 (4): 1–17.

Connell, John. 1991. "Compensation and Conflict: The Bougainville Copper Mine, Papua New Guinea." In *Mining and Indigenous Peoples in Australasia,* edited by John Connell and Richard Howitt, 55–76. Sydney: Sydney University Press.

Conservation International. 1995. "Makira Communities Reject Logging Firm." *CI News from the Front* 1 (2).

Cook, Samuel R. 2015. "The Activist Trajectory and Collaborative Context: Indigenous Peoples in Virginia and the Formation of an Anthropological Tradition." *Collaborative Anthropologies* 7 (2): 115–41.

Cookson, Michael Benedict. 2008. "Batik Irian: Imprints of Indonesian Papua." PhD diss., Australian National University.

Cooley, Alexander, and James Ron. 2002. "The NGO Scramble: Organizational Insecurity and the Political Economy of Transnational Action." *International Security* 27 (1): 5–39.

Coombe, Rosemary J. 1998. *The Cultural Life of Intellectual Properties: Authorship, Appropriation, and the Law.* Durham, NC: Duke University Press.

Coumans, Catherine. 2004. "'Beware of Anthropologists': Conflict, Social Acceptability and Anthropological Brokerage in Mining." Presented at the Society for Applied Anthropology meeting in Dallas, Texas, April.

———. 2011. "Occupying Spaces Created by Conflict: Anthropologists, Development NGOs, Responsible Investment, and Mining." *Current Anthropology* 52 (S3): S29–43.

Cove, John J. 1996. "Playing the Devil's Advocate: Anthropology in *Delgamuukw.*" *Political and Legal Anthropology Review* 19:53–57.

Creed, Gerald W., ed. 2006. *The Seductions of Community.* Santa Fe: SAR.

Cronon, William. 1983. *Changes in the Land: Indians, Colonists, and the Ecology of New England.* New York: Hill and Wang.

———. 1995. "The Trouble with Wilderness; or, Getting Back to the Wrong Nature." In *Uncommon Ground: Rethinking the Human Place in Nature,* edited by William Cronon, 69–90. New York: W. W. Norton.

Daley, Paul. 2000. "Australians in PNG Guns-for-Drugs Deals." *Sydney Morning Herald.*

Das, Veena. 1989. "Subaltern as Perspective." In *Subaltern Studies: Writings on South Asian History and Society,* vol. 6, edited by Ranajit Guha, 310–24. New Delhi: Oxford University Press.

Davenport, William. 1960. "Marshall Island Navigational Charts." *Imago Mundi* 15:19–26.

Davenport, William H., and Gülbün Çoker. 1967. "The Moro Movement of Guadalcanal, British Solomon Islands Protectorate." *Journal of the Polynesian Society* 76:123–75.

Dean, Bartholomew, and Jerome M. Levi, eds. 2003. *At the Risk of Being Heard: Indigenous Rights, Identity, and Postcolonial States.* Ann Arbor: University of Michigan Press.

Desowitz, Robert. 1981. *New Guinea Tapeworms and Jewish Grandmothers: Tales of Parasites and People.* London: W. W. Norton.

Detheridge, Alan, and Noble Pepple. 1998. "A Response to Frynas." *Third World Quarterly* 19 (3): 479–86.

Dirlik, Arif. 2001. Comment on "Lost Worlds: Environmental Disaster, 'Culture Loss,' and the Law" by Stuart Kirsch. *Current Anthropology* 42 (2): 181–82.

Dominguez, Virginia. 1986. *White by Definition: Social Classification in Creole Louisiana*. New Brunswick, NJ: Rutgers University Press.

Dooley, Kate, and Tom Griffiths, eds. 2014. *Indigenous Peoples' Rights, Forests and Climate Policies in Guyana: A Special Report*. Georgetown, Guyana: Amerindian Peoples Association and Moreton-in-Marsh, U.K.: Forest Peoples Programme.

Dove, Michael. 1993. "A Revisionist View of Tropical Deforestation and Development." *Environmental Conservation* 20 (1): 17–56.

———. 1996. "Center, Periphery, and Biodiversity: A Paradox of Governance and a Developmental Challenge." In *Valuing Local Knowledge: Indigenous People and Intellectual Property Rights,* edited by Stephen B. Brush and Doreen Stabinsky, 41–67. Washington, DC: Island Press.

Dunkerley, David L., and Neil D. Hallam. 1997. "Gold Ridge and Surroundings, Guadalcanal, Solomon Islands: An Environmental Assessment." Unpublished report, Monash University, Australia.

Eckert, Julia, Brian Donahoe, Zerrin Özlem Biner, and Christian Strümpell. 2012a. "Introduction: Law's Travels and Transformations." In *Law against the State: Ethnographic Forays into Law's Transformations,* edited by Eckert, Donahoe, Biner, and Strümpell, 1–22. Cambridge Studies in Law and Society. Cambridge: Cambridge University Press.

———, eds. 2012b. *Law against the State: Ethnographic Forays into Law's Transformations.* Cambridge Studies in Law and Society. Cambridge: Cambridge University Press.

Edmond, Gary. 2004. "Thick Decisions: Expertise, Advocacy and Reasonableness in the Federal Court of Australia." *Oceania* 74:190–230.

Ellen, Roy. 1998. Comment on "The Development of Indigenous Knowledge" by Paul Sillitoe. *Current Anthropology* 39:238–39.

Elmslie, J. 2002. *Irian Jaya under the Gun: Indonesian Economic Development versus West Papuan Nationalism.* Honolulu: University of Hawai'i Press.

———. 2010. "West Papuan Demographic Transition and the 2010 Indonesian Census: 'Slow Motion Genocide' or Not?" CPACS Working Paper No. 11/1. University of Sydney.

Epstein, T. S. 1968. *Capitalism, Primitive and Modern: Some Aspects of Tolai Economic Growth.* Manchester, U.K.: Manchester University Press.

Eriksen, Thomas Hylland. 2006. *Engaging Anthropology: The Case for a Public Presence.* Oxford: Berg.

Erikson, Patricia Pierce. 2008. "Decolonizing the 'Nation's Attic': The National Museum of the American Indian and the Politics of Knowledge-Making in a National Space." In *The National Museum of the American Indian: Critical Conversations,* edited by Amy Lonetree and Amanda J. Cobb-Greetham, 43–83. Lincoln: University of Nebraska Press.

Escobar, Arturo. 1995. *Encountering Development: The Making and Unmaking of the Third World.* Princeton, NJ: Princeton University Press.

———. 2001. Comment on "Lost Worlds: Environmental Disaster, 'Culture Loss,' and the Law" by Stuart Kirsch. *Current Anthropology* 42 (2): 183–84.

———. 2008. *Territories of Difference: Place, Movements, Life, Redes*. Durham, NC: Duke University Press.

Ethnography-as-Activism Workshop. 2010. "Ethnography-as-Activism Manifesto." Unpublished manuscript, January. Ann Arbor, MI.

Evans, Daniel. 2010. "Tensions at the Gold Ridge Mine, Guadalcanal, Solomon Islands." *Pacific Economic Bulletin* 25 (3): 121–34.

Farhadian, Charles E., ed. 2007. *The Testimony Project: Papua. A Collection of Personal Histories in West Papua*. Jakarta, Indonesia: Suwaan Langoan Indah.

Farmer, Paul. 2004. *Pathologies of Power: Health, Human Rights, and the New War on the Poor*. Berkeley: University of California Press.

Fassin, Didier. 2013. "Why Ethnography Matters: On Anthropology and Its Publics." *Cultural Anthropology* 28 (4): 621–46.

Feeley-Harnik, Gillian. 1991. *A Green Estate: Restoring Independence in Madagascar*. Washington, DC: Smithsonian Institution Press.

Feeny, David, Fikret Berkes, Bonnie J. McCay, and James M. Acheson. 1990. "The Tragedy of the Commons: Twenty-Two Years Later." *Human Ecology* 18 (1): 1–19.

Fergie, Deane. 2004. "Reflections on 'Thick Decisions': The Importance of Power, Privilege and Textual Analysis in Responding to the Legal Colonisation of Anthropology." *Oceania* 75 (1): 49–56.

Ferguson, James. 1990. *The Anti-Politics Machine: "Development," Depoliticization, and Bureaucratic Power in Lesotho*. Cambridge: Cambridge University Press.

———. 1999. *Expectations of Modernity: Myths and Meanings of Urban Life on the Zambian Copperbelt*. Berkeley: University of California Press.

Filer, Colin. 1990. "The Bougainville Rebellion, the Mining Industry and the Process of Social Disintegration in Papua New Guinea." In *The Bougainville Crisis,* edited by R.J. May and M. Spriggs, 73–112. Bathurst, Australia: Crawford House.

———. 1996. "Global Alliances and Local Mediations." *Anthropology Today* 12 (5): 26.

———. 1997a. "The Melanesian Way of Menacing the Mining Industry." In *Environment and Development in the Pacific Islands,* edited by Ben Burt and Christian Clerk, 91–122. Pacific Policy Paper 25. Canberra: Australian National University; Port Moresby: University of Papua New Guinea Press.

———, ed. 1997b. *The Political Economy of Forest Management in Papua New Guinea*. NRI Monograph 32. Boroko, PNG: National Research Institute.

———. 1997c. "West Side Story: The State's and Other Stakes in the Ok Tedi Mine." In *The Ok Tedi Settlement: Issues, Outcomes and Implications,* edited by Glenn Banks and Chris Ballard, 56–93. Pacific Policy Paper 27. Canberra: National Centre for Development Studies and Resource Management in Asia-Pacific, Australian National University.

———. 1999. "The Dialectics of Negation and Negotiation in the Anthropology of Mineral Resource Development in Papua New Guinea." In *The Anthropology of Power: Empowerment and Disempowerment in Changing Structures,* edited by Angela Cheater, 88–102. ASA Monographs 36. New York: Routledge.

Filer, Colin, Glenn Banks, and John Burton. 2008. "The Fragmentation of Responsibilities in the Melanesian Mining Sector." In *Earth Matters: Indigenous Peoples, Extractive Industries and Corporate Social Responsibility,* edited by Ciaran O'Faircheallaigh and Saleem Ali, 163–79. Sheffield, UK: Greenleaf.

Filer, Colin, and Wari Iamo. 1989. "Base-Line Planning Study for the Lakekamu Gold Project, Gulf Province." Department of Anthropology and Sociology, University of Papua New Guinea, Port Moresby. January (revised draft). Mimeo.

Filer, Colin, and Benedict Imbun. 2009. "A Short History of Mineral Development Policies in Papua New Guinea, 1972–2002." In *Policy Making and Implementation: Studies from Papua New Guinea,* edited by R. J. May, 75–116. Canberra: Australian National University Press.

Fine-Dare, Kathleen S. 2002. *Grave Injustice: The American Indian Repatriation Movement and NAGPRA.* Lincoln: University of Nebraska Press.

Finney, Ben. 1994. *Voyage of Rediscovery: A Cultural Odyssey through Polynesia.* Berkeley: University of California Press.

Forest Peoples Programme. 2016. "Indigenous Peoples in Suriname Win Important Case in the Inter-American Court of Human Rights." February 23. Moreton-in-Marsh, U.K.: Forest Peoples Programme. www.forestpeoples.org/topics/inter-american-human-rights-system/news/2016/02/indigenous-peoples-suriname-win-important-cas.

Forsyth, Timothy. 1998. Comment on "The Development of Indigenous Knowledge" by Paul Sillitoe. *Current Anthropology* 39:240–41.

Fortun, Kim. 2001. *Advocacy after Bhopal: Environmentalism, Disaster, New Global Orders.* Chicago: University of Chicago Press.

Foster, H., and A. Grove. 1993. "Looking behind the Masks: A Land Claims Discussion Paper for Researchers, Lawyers and Their Employers." *University of British Columbia Law Review* 27:213–55.

Fraenkel, Jon. 2004. *The Manipulation of Custom: From Uprising to Intervention in the Solomon Islands.* Canberra: Australian National University Press.

Franky, Y. L., and Selwyn Morgan, eds. 2015. "Papua Oil Palm Atlas: The Companies behind the Plantation Explosion." March. https://awasmifee.potager.org/uploads/2015/04/atlas-sawit-en.pdf.

Fritzsche, Marcus. 1988. "Serological Survey on Human Cysticercosis in Irianese Refugee Camps, Papua New Guinea." Inaugural-Dissertation zur Erlangung der Doktorwurde der Medizinischen Fakultat der Universitat Zurich. Institut fur Parasitologie der Universitat Zurich.

Frynas, Jedrzej George. 1998. "Political Instability and Business: Focus on Shell in Nigeria." *Third World Quarterly* 19 (3): 457–78.

———. 2000. "Shell in Nigeria: A Further Contribution." *Third World Quarterly* 21 (1): 157–64.

Gabia Gagarimabu v. BHP and Ok Tedi Mining. 2001. Supreme Court of Victoria. Transcript of Proceedings. Melbourne. August 6.

Garner, Bryan A., ed. 1999. *Black's Law Dictionary.* 7th ed. St. Paul, MN: West.

Geertz, Clifford. 1973. *The Interpretation of Cultures: Selected Essays.* New York: Basic Books.

———. 1984. "'From the Native's Point of View': On the Nature of Anthropological Understanding." In *Culture Theory: Essays on Mind, Self, and Emotion,* edited by Richard Shweder and Robert Levine, 123–36. Cambridge: Cambridge University Press.

———. 1988. *Works as Lives: The Anthropologist as Author.* Stanford, CA: Stanford University Press.

———. 1998. "Deep Hanging Out." *New York Review of Books* 45 (16): 69.

Genz, Joseph. 2011. "Navigating the Revival of Voyaging in the Marshall Islands: Predicaments of Preservation and Possibilities of Collaboration." *Contemporary Pacific* 23 (1): 1–34.

Gerritsen, Rolf, and Martha Macintyre. 1991. "Dilemmas of Distribution: The Misima Gold Mine, Papua New Guinea." In *Mining and Indigenous Peoples in Australasia,* edited by John Connell and Richard Howitt, 35–54. Sydney: Sydney University Press.

Gewertz, Deborah, and Frederick Errington. 1991. *Twisted Histories, Altered Contexts in Papua New Guinea: On Ethnography and Chambri Lives in a World System.* Cambridge: Cambridge University Press.

Gilbert, Jérémie. 2016. *Indigenous Peoples' Land Rights under International Law: From Victims to Actors.* 2nd rev. ed. Leiden, NL: Brill, Nijhoff.

———. 2017. *Strategic Litigation Impacts: Indigenous Peoples' Land Rights.* New York: Open Society Foundations. www.opensocietyfoundations.org/reports/strategic-litigation-impacts-indigenous-peoples-land-rights.

Gillison, Gillian. 2001. "Reflections on Pigs for the Ancestors." In *Ecology and the Sacred: Engaging the Anthropology of Roy A. Rappaport,* edited by Ellen Messer and Michael Lambek, 291–99. Ann Arbor: University of Michigan Press.

Ginsburg, Faye. 1997. "From Little Things, Big Things Grow: Indigenous Media and Cultural Activism." In *Between Resistance and Revolution: Cultural Politics and Social Protest,* edited by Richard G. Fox and Orin Starn, 118–44. New Brunswick, NJ: Rutgers University Press.

———. 1998. *Contested Lives: The Abortion Debate in an American Community.* Updated ed. Berkeley: University of California Press.

Glazebrook, Diana. 2004. "Teaching Performance Art Is Like Sharpening the Blade of a Knife." *Asia Pacific Journal of Anthropology* 5 (1): 1–14.

———. 2008. *Permissive Residents: West Papuan Refugees Living in Papua New Guinea.* Canberra: Australian National University Press.

Goffman, Erving. 1974. *Frame Analysis: An Essay on the Organization of Experience.* New York: Harper Colophon.

Golden, Brigham. 2003. "Political Millenarianism and the Economy of Conflict: Reflections on Papua by an Activist Anthropologist." *Asia Source.* June 23.

Goldman, Laurence R., ed. 2000. *Social Impact Analysis: An Applied Anthropology Manual.* Oxford: Berg.

Goldman, Laurence, and Scott Baum. 2000. Introduction to *Social Impact Analysis: An Applied Anthropology Manual,* edited by Laurence Goldman, 1–31. Oxford: Berg.

Goldstein, Daniel M. 2012. *Outlawed: Between Security and Rights in a Bolivian City.* Durham, NC: Duke University Press.

Goodale, Mark. 2009. *Surrendering to Utopia: An Anthropology of Human Rights.* Stanford, CA: Stanford University Press.

———. 2016. "Dark Matter: Toward a Political Economy of Indigenous Rights and Aspirational Politics." *Critique of Anthropology* 36 (4): 439–57.

Goodland, Robert, ed. 2009. *Suriname's Bakhuis Bauxite Mine: An Independent Review of SRK's Impact Assessment.* Paramaribo, Suriname: Bureau VIDS.

Gordon, John. 1997. "The Ok Tedi Lawsuit in Retrospect." In *The Ok Tedi Settlement: Issues, Outcomes and Implications,* edited by Glenn Banks and Chris Ballard, 141–66. Pacific Policy Paper 27. Canberra: National Centre for Development Studies and Resource Management in Asia-Pacific, Australian National University.

Gough, Kathleen. 1968. "New Proposals for Anthropologists." *Current Anthropology.* 9 (5): 403–35.

Government of Guyana. 2013. "Response to the Request for Precautionary Measures: Request for Information re: Akawaio Indigenous Community of Isseneru and the Amerindian Peoples' Association (APA)." Submitted to the Inter-American Commission on Human Rights, MC-283–13. November 30.

———. 2014. "Submission of Additional Information to the Inter-American Commission on Human Rights with Regard to the Petition by the Amerindian Peoples' Association (APA) and the Akawaio Indigenous Community of Isseneru." Submitted to the Inter-American Commission on Human Rights, MC-283–13. June 5.

Graham, Bill, and David Lowe. 1998. "Statement of Periods of Denied Use and Comments on Valuation Process." Before the Nuclear Claims Tribunal, Republic of the Marshall Islands. In the matter of the Alabs of Rongelap et al., claimants for compensation (NCT No. 23–02440), in the matter of Jabon on Rongelap Atoll (NCT No. 23–05443-B), in the matter of Rongerik Atoll by Iroij Anjua Loeak et al., claimants for compensation (NCT No. 23–05445-B) and in the matter of Iroij Imata Jabro Kabua, Rongelap Atoll, claimant for compensation (NCT No. 23–00501).

Greely, H. T. 1998. "Legal, Ethical, and Social Issues in Human Genome Research." *Annual Review of Anthropology* 27:473–502.

Griffiths, Tom. 2003. "Ownership, Use, Occupation and Management of Ancestral Akawaio and Arekuna Territory in the Upper Mazaruni, Guyana: A Study of Traditional Tenure over Lands and Territory Covered by the 1959 Upper Mazaruni Amerindian District." Unpublished expert report on land tenure.

Haan, Raphael den. 1955. "Het Varkensfeest zoals het Plaatsvindt in het Gebied van de Rivieren Kao, Muju en Mandobo (Ned. Nieuw Guinea)." *Bijdragen tot de Taal-, Land- en Volkenkunde* 111:92–106, 162–90.

Hale, Charles R. 2006. "Activist Research v. Cultural Critique: Indigenous Land Rights and the Contradictions of Politically Engaged Anthropology." *Cultural Anthropology* 21 (1): 96–120.

———. 2007. "'In Praise of Reckless Minds': Making a Case for Activist Anthropology." In *Anthropology Put to Work,* edited by Les Field and R. G. Fox, 103–27. Oxford: Berg.

Hallet, Judith, prod. 1994. *Lords of the Garden.* New York: Arts and Entertainment Network and Paris: Tele-Image. DVD.

Hallpike, C. R. 1977. *Bloodshed and Vengeance in the Papuan Mountains.* Oxford: Oxford University Press.

Hammar, Lawrence James. 2010. *Sin, Sex and Stigma: A Pacific Response to HIV and AIDS.* Oxon, UK: Sean Kingston.

Hann, C. M. 1998. "Introduction: The Embeddedness of Property." In *Property Relations: Renewing the Anthropological Tradition,* edited by C. M. Hann, 1–47. Cambridge: Cambridge University Press.

Haraway, Donna. 1988. "Situated Knowledges: The Science Question in Feminism and the Privilege of Partial Perspective." *Feminist Studies* 14:575–99.

Hardin, Garrett. 1968. "The Tragedy of the Commons." *Science* 62:1243–48.

Harmon, Amy. 2010. "Indian Tribe Wins Fight to Limit Research of Its DNA." *New York Times,* April 21. www.nytimes.com/2010/04/22/us/22dna.html?adxnnl=1&adxnnlx=1311889212-EQfpdyT5vCEbZtIuRU+qTg.

Harrison, Simon. 1999. "Cultural Boundaries." *Anthropology Today* 15 (5): 10–13.

Harvey, David. 2003. *The New Imperialism.* Oxford: Oxford University Press.

Hau'ofa, Epeli. 1981. *Mekeo: Inequality and Ambivalence in a Village Society.* Canberra: Australian National University Press.

Henare, Amiria, Martin Holbraad, and Sari Wastell, eds. 2006. *Thinking through Things: Theorising Artefacts in Ethnographic Perspective.* New York: Routledge.

Hennessy, Logan. 2014. "Where There Is No Company: Indigenous Peoples, Sustainability, and the Challenges of Mid-stream Mining Reforms in Guyana's Small-Scale Gold Sector." *New Political Economy* 20 (1): 1–28.

Hernawan, Budi. 2013. "From the Theatre of Torture to the Theatre of Peace: The Politics of Torture and Reimagining Peacebuilding in Papua, Indonesia." PhD diss., Australian National University.

———. 2014. "Torture as a Mode of Governance: Reflections on the Phenomenon of Torture in Papua, Indonesia." In *From "Stone-Age" to "Real Time": Exploring Papuan Temporalities, Mobilities and Religiosities,* edited by Martin Slama and Jenny Munro, 195–220. Canberra: Australian National University Press.

Herzfeld. Michael. 1997. *Cultural Intimacy: Social Poetics in the Nation-State.* New York: Routledge

Heyman, Josiah McC. 2010. "Activism in Anthropology: Exploring the Present through Eric R. Wolf's Vietnam-Era Work." *Dialectical Anthropology* 34:287–93.

Higuchi, Toshihiro. 2008. "An Environmental Origin of Antinuclear Activism in Japan, 1954–1963: The Government, the Grassroots Movement, and the Politics of Risk." *Peace and Change* 33 (3): 333–67.

Hill, Jane H., and Kenneth C Hill. 1986. *Speaking Mexicano: Dynamics of Syncretic Language in Central Mexico.* Tucson: University of Arizona.

Hilson, Gavin, and Timothy Laing. 2017a. "Gold Mining, Indigenous Land Claims and Conflict in Guyana's Hinterland." *Journal of Rural Studies* 50:172–87.

———. 2017b. "Guyana Gold: A Unique Resource Curse?" *Journal of Development Studies* 53 (2): 229–48.

Hirsch, Eric. 1995. Introduction to *The Anthropology of the Landscape: Perspectives on Space and Place,* edited by Eric Hirsch and Michael O'Hanlon, 1–30. Oxford: Clarendon.

———. 2001. "New Boundaries of Influence in Highland Papua: 'Culture,' Mining and Ritual Conversations." *Oceania* 71 (4): 298–312.

Hirsch, Eric, and Marilyn Strathern, eds. 2004. *Transactions and Creations: Property Debates and the Stimulus of Melanesia.* Oxford: Berghahn.

Hoesterey, James B. 2012. "The Adventures of Mark and Olly: The Pleasures and Horrors of Anthropology on TV." In *Human No More: Digital Subjectivities, Unhuman Subjects and the End of Anthropology,* edited by Neil Whitehead and Michael Wesch, 245–77. Boulder: University of Colorado Press.

Hogbin, Ian. 1964. *A Guadalcanal Society: The Kaoka Speakers.* New York: Holt, Rinehart and Winston.

Hohfeld, Wesley N. 1913. "Some Fundamental Legal Conceptions as Applied in Judicial Reasoning." *Yale Law Journal* 23 (1): 16–59.

Holland, H. Russel. 1996. Letter to the editor. *American Indian Culture and Research Journal* 20 (3): 167–70.

Hookey, J. F. 1973. "The Establishment of a Plantation Economy in the British Solomon Island Protectorate." *The History of Melanesia.* Second Waigani Seminar (1968), 229–38. Port Moresby: University of Papua and New Guinea.

Howard, Michael C. 1991. *Fiji: Race and Politics in an Island State.* Vancouver: University of British Columbia Press.

———. 1993. "Competing Views of the Environment and Development in Irian Jaya." Presented at the Annual Meeting of the American Anthropological Association, Washington, DC, November.

HRC (Human Rights Committee). 2004. "Concluding Observations of the Human Rights Committee: Suriname." UN Doc. CCPR/CO/80/SUR, May 4.

Hughes, Ian. 1977. *New Guinea Stone Age Tools.* Terra Australis 2. Canberra: Research School of Pacific Studies, Australian National University.

Hyndman, David. 1987. "How the West (Papua) Was Won: Cysticercosis and Indonesian Counter-insurgency in a Continuing Fourth World War." *Cultural Survival Quarterly* 11 (4): 8–13.

———. 1988. "Ok Tedi: New Guinea's Disaster Mine." *Ecologist* 18 (1): 24–29.

International Commission of Jurists, Australian Section. 1985. *The Status of Border Crossers from Irian Jaya to Papua New Guinea.* Sydney: Australia Section of the International Commission of Jurists.

Jackson, Richard. 1992. "Undermining or Determining the Nature of the State?" In *Resources, Development and Politics in the Pacific Islands,* edited by Stephen Henningham and R. J. May, 79–89. Bathurst, Australia: Crawford House.

———. 1998. "David and Goliath on the Fly." *Journal of Pacific History* 33 (3): 307–11.

Jakarta Post. 1991. "Korowai Tribe in Irian Jaya Not All Female." March 20.

Jameson, Frederick. 1994. *The Seeds of Time.* New York: Columbia University Press.

Johnston, Barbara Rose, and Holly M. Barker. 2008. *Consequential Damages of Nuclear War: The Rongelap Report.* New York: Routledge.

Jolly, Margaret, and Lenore Manderson. 1997. Introduction to *Sites of Desire /Economies of Pleasure: Sexualities in Asia and the Pacific,* edited by Lenore Manderson and Margaret Jolly, 1–26. Chicago: University of Chicago Press.

Jorgensen, Daniel. 1981. "Taro and Arrows: Order, Entropy and Religion among the Telefolmin." PhD diss., University of British Columbia.

Jorgensen, Joseph G. 1995. "Ethnicity, Not Culture? Obfuscating Social Science in the *Exxon Valdez* Oil Spill Case." *American Indian Culture and Research Journal* 19 (4): 1–124.

Juris, Jeffrey. 2008. *Networking Futures: The Movements against Corporate Globalization.* Durham, NC: Duke University Press.

Justinian. 2002. "Slater & Gordon's Tropical Nightmare." September. www.justinian.com.au/archive/slater-gordons-tropical-nightmare.html.

Kabar-Irian (Irian newsletter). 1999a. "AIDS in Timika." May 11. Email newsgroup distributed by IRJA.org.

———. 1999b. "AIDS Suspected in Thai's Death." September 5. Originally published in *Jakarta Post.* Email newsgroup distributed by IRJA.org.

———. 1999c. "Governor Concerned by HIV in Province." September 28. Email newsgroup distributed by IRJA.org.

———. 1999d. "People Survey." April 22. Email newsgroup distributed by IRJA.org.

Kabutaulaka, Tarcisius Tara. 2001. "Beyond Ethnicity: The Political Economy of the Guadalcanal Crisis in Solomon Islands." State, Society and Governance in Melanesia Working Paper no. 1. Australian National University, Canberra. http://hdl.handle.net/1885/41949.

Kahn, Miriam. 2009. Review of *Consequential Damages of Nuclear War,* by Barbara Rose Johnston and Holly M. Barker. *Contemporary Pacific* 21 (2): 401–4.

Kaipman, Paskalis. 1974. "Some Notes about the Muyu People in Jayapura." *Irian: Bulletin of Irian Jaya Development* 3 (1): 21–25.

Kaliña and Lokono Peoples v. Suriname. 2015. "Merits, Reparations and Costs." Judgment of November 25, 2015. Inter-American Court of Human Rights. Series C. No. 309. www.corteidh.or.cr/docs/casos/articulos/seriec_309_ing.pdf.

Kalinoe, Lawrence. 2003. "Independent Review Report on the Ok Tedi Community Mine Continuation Agreements and Related Matters." Prepared for Oxfam Community Aid Abroad, Australia.

Kama, Thomas. 1979. "Guadalcanal Plains." In *Land Research in Solomon Islands,* edited by Ian C. Heath, 150–58. Honiara, Solomon Islands: Ministry of Agriculture and Lands.

Kambel, Ellen-Rose. 2002. "Resource Conflicts, Gender, and Indigenous Rights in Suriname: Local, National and Global Perspectives." PhD diss., University of Leiden.

Kambel, Ellen-Rose, and Fergus MacKay. 1999. *The Rights of Indigenous Peoples and Maroons in Suriname.* IWGIA Document No. 96. Copenhagen: International Work Group for Indigenous Affairs.

Keck, Margaret E., and Kathryn Sikkink. 1998. *Activists beyond Borders: Advocacy Networks in International Politics.* Ithaca, NY: Cornell University Press.

Keck, Verena. 1998. Introduction to *Common Worlds and Single Lives: Constituting Knowledge in Pacific Societies,* edited by Verena Keck, 1–29. Oxford: Berg.

Keesing, Roger. 1989. "Creating the Past: Custom and Identity in the Contemporary Pacific." *Contemporary Pacific* 1 (1–2): 19–42.

Ketan, Joseph [with Stuart Kirsch]. 1989. "Blood Brothers Separated by the Border." *Niugini Nius* (May 24), 27 (923): 7.

King, David. 1997. "The Big Polluter and the Constructing of Ok Tedi: Eco-imperialism and Underdevelopment along the Ok Tedi and Fly Rivers of Papua New Guinea." In *The Ok Tedi Settlement: Issues, Outcomes and Implications,* edited by Glenn Banks and Chris Ballard, 94–112. Pacific Policy Paper 27. Canberra: National Centre for Development Studies and Resource Management in Asia-Pacific, The Australian National University.

King, Peter. 2004. *West Papua and Indonesia since Suharto: Independence, Autonomy or Chaos?* Sydney, Australia: University of New South Wales Press.

Kirksey, Eben. 2012. *Freedom in Entangled Worlds: West Papua and the Architecture of Global Power.* Durham, NC: Duke University Press.

Kirsch, Stuart. 1989a. "Ok Tedi River a Sewer." *Times of Papua New Guinea,* June 1–7, 491:3.

———. 1989b. "The Yonggom, the Refugee Camps along the Border, and the Impact of the Ok Tedi Mine. *Research in Melanesia* 12:30–61.

———. 1993. "Yonggom of Papua New Guinea." *Cultural Survival Quarterly* 17 (3): 40.

———. 1995. "Social Impact of the Ok Tedi Mine on the Yonggom Villages of the North Fly, 1992." *Research in Melanesia* 19:23–102. Originally appeared as Ok-Fly Social Monitoring Programme, Report 5. Port Moresby: Unisearch PNG.

———. 1996a. Anthropologists and Global Alliances. *Anthropology Today* 12 (4): 14–16.

———. 1996b. "Refugees and Representation: Politics, Critical Discourse and Ethnography along the New Guinea Border." In *Mainstream(s) and Margins:*

Cultural Politics in the 90s, edited by Michael Morgan and Susan Leggett, 222–36. Westport, CT: Greenwood Press.

———. 1997a. "Cannibal Tales." Film review essay of *Lords of the Garden. Pacific Studies* 20 (2): 170–79.

———. 1997b. "Indigenous Response to Environmental Impact along the Ok Tedi." In *Compensation for Resource Development in Papua New Guinea,* edited by Susan Toft, 143–55. Law Reform Commission of Papua New Guinea Monograph 6 and Pacific Policy Paper 24. Canberra: Australian National University Press.

———. 1997c. "Is Ok Tedi a Precedent? Implications of the Settlement." In *The Ok Tedi Settlement: Issues, Outcomes and Implications,* edited by Glenn Banks and Chris Ballard, 118–40. Pacific Policy Paper 27. Canberra: National Centre for Development Studies and Resource Management in Asia-Pacific, Australian National University.

———. 1997d. "Lost Tribes: Indigenous People and the Social Imaginary." *Anthropological Quarterly* 70 (2): 58–67.

———. 1997e. "Regional Dynamics and Conservation in Papua New Guinea: The Lakekamu River Basin Project." *Contemporary Pacific* 9 (1): 97–121.

———. 2001. "Lost Worlds: Environmental Disaster, 'Culture Loss,' and the Law." *Current Anthropology* 42 (2): 167–98.

———. 2002a. "Anthropology and Advocacy: A Case Study of the Campaign against the Ok Tedi Mine." *Critique of Anthropology* 22 (2): 175–200.

———. 2002b. "Litigating Ok Tedi (Again)." *Cultural Survival Quarterly* 26 (3): 15–19.

———. 2002c. "Rumour and Other Narratives of Political Violence in West Papua." *Critique of Anthropology* 22 (1): 53–79.

———. 2003. "Mining and Environmental Human Rights in Papua New Guinea." In *Transnational Corporations and Human Rights,* edited by George Jedrzej Frynas and Scott Pegg, 115–36. London: Palgrave.

———. 2004a. "No Justice in Ok Tedi Settlement. *Cultural Survival Quarterly* 28 (2): 52–53.

———. 2004b. "Property Limits: Debates on the Body, Nature, and Culture." In *Transactions and Creations: Property Debates and the Stimulus of Melanesia,* edited by Eric Hirsch and Marilyn Strathern, 21–39. Oxford: Berghahn.

———. 2006. *Reverse Anthropology: Indigenous Analysis of Social and Environmental Relations in New Guinea.* Stanford, CA: Stanford University Press.

———. 2007. "Indigenous Movements and the Risks of Counterglobalization: Tracking the Campaign against Papua New Guinea's Ok Tedi Mine." *American Ethnologist* 34 (2): 303–21.

———. 2008. "Social Relations and the Green Critique of Capitalism in Melanesia." *American Anthropologist* 110 (3): 288–98.

———. 2009a. "Comments on the Bakhuis Draft Environmental and Social Impact Report." In *Suriname's Bakhuis Bauxite Mine: An Independent Review of SRK's Impact Assessment,* edited by Robert Goodland, 28–59. Paramaribo, Suriname: Bureau VIDS.

———. 2009b. "Freedom and Development in Suriname." In "Indigenizing Development," edited by Alcida Ramos, Rafael Osorio, and José Pimenta. Special issue, *Poverty in Focus* 17:12–13.

———. 2009c. "Moral Dilemmas and Ethical Controversies." *Anthropology Today* 25 (6): 1–2.

———. 2010a. "Ethnographic Representation and the Politics of Violence in West Papua." *Critique of Anthropology* 30 (1): 3–22.

———, ed. 2010b. "Ethnography-as-Activism: Student Experiments, Dilemmas from the Field." *Collaborative Anthropologies* 3:69–154.

———. 2011. "Science, Property, and Kinship in Repatriation Debates." *Museum Anthropology* 34 (2): 91–96.

———. 2014. *Mining Capitalism: The Relationships between Corporations and Their Critics.* Berkeley: University of California Press.

———. 2015. "Affidavit, Kaliña and Lokono Peoples v. The Republic of Suriname." Case 12.639 of the Inter-American Court of Human Rights. January 27.

———. 2016. "Expert Report, Akawaio Indigenous Community of Isseneru and the Amerindian Peoples Association of Guyana." Petition 1424–13, Inter-American Commission on Human Rights. July 14.

Kirsch, Stuart, and Jennifer Moore. 2016. *Mining, Corporate Social Responsibility, and Conflict: The El Dorado Foundation and OceanaGold in El Salvador.* San Salvador, El Salvador: La Mesa; Washington, DC: Institute for Policy Studies. www.ips-dc.org/wp-content/uploads/2016/03/El-Dorado-Foundation-Report-2016-ENG-lowres.pdf.

Kiste, Robert C. 1974. *The Bikinians: A Study in Forced Migration.* Menlo Park, CA: Cummings.

Kopytoff, Igor. 1986. "The Cultural Biography of Things: Commoditization as Process." In *The Social Life of Things: Commodities in Cultural Perspective,* edited Arjun Appadurai, 64–91. Cambridge: Cambridge University Press.

Kroeber, Theodora. 1976. *Ishi in Two Worlds: A Biography of the Last Wild Indian in North America.* Berkeley: University of California Press.

Kundera, Milan. 1983. *The Joke.* New York: Penguin.

Lal, Brij V. 1992. *Broken Waves: A History of the Fiji Islands in the Twentieth Century.* Honolulu: University of Hawai'i Press.

Lasaqa, I. Q. 1972. *Melanesian's Choice: Tadhimboko Participation in the Solomon Islands Cash Economy.* New Guinea Research Bulletin no. 46. Canberra: New Guinea Research Unit, Australian National University.

———. 1984. *The Fijian People: Before and After Independence.* Canberra: Australian National University Press.

Lassiter, Luke Eric. 2005. "Collaborative Ethnography and Public Anthropology." *Current Anthropology* 46 (1): 83–106.

Latour, Bruno. 1993. *We Have Never Been Modern.* Translated by Catherine Porter. Cambridge, MA: Harvard University Press.

———. 2004. "Why Has Critique Run Out of Steam? From Matters of Fact to Matters of Concern." *Critical Inquiry* 30:225–48.

Lazarus, Heather. 2012. "Sea Change: Island Communities and Climate Change." *Annual Review of Anthropology* 41:175–94.

Lees, Annette. 1995. "Makira Project Profile." In *Conservation International Annual Report.* Washington, DC: Conservation International.

Leith, Denise. 2003. *The Politics of Power: Freeport in Suharto's Indonesia.* Honolulu: University of Hawai'i Press.

Lessig, Lawrence. 2001. *The Future of Ideas: The Fate of the Commons in a Connected World.* New York: Random House.

Li, Tania Murray. 2000. "Articulating Indigenous Identity in Indonesia: Resource Politics and the Tribal Slot." *Comparative Studies in Society and History* 42 (1): 149–79.

———. 2002. "Engaging Simplifications: Community-Based Resource Management, Market Processes and State Agendas in Upland Southeast Asia." *World Development* 30 (2): 265–83.

———. 2007. *The Will to Improve: Governmentality, Development, and the Practice of Politics.* Durham, NC: Duke University Press.

———. 2014. *Land's End: Capitalist Relations on an Indigenous Frontier.* Durham, NC: Duke University Press.

Lindstrom, Lamont, and Geoffrey M. White. 1997. "Introduction: Chiefs Today." In *Chiefs Today: Traditional Pacific Leadership and the Precolonial State,* edited by Geoffrey M. White and Lamont Lindstrom, 1–18. Stanford, CA: Stanford University Press.

Locke, John. [1689] 1947. *Two Treatises of Government.* Edited by Thomas Ira Cook. New York: Hafner.

Loperena, Chris. 2016. "A Divided Community: The Ethics and Politics of Activist Research." *Current Anthropology* 57 (3): 332–46.

Lovell, Nadia. 1998. Introduction to *Locality and Belonging,* edited by Nadia Lovell, 1–24. London: Routledge.

Low, Sam. 2013. *Hawaiki Rising: Hokule'a, Nainoa Thompson, and the Hawaiian Renaissance.* Waipahu, HI: Island Heritage.

Low, Setha M., and Sally Engle Merry. 2010. "Engaged Anthropology: Diversity and Dilemmas." *Current Anthropology* 51 (2): S203–S26.

Lucas, Anton, and Carol Warren. 2003. "The State, the People, and Their Mediators: The Struggle over Agrarian Law Reform in Post–New Order Indonesia." *Indonesia* 76:87–126.

Lynch, Owen J., and Janis B. Alcorn. 1994. "Tenurial Rights and Community-Based Conservation." In *Natural Connections: Perspectives in Community-Based Conservation,* edited by David Western, R. Michael Wright, and Shirley Strum, 373–92. Washington, DC: Island Press.

Macdonald, Gaynor. 2002. "Ethnography, Advocacy and Feminism: A Volatile Mix; a View from a Reading of Diane Bell's *Ngarrindjeri Wurruwarrin.*" *Australian Journal of Anthropology* 13 (1): 88–110.

MacDougall, John A. 1987. Review of *Indonesia's Secret War,* by Robin Osbourne. *Indonesia* 43:101–4.

Macintyre, Martha. 2015. "Unruly Monsters." *Current Anthropology*. 56 (1): 143–44.

Macintyre, Martha, and Simon Foale. 2004. "Politicized Ecology: Local Responses to Mining in Papua New Guinea." *Oceania* 74 (3): 231–51.

Mack, Andy L., ed. 1998. *A Biological Assessment of the Lakekamu Basin, Papua New Guinea*. Washington, DC: Conservation International.

MacKay, Fergus. 2016. "Case of the Kaliña and Lokono Peoples v. Suriname: Summary and Reflections." Unpublished report.

———. 2013–14. *Indigenous Peoples and United Nations Human Rights Bodies: A Compilation of UN Treaty Body Jurisprudence, Reports and Special Procedures of the Human Rights Council, and the Advice of the Expert Mechanism on the Rights of Indigenous Peoples*. Vol. 6. Moreton-in-Marsh, U.K.: Forest Peoples Programme.

Maclellan, Nic. 2015. "Pacific Diplomacy and Decolonization in the 21st Century." In *The New Pacific Diplomacy*, edited by Greg Fry and Sandra Tate, 263–81. Canberra: Australian National University Press.

MacLeod, Jason. 2016. *Merdeka and the Morning Star: Civil Resistance in West Papua*. Brisbane, Australia: University of Queensland Press.

MacLeod, Jason, Rosa Moiwend, and Jasmine Pilbrow. 2016. *A Historic Choice: West Papua, Human Rights and Pacific Diplomacy at the Pacific Island Forum and Melanesian Spearhead Group*. United Liberation Movement for West Papua. www.ulmwp.org/historic-choice-west-papua-human-rights-pacific-diplomacy-pacific-island-forum-melanesian-spearhead-group.

Macpherson, C. B. 1964. *The Political Theory of Possessive Individualism: Hobbes to Locke*. Oxford: Clarendon.

Maest, Anne. 2009. "Comments on Environmental Aspects of the Bakhuis Environmental and Social Impact Report." In *Suriname's Bakhuis Bauxite Mine: An Independent Review of SRK's Impact Assessment*, edited by Robert Goodland, 61–92. Paramaribo, Suriname: Bureau VIDS.

Maine, Henry Sumner. [1861] 1986. *Ancient Law*. Tucson: University of Arizona Press.

Makhijani, Arjun. 2010. "The Never-Ending Story: Nuclear Fallout in the Marshall Islands." Review of *Consequential Damages of Nuclear War*, by Barbara Rose Johnston and Holly M. Barker. *Nonproliferation Review* 17 (1): 197–204.

Malinowski, Bronislaw. 1935. *Coral Gardens and Their Magic: A Study of the Methods of Tilling the Soil and of Agricultural Rites in the Trobriand Islands*. Vol. 1. London: Routledge.

Marcus, George, and Michael M. J. Fischer. 1986. *Anthropology as Cultural Critique: An Experimental Moment in the Human Sciences*. Chicago: University of Chicago Press.

Martin, Keir. 2013. *The Death of the Big Men and the Rise of the Big Shots: Custom and Conflict in East New Britain*. Oxford: Berghahn.

Martinez-Alier, Joan. 2003. *The Environmentalism of the Poor: A Study of Ecological Conflicts and Valuation*. Northampton, MA: Edward Elgar Publishing.

Matbob, Patrick, and Evangelia Papoutsaki. 2006. "West Papuan 'Independence' and the Papua New Guinea Press." *Pacific Journalism Review* 12 (2): 87–105.

Matthews, James. 1992. "Hot Spot." *Rolling Stone* (Australia) 473:71–73, 95.

Maun, Alex. 1997. "The Impact of the Ok Tedi Mine on the Yonggom People." In *The Ok Tedi Settlement: Issues, Outcomes and Implications,* edited by Glenn Banks and Chris Ballard, 113–17. Pacific Policy Paper 27. Canberra: National Centre for Development Studies and Resource Management in Asia-Pacific, Australian National University.

May, R. J. 1986. *Between Two Nations: The Indonesia–Papua New Guinea Border and West Papuan Nationalism.* Bathurst, Australia: Robert Brown.

McArthur, Margaret. 1971. "Men and Spirits in the Kunimaipa Valley." In *Anthropology in Oceania: Essays Presented to Ian Hogbin,* edited by L. R. Hiatt and C. Jayawardena, 155–89. San Francisco: Chandler.

McCallum, Rob, and Nikhil Sekhran. 1997. *Race for the Rainforest: Evaluating Lessons from an Integrated Conservation and Development Experiment in New Ireland, Papua New Guinea.* Port Moresby: PNG Biodiversity Conservation and Resource Management Programme.

McDougall, Debra. 2016. *Engaging with Strangers: Love and Violence in the Rural Solomon Islands.* Oxford: Berghahn.

McGovern, Mike. 2011. *Making War in Côte d'Ivoire.* Chicago: University of Chicago Press.

McLaren, John, A. R. Buck, and Nancy E. Wright, eds. 2005. *Despotic Dominion: Property Rights in British Settler Societies.* Vancouver: University of British Columbia Press.

McLennan, John F. 1865. *Primitive Marriage.* Edinburgh: Adam and Charles Black.

McWilliams, Edmund. 2007. Introduction to *The Testimony Project: Papua,* edited by Charles E. Farhadian, 13–17. Jakarta, Indonesia: Suwaan Langoan Indah.

Merlan, Francesca. 2001. Comment on "Lost Worlds: Environmental Disaster, 'Culture Loss,' and the Law," by Stuart Kirsch. *Current Anthropology* 42 (2): 187.

Mihesuah, Devon A., ed. 2000. *Repatriation Reader: Who Owns American Indian Remains?* Lincoln: University of Nebraska Press.

Moiwana Community v. Suriname. 2005. "Preliminary Objections, Merits, Reparations and Costs." Judgment of June 15, 2005. Inter-American Court of Human Rights. Series C, no. 124. www.corteidh.or.cr/docs/casos/articulos/seriec_124_ing.pdf.

Moiwend, Rosa, and Paul Barber. 2011. "Internet Advocacy and the MIFEE Project in West Papua." In *Comprehending West Papua,* edited by Peter King, Jim Elmslie, and Camellia Webb-Gannon. Sydney: West Papua Project, Centre for Peace and Conflict Studies. http://sydney.edu.au/arts/peace_conflict/practice/Comprehending%20West%20Papua.pdf.

Monson, Rebecca. 2015. "From Taovia to Trustee: Urbanisation, Land Disputes and Social Differentiation in Kakabona." *Journal of Pacific History* 50 (4): 437–49.

Moore, Clive. 2004. *Happy Isles in Crisis: The Historical Causes for a Failing State in Solomon Islands, 1998–2004.* Canberra: Asia-Pacific Press.

Moran, Robert E. n.d. "Cyanide in Mining: Some Observations on the Chemistry, Toxicity, and Analysis of Mining-Related Waters." Unpublished paper. www.earthworksaction.org/files/publications/morancyanidepaper.pdf.

Morgan, Lewis Henry. 1870. *Systems of Consanguinity and Affinity of the Human Family.* Washington, DC: Smithsonian Institution.

Morrissey, James, and Anthony Oliver-Smith. 2013. "Perspectives on Non-economic Loss and Damage: Understanding Values at Risk from Climate Change." In *Loss and Damage in Vulnerable Countries Initiative Report,* edited by Koko Warner and Sönke Kreft. Bonn: United Nations University. September. www.lossanddamage.net/download/7213.pdf.

Mosko, Mark. 1985. *Quadripartite Structures: Categories, Relations and Homologies in Bush Mekeo Culture.* New York: Cambridge University Press.

Mosse, David, ed. 2013. *Adventures in Aidland: The Anthropology of Professionals in International Development.* Oxford: Berghahn.

Murray, Gavin, and Ian Williams. 1997. "Implications for the Australian Minerals Industry: A Corporate Perspective." In *The Ok Tedi Settlement: Issues, Outcomes and Implications,* edited by Glenn Banks and Chris Ballard, 196–204. Pacific Policy Paper 27. Canberra: National Centre for Development Studies and Resource Management in Asia-Pacific, Australian National University.

Nadasdy, Paul. 2005. *Hunters and Bureaucrats: Power, Knowledge, and Aboriginal-State Relations in the Southwest Yukon.* Vancouver: University of British Columbia Press.

Naitoro, John. 1989. "Documentation of Traditional Land Tenure: Key to Adaptation in Modern Society." *'O'o: A Journal of Solomon Islands Studies* 2 (1): 48–56.

Nanau, Gordon Leua. 2014. "Local Experiences with Mining Royalties, Company and the State in the Solomon Islands." *Journal de la Société des Océanistes* 138–39 (1): 77–92.

———. 2017. Review of *Greed and Grievance,* by Matthew G. Allen. *Contemporary Pacific* 29 (1): 207–9.

Nathansohn, Regev. 2009. "Ethnography-as-Activism Meeting with Native American Graduate Student Caucus Members." November 3. Unpublished notes.

Nelson, Diane. 1999. *A Finger in the Wound: Body Politics in Quincentennial Guatemala.* Berkeley: University of California Press.

Nelson, Hank. 1976. *Black, White and Gold: Gold Mining in Papua New Guinea, 1878–1930.* Canberra: ANU Press.

Nepstad, Daniel C., and Stephan Schwartzman, eds. 1992. *Non-timber Products from Tropical Forests: Evaluation of a Conservation and Development Strategy.* Advances in Economic Botany, 9. New York: New York Botanical Garden.

New York Times. 2015. "Lost Voices of the World's Refugees." June 13. www.nytimes.com/2015/06/14/opinion/lost-voices-of-the-worlds-refugees.html.

Nietschmann, Bernard, and Thomas J. Eley. 1987. "Indonesia's Silent Genocide against Papua Independence." *Cultural Survival Quarterly* 11 (1): 75–78.

Niezen, Ronald. 2003. *The Origins of Indigenism: Human Rights and the Politics of Identity.* Berkeley: University of California Press.

Nixon, Rob. 2011. *Slow Violence and the Environmentalism of the Poor.* Cambridge, MA: Harvard University Press.

Nowotny, Helga, Peter Scott, and Michael Gibbons. 2001. *Re-thinking Science: Knowledge and the Public in an Age of Uncertainty.* Cambridge, UK: Polity.

Nuclear Claims Tribunal. 1999a. Testimony of Dr. Laurence M. Carucci before the Nuclear Claims Tribunal in re: the people of Enewetak's claim for consequential damages (including questions from Davor Pevec, attorney for the people of Enewetak, Philip Okney, Defender of the Fund, and the Tribunal Judges), April, 20, 1999, in Majuro, Republic of the Marshall Islands. Video.

———. 1999b. Testimony of Dr. Nancy J. Pollock before the Nuclear Claims Tribunal in re: the people of Enewetak's Claim for consequential damages (including questions from Davor Pevec, attorney for the people of Enewetak, Philip Okney, Defender of the Fund, and the Tribunal Judges), April 21, 1999 in Majuro, Republic of the Marshall Islands. Video.

Nuti, Paul J. 2007. "Reordering Nuclear Testing History in the Marshall Islands." *Anthropology News* 48 (6): 42–43.

Okney, Philip A. 1999. "Memorandum of Points and Authorities in Opposition to an Award of Damages for Relocation as a Separate Category of Damages." Nuclear Claims Tribunal No. 23–0902 in the Matter of the People of Enewetak et al., Claimants for Compensation.

Oldfield, Sophie. 2015. "Between Activism and the Academy: The Urban as Political Terrain." *Urban Studies* 52 (11): 2072–86.

Olwig, Karen Fog, and Kirsten Hastrup, eds. 1997. *Siting Culture: The Shifting Anthropological Object.* New York: Routledge.

Ondawame, Otto. 2000. "Indonesian State Terrorism: The Case of West Papua." In *Reflections on Violence in Melanesia,* edited by Sinclair Dinnen and Allison Ley, 277–89. Leichhardt, Australia: Hawkins Press; Canberra: Asia Pacific Press.

———. 2010. *One People, One Soul: West Papuan Nationalism and the Organisasi Papua Merdeka.* Bathurst, Australia: Crawford House.

Orsak, Larry. 1991. *The Wau Ecology Institute's "Insect Ranch" Programme.* Wau, Papua New Guinea: Wau Ecology Institute.

Ortner, Sherry B. 1995. "Resistance and the Problem of Ethnographic Refusal." *Comparative Studies in Society and History* 37 (1): 173–93.

———. 2016. "Dark Anthropology and Its Others: Theory since the Eighties." *Hau* 6 (1): 47–73.

Osborne, Lawrence. 2005. "Strangers in the Forest: Contacting an Isolated People—on a Guided Tour." *New Yorker* (April 18): 124–30.

Osborne, Robin. 1985. *Indonesia's Secret War: The Guerilla Struggle in Irian Jaya.* Boston, MA: Allen and Unwin.

Osterweil, Michal. 2013. "Rethinking Public Anthropology through Epistemic Politics and Theoretical Practice." *Cultural Anthropology* 28 (4): 598–620.

Ostrom, Elinor. 1990. *Governing the Commons: The Evolution of Institutions for Collective Action.* Cambridge: Cambridge University Press.

Page, Samantha, and Marilyn Strathern. 2016. "The Impact Agenda and Its Impact on Early Career Researchers: A Discussion with Marilyn Strathern." *Anthropology in Action* 26:46–51.

Paine, Robert. 1996. "In Chief Justice McEachern's Shoes: Anthropology's Ineffectiveness in Court." *Political and Legal Anthropology Review* 19:59–70.

Pálsson, Gísli. 2007. *Anthropology and the New Genetics.* Cambridge: Cambridge University Press.

Pania, Dalcy Tovosia. 2000. "Peacemaking in Solomon Islands: The Experience of the Guadalcanal Women for Peace Movement." *Development Bulletin* 53:47–48.

Peacock, James. 2002. *The Anthropological Lens: Harsh Light, Soft Focus.* Cambridge: Cambridge University Press.

Pearl, Mary C. 1994. "Local Initiatives and the Rewards for Biodiversity Conservation: Crater Mountain Wildlife Management Area, Papua New Guinea." In *Natural Connections: Perspectives in Community-Based Conservation,* edited by David Western, R. Michael Wright, and Shirley Strum, 193–214. Washington, DC: Island Press.

Peluso, Nancy L., and Michael Watts, eds. 2001. *Violent Environments.* Ithaca, NY: Cornell University Press.

Peters, Emrys. 1963. "Aspects of Rank and Status among Muslims in a Lebanese Village." In *Mediterranean Countrymen: Essays in the Social Anthropology of the Mediterranean,* edited by Julian Alfred Pitt-Rivers, 159–200. Paris: Mouton.

———. 1972. "Shifts in Power in a Lebanese Village." In *Rural Power and Social Change in the Middle East,* edited by Richard T. Antoun and Iliya Hayek, 165–97. Bloomington: University of Indiana Press.

Pierpont, Claudia Roth. 2004. "The Measure of America: How a Rebel Anthropologist Waged War on Racism." *New Yorker* (March 8): 48–63.

Piven, Frances Fox, and Richard A. Cloward. 1978. *Poor People's Movements: Why They Succeed, How They Fail.* New York: Vintage.

Plasman, James H., and Gregory J. Danz. 2007. "Memorandum of Decision and Order." Nuclear Claims Tribunal Nos. 23–02440, 23–05443-B, 23–05445-B, and 23–00501 in the Matter of the Alabs of Rongelap et al., Jabon on Rongelap Atoll and Rongerik Atoll by Iroij Anjua Loeak et al., and Iroij Imata Jabro Kabua, Rongelap Atoll, Claimants for Compensation. April 17. Majuro, Republic of the Marshall Islands.

Plemmons, Dena, and Alex W. Barker. 2016. "Background and Context to the Current Revisions." In *Anthropological Ethics in Context: An Ongoing Dialogue,* edited by Dena Plemmons and Alex W. Barker, 39–74. Walnut Creek, CA: Left Coast Press.

PNG NSO (Papua New Guinea National Statistics Office). 1991. *Final Figures: Census Unit Populations, Morobe and Gulf Provinces.* Port Moresby, PNG: National Statistics Office.

Pocock, J. G. A. 1992. "Tangata Whenua and Enlightenment Anthropology." *New Zealand Journal of History* 26 (1): 28–53.

Pollock, Nancy J. 1992. *These Roots Remain: Food Habits in Islands of the Central and Eastern Pacific since Western Contact.* Laie, Hawaii: Institute for Polynesian Studies.

———. 1999. "A Perspective on Cultural Loss by the Enewetak People." Report submitted to the Office of the Defender of the Fund, Nuclear Claims Tribunal, March 9.

———. 2016. "Reproductive Anomalies in the Marshall Islands." In *Missing the Mark? Women and the Millennium Development Goals in Africa and Oceania,* edited by Naomi M. McPherson, 264–85. Bradford, Ontario: Demeter.

Povinelli, Elizabeth A. 2002. *The Cunning of Recognition.* Durham, NC: Duke University Press.

Pratt, Mary Louise. 1992. *Imperial Eyes: Travel Writing and Transculturation.* London: Routledge.

Price, Richard. 2011. *Rainforest Warriors: Human Rights on Trial.* Philadelphia: University of Pennsylvania Press.

Rabinow, Paul. 1977. *Reflections on Fieldwork in Morocco.* Berkeley: University of California Press.

———. 1996. *Essays on the Anthropology of Reason.* Princeton, NJ: Princeton University Press.

———. 2002. "Midst Anthropology's Problems." *Cultural Anthropology* 17 (2): 135–49.

Radin, Margaret Jane. 1993. *Reinterpreting Property.* Chicago: University of Chicago Press.

Radio New Zealand. 2017. "Solomon Landowners Discuss Concerns on Reopening Gold Mine." May 10. https://ramumine.wordpress.com/2017/05/11/solomons-landowners-discuss-concerns-on-reopening-gold-mine/.

Ramos, Alcida Rita. 1999. "Anthropologist as Political Actor." *Journal of Latin American Anthropology* 4 (2): 172–89.

———. 2008. "Disengaging Anthropology." In *A Companion to Latin American Anthropology,* edited by Deborah Poole, 266–84. Oxford: Blackwell.

Rappaport, Roy A. 1968. *Pigs for the Ancestors.* New Haven, CT: Yale University Press.

———. 1993. "The Anthropology of Trouble." *American Anthropologist* 95 (2): 293–303.

Read, Peter. 1996. *Returning to Nothing: The Meaning of Lost Places.* Cambridge: Cambridge University Press.

Redford, Kent H. 1991. "The Ecologically Noble Savage." *Cultural Survival Quarterly* 15 (1): 46–48.

Regenvanu, Ralph, Stephen W. Wyatt, and Luca Tacconi. 1997. "Changing Forestry Regimes in Vanuatu: Is Sustainable Management Possible?" *Contemporary Pacific* 9 (1): 73–96.

Rex Dagi v. BHP and OTML. 1995. Supreme Court of Victoria. No. 5782 of 1994. Judgment. November 10. Melbourne.

Richards, Janet. 2010. "Spatial and Verbal Rhetorics of Power: Constructing Late Old Kingdom History." *Journal of Egyptian History* 3 (2): 339–66.

Richards, Janet, and Terry Wilfong. 1995. *Preserving Eternity: Modern Goals, Ancient Intentions.* Ann Arbor, MI: Kelsey Museum of Archaeology.

Riding In, James. 2000. "Repatriation: A Pawnee's Perspective." In *Repatriation Reader: Who Owns American Indian Remains?* edited by Devon A. Mihesuah, 106–22. Lincoln: University of Nebraska Press.

Robbins, Joel. 2013. "Beyond the Suffering Subject: Towards an Anthropology of the Good." *Journal of the Royal Anthropological Institute* 19 (3): 447–62.

Rodríguez-Garavito, César, and Diana Rodríguez-Franco. 2015. *Radical Deprivation on Trial: The Impact of Judicial Activism on Socioeconomic Rights in the Global South.* Cambridge: Cambridge University Press.

Rose, Carol M. 1994. *Property and Persuasion: Essays on the History, Theory, and Rhetoric of Ownership.* Boulder, CO: Westview Press.

Rose, Deborah Bird. 1996. *Nourishing Terrains: Australian Aboriginal Views of Landscape and Wilderness.* Canberra: Australian Heritage Commission.

Rose, Mark. 1993. *Authors and Owners: The Invention of Copyright.* Cambridge, MA: Harvard University Press.

Rosen, Lawrence. 2001. Comment on "Lost Worlds: Environmental Disaster, 'Culture Loss,' and the Law," by Stuart Kirsch. *Current Anthropology* 42 (2): 188–89.

Rosengren, Dan. 2002. "On 'Indigenous' Identities: Reflections on a Debate." *Anthropology Today* 18 (1): 25.

Rubel, Paula G., and Abraham Rosman. 1978. *Your Own Pigs You May Not Eat: A Comparative Study of New Guinea Societies.* Chicago: University of Chicago Press.

Ruddle, Kenneth, Patricia K. Townsend, and John D. Rees. 1978. *Palm Sago: A Tropical Starch from Marginal Lands.* Honolulu: University of Hawai'i Press.

Rudiak-Gould, Peter. 2013. *Climate Change and Tradition in a Small Island State: The Rising Tide.* New York: Routledge.

Rumbiak, John. 2003. "Europe in the World: EU External Relations and Development." Remarks on EU Foreign Policy Conference, Brussels. May 19.

Rutherford, Danilyn. 1996. "Of Birds and Gifts: Reviving Tradition on an Indonesian Frontier." *Cultural Anthropology* 11 (4): 577–616.

———. 1999. "Waiting for the End in Biak: Violence, Order, and a Flag-Raising." *Indonesia* 67:39–59.

———. 2002. *Raiding the Land of the Foreigners: The Limits of the Nation on an Indonesian Frontier.* Princeton, NJ: Princeton University Press.

———. 2005. "Nationalism and Millenarianism in West Papua: Institutional Power, Interpretive Practice, and the Pursuit of Christian Truth." In *Social Movements: An Anthropological Reader,* edited by June Nash, 146–67. London: Blackwell.

———. 2012. *Laughing at Leviathan.* Chicago: University of Chicago Press.

———. 2014. "Demonstrating the Stone Age in New Guinea." In *From "Stone-Age" to "Real-Time": Exploring Papuan Temporalities, Mobilities and Religiosities,* edited by Martin Slama and Jenny Munro, 39–58. Canberra: Australian National University Press.

Ruthven, David. 1979. "Land Legislation from the Protectorate to Independence." In *Land in the Solomon Islands,* edited by Peter Larmour, 239–48. Suva, Fiji: Institute of Pacific Studies, University of South Pacific.

Sahlins, Marshall. 1963. "Poor Man, Rich Man, Big Man, Chief: Political Types in Melanesia and Polynesia." *Comparative Studies in Society and History* 5:285–303.

———. 1993. "Goodbye to *Tristes Tropes:* Ethnography in the Context of Modern World History." *Journal of Modern History* 65 (1): 1–25.

———. 1999. "What Is Anthropological Enlightenment? Some Lessons of the Twentieth Century." *Annual Review of Anthropology* 28: i–xxiii.

———. 2000. *Culture in Practice: Selected Essays.* New York: Zone Books.

Said, Edward W. 1978. *Orientalism.* New York: Pantheon.

———. 1989. "Representing the Colonized: Anthropology's Interlocutors." *Critical Inquiry* 15 (2): 205–25.

Sakharov, Andrei. 1968. "Reflections on Progress, Peaceful Coexistence, and Intellectual Freedom." *New York Times,* July 22.

Sakulas, Harry. 2012. "An Evaluation of Integrated Conservation and Development Projects in PNG." PhD diss., Charles Sturt University, Albury, Australia.

Sánchez, Eduardo, and Daniel Myrick, dirs. 1999. *Blair Witch Project.* Santa Monica, CA: Artisan Entertainment. DVD.

Santos, Boaventura de Sousa, and César A. Rodríguez-Garavito. 2005. "Law, Politics, and the Subaltern in Counter-hegemonic Globalization." In *Law and Globalization from Below,* edited by Boaventura de Sousa Santos and César A. Rodríguez-Garavito, 1–26. Cambridge: Cambridge University Press.

Saramaka People v. Suriname. 2007. "Preliminary Objections, Merits, Reparations and Costs." Judgment of November 28, 2007. Inter-American Court of Human Rights. Series C. No. 172. www.corteidh.or.cr/docs/casos/articulos/seriec_172_ing.pdf.

Saramaka People v. Suriname. 2008. "Interpretation of the Judgment on Preliminary Objections, Merits, Reparations and Costs." Judgment of August 12. Inter-American Court of Human Rights. Series C. No. 185. www.corteidh.or.cr/docs/casos/articulos/seriec_185_ing.pdf.

Saulei, Simon. 1987. "Forest Exploitation in Papua New Guinea." *Contemporary Pacific* 9 (1): 25–38.

Sawyer, Suzana. 2004. *Crude Chronicles: Indians, Multinational Oil, and Neoliberalism in Ecuador.* Durham, NC: Duke University Press.

Sax, Joseph L. 2001. *Playing Darts with a Rembrandt: Public and Private Rights in Cultural Treasures.* Ann Arbor: University of Michigan Press.

SBS Australia. 2016. "Major Tailings Dam Spill at Solomon Islands 'Disaster' Gold Mine." April 8. *SBS Australia.* www.sbs.com.au/news/article/2016/04/08/major-tailings-dam-spill-solomon-islands-disaster-gold-mine.

Scheper-Hughes, Nancy. 1979. *Saints, Scholars and Schizophrenics: Mental Illness in Rural Ireland.* Berkeley: University of California Press.

———. 1989. *Death without Weeping: The Violence of Everyday Life in Brazil.* Berkeley: University of California Press.

———. 1995. "The Primacy of the Ethical: Propositions for a Militant Anthropology." *Current Anthropology* 36 (3): 409–20.

———. 2000. "Ire in Ireland." *Ethnography* 1 (1): 117–40.

———. 2005. "The Last Commodity: Post-human Ethics and the Global Traffic in 'Fresh' Organs." In *Global Assemblages: Technology, Politics, and Ethics as Anthropological Problems,* edited by Aihwa Ong and Stephen J. Collier, 145–68. Oxford: Blackwell.

———. 2009. "Making Anthropology Public." *Anthropology Today* 25 (4): 1–3.

Schieffelin, Edward L. 1976. *The Sorrow of the Lonely and the Burning of the Dancers.* New York: St. Martin's.

———. 1997. "History and the Fate of the Forest on the Papuan Plateau." *Anthropological Forum* 7 (4): 575–97.

Schneider, David Murray. 1980. *American Kinship: A Cultural Account.* Chicago: University of Chicago Press.

Schoorl, J. W. [1957] 1993. *Culture and Change among the Muyu.* KITLV Translation Series 23. Leiden, NL: KITLV Press.

———. 1988. "Mobility and Migration in Muyu Culture" *Bijdragen to de Taal-, Land- en Volkenkunde* 145:540–56.

Scott, James C. 1987. *Weapons of the Weak: Everyday Forms of Peasant Resistance.* New Haven, CT: Yale University Press.

———. 2010. *The Art of Not Being Governed: An Anarchist History of Upland Southeast Asia.* New Haven, CT: Yale University Press.

Sen, Amartya. 1999. *Development as Freedom.* Cambridge, MA: Harvard University Press.

Serdeczny, Olivia, Eleanor Waters, and Sanders Chan. 2016. "Non-economic Loss and Damage: Addressing the Forgotten Side of Climate Change Impacts." Briefing paper. Bonn: Deutsches Institute für Entwicklungspolitik. www.die-gdi.de/uploads/media/ BP_3.2016_neu.pdf.

Shelton, Dinah. 2015. "The Rules and the Reality of Petition Procedures in the Inter-American Human Rights System." *Notre Dame Journal of International Comparative Law* 5:1–28.

Shryock, Andrew. 2004. "Introduction: Other Conscious/Self Aware; First Thoughts on Cultural Intimacy and Mass Mediation." In *Off Stage/On Display: Intimacy and Ethnography in the Age of Public Culture,* edited by Andrew Shryock, 3–28. Stanford, CA: Stanford University Press.

Sillitoe, Paul. 1998. "The Development of Indigenous Knowledge: A New Applied Anthropology." *Current Anthropology* 39:223–52.

Silverman, Raymond, and Carla Sinopoli. 2011. "Besieged! Contemporary Political, Cultural, and Economic Challenges to Museums in the Academy as Seen from Ann Arbor." *University Museums and Collections Journal* 4:19–31.

Simmel, Georg. 1978. *The Philosophy of Money.* Translated by Tom Bottomore and David Frisby. London: Routledge and Kegan Paul.

Simpson, Audra. 2014. *Mohawk Interruptus: Political Life across the Borders of Settler States.* Durham, NC: Duke University Press.

Sinopoli, Carla. 2010. "NAGPRA Spurs Potential Collaboration between U-M Museum and Native Tribes." *Consider* 24 (9): 2.

Slama, Martin, and Jenny Munro. 2014. Introduction to *From "Stone-Age" to "Real-Time": Exploring Papuan Temporalities, Mobilities and Religiosities,* edited by Martin Slama and Jenny Munro, 1–38. Canberra: Australia National University Press.

Smith, Alan, and Kevin Hewison. 1986. "1984: Refugees, 'Holiday Camps' and Deaths." In *Between Two Nations: The Indonesia–Papua New Guinea Border and West Papua Nationalism,* edited by R. J. May, 200–17. Bathurst, Australia: Robert Brown.

Smith, Andrea. 2005. *Conquest: Sexual Violence and American Indian Genocide.* Cambridge, MA: South End.

Smith, Michael French. 1994. *Hard Times on Kairiru Island: Poverty, Development, and Morality in a Papua New Guinea Village.* Honolulu: University of Hawai'i Press.

Smith-Norris, Barbara. 2016. *Domination and Resistance: The United States and the Marshall Islands during the Cold War.* Honolulu: University of Hawai'i Press.

Somare, Sir Michael. 2015. "Melanesian Spearhead Group: The Last 25 Years." In *The New Pacific Diplomacy,* edited by Greg Fry and Sandra Tate, 291–98. Canberra: Australian National University Press.

Sontag, Susan. 1963. "A Hero of Our Time." *New York Review of Books.* November 28. www.nybooks.com/articles/1963/11/28/a-hero-of-our-time/.

———. 1966. "Anthropologist as Hero." In *Against Interpretation,* by Susan Sontag, 69–81. New York: Farrar, Straus and Giroux.

Speed, Shannon. 2007. *Rights in Rebellion: Indigenous Struggle and Human Rights in Chiapas.* Stanford, CA: Stanford University Press.

Spennemann, Dirk H. R. 1998. "Marshallese Canoes." Essays on the Marshallese Past, Digital Micronesia. http://marshall.csu.edu.au/Marshalls/html/essays/es-tmc-1.html.

SRIP (Special Rapporteur on Indigenous Peoples). 2003. *Report of the Special Rapporteur on the Situation of Human Rights and Fundamental Freedoms of Indigenous People.* Rodolfo Stavenhagen, submitted in accordance with Commission resolution 2001/65. UN Doc. E/CN.4/2003/90, January 21.

SRK Consulting. 2005. "Environmental Sensitivity Analysis of the Wane 4 Concession." Report prepared for NV BHP Billiton Maatschappij Suriname. Report No. 346204/1, July 2005.

Staats, Susan. 1996. "Fighting in a Different Way: Indigenous Resistance through the Alleluia Religion of Guyana." In *History, Power, and Identity: Ethnogenesis in the Americas, 1492–1992,* edited by Jonathan D. Hill, 161–79. Iowa City: University of Iowa Press.

Starn, Orin. 1991. "Missing the Revolution: Anthropologists and the War in Peru." *Cultural Anthropology* 6 (1): 63–91.

———, ed. 2015. *Writing Culture and the Life of Anthropology.* Durham, NC: Duke University Press.

Start, Daniel. 1997. *The Open Cage: The Ordeal of the Irian Jaya Hostages.* New York: HarperCollins.

Stasch, Rupert. 2001. "Giving Up Homicide: Korowai Experience of Witches and Police (West Papua)." *Oceania* 72 (1): 33–52.

———. 2005. Osborne/Kombai/New Yorker. Post to ASAONET, Association for Social Anthropology in Oceania Bulletin Board (asaonet@listserv.uic.edu). April 16.

———. 2007. "Demon Language: The Otherness of Indonesian in a Papuan Community." In *Consequences of Contact: Language Ideology and Sociocultural Transformations in Pacific Societies,* edited by Miki Makihara and Bambi B. Schieffelin, 96–124. Oxford: Oxford University Press.

———. 2011. "Textual Iconicity and the Primitivist Cosmos: Chronotopes of Desire in Travel Writing about Korowai of West Papua." *Journal of Linguistic Anthropology* 21 (1): 1–21.

———. 2014. "From Primitive Other to Papuan Self: Korowai Engagement with Ideologies of Unequal Human Worth." In *From "Stone-Age" to "Real-Time": Exploring Papuan Temporalities, Mobilities and Religiosities,* edited by Martin Slama and Jenny Munro, 59–94. Canberra: Australian National University Press.

———. 2016. "Dramas of Otherness: 'First Contact' Tourism in New Guinea." *Hau* 6 (3): 7–27.

Stephen, Michele. 1995. *A'isa's Gifts: A Study of Magic and the Self.* Berkeley: University of California Press.

Stillman, Amy Ku'uleialoha. 2009. "Access and Control: A Key to Reclaiming the Right to Construct Hawaiian History." In *Music and Cultural Rights,* edited by Andrew N. Weintraub and Bell Yung, 86–109. Champaign: University of Illinois Press.

Stoler, Ann Laura. 1992. "'In Cold Blood': Hierarchies of Credibility and the Politics of Colonial Narratives." *Representations* 37:151–89.

Strathern, Marilyn. 1987. "An Awkward Relationship: The Case of Feminism and Anthropology." *Signs* 12 (2): 276–92.

———. 1988. *Gender of the Gift: Problems with Women and Problems with Society in Melanesia.* Berkeley: University of California Press.

———. 1992. *Reproducing the Future: Essays on Anthropology, Kinship and the New Reproductive Technologies.* Manchester, UK: Manchester University Press.

———. 1995. "The Nice Thing about Culture Is That Everyone Has It." In *Shifting Contexts: Transformations in Anthropological Knowledge,* edited by Marilyn Strathern, 153–76. New York: Routledge.

———. 1999. *Property, Substance and Effect: Anthropological Essays on Persons and Things.* London: Athlone.

———. 2004. *Partial Connections.* New York: AltaMira.

———. 2005. *Kinship, Law and the Unexpected: Relatives Are Always a Surprise.* Cambridge: Cambridge University Press.

———. 2006. "A Community of Critics? Thoughts on New Knowledge." *Journal of the Royal Anthropological Institute* 12:191–209.

Strathern, Marilyn, and Eric Hirsch. 2004. Introduction to *Transactions and Creations: Property Debates and the Stimulus of Melanesia,* edited by Eric Hirsch and Marilyn Strathern, 1–18. Oxford: Berghahn.

Stuesse, Angela. 2016. *Scratching Out a Living: Latinos, Race, and Work in the Deep South.* Berkeley: University of California Press.

Sunder, Madhavi. 2001. Comment on "Lost Worlds: Environmental Disaster, 'Culture Loss,' and the Law," by Stuart Kirsch. *Current Anthropology* 42 (2): 189–90.

Sutherland, William. 1992. *Beyond the Politics of Race: An Alternative History of Fiji to 1992.* Canberra: Department of Political and Social Change, Research School of Pacific Studies, Australian National University.

Swartzendruber, J. F. 1993. *Papua New Guinea Conservation Needs Assessment: Synopsis Report.* Washington, DC: Biodiversity Support Program; Boroko: Department of Conservation and Environment, Government of Papua New Guinea.

Tait, Nikki. 1996. "Ok Tedi Copper Mine Damage Claim Settled." *Financial Times,* June 12.

Tapsell, Ross. 2015. "The Media and Subnational Authoritarianism in Papua." *South East Asia Research* 23 (3): 319–34.

Tate, Winifred. 2007. *Counting the Dead: The Culture and Politics of Human Rights Activism in Colombia.* Berkeley: University of California Press.

———. 2013. "Proxy Citizenship and Transnational Advocacy: Colombian Activists from Putumayo to Washington, DC." *American Ethnologist* 40 (1): 55–70.

Tax, Sol. 1975. "Action Anthropology." *Current Anthropology* 16 (4): 514–17.

Teaiwa, Teresia K. 1994. "Bikinis and Other S/Pacific N/Oceans." *Contemporary Pacific* 6 (1): 87–109.

Tebay, Neles. 2005. *West Papua: The Struggle for Peace with Justice.* London: Catholic Institute for International Relations.

Theidon, Kimberly. 2001. "Terror's Talk: Fieldwork and War." *Dialectical Anthropology* 26:19–35.

———. 2006. "The Mask and the Mirror: Facing Up to the Past in Postwar Peru." *Anthropologica* 48 (1): 87–100.

Thomas, David Hurst. 2000. *Skull Wars: Kennewick Man, Archaeology, and the Battle for Native American Identity.* New York: Basic Books.

Tingay, Alan. 2007. "The Ok Tedi Mine, Papua New Guinea: A Summary of Environmental and Health Issues." November. Unpublished report sponsored by Ok Tedi Mining, Ltd.

Toft, Susan, ed. 1997. *Compensation for Resource Development in Papua New Guinea.* Law Reform Commission of Papua New Guinea Monograph 6 and Pacific Policy Paper 24. Canberra: Australian National University Press.

Torpey, John. 2001. "'Making Whole What Has Been Smashed': Reflections on Reparations." *Journal of Modern History* 73 (2): 333–58.

Toyosaki, Hiromitsu. 1986. *Good-Bye Rongelap!* Translated by Masayuki Ikeda and Heather Ikeda. Tokyo: Tsukiji Shokan.

Trask, Haunani-Kay. 1991. "Natives and Anthropologists: The Colonial Struggle." *Contemporary Pacific* 3 (1): 111–17.

Trope, Jack F., and Walter R. Echo-Hawk. 2000. "Native American Graves Protection and Repatriation Act: Background and Legislative History." In *Repatriation Reader: Who Owns American Indian Remains?* edited by Devon A. Mihesuah, 123–66. Lincoln: University of Nebraska Press.

Trouillot, Michel-Rolph. 1991. "Anthropology and the Savage Slot: The Poetics and Politics of Otherness." In *Recapturing Anthropology,* edited by Richard Fox, 17–44. Santa Fe, NM: SAR Press.

Tsing, Anna Lowenhaupt. 1993. *In the Realm of the Diamond Queen: Marginality in an Out-of-the-Way Place.* Princeton, NJ: Princeton University Press.

Tsing, Anna Lowenhaupt, J. Peter Brosius, and Charles Zerner. 2005. "Introduction: Raising Questions about Communities and Conservation." In *Communities and Conservation: Histories and Politics of Community-Based Natural Resource Management,* edited by J. Peter Brosius, Anna Lowenhaupt Tsing, and Charles Zerner, 1–34. New York: AltaMira.

Turner, Terence. 1991. "Representing, Resisting, Rethinking: Historical Transformations of Kayapo Culture and Anthropological Consciousness." In *Colonial Situations: Essays in the Contextualization of Ethnographic Knowledge,* edited by George W. Stocking, 285–313. Madison: University of Wisconsin Press.

U.S. Government. 2010. "Native American Graves Protection and Repatriation Act Regulations: Disposition of Culturally Unidentifiable Human Remains; Final Rule." March 15. *Federal Register* 75 (49): 12377–405.

Veur, Paul W. van der. 1966. *Search for New Guinea's Boundaries: From Torres Strait to the Pacific.* Canberra: Australian National University Press.

VIDS (Vereniging van Inheemse Dorpshoofden in Suriname, Association of Indigenous Village Leaders in Suriname). 2009. "Securing Indigenous Peoples' Rights in Conservation in Suriname: A Review." Forest Peoples Programme Series on Forest Peoples and Protected Areas. Moreton-in Marsh, UK: Forest People Programme.

Voice of America. 2009. "UN Expert Says Action Needed to Prevent Genocide in Several African Countries." October 31. www.voanews.com/a/a-13-2006-01-27-voa58/323573.html.

Walker-Said, Charlotte. 2015. "Introduction: Power, Profit, and Social Trust." In *Corporate Social Responsibility? Human Rights in the New Global Economy,* edited by Charlotte Walker-Said and John D. Kelly, 1–26. Chicago: University of Chicago Press.

Wardlow, Holly. 2006. *Wayward Women: Sexuality and Agency in a New Guinea Society.* Berkeley: University of California Press.

Warner, Koko, and Kees van der Geest. 2013. "Loss and Damage from Climate Change: Local-Level Evidence from Nine Vulnerable Countries." *International Journal of Global Warming* 5 (4): 367–86.

Watts, Michael. 2010. "Blind Faith: Some Personal Reflections on Nigerian Fieldwork." *Journal of Cultural Geography* 27 (3): 275–85.

Webb-Gannon, Camellia. 2014. "Merdeka in West Papua: Peace, Justice and Political Independence." *Anthropologica* 56 (2): 353–67.

———. 2017. "Effecting Change through Peace Research in a Methodological 'No-Man's Land': A Case Study of West Papua." *Asia Pacific Journal of Anthropology* 18 (1): 18–35.

Webster, David. 2001–2. "'Already Sovereign as a People': A Foundational Moment in West Papuan Nationalism." *Pacific Affairs* 74 (4): 507–28.

Weiner, Annette. B. 1976. *Women of Value, Men of Renown: New Perspectives in Trobriand Exchange.* Austin: University of Texas Press.

———. 1992. *Inalienable Possessions: The Paradox of Keeping While Giving.* Berkeley: University of California Press.

Weiner, James F. 1999. "Culture in a Sealed Envelope: The Concealment of Australian Aboriginal Heritage and Tradition in the Hindmarsh Island Bridge Affair." *Journal of the Royal Anthropological Institute* 5:193–210.

Weisgall, Jonathan M. 1994. *Operation Crossroads: The Atomic Tests at Bikini Atoll.* Annapolis, MD: Naval Institute Press.

Wells, Michael, and Katrina Brandon, with Lee Jay Hannah. 1992. *People and Parks: Linking Protected Area Management and Local Communities.* Washington, DC: World Bank.

Welsch, R. L. 1994. "Pig Feasts and Expanding Networks of Cultural Influence in the Upper Fly–Digul Plain." In *Migration and Transformations: Regional Perspectives on New Guinea,* edited by A. J. Strathern and G. Stürzenhofecker, 85–119. Pittsburgh, PA: University of Pittsburgh Press.

West, Paige. 2005. *Conservation Is Our Government Now: The Politics of Ecology in New Guinea.* Durham, NC: Duke University Press.

———. 2006. "Environmental Conservation and Mining: Strange Bedfellows in the Eastern Highlands of Papua New Guinea." *Contemporary Pacific* 18 (2): 295–313.

West, Paige, and Enock Kale. 2015. "The Fate of Crater Mountain: Forest Conservation in the Eastern Highlands of Papua New Guinea." In *Tropical Forests of Oceania: Anthropological Perspectives,* edited by Joshua A. Bell, Paige West, and Colin Filer, 155–78. Canberra: Australian National University Press.

White, Geoffrey M. 1997. "The Discourse of Chiefs: Notes on a Melanesian Society." In *Chiefs Today: Traditional Pacific Leadership and the Postcolonial State,* edited by Geoffrey M. White and Lamont Lindstrom, 211–28. Stanford, CA: Stanford University Press.

White, Geoffrey M., and Lamont Lindstrom, eds. 1997. *Chiefs Today: Traditional Pacific Leadership and the Precolonial State.* Stanford, CA: Stanford University Press.

Wolfers, Edward P., ed. 1988. *Beyond the Border: Indonesia and Papua New Guinea, South-East Asia and the South Pacific.* Waigani, PNG: University of Papua New Guinea; Suva, Fiji: Institute of Pacific Studies, University of the South Pacific.

Ziman, John. 2000. *Real Science: What It Is, and What It Means.* Cambridge: Cambridge University Press.

Zocca, Franco. 2008. "Mobility and Changes in Cultural Identity among the West Papuan Refugees in Papua New Guinea." *Catalyst* 38 (2): 121–51.

Zoleveke, Gideon. 1979. "Traditional Ownership and Land Policy." In *Land in Solomon Islands,* edited by Peter Larmour, 1–9. Suva, Fiji: Institute of Pacific Studies, University of South Pacific.
Zorn, Jean G. 1993. "The Republic of the Marshall Islands." In *South Pacific Islands Legal Systems,* edited by Michael A. Ntumy, 100–141. Honolulu: University of Hawai'i Press.
Zubrinich, Kerry. 1997. "Cosmology and Colonisation: History and Culture of the Asmat of Irian Jaya." PhD thesis, Charles Sturt University, Bathurst, Australia.

INDEX

NOTE: Page numbers in *italics* denote maps and illustrations. Papua New Guinea is abbreviated as PNG.